THE
MALLINCKRODT - BISCHOFF
PARTNERSHIP

First published in Great Britain 2004
by Bernard Dewe Mathews
112 Castelnau, Barnes
London SW13 9EU
Tel/fax : 020 8748 7669
E-mail Bernard@dewemathews.freeserve.co.uk

ISBN 0-9546473-0-0

Printed in Great Britain by Bath Press
Design by design principals, Warminster

This book is dedicated to:

Jackie, Laura, Chloe and Freddie

and all my colleagues at Schroders and their
clients who made Schroders such a congenial
place in which to work.

By the same Author

BLOWING MY OWN TRUMPET
The Memoirs of Bernard Dewe Mathews

ISBN 0-9546473-1-9

Tim
with best mother
Bernard

THE
MALLINCKRODT - BISCHOFF
PARTNERSHIP

A HISTORY OF
SCHRODERS
1973 – 2000

BERNARD DEWE MATHEWS

CONTENTS

PART 3 BISCHOFF 1995-2000

ANNEXES

INTRODUCTION

My objectives in writing this book have been threefold. First, to explain why Schroders, arguably the most successful British merchant bank in the City of London in the last decade of the twentieth century, failed to maintain its independence as an investment bank and had to sell this its most visible business to Citigroup in 2000. Secondly, I have attempted to provide those who were at Schroders at the time with a reasonably accurate description of what happened and the contribution made by them and their colleagues. And thirdly from this to show their families why they spent far too much of their time away from home. An added bonus would be to give a better understanding to those who were not there and are rather mystified about what a large British merchant bank did.

Working in chronological order from 1973, the first part of the book starts with the departure of Schroders' chairman Gordon Richardson to become the Governor of the Bank of England. It briefly describes the earlier history of Schroders, including its successful merger with Helbert, Wagg and the development of a particularly well regarded corporate finance business. Over the following twelve years under the chairmanship of Michael Verey and the Earl of Airlie, Schroders' profits continued to grow, despite difficult economic conditions, with its many diverse activities. Unfortunately, during this period it suffered a rapid decline in its reputation as a corporate financier largely due to a lack of leadership and a certain amount of complacency leading to the loss of many valued clients. At this point the bank came under the management of George Mallinckrodt, who was married to the sister of Bruno Schroder, the leading member of the Schroder family that was the controlling shareholder, as chairman and Win Bischoff as the chief executive. The partnership between these two very different characters over the next ten years saw Schroders' reputation brought back to and exceed its earlier pre-eminence.

The second part of the book deals with the period from 1985 to 1994 when Mallinckrodt was the chairman and Bischoff the chief executive. Their early life and careers at Schroders prior to them taking over the management illustrate their very different upbringings and work experiences. The development of the partnership between them and how they divided up their responsibilities is explained. This is followed by a description of the changing fortunes of the different businesses and the overseas companies. Particular emphasis is given to the struggles to turn the corporate finance business into a globally competitive investment banking business and the resulting changes to the culture of the firm.

The period from 1995 to 2000 is covered in the third part of the book, from when Bischoff became chairman of Schroders until the investment bank was sold. It shows how Schroders fought to remain independent but finally had to bow to the overwhelming competition of the strongly capitalised US investment banks and break up with the glamorous and more risky investment bank being sold for a handsome profit to Citigroup, leaving Schroders as an asset management business.

In the last chapter with the benefit of hindsight I have examined the reasons for Schroders failing to achieve its objective of becoming a fully integrated global investment bank like its competitors in New York.

It is important to understand that merchant banks comprise a multitude of different businesses often not related to each other but all there to make money. Some thrive, others fail and many new businesses are created. This is the story of the ups and downs in the business under the pressures of market forces during those 27 years.

The book is about the people who worked at Schroders and the roles they played in its development and success rather than about the economic conditions that prevailed, although these are referred to. The firm decided not to give me access to any of its papers without editorial control and so I had to confine myself to publicly available information. As a result there are inevitable gaps in my knowledge and this might lead to Schroders not necessarily sharing my views on some of the critical issues. And so I embarked on the book without their support but with my independence. As I approached my former colleagues, stating that I wished to preserve editorial control, I found them to be unanimously supportive and far more open than I had expected. Surprisingly only 6 out of 93 former colleagues were unwilling to be interviewed.

The more I spoke to the people involved the more I realised that we are all fallible and that many things go wrong, some people are not as able as hoped for or are in the wrong place at the wrong time despite their good intentions, circumstances change and are not understood and the competition is better or stronger. Success is therefore a triumph of fortune and hard work over adversity with the successes outweighing the failures. This is the nature of any business.

The opinions expressed in the book are drawn from the views of those I interviewed rather than my own except where specifically stated otherwise. Having said that it was I who chose which of their views to include largely on the basis that they were corroborated by others. The last chapter however is purely my own.

I would like to thank all the people I interviewed whose names are listed below, divided between colleagues, clients and competitors as well as a few of Win's and Gowi's personal friends and relations to all of whom I dedicate this book. Should they disagree with what I have written I hope they will forgive me. Finally I would like to thank Adam Broadbent and Ian Strachan for their helpful comments on the structure and contents of the book and my daughter Laura who scanned and arranged the photographs.

Bernard Dewe Mathews
Souldern Mill, Oxfordshire
December 2003

LIST OF THOSE INTERVIEWED

SCHRODERS

Chairmen
The Earl of Airlie, Sir Win Bischoff, John Hull, George Mallinckrodt,
Bruno Schroder

Non-Executive Directors
Charles Sinclair, Bill Turner, Alva O Way

Corporate Finance
Hugh Ashton, Adam Broadbent, David Challen, Patrick Drayton,
Sir Patrick Fairweather, Gerry Grimstone, Guy Harington, David Murison,
Derek Netherton, Philip H Robinson, Will Samuel, Robert Swannell,
Panfilo Tarantelli, Geoffrey Williams

Securities
Rupert Caldecott, Ruth Sack, Ivan Sedgwick, Richard Watkins, Richard Wyatt

Capital Markets
Philip Mallinckrodt, Paul Sauvary, William Slee, Andrew Williams

Project Finance
John Burnham, Read Gomm, Philip C Robinson, George Wadia

Investment Management
Hugh Bolland, Jim Cox, John de Havilland, Richard Foulkes, John Govett,
Jeremy Hill, Keith Niven, Peter Sedgwick, Peter Walton

Ventures
Gordon Byrn, Veronica Eng, Nicholas Ferguson, Jon Moulton, Ivor O'Mahony,
Charles Sherwood, Peter Smitham

Banking/Treasury
Bernard Barham, John Rock, Jean Solandt, Andrew Sykes

THE MALLINCKRODT – BISCHOFF PARTNERSHIP

Finance and Administration

David Caruth, Sue Cox, Andrew Gaulter, Hon Nicholas MacAndrew, Agnes May, David Morris, Richard Sadleir

Schrobanco

Marion Gilliam, Ajit Hutheesingh, Matt Snyder

Wertheim

James Harmon, Steven Kotler, Arthur Rebell, Barry Tarasoff

Asia

Ian Boyce, Arthur Charles, Giles Elliott, Brian Gatfield, John Gerahty, Michael Gleeson-White, Richard Griffin, Mark Hopkinson, Peter Mason, Kerry Smith, Robin Tomlin

Former Schroders

Gary Brass, Alison Carnwath, Bill Harrison, Nicholas Jones, Anthony Loehnis, Nick Roditi, Robert Whyte

CLIENTS

Charles Allen-Jones, John Baker, Baroness Lydia Dunn, Frank Frame, Sir Roger Gibbs, Sir Peter Graham, Antony Hichens, Hon Michael Kadoorie, James Kelly, Jeremy Lancaster, David Millar, Sir Michael McWilliam, Sir William Purves, John Richardson, Sir Nigel Rudd, Lord Simon of Highbury, David Stileman, Ian Strachan, Lord Young of Graffham

COMPETITORS

David Clarke, Sir John Craven, Henry Keswick, Michael Klein, David Mayhew, Simon Robertson, Sir David Scholey, John Thornton, Andrew Tucke.

FAMILY AND FRIENDS

Nat & Jewelle Bickford, Lady Bischoff, Charles Bischoff, Christopher Bischoff, Christian Bischoff, Sir Alastair Goodlad, Dr Roland Horster, Sir David Kinlock, David Leathers, Ronald and Hon Rita McAulay, Anita Volz Wien, Charmaine Mallinckrodt, Lindy Leschallas

LIST OF ILLUSTRATIONS

PART 1
AFTER RICHARDSON
1973 – 1984

CHAPTER 1

'HE WAS A GOD'

1973 – 1977

Halfway between the Bank of England and St Paul's Cathedral in the City of London lies what used to be the head office of Schroders Plc at 120 Cheapside. As you entered the eight storey marble-faced building that was built in 1964 through a pair of glass doors you saw, soaring above the receptionist in front of you against a mahogany clad wall, a world time clock with a great wheel, ten feet in diameter, surrounded by the names of the cities around the world where Schroders had offices, indicating the time at each of them. It was believed to be the largest clock wheel in the world and turned once every 24 hours when it was working!

If you were a client the receptionist sent you up to the seventh floor where you were greeted by a butler, dressed in pinstriped trousers and a black coat, and led into a meeting room where you were served a cup of coffee or tea. Merchant bankers rarely greeted their guests in their private offices. The exception was those who occupied the top floor, which was where the chairman and his most senior colleagues were located. To visit them you turned right out of the lifts. If you turned left you entered the boardroom where many of the major decisions were taken.

The boardroom was 100 metres square with eight large plate glass windows on opposite walls facing the front and the rear of the building. Hung on the other two walls were four life-size oil paintings of members of the Schroder family who were senior partners or chairmen of Schroders – Johann Heinrich Schröder (1818-1883), Baron Sir John Henry Schröder Bt. (1849-1910), Baron Bruno Schröder (1895-1940) and Helmut Schroder (1926-1965). J Henry Schroder & Co was formed in 1818 and was a partnership until 1957, directors being appointed thereafter. The holding company, Schroders Limited, acquired the business of Helbert, Wagg & Co in 1962 and merged it with J Henry Schroder & Co to form J Henry Schroder Wagg & Co Limited (known as Schroder Wagg). It also owned another banking business in New York called J Henry Schroder Banking Corporation (known as Schrobanco). (Organisation charts of the Schroder Group showing the main subsidiary and associated companies before and after the sale of Schrobanco are attached as Annex 1) Because of the skilful way in which the acquisition had been financed, the Schroder family remained the owners of approximately 48% of the ordinary shares of the publicly listed company, only diluting its shareholding by 4%. [1] Helmut Schroder was the first chairman of Schroders Limited, and was succeeded by Gordon Richardson (later Baron Richardson of Duntisbourne) in 1965, when the bank moved from Leadenhall Street to Cheapside. He had been recruited by Helmut in 1957.[2]

Helbert, Wagg was clearly a very good business fit. The *Financial Times* said, 'the marriage is a very natural one. It is an almost classic link-up between the predominantly 'banking' bank (Schroders) and the predominantly 'industrial' bank (Helbert, Wagg)'. Schroders was essentially a banking house with a tiny investment management and corporate finance capability. Helbert, Wagg was a corporate finance and investment management business with virtually no banking capability and so the two dovetailed perfectly with no rivalries. The houses were managed very differently. The partners of Schroders were responsible for producing the business for the managers to execute, some of whom, like David Forsyth and Alec Cairns [3], became partners. The Schroder managers were given a good allocation of shares and retired financially secure. At Helbert, Wagg, the partners wrote their own letters and managed the business, the other staff doing the back office work and having little prospect of becoming partners. From the outset the combined business hummed. It was the most effective merger in the City in the 1960s and could be compared with SG Warburg's merger with Akroyd & Smithers, Rowe & Pitman and Mullens in the 1980s.

Richardson, the formidable chairman of Schroders from 1965 to 1973, was regarded by many as the outstanding man of his generation in the City. He transformed the way in which the merchant banks conducted corporate finance and turned Schroders into the leading merchant bank in the City. In the words of a client, Charles Gordon, he turned Schroders into 'one of the smoothest, best operated merchant banks in the City', with the general tenor being 'overall expansion, little publicity, less fanfare, superb results. A natural leader and a natural banker' (Charles Gordon, *Two Tycoons*). Sir Siegmund Warburg, the founder of SG Warburg, saw Schroders as having a 'well ordered system run on gold ball bearings'. John Kinross, a colleague of Richardson from ICFC, said, 'he had a first class brain, moral courage, persistence, a strong personality, a very shrewd man, a very nice man, but he could be as hard as nails' (personal interview). Sir Henry Benson, after retiring as senior partner of Coopers & Lybrand, described Richardson as both 'a man of scrupulous integrity' and 'a perfectionist'. Furthermore, he said,

> he has a very gentle demeanour, but there is an iron fist in the velvet glove. Once he's made up his mind on an issue of principle, nothing will change it. There are some disadvantages in this in the sense that because he was a perfectionist he sometimes delayed decisions, some for a little too long, while he was making up his mind and satisfying himself that the decision was the right one. But once he'd made up his mind then that was that. (David Kynaston, *The City of London Vol. IV, A Club No More*)

Closer to home Win Bischoff said, 'he was outstanding, success resided in him, he was a god to many people, highly professional, very thoughtful, dedicated to getting in new clients through his force of intellect and personality'. With such a reputation he was clearly going to be a hard act to follow.

Richardson appeared to have made no plans for his succession, despite having hoped that he would be appointed Governor of the Bank of England in 1971. This hope was frustrated by Sir Leslie O'Brien, the incumbent, deciding to seek a second term and staying on until his 65th birthday in June 1973. Richardson had, however, built around him what was referred to by a former Helbert, Wagg director as 'Richardson's court', comprising John Bayley [4], John Hull [5], Leslie Murphy [6], Jim Wolfensohn [7] and, later, Sir Henry Fisher [8]. With the exception of Bayley, who was more instinctive, they all had exceptionally fine intellects although very different styles. Hull, Murphy and Fisher, all of whom had been personally recruited by Richardson, were possible successors. It was thought by some that he may also have given certain undertakings to his young protégé, Wolfensohn, regarding his future succession.

Murphy, although respected, was not universally liked, as he was so clever and blatantly a socialist. He was also quite abrasive, which appealed to some but was uncomfortable for others. He never quite fitted into what became accepted as the Schroder style – which in time may have led to a loss in Schroders' market position. Fisher never came up to expectations, Bayley was never a contender and it was too early for Wolfensohn, who was still untested. Hull's view of himself was that Richardson 'was rather disappointed in me having become aware of my faults before he was able to cure them'.

Richardson had resisted making any commitment to Michael Verey, the most senior of the former Helbert, Wagg directors, who was three years his elder. Verey at the time of the merger had reserved his right to retire at 65 (in 1977) rather than at the Schroder retirement age of 60. However, as Richardson found himself having to spend increasingly more time in New York trying to resolve the intractable problems of Schrobanco, he had no alternative than to relinquish the chairmanship of Schroder Wagg to Verey – who had been pressing hard for the two chairman roles to be split – in 1972. He had handed over the chairmanship of Schrobanco in New York to Jack Howell in 1970. [9] Verey thereby became Richardson's natural successor when the latter was appointed the Governor of the Bank of England (the Bank) in July 1973.

Verey was very different to Richardson in background and in his attitude to business practice. Whereas Richardson was a self-made meritocrat, a technocrat and true professional, with no time for the old Etonian aspect of the City and always in pursuit of excellence, Verey was of the old school, described by a journalist at the time as, 'a tall, slender, elegant and patrician figure, very much the beautifully mannered Etonian merchant banker' (SA Press Cuttings, newspaper unidentified, Richard Roberts, *Schroders - Merchants & Bankers*). Verey was a buccaneer, amusing, boisterous and good fun to be with and he surrounded himself with a different group of colleagues, mostly former Helbert, Wagg partners like Sir Ashley Ponsonby and Bobby Holland. Richardson's inner group was quickly displaced – Fisher left shortly after Richardson to become president of Wolfson College, Oxford, and Murphy became deputy chairman of the newly created National Enterprise Board for which he subsequently received a knighthood in 1978. Bayley remained in New York as group finance director until he retired in 1983. Although Verey recognised Wolfensohn's skills, he did not think he had the right background to run an institution of Schroders' calibre and was glad to see him preoccupied in New York as president of Schrobanco. Only Hull, who got on well with Verey, remained, having been appointed deputy chairman of Schroder Wagg on his return at the end of 1974 from a three-year secondment to the Take-over Panel as its second director general.

Verey's main interest was in becoming the senior partner of Helbert, Wagg – he was not interested in matters outside of the City of London and did not care for travelling overseas. He probably would have preferred to remain chairman of Schroder Wagg but having fought Richardson for that position, he could hardly retain it when he became chairman of Schroders. He therefore appointed the Earl of Airlie [10], who had succeeded him as head of Investment Management in 1972, as chairman of Schroder Wagg, which represented 80% of the group's activities. This deeply upset Wolfensohn who had serious ambitions if not expectations to become the next chairman. By way of compromise, Wolfensohn was appointed executive deputy chairman of Schroders Limited.

During Verey's chairmanship the Earl of Perth, a long-standing non-executive director and a supporter of Wolfensohn, reluctantly resigned and was replaced by Sir Ernest Woodroofe, a former chairman of Unilever. Verey also appointed three new executive directors, David Forsyth, the head of Banking, from which most of the profits were earned, Mark Maged [11], Wolfensohn's successor as president of Schroders Inc, and Geoffrey Williams [12], the head of the Corporate Finance.

Verey was dealt a continuously bad set of cards during his chairmanship. Following Richardson's departure to the Bank in July 1973, the City was hit by the collapse of property values and share prices and the failure of many property companies and secondary banks. This became known as the secondary banking crisis and required the Bank to organise a 'lifeboat' to save the situation. The crisis had been fuelled earlier by Heath's reckless pursuit of economic growth at all costs and the Barber boom, together with a relaxation of lending limits by the Bank under its *Competition and Credit Controls* policies. This was accompanied by the rise of aggressive financial conglomerates, such as Slater Walker, First National Finance Corporation (FNFC) and Keyser Ullmann, who were challenging the more staid and established financial institutions, such as Schroders. At the same time, a quadrupling of oil prices led to inflation and recession in all the industrial nations. In the United Kingdom, following years of mismanagement of the economy, there was inflation, strikes and rising unemployment. These were difficult times to take over from Richardson. They were also testing times for Richardson, then new as Governor of the Bank.

With the incoming Labour government under Harold Wilson in the autumn of 1974 came pressure for the City to direct its funds towards industry. This was followed by the sterling crisis, which drove the government into the hands of the International Monetary Fund (IMF). The government had to swallow the IMF medicine of cutting back on the public sector borrowing requirement and this, at last, brought about a stabilisation of sterling and a rise in the stock market. As chairman of the Accepting Houses Committee, Verey played an important role in persuading the large insurance companies to underwrite new issues and thereby help to resuscitate industry. In October 1974, when the City was in the depths of depression, he persuaded Commercial Union, where he was vice-chairman, to make a rights issue of £62 million (at a dividend yield of about 16%!) saying, without consulting his colleagues at Schroders, that Schroder Wagg would underwrite the issue. It proved to be a great success and played a crucial part in restoring confidence in the City and paved the way for the stock market recovery and a flood of rights issues in 1975. Verey's faith was vindicated and much-needed heart was put into the City.

Verey's feel for the market was uncanny and is well illustrated by the experience of Roger Gibbs (later knighted) of Gerrard & National, a leading London discount house,

During the first week of December 1976 we went into the hands of the IMF. Surprisingly in the first twenty-four hours after the announcement, the gilt market fell sharply. As the UK was now going to be run on lines approved by the IMF, it seemed certain that long-term interest rates of more than 14% were bound to fall. At Gerrards we decided to buy. We were so convinced that it was going to be one of the great bull markets in gilts that we set aside a magnum of Krug '62 as the prize for the person who forecast how low minimum lending rate (MLR) would fall in 1977. Most experts seemed to think there was a chance that MLR could fall from a high of 15% to 12% or even 11%. There was one person who forecast that interest rates would fall to 7% or even lower by the autumn – in fact, MLR fell to 5% on 7 October 1977. It was Michael Verey who was the optimist and collected the magnum of Krug.

But for Verey it was too late – his time as chairman was up. Despite no longer being chairman of Schroder Wagg, Verey had retained his role as chairman of the Accepting Houses Committee, the most prestigious role for a merchant banker in the City, where he played a major part in leading the City out of a depression. When he retired, John Baring, the new chairman and a man of similar ilk, gave a dinner for Verey at which he said rather euphorically, 'there is no-one, my dear Michael, in the City of London held in greater regard or greater affection than you are' (*Wagtail* 1977). He was probably the leading figure in the City in the domestic issuance business. He also fought the Stock Exchange over the unreasonably high commission rates being charged for large transactions and achieved significant reductions. This was his milieu – the club atmosphere of the old City establishment.

The difficulties of the mid-1970s were to some extent reflected in the performance of Schroders during the four years of Verey's chairmanship with the profits only increasing from £2.4 million to £3.5 million. Shareholders' funds, however, did better, increasing from £25.9 million to £44.9 million (i.e. the return on shareholders' funds fell from 9.2% to 7.8%). Market capitalisation declined from £33.0 million to £31.8 million – in contrast the FTSE All Share index rose from 150 to 215, up 40%. (During Richardson's eight-year chairmanship profits and shareholders' funds were tripled and doubled respectively.) It is perhaps worth mentioning that merchant banking profits can be misleading in that the true profits were not fully disclosed until 1992 – until then they were privileged in being allowed under the Companies Act to smooth the annual profits by making reasonable transfers to (and from) inner reserves – a trifle embarrassing to the corporate financiers who were advising their clients to be more open with the market and their shareholders!

Both Verey and Airlie, who followed him as chairman in 1977 to the end of 1983, had to deal with the perennial problem of Schrobanco's poor return on capital, a decline in Schroders' stature as a corporate finance advisor in London and the undramatic but steady fall in the profitability of the banking business, which had been financing most of the other activities. These were only partially offset by the development of a successful treasury business, the emergence of the investment management business and a modest expansion outside the United Kingdom and the United States. It is easier therefore to follow the course of each of these activities through the period of both chairmanships.

It is necessary to appreciate that the British merchant banks comprised a series of different businesses that were often only tangentially related. They grew up through the skill of talented people who wanted to build new business and were encouraged to do so and given a lot of room by the chairman and his colleagues. Each business was dependent on different markets and so as some went through bad times others might counter-balance them. This also partially explains why profits could continue to grow despite bad economic climates. The key to achieving success was to attract talented and entrepreneurial people who could be trusted to develop and expand new and existing businesses so that over the cycle they grew into different and more successful activities. Whereas Richardson's most obvious failure was not finding a successor in his own mould, his great legacy was the extraordinary amount of able people he personally hired – it was largely they who ran the businesses during their resurgence in the mid-1980s and 1990s. He introduced graduate recruitment, which led in time to the merchant banks becoming the first choice for people who in previous generations went to the Foreign Office and the Treasury.

Corporate Finance

When Richardson left, Schroders lost a great leader. Those that he brought into the firm at a senior level failed to develop to fill the gap and there was no leadership in Corporate Finance. Hull and Williams, by their own admission, were lawyers rather than entrepreneurial merchant bankers. Within Corporate Finance it had become the custom to rotate the head of the division every five years. Hull had handed over to Williams in 1968 and Francis Cator, a former Helbert, Wagg partner and friend of Verey, who was an accountant and landowner from Norfolk, succeeded Williams in 1973 when Verey became the chairman of Schroders and Airlie chairman of Schroder Wagg.

During the secondary banking crisis, Schroders received a lot of corporate finance work from the Bank of England under Richardson, helping to restructure companies like FNFC under Pat Matthews, which were in the 'lifeboat' being overseen by the Bank and financed reluctantly by the clearing banks, particularly Tuke of Barclays. As a result Schroders managed to maintain its name and became known as the 'bankers' bank'. Williams, who as deputy chairman of Schroder Wagg remained involved with clients, led most of this work, which required advice to the support group of banks and recommendations on how to reconstruct the banks in the 'lifeboat', often refinancing them by means which resulted in the supporting banks owning substantially all the equity. David Challen, then an assistant to Hugh Ashton, Cator's successor, learnt a great deal from the 'lifeboat' regarding the fundamentals of banking and the lack of risk management with too much exposure to a single sector.

Cator was not a dynamic leader. He lacked the charisma and leadership as well as the imagination to make an impact on the clients. Every year when the budgets were discussed, he always forecast no profit, saying he knew his costs but had no idea of his income. The board meetings of Norwich Union were always held on Fridays and Cator was invariably in attendance rather than being in the office. It was a thin time.

Although Schroders probably had the most impressive client list of UK companies of all the merchant banks, and retained a leading position in both mergers and acquisitions (M&A) and equity underwriting, there was a significant decline in these activities during the mid-1970s and Schroders had to batten down the hatches. More importantly Schroders' reputation as a corporate finance adviser began to decline. Its directors were complacent, simply milking the Richardson inheritance and doing no marketing. They were driven by neither greed nor fear nor pride and there was a lack of leadership, Verey having little knowledge or interest in corporate finance. Despite Verey being on the board of British Petroleum in 1977 and Lazards being its normal advisor, SG Warburg under David Scholey (later knighted) was appointed to lead the £564 million government's sale of its 17% stake in BP. As a result SG Warburg, particularly linked to the name of Scholey, was now widely recognised as London's premier merchant bank. In a space of four years Schroders had lost its place as one of the top advisors (David Kynaston, *The City of London Vol. IV, A Club No More*). Richardson left Schroders with probably the finest execution capability in the City, but to be fully exploited it needed people with business creativity, energy and entrepreneurialism and this was totally lacking. Around the corner at SG Warburg it was very different. Siegmund Warburg had created SG Warburg from scratch into one of the leading and most progressive merchant banks in the City with a heavy emphasis on Europe (see the section on *International Department* below). He made SG Warburg the most entrepreneurial merchant bank in the City and developed a new way of doing business, which had to be emulated by his competitors. He had also nursed a brilliant successor in Scholey who over the next 15 years became the leading figure in corporate finance, as Richardson had been before him. SG Warburg had an ambivalent relationship with

Schroders. It was good at the working level but the feeling was that the senior management treated the Warburg people *de haute en bas*. Schroders was to pay heavily for this complacency over the next few years as described in the next chapter.

The style of Corporate Finance at the time is reflected in Garry Brass' views. Garry Brass joined Schroders in 1971 as a very young accountant from Glasgow. He started in Corporate Finance under Sir Charles Pickthorn and found Schroders to be honest, fair and transparent, responsive, client-driven and mainly an advisory business doing M&A, general advice and rights issues. There was a great client list but the cracks were beginning to appear by the time he left in 1978. His biggest assignment was supporting Wolfensohn and Ashton on the restructuring of Burmah Oil which, having gone bust, had dropped Barings for Schroders and appointed Sir Alastair Down from BP as its chairman. Over an 18-month period Brass worked on developing a strategy for survival including the sale of assets and major negotiations with the Department of Energy and the Bank of England concerning the mismatch of tanker liabilities. He had a great admiration for Wolfensohn, whom he found refreshing and very perceptive. He recalls him poking his nose into Down's office to find him immersed in a great pile of papers looking very depressed. Wolfensohn immediately lifted the gloom with his disarming charm.

Alastair Down looked up so pleased to see Jim and said, 'Is there any chance that we will get through this?' to which Jim responded, 'I really don't know'. He did not have the typical merchant bankers' serious reply of a set of alternative strategies. Down knew he had a friend on his side who would do all in his power to help. He could make a client feel he was not alone in a crisis. He had an affinity with his clients and treated his colleagues with respect always asking the most junior member of the team his views.

This was a taxing assignment and Brass had a high regard for Ashton, who was to succeed Cator, saying 'he was the ultimate gentleman, always defended the troops and never embarrassed them in public taking them aside quietly to point out an error. He was genuinely honest. He gave instant responses and was perhaps not as brilliant as others.' Here was a glimmer of the client-drawing power of Wolfensohn who had never been allowed to challenge the order in Corporate Finance in London. What a formidable competitor to Scholey he might have been.[13]

International Department

One of Wolfensohn's creations under Richardson when he arrived from Australia in 1968 was the international department, which was responsible for developing Schroders' Eurobond business. This relatively new market was dominated by SG Warburg, NM Rothschild and White Weld and was therefore an uphill task for Schroders. When Wolfensohn went to New York in 1970, Williams became the nominal head and was followed by Gowi Mallinckrodt, Bruno Schroder's brother-in-law (see Chapter 3) in 1973. The senior members of the team, comprising Anthony

Loehnis, Christopher Gladstone and Tony Asseily, had to find clients wanting to issue Eurodollar bonds.

Loehnis was a high flier having joined Schroders as personal assistant to Richardson from the Foreign Office in 1967. He was introduced to Richardson by his friend from Oxford, John Cooper, then Richardson's personal assistant and looking to move into a mainline function of the bank. Loehnis was immediately attracted by Richardson's intelligence, huge charm and ability. 'He had masterminded the tax affairs of the Schroder family and the merger and with his knowledge of tax and his powers of persuasion he was able to seduce people into becoming clients. The merger of Schroders and Helbert, Wagg was much more effective than Kleinwort and Robert Benson Lonsdale – it was a good mix with little rivalries.'

In the late 1960s, Schroders had, with much hubris, entered the Euromarket without bringing in the major underwriters, such as Deutsche Bank and Morgan Stanley as co-managers, and thereby lost out on future reciprocity. Early in 1971, Schroders attempted to arrange a Eurobond issue for ICI in bad market conditions but received little support from the co-managers and having virtually no placing power in the after market pulled the issue when it was just about fully subscribed, much to everyone's shock. One has to ask why Richardson did not see the foolhardiness of this. Shortly afterwards, ICI issued the bond, which was successfully underwritten and sold by SG Warburg. Schroders always floundered in the Eurobond market after that. SG Warburg, which in the early 1970s was well behind the leading merchant banks and wondering how it might break into this clique with its established set of clients, decided to concentrate on the Eurobond market. Schroders did not appear to them to believe the market would survive and was doing nothing about it. By working hard, they built a formidable capability in the market and through doing so got to understand the workings of the primary and secondary markets. This was to put them in good stead for the securities market, the key to building a successful investment banking business in the 1980s.

When ICI later moved from Schroders to SG Warburg for its domestic issues, it was a clear demonstration that SG Warburg had become the most successful of all the merchant banks. Schroders thereafter lacked the placing power to secure Eurobond mandates for overseas issuers and did not get invited into the mandates of others and this became a vicious circle. There were some sterling dollar convertible mandates for US companies like Conoco introduced by Murphy, a number of Japanese companies and other minor players in a market, which was becoming increasingly more professional and commodity driven. Schroders lost out as a result of not being competitive and not having the scale or the skills. There were a series of set backs and Schroders was unable to build the critical mass of successes – it did not have a feel for the market and did not know the investors. The Western Mining issue was the final straw. This company was a long-standing client of Schroder Darling in Australia and Schroder Wagg and was persuaded by Tyo van Marle [14], who had succeeded Loehnis in managing the department in 1977 [15], to issue a $25 million bond. Market conditions were terrible and the issue was being taken up very slowly but van Marle remained publicly optimistic that there would be further applications. On the day of the issue, much to the embarrassment and annoyance of Western Mining, Schroders cut the issue from $25 million to $15 million. Western Mining never gave Schroders any further business. With the business going from bad to worse, the international department lost its independence and was put under the management of Cator and Ashton in Corporate Finance. One might ask why none of the people involved were fired. It was not in the Schroder culture to fire people who failed – they were simply moved aside on the basis that responsibility was collective.

Investment Management

Another of Schroders' principal activities, in which both Verey and Airlie started their careers, was Investment Management. Verey, with Airlie's help, sowed the seeds of the future success of the Investment Management business. His clients such as BP, Boots, the BBC and Commercial Union, formed the bedrock for the pension fund business. Verey, unlike Sir Siegmund Warburg, saw the benefits of managing other peoples' money. He was a market man and a shrewd investor – personable and amusing but belonging to a different era. He said that one should never visit a stockbroker – brokers always came to you! He came from a world in which it was accepted practice for people in the City to take advantage of any information available to make a profit for their firm and for themselves. Richardson strongly disapproved of this practice, regarding it as being 'on the make' and he and Verey did not get on as a result. In those days insider trading, as it became known, was widely believed to be endemic in the City and had been raised as a matter of concern by certain members of the Take-over Panel with the Secretary of State for Trade and Industry in February 1973 (Ian Fraser, *The High Road to England*).

Airlie, although more tense than Verey, had an equally good nose for investment and, as head of Investment Management, was respected for being conscientious and committed although it was said that some good staff left due to not having been promoted through not having come from the right background. He and Gordon Popham were behind the move into unit trusts and set up the Capital and Income Funds followed by the General Fund. This proved to be a meaningful business. When Airlie became chairman of Schroder Wagg in 1973, Popham succeeded him as head of Investment Management and remained so for the next twelve years. Popham had joined Helbert, Wagg in 1951 and become a director of Schroder Wagg in 1967. Airlie regarded him very highly saying he was, 'one of the shrewdest investors I've ever known, with a real feel for the market. Despite this he was almost totally inarticulate and you had to listen to him very carefully, as he threw his hands into the air, to pick up the point he was making.'

In the early 1970s Investment Management was making very little profit as most of the underwriting fees went to Corporate Finance rather than being shared. Profits often depended on the skills of John de Havilland [16], who had a tremendous feel for the market. In 1967 he became an assistant to Popham who was responsible for managing the firm's book (Schroders' money as opposed to its clients') and in 1969 it was handed over to him, as Airlie said, 'you have a knack of turning one penny into two.' From then on, he became the firm's trader by taking positions in gilts and commodities. He avoided equities due to perceiving a conflict of interest with clients – at the same time he stopped managing equity portfolios for clients, managing bond portfolios instead. In managing the firm's book he said modestly 'I had a lucky run with only a loss in one year in the late 1980s.' He never took very big positions. Airlie and Popham would say 'don't lose more than £400,000' and he would tailor the positions he took to what he could afford to lose. Most of the profits came from gilts and in one year he made a spectacular profit of £2 million, much of which was in sugar. He kept Investment Management in profit through the difficult years.

The year 1974 was a particularly difficult time for everyone in the City with a real fear that capitalism was under deliberate attack from the Wilson government. The taxation of corporate profits, which were overstated as a result of high inflation, left companies with insufficient cash flow to finance their operations. If allowed to continue much longer, more and more companies would have had to be rescued by the government in some sort of back door nationalisation. The economic climate created great difficulties for Investment Management. NM Rothschild had done very well with its gold investments and was crowing in the press – it proved to be their death knell as from then on they never did as well again in investment management. The bear market of 1973/4 resulted in equities falling as inflation rose resulting in large negative returns on pension funds. Most of the clients questioned whether their companies should even have pension funds. With the four-day week and the All Share index at 145, Popham, who had held his nerve and stuck with equities during the bear market, gave instructions to put everything into equities saying, 'if it is the end of the world it does not matter but if it goes well we will do very well indeed.' Schroders stepped up its equities in the last quarter of 1974. Burmah Oil had recently gone bust and there were rumours of many institutions going to the wall. Shortly afterwards there was a massive turn round in the market and one could not get into the market as it was rising too fast.

As Schroders was in the equity markets early, the returns in 1975 in absolute and relative terms were exceptional compared to the competitors. At the same time consultancy firms were emerging who were asked by the pension fund trustees to advise on the merits of the managers. The year 1975, in which Schroders did so well, was the base year on which Wood Mackenzie set its future performance statistics. Schroders' strong track record in 1975 and 1976 made it one of the best of the top performers and gave it the opportunity to secure a lot of new business through to the end of the 1970s – 'whatever they say about individuals and systems in the end it is past performance which is the deciding factor in the choice of an investment manager.' Airlie and Popham created the team that would later build Investment Management into a world force. They hired John Govett, Jeremy Hill, David Mumford, Keith Niven, Richard Foulkes and Peter Sedgwick. In particular Popham realised that things were changing and brought in people for what they were rather than who they were, for example Sedgwick, Niven and Hugh Bolland. They brought a commercial approach to the business and started to build relationships by entertaining their clients at such events as the European Open Golf Competition. The more senior directors of the old school like Sir Ashley Ponsonby and Sir Richard Baker Wilbraham, who had very good client relationships, were supported by a new breed of professionals and the clients were impressed by this combination.

Popham initiated a number of new businesses for Investment Management that were to prove very beneficial over the next 20 years. In 1968, much to the horror of the haughty board, Popham suggested that he start a unit trust business for the 'middling rich' with minimum investments of £2,500 (in today's terms £50,000). The board thought that it was far too *infra dig.* to deal with such people. Popham held his corner and put his job on the line should it fail, the Capital Fund and the Income Fund being launched in the same year. Needless-to-say it was a resounding success – every telephone line was engaged through the heavy demand and Richard Foulkes, recently hired from Cambridge, was given the task of answering 30 to 40 calls each day explaining the process. He learnt a huge amount and built his very successful career on the experience he gained over the next two years. In 1972 Schroder Life was formed. It sold unit-linked policies, a relatively new concept for the life assurance industry but one gaining rapidly in popularity. Rather than the opaque nature of traditional with profits policies, unit-linked policies offered sums assured related directly to the published prices of unitised managed funds. Schroder Life, whose value to Schroders was in its future income stream, gave great momentum to the inflow of funds. Popham built up a range of funds but had to keep pushing the board to agree to make available the capital needed as it built assets rather than profits.[17]

Another important initiative was the creation of the first property unit trust in 1966, the Pension Fund Property Unit Trust (PFPUT) that was set up as an independently managed fund with its own management committee, including Barrie Johnston from Schroders, and employing its own team of chartered surveyors. In 1971 Popham won agreement that Schroders should launch its own property unit trust, and hired Roy Coombes, a chartered surveyor from the Prudential, to run it. It grew very quickly and when in 1984 Haslemere took over PFPUT, the Schroder fund became the largest PUT in the UK, which it still is today with a value over £1.2 billion, under the able management of William Hill.[18]

Although still not very profitable, Investment Management was quietly emerging as an important and reliable business.

Banking

The banking business generated around 60% of Schroder Wagg's profits and was therefore a critical part of the business. The secondary banking crisis, rapidly increasing competition in the inter-bank market, OPEC-led inflation, worldwide recession and the poor state of the UK economy presented enormous challenges to the bankers. Fortunately, due to the cautious credit policies of David Forsyth, the head of Banking, Schroders suffered no bad debts – a remarkable achievement. Forsyth was a traditional colonial banker from the Hongkong and Shanghai Banking Corporation (HSBC). He was very cautious and believed that loan commitments were best made on the basis of a judgement of the people responsible within the client company – he was invariably right in these judgements and was a prudent and good chairman of the Credit Committee. He was a quiet man with great courtesy and much liked by all his colleagues.

Forsyth was supported by four directors: Gowi Mallinckrodt (responsible for North America and continental Europe); Peter Bulfield [19] (the UK, Australasia and Japan); Sir John Hall (Scandinavia and Latin America); and Ernest Ingold (foreign exchange trading). They all shared a room like partners. Mallinckrodt had good contacts in Germany and used Jean Solandt in London and Ulf Sudeck, Schroders' representative in Frankfurt, to conduct most of the banking business under his supervision. Mallinckrodt spent much of his time marketing to the major companies in the United States where he was more comfortable than in England – he travelled very extensively and also arranged many secondments of senior officers from Schrobanco to London. Schroder Wagg had identified the United States as being an important market for banking business and had an ambitious joint marketing programme taking advantage of the restrictions on foreign investment by US corporations, introduced in 1968 and monitored by the Office of Foreign Direct Investment (OFDI), to get business. This caused some friction with Schrobanco as most of the business opportunities came to London. It required a lot of goodwill and Mallinckrodt was the ideal person to be involved, since he was trusted in New York having spent many years there earlier in the 1950s. He was also spending an increasing amount of time with the international department under Wolfensohn (see Chapter 3).

Although Schroder Wagg managed to escape reasonably unscathed from the secondary banking crisis, it was caught out by the sharp rise in interest rates. The Barber boom and the Competition and Credit Controls policy from the Bank of England led to high interest rates being used as the main method of controlling credit – interest rates were pushed up successively to unprecedented levels from 9% to 13% in October 1973. John Cooper, the head of treasury operations up to the end of 1972 and formerly personal assistant to Richardson, had, in the previous year, when interest rates were relatively low, built up holdings in the region of $120 million of dollar certificates of deposit (CDs) with maturities of up to five years at fixed interest rates, which were being funded by short-term borrowing at variable interest rates in the inter-bank market. Bulfield, the head of UK banking, had built up a similar amount in sterling CDs. When these commitments were made the bank was making a healthy margin of 2%. However, with the surge in interest rates to levels double the locked-in fixed rates, the CDs became illiquid making it impossible to unwind the position. To do so, had it been possible, would have cost the bank £10 million, a third of its shareholders funds. No wonder Forsyth was deeply shocked and Airlie extremely worried. The problem was that nobody, including Forsyth, understood the treasury function save for Jean

Solandt who had been trained as a foreign exchange dealer at Société Générale in Paris before joining Schroder Wagg in 1968. With the firm losing up to £20,000 each day, Airlie asked Solandt, still an assistant director [20], to resolve the crisis. Cooper had left the previous year for Singer & Friedlander and Bulfield was asked to confine his activities to lending, which was where his strengths lay. To resolve the problem Solandt, with the support of Richard Bown, did more of the same and increased the amount of CDs by 50% as interest rates fell, building huge positions to offset the existing liabilities and at the same time increasing the average yield of the total portfolio. In parallel they carried out judicious foreign exchange trading which together enabled a break-even position to be achieved the following year. This led to profits for both sterling and foreign currencies which eventually turned into profits overall. Treasury management became an increasingly important source of Banking's profits. Airlie said Solandt was, 'superb. He, more than anyone, should take credit for seeing us through that difficult period. He had my total confidence and admiration.'

With the high interest rates, the good quality bank-lending book was increased particularly in the UK and Australia under Bulfield, a very competent lending banker and much liked by his customers. The long-established Latin American business, which rarely involved loans over six months and only to corporate names, also grew in line with the rest of the lending book under Hall and Tony Lesser [21]. Occasionally, to test the credit standing of Latin American borrowers, Forsyth used not to renew their facilities to see whether they could borrow elsewhere and then only renew them if they were successful, even at the risk of losing them as a customer.

Another activity that came under Banking was Schroder Leasing, which provided new lending opportunities with higher margins but where credit risks could be contained. Over the years this business was developed to become the market leader in small ticket sales and leasing. There was not much synergy with Banking but it made a good return on capital and was very profitable.

An export credit unit was set up under Ansell Egerton, which focused on fee-earning advisory services, based on arranging syndicated loans for exporters, guaranteed by the British government. Egerton, a former university economics professor and journalist hired by Verey, was bright and ambitious despite being rather lazy. He built up a good business financing UK exports to South Africa, including two of the largest export lines of credit for ISCOR, the government steel corporation and Industrial Development Corporation which financed large British contracts for capital goods to South African companies. They gave Schroders access to some of the main British exporters who were clients of Hill Samuel and Lazards – the leaders in the UK export credit business – and would otherwise not have dealt with Schroders. The other members of the team were Alastair Forsyth, Bernard Dewe Mathews and Eric Jones, an able drafter of loan agreements. Forsyth was the key member of the team as he had been in United Steel and AEI before it was acquired by GEC. He therefore knew the main exporters and also how they won and financed their contracts. The early years were difficult and little progress was made outside South Africa, despite a lot of hard work. Projects were followed with great diligence in Jamaica, Egypt, Iran and Brazil to name only a few but all to no avail. It was all very frustrating and depressing for those involved.

In 1977, following one of Wolfensohn's initiatives, the setting up of a joint-venture merchant bank with the Standard Bank in Nigeria, Egerton and Alastair Forsyth decided to move to Lagos, perhaps because they saw no future in Schroders' export credit business. When the Nigerian government enacted an indigenisation decree enforcing all banks to sell 50% of their shares to the government, Schroders decided to withdraw. Egerton left to become the managing director of Standard Chartered Bank's merchant banking businesses in London. Forsyth went to Venezuela to open a representative office in Caracas for Banking under Lesser.

Schrobanco

The largest part of Schroders' limited capital in 1973 was invested in Schrobanco and this increased as the dollar appreciated against sterling. However, the nominal return on equity of around 8% was low and a matter of serious concern. In Bruno's view Schroders made a mistake in never taking out a dividend from Schrobanco and this was a bad discipline for the management, as they were never expected to achieve target returns on their capital. In his last few years at Schroders, Richardson had spent a lot of his time trying to find a way through the problems of the Glass-Steagall Act (which prevented US commercial bankers from underwriting stock market issues) by seeing a lot of the leading lawyers on Wall Street. He found this intellectually interesting but it proved unproductive. After Richardson departed for the Bank of England, Verey largely left Schrobanco to Wolfensohn. He used to visit New York for board meetings but returned to London immediately afterwards. Most of the London management had little time for Schrobanco, thinking that they were lightweight second-class bankers. The Schroder family, however, had a strong emotional commitment to them as the firm, which had large debts outstanding in Germany after the war, would have failed but for the solvency of Schrobanco and so Bruno would have nothing to do with those who wished to sell it. Verey had regular arguments with Bruno over the subject and acquired his nickname 'the butler' as a result of saying 'I have had enough of being treated like the family's butler.' He therefore left it to Wolfensohn.

In fact Schrobanco had earlier been a very interesting institution that had attracted a lot of senior ex-government people. In the early 1950s, 90% of Schroders' profits had come from New York, but this percentage started to erode from 1958 with the acute 'funding squeeze' on banks in New York and the emerging competition from the large domestic banks in New York in the international markets. Due to its parentage Schrobanco had far more experience of international markets than its larger competitors in New York, which were much more focused on the domestic market. Ford Motor Company had a policy that all exports had to be financed externally and Schrobanco was appointed as one of the banks to finance its operations in South America, mainly involving short-term finance for shipping exports in Venezuela. In Asia, feeding on Schroders' 150-year history and Schroder Wagg's contacts, much business was done by Matt Snyder [22] in Japan and particularly in Taiwan and Korea where Schrobanco played an intermediary role in the financing of US support programmes for the export of food. Schrobanco acted as the lead bank and agent of many multinational loans to Latin American and Asian borrowers since it could understand the credits, which were not based on conventional balance sheets. Schrobanco only took a small participation in each loan syndicating the rest to US banks, many of them from the states outside New York. Some of the colour of the firm at the time is described in the note at the end of the chapter by Marion Gilliam who joined Schrobanco as assistant to the general counsel in 1966 and left after Wolfensohn departed in 1977. [23]

Wolfensohn's appointment as president of Schrobanco in 1970, aged 36, initially caused a lot of unrest among the senior executives in New York. It was during a shifting regulatory environment particularly concerning the foreign-owned banks. The problem with Schrobanco was profitability – it was too small to succeed in its domestic market as it had insufficient capital to become a lead bank. It had a good reputation for ingenuity and creativity as a specialist international banking firm with its main clientele being in Europe, Latin America and Asia. It also had some impressive US clients, including General Motors, IBM and General Electric, and it concentrated on serving them in the international markets. However, as the large New York banks increased their overseas activities Schrobanco was gradually squeezed out. Throughout there was a continuing desire to move into investment banking. At one stage Richardson and Wolfensohn considered the sale of Schrobanco with a view to purchasing 25% of First Boston but this was rejected in favour of Schroders remoulding Schrobanco under its own ownership. Wolfensohn emphasised expanding the non-banking activities and cut costs to increase profitability. He also put a lot of effort into expanding the overseas presence in places like Brazil, Colombia and Venezuela. He even initiated the purchase of a small stake in PDFCI, a development bank in Indonesia sponsored by the International Finance Corporation (IFC), the private sector arm of the World Bank. After people had got used to him he was seen as the main agent for change, the visionary and the driving force. He was not best pleased when Verey told him to 'batten down the hatches'.

Despite this, Wolfensohn continued to inspire all those around him. Following the oil crisis in 1973 and the substantial increases in the revenues of the oil producers, Wolfensohn suggested to the Central Bank of Venezuela, for whom Schrobanco had arranged a gold-backed loan, that Schroders assist it with the management of its funds as it lacked the skills in-house. Wolfensohn was asked to develop proposals and he assembled a team that included Solandt, Erik Gasser, the general manager of Schroders AG, Geoffrey Bell, a former personal assistant to Richardson based in New York, and various others from the Group. All of the competitors were asked to make presentations and as a result Schroders was awarded a contract, which although relatively small was extremely prestigious. Solandt said, 'I have never been as motivated – it was a wonderful experience with Jim a great inspiration.' It was also the start of the Reserve Asset Management Programme (RAMP), a group effort comprising colleagues from New York under Bell, London under Henry Blackie, and others from Zurich and Beirut, that marketed fund management services to central banks around the world and then extended its services to industrial companies. It was one of many examples of group-wide efforts initiated by Wolfensohn, although it has to be said it did more for Schroders' reputation with the central banks than its profits. Unfortunately Wolfensohn failed to select a good leader and the concept was picked up and exploited to the full by SG Warburg, Lehman and Lazard Frères, who as a triumvirate made an enormous success of the business acting for many governments, the most prestigious being a long-term contract in Indonesia.

In 1974 Verey appointed Wolfensohn as group chief executive and this required him to move back to London. Mark Maged, who had been hired by Wolfensohn as the general counsel of Schroders in New York, succeeded him as president of Schroders Inc in 1974 and became a director of Schroders Ltd the following year. A lawyer by background with no banking experience and lacking Wolfensohn's genius, Maged handed over the presidency of Schrobanco to Martin Witschi, a Swiss-born banker with a reputation for being very careful and who had been at Schrobanco since 1950, so that he could concentrate on the development and expansion of the investment banking activities. Wolfensohn had hired a number of people from outside to support Maged in building the new investment banking business within Schrocorp, including Steve Petchek, a partner of a leading law firm specialising in mergers and acquisitions and Ajit Hutheesing, the marketing director of IFC. Jim Collinson was another member of the team concentrating on venture capital. Hutheesing's experiences give a feel for the atmosphere at Schrocorp at the time. [24] He was asked to develop a plan to do new business in the United States that differentiated Schroders from Morgan Stanley, the leading investment bank in New York at the time. Not long afterwards Wolfensohn was drawn back to London where his life became

> increasingly difficult, as his efforts were continually frustrated. Although Mark was meant to run the show, it was Jim who was the driving force coming up with all the initiatives, many of which ran into the sand. Mark was not a good judge of projects. Jim was always on an aeroplane, often accompanied by his cello in the next seat, and therefore was difficult to access. Any problems had to be dealt with through Bayley, who did not have a good reputation with the officers in New York, being regarded as too superficial. There was no leadership at the top – Jim may not have been good at selecting his senior colleagues. His position in London was becoming increasingly untenable despite being the chief executive.

The Wolfensohn Affair
In 1977 Verey's time was up and this led to a major battle over who should be his successor. Verey was absolutely determined to stop Wolfensohn – 'over my dead body'

he said. Why had he changed his mind about Wolfensohn? He and his wife Mary had been travelling in China with Anthony and Jenny Loehnis in 1974, at which time he was very relaxed about Wolfensohn being his successor. Prior to that they had been separated by the Atlantic but they had quite different personalities and once in London there was increasing friction between them. There were also differences between Wolfensohn and the other senior people in London, who tended to be more conventional. The two main contenders to succeed Verey were Airlie and Wolfensohn.

As explained earlier, David Airlie had been with Schroders since 1953 and was well known, respected with a proven record in Investment Management and liked by both the Schroder and the Helbert, Wagg directors and therefore an insider. Outside Schroders he was treasurer of the Scout Association and being close to the Royal family he performed a variety of public services, mostly connected with Scotland. An Etonian and ex-Scots Guards officer, he was in looks, appearance and manner a true aristocrat. Although occasionally somewhat aloof he was known for his courtesy, which made him popular with colleagues and staff. He was the classic establishment figure, characteristic of those then running large institutions in the City. Although not a great intellect, he personified integrity and prudence and stood for continuity. He was safe and reliable. His weakness was that like Verey before him he had no experience of corporate finance, which was the key to Schroders' reputation. He was 51 years old.

Jim Wolfensohn, the group chief executive, was a protégé of Richardson but an outsider. He was an intellectually brilliant internationalist with a huge charisma and a large following of admirers in the firm, particularly among the young. He was a phenomenal business getter, being very attentive to the needs of clients. He was bright and likeable to clients and had an aura of winning. People liked to be seen in his company. He was politically shrewd with clients but not so within the bank. On the other hand, he was rather volatile and left others to carry out the execution of ideas initiated by him, often requiring them having to pick up the pieces after the many hares he had set off. He was rather domineering and his style led to him being surrounded by a select group of acolytes who tended to be loyal to him rather than to the firm. Some felt he was more of a boutique man, being a brilliant corporate adviser, than a suitable leader for a large corporation. He was exciting, erratic and a risk taker and likely to challenge cherished assumptions. He was also a natural leader, a quality lacking within Schroders. In 1977 he was still only 43.

Mallinckrodt, who had probably worked more closely with Wolfensohn than anyone else in London said,

> his sheer intelligence and imagination were formidable. The fact that he played the cello so well showed that his discipline and interpretive powers were remarkable and I think he brought these qualities to business as shown in his fertile mind and his extraordinary creativity. Few people have this ability and passion, which is often found among the most successful Jews. The fact that there are so few Jews in the

world and that they have always been a minority and continually persecuted makes it inherent in their character that they are fundamentally insecure and feel they have to defend their turf. They achieve this by their elitism through their intellectual capital. Jim had this and always wanted to be in the driving seat.

Mallinckrodt was very concerned about the impasse regarding the succession but felt it was a management issue not an ownership issue and advised Bruno Schroder that the family should not be a final arbiter. Although he was not on the board he said he would wish to be seen as neutral.

With his creative work in New York, all the management there, including Bayley, were rooting for Wolfensohn. However, the relative strength of New York had declined as the scales had been tipped by the growth and greater profitability of London through the leading reputation of Corporate Finance under Richardson and by the loss of Schrobanco's franchise in New York.

The board was evenly split on the issue with the London directors on the side of Airlie and the New York-based directors supporting, and the Schroder family being in sympathy with, Wolfensohn. The three independent non-executive directors were in the middle. They were Lord Oliver Franks, a highly distinguished former British Ambassador to Washington and chairman of Lloyds Bank and currently provost of Worcester College, Oxford University, Sir Ernest Woodroofe, a former chairman of Unilever, and Dr Harold Brown, an eminent scientist, former Secretary of the US Air Force and president of the California Institute of Technology. Wolfensohn played his hand rather badly by lobbying certain of the London directors, which made them distrust him as they did not like his style. After many indecisive meetings over a period of many months, it was put into the hands of Franks to resolve. In the meanwhile nobody was looking after the business.

In the end it came down to whether or not to reject Wolfensohn. Because of the concern raised by Verey, who was always loyal to those who worked for him, that Airlie and Hull might leave, Franks came to the conclusion that, although Wolfensohn was the more talented, Airlie was the safer option. Wolfensohn had been out-manoeuvred by Verey. It was common gossip in the City that anti-Semitism was one of the factors weighing against Wolfensohn. On leaving he wrote a letter to Gilliam saying, 'How can a Jewish boy from down under compete with a thoroughbred racehorse?' This was surprising as there was no anti-Semitism within Schroders lower down, where Wolfensohn was seen as a magnetic and inspiring figure.

The Schroder family

Bruno Schroder, aged 47 at the time, represented the Schroder family interests on the board. He was at Harvard Business School in 1960 when his father, Helmut, had his second heart attack and so decided to return to England and forsake a career in the United States. He initially started in Banking and then joined Corporate Finance but soon realised that he should concentrate his efforts on preserving the family's capital –

as in the Parable of the Talents (Matthew 25:14-30) – rather than on earning profits for the bank. He therefore became non-executive, going on to the board as a non-executive director in 1963. He was a strong advocate of Wolfensohn and was frustrated by not being able to force the issue with his family's controlling shareholding. He did not get on with Verey. Verey, a former partner of Helbert, Wagg, who was the main dissenter against the merger, felt the Helbert, Wagg directors had not been treated as well as the Schroder directors since the merger in 1962. Bruno on the other hand felt that they had been very well compensated at the time of the merger. This resulted in a bad relationship between them. Verey, having served in the war, was also openly anti-German. Bruno, however, had little influence and Verey treated him with disdain. Bruno felt very aggrieved by his failure to secure Wolfensohn's position. He was determined thereafter to ensure he was never outvoted on the board again.

Central to the story of Schroders is the role of the Schroder family as seen through the actions and attitude of Bruno, the head of the family. As explained earlier the family, which comprised Bruno, Charmaine and their cousin John, owned 48% of the shares. The Schroder family had been brought up with a Calvinistic sense of duty to the firm and to looking after the people in the firm and at Dunlossit, their estate on the Isle of Islay in Scotland. They were proud of the firm, which was the focal point of the family, and they saw it to be their duty to protect their shareholding in it. In the words of another outside shareholder, 'the Schroders believe that what they have inherited they hold in trust for the next generation. Their job is to look after it and preferably hand it on in better shape than it was when they inherited it from the previous generation.' This attitude was the result of Bruno's grandfather, Baron Bruno having been entrusted the responsibility for the firm by his uncle Sir John Henry and knowing he had not earned it, he inculcated in his son Helmut that the firm was not personal but held in trust for the next generation. This philosophy was handed down to Bruno and Charmaine who were told by their father that what was good for the firm was good for the family. They never regarded the firm in monetary terms, rarely considering the share price and never seeing themselves as being rich. It was also important for themselves and the family that they all earned a living. Through the good work of Sidney Hodgson, a lawyer from Farrows who had been recruited by Richardson to run the family office, they had been able, with his superb knowledge of tax, to maintain their shareholding despite the expansion of the firm.

Bruno saw the success of Schroders being based on three legs: choosing the right strategy; its effective implementation; and maintenance of effective control through the family shareholding. He felt that as a member of the board he could participate in the first, the second was based on having the right management and the third could be achieved by organising efficient tax structures and keeping the family together. In respect to strategy he was therefore prepared to ask endless questions and if necessary defer any answers in the quest of ensuring he made no errors. If in doubt he would prefer to see no change. Needless-to-say this exasperated the management who patiently had to go into exhausting detail to satisfy him and so with dogged determination the figures had to be broken down into ever increasing detail.

The big challenge came in 1989 when John, who had no involvement in Schroders, decided to sell all his Schroder shares, which by that time represented just over 6% of the voting shares. Fortunately, Bruno and Charmaine had secured a letter from John stating that he would offer them the shares at their market value should he decide to sell. Bruno immediately went around to Philip Wilkinson at the NatWest Bank and within 20 minutes was given a £25 million line of credit that enabled him to buy most of John's shares. He also rang Gowi, who was in Tokyo at the time, and informed him of the position saying that they needed to place some of John's shares into friendly hands. Over the next few days Gowi arranged for various Japanese banks and families close to Schroders as well as Bill Turner, then on the Schrobanco board, to purchase some of the shares. In the meanwhile Bruno and Charmaine underwrote the value of the shares, with a potential loss of up to £6.5 million. At the same time, on the suggestion of Philip, Gowi and Charmaine's son, the family divested itself of all its non-voting shares and bought voting shares. Together with their friends they were able to buy all of John's shares at the market price, finishing up with the 48.01% of the voting shares that was necessary to maintain effective control and to preserve the independence of Schroders. There were no agreements with the friendly parties regarding retention and all was done through the good relationships developed over many years. It was a major milestone that secured the independence of Schroders by protecting it from predators and gave it the freedom to rebuild itself in the face of a rapidly changing market. The Schroder family knew they could always buy 2% in the market in one year should it be necessary, although this was to change when the Take-over Panel changed the rules to stop creeping control. However, this independence brought with it the constraint of inhibiting growth though a lack of capital to make major acquisitions.

Bruno with great reluctance agreed to Airlie being appointed chairman and there was friction between them throughout his chairmanship, particularly in relation to Schrobanco. Almost immediately afterwards Mallinckrodt was made an executive member of the board and Bayley, who had strongly supported Wolfensohn and also had bad relations with Airlie, became deputy chairman. As a *quid pro quo* Airlie insisted that John Hull become chairman of Schroder Wagg and joint deputy chairman of Schroders.

Wolfensohn, after receiving $100,000 in compensation for loss of office, immediately left to join Salomon Brothers in New York. He was big enough not to show the bitterness he clearly must have felt, having turned his mind to his future at Salomons. However, when interviewed later he recalled, 'I was going to change the structure, make it more goal-orientated, more aggressive. That would have upset the apple cart. They were scared that I would do terrible things, like getting them into distribution. I had a different perception. I knew the merchant banks were vulnerable' (David Kynaston, *The City of London Vol. IV, A Club No More*). He had a brilliant career after Schroders, initially as a partner at Salomon Brothers – in which he made a lot of money when it was acquired by Philipp Brothers (Phibro) in 1981 – and then when he opened his own investment banking boutique on Wall Street, James D Wolfensohn & Associates, based on the handsome retainers he received from ten clients. Such was his reputation as a corporate financier to the most prestigious companies in the United States that, much to the envy of the whole of Wall Street, he attracted Paul Volcker, the retiring chairman of the US Federal Reserve Board. President Clinton finally nominated him to be the President of the World Bank where he was to face significantly more difficult and important challenges. Throughout he remained a good friend of Schroders and was often available, despite his horrendously busy schedule, to be of help. Looking back his departure from Schroders was the right decision for everybody but at the time it created a lot of tension and disappointment among the young who did not know Airlie.

Airlie greatly admired Wolfensohn's enormous talents and got on well with him. He was the first to agree that he was a great loss. 'Jim was an investment banker par excellence and brilliant with clients.' He felt that the best solution would have been for Wolfensohn to be the group chief executive with him as chairman but Wolfensohn was not interested in that. Had the roles been similar to those agreed between Mallinckrodt and Bischoff later on things might have been different.

NOTES

1. In 1960 Helmut Schroder had his second heart attack and various family trusts were set up to avoid death duties. The main beneficiaries were his two children Bruno and Charmaine and his nephew John Schroder. Between them they controlled fewer than 50% of the shares with John owning approximately 6%. In the event Helmut recovered and only died in 1969.

2. Gordon Richardson was called to the Bar in 1946 and, having built up a successful practice specialising in company law, decided in 1955 to pursue a career in the City by joining the Industrial and Commercial Finance Corporation (ICFC) with the expectation of succeeding Lord Piercy as chairman. When Piercy decided not to retire, despite being 71, Richardson accepted an invitation from Helmut Schroder to become a partner of J Henry Schroder & Co in 1957 and was appointed deputy chairman in 1960.

3. David Forsyth joined J Henry Schroder & Co in 1951, aged 32, having been with the Hongkong and Shanghai Banking Corporation in Asia since the war (he joined Martins Bank aged 16 in 1937 and was transferred to HSBC in 1939 before being called up). He worked on Japanese and South American banking business under Alec Cairns, the long-standing and highly respected head of Banking until 1964 when he succeeded him.

4. John Bayley, an accountant and financial controller with Sperry Gyroscope Co Ltd, had been recruited as financial controller by Richardson in 1959, aged 36, and was appointed to the board in 1966. Richardson had a high regard for his financial skills – he had a photographic memory and was strong on mental arithmetic – and he became part of

Richardson's inner circle. He played a major supporting role to Richardson in his efforts to build up Schrobanco and became largely based in New York from 1973, when he acquired his nickname 'the captain' after a film of Alec Guinness because of his endless travel between his two homes in London and New York. In 1977 he remained the highly respected group finance director and was influential. He was a strong supporter of Wolfensohn and the Schroder family but played a declining role after Richardson's departure. He remained in regular contact with Richardson and kept him in touch with developments at Schroders.

5. John Hull, who had been in chambers with Richardson, had been encouraged to leave the Bar in 1961, when aged 32, to head Schroders' small corporate finance operation, and was appointed a director in 1969.

6. Leslie Murphy, a former civil servant and private secretary to Hugh Gaitskill, the Minister of Fuel and Power (and future leader of the Labour Party) and finance director of the Iraq Petroleum Company, came to Schroder Wagg in 1964 and was appointed a director in 1970.

7. James Wolfensohn, an Australian lawyer and former partner of the Sydney stockbroker Ord, Minnett, had become a managing director of Darling & Company in 1965. He had formerly been a member of the Australian fencing team in the 1956 Olympics and was an accomplished cellist. After a row with John Broinowski, the autocratic head of Darling & Company in 1968 (see Chapter 18), Richardson arranged for him to join Schroder Wagg as head of its international bond-issuing business. In 1970 Richardson unexpectedly appointed him president of Schrobanco at the early age of 36.

8. Sir Henry Fisher, a former high court judge, became group planning director in 1971, having been persuaded by Richardson that merchant banking would be a more interesting career than remaining on the bench. Later he said wryly, 'It is always greener on the other side.'

9. John Howell joined Schrobanco in 1947, aged 30, having served in the war as a journalist and was much involved in Schrobanco's international expansion particularly in Europe. He succeeded Gerald Beal as president in 1962.

10. Lord David Ogilvy (the future Earl of Airlie) had joined the investment department of J Henry Schroder & Co in 1953 and accompanied Helmut on his historic red-carpet tour of Germany in 1954 to re-establish banking relationships with the major institutions and large companies – following the settlement of the Standstill debts in Germany which had so tested Schroders' resources immediately after the war that they had vowed never to do business with Germany again – and included a call on Dr Hermann Abs, the chairman of Deutsche Bank and the most important banker in Europe. Airlie found it interesting to revisit Germany and see how it had recovered from the war, having last been there in 1945, as an officer in the Scots Guards, when the country was totally devastated. He also assisted Richardson in his fundamental review of the firm's activities in 1957. Following the acquisition of Helbert, Wagg he was sent by Richardson to sit with Verey and Ponsonby to learn about the merchant banking business. At the time Helbert, Wagg was as good a merchant bank as any in the City and it was commonly accepted in the City and within Schroders that the people in Helbert, Wagg were significantly better than those in Schroders. Airlie recognised this and found himself in the uncomfortable position of having divided loyalties, much liking his new colleagues. He felt that the combination of Richardson's intellect, legal training and well founded views and Verey's instinctive feel for the market, which was as good as anyone's in the City, was unbeatable. And so Airlie was at the heart of the firm and close to all those who mattered. This was to have a profound effect on his future.

11. Mark Maged, who had been hired by Wolfensohn as Schroders Inc's general counsel, succeeded him as president of Schrobanco when Wolfensohn was appointed group chief executive of Schroders and chairman of Schroders Inc in November 1974.

12. Geoffrey Williams, a partner of Slaughter & May since 1961 and much involved with the affairs of J Henry Schroder from the mid-1950s, was invited by Richardson to join Schroder Wagg in 1966 and succeeded John Hull as head of Corporate Finance in 1968. He was universally admired by his colleagues and was an effective head of Corporate Finance. He was a trouble-shooter rather than a creator of business. Adam Broadbent, who became head of Corporate Finance 16 years later and greatly admired Williams, described him as having 'superlative critical intelligence and an ability to understand what made a deal and what did not. He was also extremely funny and entertaining and not at all serious – a characteristic he shared with John Hull, his closest colleague.' Nicholas Jones, one of the most highly regarded directors of Corporate Finance during the mid-1980s, 'liked Geoffrey enormously and found him immensely helpful to bounce off corporate finance problems with his superb mind and ability to get to the point immediately.' Williams remained a mentor and consultant to those in Corporate Finance until he retired in 1990, being willing to talk through their problems and to address complex and difficult problems with great clarity often adding a few amusing Schroder anecdotes if they had time to indulge in his skills as a raconteur.

13. Gary Brass had a difficult decision in 1978 when Harold Lamotte, a colleague at Schroders, asked him if he would join him in setting up a private fund management business. He felt the challenge and the likelihood of there being a life after 50 made it worthwhile sacrificing the excitement he would have had at Schroders between 32 and 50. Twenty-five years later they are still together and have built up a very successful boutique.

14. Tyo van Marle, who was born and educated in the Netherlands, had joined Schroders in 1972 from Pierson Heldring & Pierson, the Dutch merchant bank, where he had worked on domestic and international corporate finance including capital market issues.

15. At the request of Gordon Richardson, Anthony Loehnis was seconded to the Bank in

1977 where he assisted with the Wilson committee of inquiry into the Stock Exchange. Two years later, not having been offered a role he would have liked at the Bank, he was attracted back to Schroders by Airlie to become deputy to Ashton in charge of international issues. With the decline of Corporate Finance and with Michael Bentley, recruited by Airlie from Lazards, not coming up to scratch, Loehnis, who had always been seen by Verey as a potential chairman of Schroders, was clearly an important catch. Airlie was not therefore best pleased when within nine months Loehnis returned to the Bank in 1980 as the overseas director, Richardson by then having cleared his lines – Airlie may have reasonably felt that this was what Richardson had intended all along. Loehnis remained at the Bank for the next ten years before becoming vice-chairman of SG Warburg in 1989. Before leaving he was asked by Airlie to carry out a 'Whither Schroders' exercise with Richard Sadleir, Airlie's PA. The broad conclusions were to sell Schrobanco and to stop pretending Schroders was an international bank rather than a cluster of local banks.

16. John de Havilland's father, a retired professional soldier, encouraged his son to go into the City and arranged for him to have a summer job at Schroders in 1957 where he knew Sir Alex Abel-Smith and Jock Backhouse. Two years later, having finished at Cambridge, he wrote asking when and where he should report to and was surprised to receive a frosty reply. Apparently, he had failed to write a thank you letter and so was not thought a suitable person for Schroders to employ. He had to eat humble pie before being taken into the investment department where he received the best possible training by preparing, in perfect italic script, client valuations – the lady who typed them had an instinctive feel for whether there were errors and he thereby acquired a feel for what looked right. He then had to learn how to write a letter to a client and found he had to work at it. He and Airlie were the only investment managers from Schroders to join up with the former Helbert, Wagg partners.

17. Schroder Life scarcely made any profits in its 14-year life prior to it being sold to The National Mutual Association of Australasia in 1986 for £99 million from an investment of £12 million (see Chapter 2). Govett had a disagreement with Popham over the content of the sale at the time as he felt Schroders should retain the institutional based unit trusts and Schroders' own client holdings as a base for building a new business. Govett won the argument and it proved to be the key to building the institutional unit trust business. At the same time, Richard Foulkes suggested that Banking should take the client cash deposits on to the balance sheet and, against many sceptics in Banking, managed to persuade them there was a hard core of funds that would not be withdrawn. This was to change later following the Leeson affair and the collapse of Barings (see Chapter 22).

18. There were successful property management businesses in the United States under Norman Peck and in Australia under Jeremy Lewis (see Chapter 18), both run independently from London. Any future attempts to achieve synergies through integration were unsuccessful after a significant part of the equity in both businesses had been conceded to their senior managements to keep them within the Group and they had no intention of giving up the independence that this afforded them. Eventually it was agreed that the only way forward was for Schroders to sell its interest in them.

19. Peter Bulfield, a 29-year-old chartered accountant, was hired by John Bayley as the firm's internal auditor in 1959 after which he joined Banking under David Forsyth becoming a director of Schroder Wagg in 1967.

20. The title assistant director was initiated to mitigate the effects of the government's ridiculous incomes policy and was described by Richardson as 'a stepping stone for some and a resting place for others', and so it proved.

21. Antony Lesser was interviewed and accepted by Helbert, Wagg and started at Schroders in 1962, aged 23. Speaking Italian, French and Spanish, he spent most of his career on banking in Latin Europe followed by Latin America.

22. Matthew Snyder joined Schrobanco in 1968 under Peter Carpenter and found the firm enormously collegiate, almost like a partnership. He spent much time in London and had a strong relationship with those in Banking. He became a senior vice president responsible for Asia and was part of the group of enthusiastic supporters of Wolfensohn. He left in 1979 and was very successful working with Middle East institutions. He observed that most of those he knew at Schroders in New York did well after they left.

23. Marion Gilliam, whose family knew Gerry Beal, joined Schrobanco as a young lawyer in 1966. He found himself working for the general counsel who rarely appeared as he was invariably on an alcoholic binge between attending drying out clinics. He found it very challenging working with Sullivan & Cromwell, the leading commercial law practice in New York. His colleagues at Schrobanco were all slightly off-beat and attractive, many of them interesting ex-government people. It soon became apparent that Richardson's main interest was in developing an investment banking business but this was frustrated by the Glass-Steagall Act. Endless discussions were held with the leading law firms and Gilliam was asked by Richardson how Schroders could get around the Act. His conclusions were pretty straightforward, 'you will have to sell the banking operations in New York'. He was deeply impressed by Richardson's brilliant mind but found like others that he sometimes had difficulty making up his mind, always seeing every side of the argument. He first came across Richardson, shortly after being hired. Having had an agreeable conversation about books and music, he stopped at the door on his way out and apologetically asked him who he was. Later he was seconded to London to work in Corporate Finance sharing an office with Win Bischoff and immediately struck up a friendship with Wolfensohn, often going to concerts together – in his spare time Wolfensohn was managing the careers of a group of exceptional musicians including Vladimir Ashkenazy, Daniel Barenboim, Radu Lupu and André Previn. He returned to New York after his secondment to hear that, despite all the discussions with the lawyers, the Schroder family was unwilling to sell Schrobanco. From then on he worked as an assistant to Wolfensohn as corporate secretary and part of an internal advisory team.

24. Ajit Hutheesing had known Wolfensohn since his days at Loeb Rhodes in the early 1960s and had remained a friend as he moved on to SG Warburg in London and then to support the interests in India of his family, who were related to the Nehrus, and finally for ten years at IFC. At IFC he was a chief investment officer responsible for investments and loans to the southern cone countries of South America for six years. He then became the marketing director responsible for managing IFC's portfolio of investments and loans, the syndication of existing and new loans, co-financing and the public floating of equity investments, thereby releasing more funds to invest and lend to new customers. He therefore had substantial international experience and useful contacts in the developing world. In 1975 Wolfensohn asked Hutheesing to come into the real world and join Maged, Petchek and Collinson at Schroder Corporation, the vehicle used to build an investment banking business in New York. 'He painted a big picture of Schroders in New York as an international bank building on the international relationships of Schroders in London – it sounded very attractive. Jim had such magnetism that it was difficult to say no to him.'

CHAPTER 2

THE AIRLIE YEARS

1977 – 1984

Airlie's first task was to undo the damage done during the extensive debate prior to his appointment as chairman. He worked on, 'mending the fences and settling things down', particularly in New York where there was great dissension led by Bayley. Originally he would have liked to have taken on the two roles of chairman of Schroders and chairman of Schroder Wagg, but he rapidly came to the conclusion that things were continuing to go badly in New York and he therefore asked Hull to become chairman of Schroder Wagg. Hull was somewhat reluctant but agreed to take on the job for three years.

In 1969, Richardson had asked Hull to take some time off to prepare a blueprint for Schroders' future with a revised structure and business plan. He spent two weeks at home preparing the plan, which was put to the board. Hull was asked to implement the plan and was appointed group planning officer and a member of the board. 'I was therefore removed from all profitable duties and couldn't think of anyone less suited to the appointment.' He did, however, spend a lot of time in New York and came to understand what an investment bank could and could not do while owning a commercial bank in the USA. In the next twelve months he did very little apart from supporting Richardson – 'nothing happened nor was it likely to happen'. He was then 'returned to unit' as head of Corporate Finance for a year, which he greatly enjoyed. However, he had already burnt his boats with Richardson. What Hull liked most was having his own clients and seeing through transactions for them. He was particularly fond of Sir Geoffrey Crowther, the former editor of the *Economist* and then the chairman of Trust Houses, who categorised all people in public life as being 'bishops or bookmakers'. Crowther, who was clearly a bishop, now as a captain of industry saw himself as a bookmaker. Hull never made that mistake, always seeing himself as a bishop. He liked his clients and was interested in their businesses, not in 'squeezing fees' out of them. The final straw for Richardson was when in 1972 he accepted an invitation by the Bank of England to take over from Ian Fraser as full-time director general of the Take-over Panel for three years. He never regretted his decision and had the best time of his career. Ian Fraser who went on to become chairman of Lazards said of Hull, 'This was a brilliant appointment and John fulfilled it with much distinction for three years' (Ian Fraser, *The High Road to England*). He returned to Schroders at the end of 1974 and became joint deputy chairman of Schroders and chairman of Schroder Wagg in 1977. He accepted these appointments with some reluctance, as he did not want all the hassle of disagreements with the Schroder family. A close colleague said that in some ways he was the wrong man in the wrong place at the wrong time. He once told another colleague that he was far too embarrassed to be seen reading the *Financial Times* in public and so carried *The Times*. Anybody who knew John could not fail to like, respect and admire him. His exceptionally high ethical standards were an example to all.

When asked by the editor of the *Schroder Wagtail*, the house magazine, to contribute a report on the London group of companies, following his appointment as chairman of Schroder Wagg, typically he did not set out the usual litany of financial results but wrote that,

> The magazine is concerned with the most important part of our business – the people who work in it. It aims, through its record of our activities to bring us closer together, to make us feel, as we must feel if we are to have enduring success, that we are a community of people with a common dedication and loyalty to and affection for the organisation within which we work. I believe that, over the years, it has been magnificently successful in so doing. It is our people who have fashioned our business and who have created the very fine reputation that it has in the City of London and, indeed, worldwide – a reputation of which we are all justly proud.
>
> For all members of staff, 1977 has been, in personal terms, I know a very difficult year. The continuing high rate of inflation has meant real hardship for those with young families. This knowledge makes me all the more appreciative of the efforts and enthusiasm of you all, because it is your efforts and your enthusiasm which have made possible the achievements of 1977.

Whereas following Verey's appointment there were substantial changes to the board involving the removal of supporters of Wolfensohn and others associated with Richardson, Airlie did not remove anyone. Instead he united the board although his relations with Bayley and Bruno were cool. Harold Brown, the non-executive director in New York who had been part of the decision against Wolfensohn, retired at the same time as Verey and was not immediately replaced. In 1982 Jack Howell retired as chairman of Schroders Inc and was replaced by Jack Connor, a formidable American businessman, who had joined the board in 1980.[1] Murphy, who was close to the Schroder family, returned to the board as a non-executive at the end of his period at the National Enterprise Board in 1979 and was followed the next year by Baron Daniel Janssen, a leading Belgium industrialist, who was chairman of the executive committee of the chemical company Solvay and close to the Schroder family. With Mallinckrodt also a director, the Schroder family had many more votes than before the Wolfensohn saga. Apart from Mallinckrodt, the other new executive directors were Michael Bentley, Popham, head of Investment Management, and Solandt, the new head of Banking who had succeeded Forsyth when he retired in 1978. Bentley was invited by Airlie to join Schroders from Lazard Brothers where he had run their merchant bank in South Korea, having previously spent many years in SG Warburg. He was given responsibility for transatlantic investment banking but found it difficult to make much impact without having businesses directly reporting to him. Having little experience of the United States, like practically everyone else in London, did not help. Being an outsider and, worse, a potential successor to Airlie did not make his life any easier. Airlie realised quite quickly that he had made a mistake. Bentley was, however, to play a major role in developing Schroders' oil and gas expertise and in creating the highly successful venture capital business (see Chapter 13).

The economic conditions that had been so bad during Verey's time had improved by the end of 1977. The key issues dealt with during Airlie's chairmanship were: trying to halt the slide in Schroders' reputation as a corporate finance house; the continuingly difficult competitive position of Schrobanco; expansion outside the United Kingdom and the United States; and most importantly putting in place a long-term plan to secure Schroders' future and to deal with the Big Bang. This is the term used to encapsulate the changes culminating on 27 October 1986 with the abandonment of the commission agreement between members of the London Stock Exchange and of strict segregation of jobbers and brokers, the effect of which was that the banks were able to enter the securities business and buy jobbers and brokers.[2] Investment Management and Treasury laid the seeds for their future success and Banking was hit by the Latin American debt crisis.

Corporate Finance

In terms of reputation, corporate finance was what really mattered. This was the area that Richardson had made his own. Although during Verey's period there was little business, due to the bad economic conditions, and many of the clients had to be rescued, Schroders was already slipping. Cator handed over to Ashton in 1978 after Airlie became chairman and was made vice-chairman of Schroder Wagg, a largely honorary title and useful when a client wanted to feel he was being seen by someone important. His main job was being chairman of the Staff and Administration Committee. This was a new post dealing with management matters of little interest, despite their importance, to those running the main businesses – pensions and premises. This enabled him to walk the corridors of the building like a squire visiting his tenants – all with the very best intentions.

Ashton, the head of Corporate Finance, was of the old order. Regular as clockwork, he would confidently stride through the front doors at 120 Cheapside at 9.30 am wearing his bowler hat and carrying a tightly furled umbrella wishing all in sight a good morning as he swept into a lift for the sixth floor. He was not untypical of many in the bank at that time. A chartered accountant, Ashton had joined Schroders nascent corporate finance team under Hull in 1961, comprising Bernard Knight, Christopher Gladstone and Sir Charles Pickthorn, all sharing one room. He was hard-working, disciplined and diligent, with high standards and always correct in his behaviour. However, he did not impress thrusting clients, but he was the best that Schroders had at the time. At the same time he mistakenly continued with his responsibility for marketing Schroder Wagg's services in America, involving over a third of his time. He was therefore not fully concentrating on the state of the corporate finance business, which unknown to most at Schroders was going through a massive transformation. Schroders had such a formidable list of clients including three or four of the top insurance companies that if anything went wrong it was magnified. All the corporate finance directors had clients whom they liked personally and whose businesses they were interested in. They did not believe in squeezing fees out of them. They had worked for them for years without receiving a fee, which was totally uncommercial. Many were charming amateurs without the necessary technical skills, popular with the chairman but less convincing with the finance directors. It was the end of an era particularly with the arrival of Mrs Thatcher. The change was not appreciated by most. The competition, particularly SG Warburg and Morgan Grenfell, was becoming much more aggressive. Schroders was seen by its competitors to be very much part of the establishment, a bit pompous, relying on historical relationships, not fast or aggressive and very domestic with no interest in the new international world (interview with Sir John Craven). SG Warburg, which was much more freewheeling, entrepreneurial and slightly buccaneering, could see the frustration of the young at Schroders with its rather rigid and conservative style (interview with Sir David Scholey). As the profits were negligible new people were not being recruited. Fisher's earlier policy of only hiring people with first class degrees from Oxford and Cambridge was becoming a burden – such people often had no idea how to communicate with industrialists. Simon Robertson, at Kleinwort Benson, felt Schroders took too long to move from a gentleman's club to a highly professional organisation. He recalled working under Charles Ball on a transaction against Schroders in which Ball, a hard-nosed pro, got Ashton to bid four times before he declared his hand – it was a valuable lesson for Robertson, which he never forgot.

A different view of Ashton came from Sir Roger Gibbs. Ashton acted for the Gibbs family from late 1979 until the sale of Antony Gibbs & Sons Ltd in the spring of 1980, when the bank was sold to HSBC.

> The bid was announced just before Christmas when the market price of Gibbs shares was 37p. It rose to 55p on the announcement. It seemed extraordinary, in such a small deal, that HSBC did not wish to name an actual price. Ashton played on this and many other points and negotiated brilliantly. By April 1980, he had squeezed 85p cash and 90p in HSBC paper out of Michael Sandberg (HSBC chairman) – 90p being the price at which Antony Gibbs went public in 1972. The Gibbs family were extremely grateful to Ashton and to Schroders.

On the other side of the City, Morgan Grenfell adopted a policy of aggressive recruitment of their competitors' clients. Morgan Grenfell at the time was under Christopher Reeves and Graham Walsh with a small management team of accountants with no university education and no money. They all had share options, which gave them a vested interest in increasing the bank's profitability. Walsh, who had recently returned from Hull's previous job as director-general of the Take-over Panel, had acquired a 'handy knowledge of how the rules of the City Code could be warped or bypassed altogether in the interests of a client.' Armed with this knowledge Walsh embarked on an expansionist strategy, recruiting accountants and solicitors and marketing ideas aggressively to clients – a six-man team was formed solely to dream up potential deals, largely by seeking out acquisitive companies that were not already clients of the bank and showering them with take-over propositions. What was good for the profitability of the bank took precedence over disinterested advice to the client (Dominic Hobson, *The Pride of Lucifer*). This was a totally different world to that prevailing within Schroders in 1981.

Schroders with many more clients was an easy target. The bank was bogged down with run-of-the-mill work and was unconscious of the changes taking place in the manner in which corporate finance was being conducted and it did not like the new style. It failed to keep in touch with many of the clients – the directors were not lunching enough and had lost the habit of visiting clients at their premises. Schroders had become complacent. More importantly it was not bringing the clients new ideas. A criticism at the time was that there were a lot of accountants and lawyers who were good at execution, with far too much being done in-house rather than being delegated to the professional firms of accountants and lawyers. It was not difficult in these circumstances for the more aggressive competitors, particularly SG Warburg, to 'steal our clients'. SG Warburg had relatively few major clients and found rich pickings at Schroders and the other more established merchant banks. Perhaps even more importantly Schroders lacked anyone at the top with the charisma to keep and to attract new clients. The boot was now on the other foot. Nobody remembered Richardson, with his disdain for the Etonian aspects of the City some 15 years previously, saying, 'I look at Morgan Grenfell's clients today and say they will be ours tomorrow' (Anthony Sampson, *Anatomy of Britain Today*).

The first major blow was being dropped by one of the longest-standing and most loyal clients, the Thomas Tilling Group, for whom Willie Wiltshire, one of the oldest directors, was responsible. A few days before Easter in 1983, Sir Patrick Meaney, the chairman of Tilling, called on Hull to say he had received an unsolicited bid from BTR and was determined to fight it off. He arranged a meeting for the following Thursday. In the interim Wiltshire and Challen had called on Tilling to discuss the defence. Having no experience of conducting defences, they were completely at sea in showing how Schroders could support Tilling, not having a clue how to deal with press strategy. They simply floundered at the meeting and it was clear that they were totally unprepared for the new world in which Morgan Grenfell was very comfortable. Over the weekend Hull received an urgent call from de Havilland, the brilliant investment dealer, and Ian Menzies, one of the young corporate finance directors, requesting his presence at a crisis meeting in Bermuda on the same Thursday. Hull in his words, 'stupidly fell for it' and rang Meaney to say he would be away in Bermuda for 48 hours. Meaney promptly went round to see Scholey at SG Warburg and asked him to conduct the defence. Schroders had been sacked. As Francis Black, the finance director said, 'when you are fighting for your life, you need the best.' Scholey was flabbergasted and thrilled. As the BTR/Tilling contest was the first of a number of blockbuster take-over battles in the mid-1980s, for Schroders to have been so ignominiously excluded was a serious humiliation. As Hull said, 'I made a mistake. I did not expect them to react like that as I did not know them very well.' Hull, unlike Richardson, Verey and Airlie lacked the killer instinct.

On 6 April 1983, John Thornton, a 28-year-old executive in Goldman Sachs' prestigious M&A team in New York, educated at Harvard, Oxford and the Yale School of Management, was paying a routine visit to London. Having checked into Claridges Hotel, he saw on front of the *Financial Times* that Owen Green of BTR had made a dawn raid on Tilling's shares – this was followed six days later by a full bid of £576 million, the largest bid ever attempted on the London Stock Exchange. It so happened that he knew Colin Draper, the deputy chairman, as he had recently sold him a New Jersey company that manufactured industrial glue. He rang Draper asking if he could call on him to discuss the bid observing that as Tilling had many assets in the United States he might be able to help. Within the hour Thornton was at Crewe House, Tilling's imposing offices in Curzon Street, sitting with Draper and Black. Goldman Sachs, unlike most of its competitors, had set up an M&A team comprised of people who only worked on M&A deals. 'They were the brain surgeons by comparison with the general practitioners who were generalist corporate financiers.' Furthermore, Goldman Sachs was renowned for being the leading house in the United States for defending take-overs, the bank having a declared policy not to act for hostile bidders. Whereas BTR's hostile bid was unusual in the United Kingdom such bids were quite common in the United States and Goldman Sachs had much experience of them.

Thornton was amazed to hear that Tilling had not heard from Schroders. After three days, SG Warburg and Goldman Sachs were appointed joint advisers together with Rowe & Pitman, the stockbrokers, with Scholey, then chairman, leading for SG Warburg. Even though Thornton was there first it was a bridge too far for Goldman Sachs to be appointed sole adviser. The explanation of what follows, although maybe one-sided and not wholly in accord with the view of SG Warburg, typifies the contrasting styles and methods of work of the British merchant banks and the US investment banks at the time and, as it was to have such an important impact on the future of the City, it is spelt out in some detail. To Thornton and his colleagues in New York, with their depth of experience of such defences, it was clear that a high bid would win in the absence of a more attractive financial alternative to the shareholders generated by the company. They therefore came back with specific actions which would increase Tilling's share price and make it uneconomic for BTR to continue, including the suggestion that Tilling announce that it was going to float off all its medical businesses in one package to the shareholders. Being a conglomerate, all its businesses were trading at a discount but, if separated, would individually command a much higher price and therefore would collectively have a greater value. This recommendation was submitted within three days but when suggested by Black to a director of SG Warburg the response was, 'I would not want to be too precipitous.'

The work was divided between Goldman Sachs and SG Warburg, with Goldman being responsible for advising on the US companies, Warburg the UK companies and the others jointly. Within a few days Thornton called for a meeting to discuss the values attributed to each of the US companies by his firm. It was a typical piece of work with the analysis for each company running to 30 pages or so – technical, quantitative and computer driven, it included a full industrial and (stock) market analysis. At the meeting at Tilling were two representatives from SG Warburg, two from Goldman Sachs and one from Rowe & Pitman. Thornton started with his presentation, which took nearly three hours finishing with a total value for all the companies. SG Warburg followed starting with Cornhill Insurance. The Warburg man turned to his colleague from Rowe & Pitman and asked what he thought the value would be, to which he picked up his copy of the *Financial Times,* looked down the general insurance section of the closing prices and read off the net asset value suggesting that a bid premium of 30% be added. All the companies were valued in ten minutes. Thornton was so surprised, it was so alien to his culture, that he thought it must be a joke. He also noted that SG Warburg, in deferring to the broker, might not be familiar with the market and that the Rowe & Pitman did not differentiate between the merger market and the public market. Goldman Sachs knew what insurance companies traded for in the merger market in New York. With the absence of the analytical tools with which Thornton was familiar, there also did not appear to be any substantial intellectual underpinning of their views. Thornton's recommendations regarding the float of the medical companies were rejected.

In the meanwhile the 60-day timetable was running out. 'It was like a ballet dance to the death.' He felt he was being marginalized and as they reached the forty-sixth day he knew they could do no more as it was now over to the shareholders to decide on the BTR bid, which by that time had been increased to £655 million. In desperation Tilling announced that it would be selling most of its marketable securities, Cornhill and Inter Med, its healthcare group, for £175 million, discreetly dropping its slogan, 'the sum of our parts makes us strong' (Dominic Hobson, *Pride of Lucifer*). From this point under the take-over rules, neither party was able to say or do anything unless there was a counter-bidder. Thornton suggested putting together a leveraged buy out with the management being supported by a group like Kohlberg, Kravis, Roberts (KKR), the buyout specialists in New York. As nobody was familiar with such bids, he went into the mechanics in detail explaining about the debt and the subsequent sale of assets to repay the debt. He said that the worst that could happen was that the KKR counter-bid would win, in which case it would be good for everybody. Alternatively BTR would have to increase its price but it might go away. Tilling was beginning to get worried and Black arranged for Thornton to speak to a sub-committee of the board. He finished his presentation by saying, 'You either accept a KKR approach or you will lose your company.' He rang Henry Kravis and explained the situation asking him to come to London to see Tilling warning him that it was likely to be begrudging. Kravis rang back to say he would come to London two days later with his partners. The next day Thornton saw Black who said Tilling would not meet KKR – they had been unwound by SG Warburg and Rowe & Pitman. Six days later BTR's bid was successful with a 61% acceptance. Within two weeks, 44 of the top 50 Tilling management were sacked and their imperious headquarters, Crewe House, was put on the market and subsequently sold for £36 million to Saudi Arabia to become its embassy in London. More importantly for Schroders and the other British merchant banks, Goldman Sachs changed its humble goal for London of 'developing more systematic business with European companies wanting to do things in the US' to the more ambitious goal of 'competing for indigenous business in each indigenous country in Europe.' Thornton could see that the domestic competition was far weaker than he had realised. 'The results were dire for all the merchant banks including Schroders, although they put up a good fight but only in the UK. It was the very nascent stage of the development of a global market with its own rules of engagement and ways of behaviour that were to be superimposed on the UK market.'

Not long after Morgan Grenfell's successful support of BTR, Jeffrey Sterling, newly installed as the chief executive of P&O, another long-standing client of Schroders advised by Williams, decided to move to Morgan Grenfell. He explained publicly in a press announcement that was headlined the following morning in the *Financial Times*, 'I decided I wanted to work with people more in tune with my style.' This was deeply mortifying for Schroders. Morgan Grenfell promoted itself as being able to go to the brink in fighting for its clients and had won a lot of business as a result. Schroders regarded them as sailing too close to the (regulatory) wind and although Morgan Grenfell had won a lot of bids through these aggressive tactics they were not acceptable to Schroders. The press were not kind to Schroders. By the end of 1983 Morgan Grenfell had overtaken SG Warburg not only as the undisputed take-over champions of the City of London, a title they were to maintain for the next five years, but also as the biggest underwriter of rights issues, handling 19 worth £485 million (Dominic Hobson, *The Pride of Lucifer*).

These were serious blows and fully exploited by the competitors who said Schroders was old fashioned. Schroders was too high-minded and out of touch. In a changing world Schroders neither appreciated nor liked the new world. More unforgiveable, many were uninterested. There was a sense that if clients were foolish enough they could leave but they would regret it later – there was no sense that Schroders had made any errors. Typical of Schroders at the time was its attitude to fees. Schroders only discussed the fee with the client after the transaction was concluded on the basis that its quantum would reflect the satisfaction of the client with the quality of Schroders' work. Six years earlier in 1977, Dewe Mathews attended a lunch given by Sir Arnold Weinstock, the all-powerful managing director of GEC, for Sir Lawrence Kadoorie and Sir Sidney Gordon, chairman and finance director of China Light & Power Company of Hong Kong, to celebrate the successful financing of GEC's contract to build the Castle Peak power station (see Chapter 4). Dewe Mathews' friends in GEC wanted him to have some exposure to Weinstock and Sir Kenneth Bond, the impressive finance director, and so he was placed between them. At the time Schroders was defending Avery, the weighing machine company, against a hostile and increasingly acrimonious bid from GEC. Weinstock was very irritated by Schroders' advice, which led to GEC having to increase the price of its offer. When Weinstock realised Dewe Mathews was a director of Schroder Wagg he rounded on him with the threat that once he had acquired Avery he would stop the payment of the Schroders' fee. On returning to the office, Dewe Mathews contacted Loehnis, the director responsible for the defence and warned him of Weinstock's threat and suggested that he secure a board approval to Schroders' fee. Amazingly Airlie stopped Loehnis agreeing a fee with Avery saying Schroders did not behave like that. Schroders was living in another world. Noble words but Weinstock adhered to his threat by stopping the fee. Later Bond offered to pay a fee of £250,000, which was rejected by Schroders as being derisory.

The other area, where the corporate finance directors completely failed to see change, was the social revolution arising from what became known as Thatcherism. Unlike Kleinwort Benson, NM Rothschild and SG Warburg, Schroders largely ignored privatisation and failed to cultivate the government, although this was rectified later.

By 1983 Airlie had lost all confidence in Ashton and had tried earlier to move him but this was resisted by Hull. Airlie had hired Bentley from Lazards to take over the international corporate finance business. He was heavy-handed with Ashton in unceremoniously taking over his responsibilities for marketing in the United States, after ten years of hard toil. Not long afterwards, Ashton was replaced by his young former trainee, Win Bischoff, who had recently returned from Hong Kong (see Chapter 4). Ashton then had the indignity of being the first head of Corporate Finance not to be made a vice-chairman. It was a bitter blow for him – he had worked so hard over so many years. A few months later he was offered a seat on the board of his old client Hanson and he left Schroders after 23 years service. He was admired by many for behaving with such great dignity and remained friends with them. He had taken the rap for the serious decline of Corporate Finance for which he was not solely responsible – it was not long before many other heads would fall. Challen, who became head of Corporate Finance in 1990, said that despite the failures a considerable debt of gratitude was owed by corporate finance directors and staff to Hull and Ashton for the very high professional standards of work and the strong sense of integrity and ethics they had embedded in the division and the young, as this was to stand them in good stead when it came to them having to stand up against the excesses of bad practice in the mid-1980s.

Bentley, as the titular head of Corporate Finance worldwide, had been effectively frozen out by Corporate Finance in London and turned to the United States. There he created London American Energy, an exploration and production company whose purpose was to invest in joint venture with independent E & P companies in Texas, for which he raised $100 million, mainly in London. He followed this up with another $70 million for American Petroleum Production, for investments in production assets. An energy advisory business, Schroder Energy Associates, was formed and subsequently it was merged into a joint venture with Torchmark Corporation under the name Schroder Torch Energy Advisors to provide investment advisory and corporate financial services to foreign and domestic investors in the US energy field. These were the beginnings of Schroders' activities in the oil and gas sector and the launching pad for building corporate finance's expertise in the energy sector.

Investment Management

The period between 1977 and 1984 saw the rapid growth and emerging profitability of Investment Management, still under Popham, who continued to introduce new initiatives. After 1977 more funds were being secured through performance rather than connections. Clients were carefully targeted and marketed on the basis of the good track record. 'Beauty parades' became more common and the business was being run more professionally. Most of the clients were the large companies. Schroders had none of the lucrative local authority business until 1981 when Popham, Govett and Niven secured half the £100 million pension fund from Strathclyde Region, where Niven had been educated. This was a large amount at the time. The following year they got £75 million from Lancashire and this led to Schroders eventually becoming the largest manager of local authority pension funds by the late 1980s.

In 1978 the investment management people at Schroder Naess & Thomas in New York told Baker Wilbraham, who was responsible for the US market in London, that the US pension fund managers were planning to divest a small part of their investments abroad. SG Warburg, having looked into it, had decided not to pursue it but Richard Foulkes and Charles Tallents under Jeremy Hill's direction were impressed with the potential. They were amazed to find that Schroders' name was virtually unknown outside New York and so they had to work from scratch. However, after a lot of marketing they began to pick up the odd account including $25 million from Vanguard. With Hill's increasing responsibilities in Asia including setting up a new stockbroking business (see Chapter 11) he withdrew from Schroder Capital Management International (SCMI) in 1982 and handed over to Sedgwick, who had just been appointed a director. Despite hating it initially, within six months Sedgwick was so enthusiastic that it helped him vault into being Popham's successor in 1985.

Over Easter 1984 Popham decided to stand down and together with Airlie, he decided that Nick Ferguson, who was then running SIMBL and only aged 35 at the time, should succeed him (see Chapter 17). In fact Airlie, who saw Ferguson as a future chairman, and Popham had already informed Ferguson of his appointment. Popham told the senior investment directors of his decision. None of them were interested in being appointed and Hill thought that Investment Management had become rather fuddy-duddy and needed some fresh air. Popham was firmly sat on by Govett, Sedgwick and Mumford in particular, who would have none of it. There was not a warm feeling towards Ferguson who was seen as an outsider, never having been in Investment Management for a meaningful period. Nobody doubted his abilities however. Govett and Mumford supported by Salisbury and Niven, two bright assistant directors, agreed that Sedgwick, the newest director, should become their head and informed Popham of their choice, virtually as an ultimatum. They were upset, as they had just got the business going, and saw the imposition of Ferguson as a slap in their face. They respected Sedgwick with his honesty and common sense and his willingness to speak his mind. Popham, after a half-hearted attempt to agree a compromise of joint leadership, conceded and Sedgwick was invited by Airlie to take over the division. This was the start of many changes that were to come within Schroders.

Despite the progress being made in building the investment management business it was still a Cinderella business overshadowed by the glamour and press coverage of Corporate Finance where Schroders was seriously in decline. Popham, who had become group managing director of investment management worldwide unexpectedly died in 1986. During his time as head of Investment Management at Schroder Wagg from 1973 to 1984 the total value of funds under management were built up from about £1 billion to £10.3 billion. The FT All Share index rose from 150 to 593 during the same period, showing that the increase in the value of the funds under management was mainly due to attracting new funds – increases in funds under management are a function of new money received and an increase in its value due to a rise in the market and good management. Perhaps of even greater importance, he had set in train a wide range of initiatives from which the business could expand to become the dominant activity within Schroders in terms of profitability and value.

Banking

Although economic conditions had improved in the United Kingdom, the ferocity of the competition and the declining margins on lending and acceptance business meant that Schroders' traditional banking business, which hitherto had made the lion's share of the profits, was becoming increasingly less profitable. These were offset by the treasury operations under Solandt, which became increasingly more profitable because of trading and arbitrage opportunities. The money books had a successful time, with good profits being made as interest rates fell. Opportunities were exploited and bad times avoided.

On Forsyth's retirement in 1977, Airlie appointed Solandt, the youngest director, to be head of Banking against Forsyth's advice that Bulfield should be his successor. At the same time Bulfield replaced Egerton as head of export credit, which had become known as Project Finance. Solandt was a good lending banker and he brought to Schroders knowledge of the foreign exchange markets unmatched by others. Schroders was entering into a much more difficult period of banking and he was the right man to manage the change. He was also exceptionally polite and courteous. He appointed John Rock and Bernard Barham, both of whom had joined Schroders when aged 16, directors responsible for Bulfield's portfolio. Lesser, who had taken over the Latin American business from Hall, who had joined Bank of America, was spending more time with Czarnickow Schroder, the specialised oil futures broking business, leaving Michael Ladenburg in charge of Latin America. Regrettably Lesser died suddenly in 1985, aged only 47 and at the height of his career.

By 1979 lending margins were being substantially eroded by the huge influx of petrodollar deposits following another massive hike in oil prices and increasing competition from the foreign banks, whose London branches nearly doubled between 1973 and 1982. In order to find a home for the surplus dollar funds available in the market, lending bankers raced around the world meeting the demands of every country, irrespective of their credit standing, to fund their financially unviable import substitution projects at increasingly low interest margins. With the Falklands War and the emerging balance of payments problems, the currencies of the Latin American countries fell against the dollar making it impossible for them to service their debts. There followed a worldwide debt crisis with defaults all over the developing world particularly in Latin America where Schroders had a large exposure. Fortunately the Credit Committee had strict limits for countries where it was deemed that there were risks of non-payment, that is all countries save for the USA, and so the damage was contained. However, substantial provisions had to be made on the outstanding loans and all lending was stopped. Ladenburg set about collecting as many debts as possible. Bulfield, who had been replaced by Dewe Mathews as head of Project Finance in 1983, was put in charge of a separate team set up to manage the debt collection and the losses were isolated from the profits of Banking. He was supported by Alastair Forsyth who was called back from Caracas. At the same time, much to the disappointment of Rock and Barham, Ladenburg, who was well regarded by Airlie, had been made deputy head of Banking by Solandt.

Project Finance

With Bulfield taking over the export credit and project finance unit, it acquired a separate and grander identity – the Schroder Projects Division, or as it was known, SPD. Bulfield had built up a strong reputation as a competent and shrewd banker, particularly in Japan and in Australia. He arranged a number of project financings in Australia in the late 1960s for The Aluminium Company of America (ALCOA) and Western Mining, which involved some of the principles of limited recourse financing – that is financing projects without recourse to the guarantee of shareholders or project sponsors. He therefore brought to Project Finance a record of success and much needed credibility with the clients. Under Bulfield, financings were arranged in Hong Kong, Singapore, South Africa, Colombia and Venezuela, and more notably the Ranger uranium mine in Australia, which was a landmark financing.

Bulfield concentrated his efforts on Latin America and Australia, with Howard Hunt and Alan Bristow doing much of the legwork in Brazil, Colombia, Trinidad and Venezuela. After the aborted Nigerian venture, Forsyth had gone out to Caracas to set up a representative office covering Colombia, Ecuador, Trinidad and Venezuela and was therefore able to open doors and support the project finance effort. They worked extensively on various aluminium projects in Venezuela where some welcome advisory fees were received. However, none of these projects came to fruition despite all the hard work. Bulfield and Hunt therefore turned their attention to Australia where Bulfield secured the mandate to arrange the financing for the Ranger uranium mine in the Northern Territories of Australia from Peko Walsend and EZ Resources, the project sponsors. It was complicated and took over four years to complete, not least because of the political controversy involved in the Labour government having to support the purchase of uranium being mined on land claimed by the Aboriginals. This financing, which was finally completed in 1981, was important as it not only brought in some good fees but it also re-established Project Finance's credentials for mining finance.

In the meanwhile Dewe Mathews spent his time working on projects in Hong Kong and South East Asia as is described in Chapter 4 below. After completing the financing of the Castle Peak power station in 1977, he was appointed deputy head of Project Finance with responsibility for Asia, the Middle East and Africa.[3] Within Project Finance, there was a certain amount of tension, due to Dewe Mathews' open disagreement with Bulfield over how the business should be run. Bulfield played things by ear in the old way and was rather dismissive of modern management techniques like forward planning and the monthly reporting of performance and profits. Dewe Mathews, being an accountant and former management consultant, introduced a detailed management information system based on the completion of weekly time sheets, which provided useful information on the costs and profitability for each project, client and overseas market, enabling rational decisions to be made on the redirection of the business towards a more profitable activity. He also arranged away-day planning sessions for the people in his team to agree the way forward.

Earlier in 1976 Philip C Robinson (not to be confused with Philip H Robinson, Schroders' overlord for Asia – see Chapter 4), a sound banker with a collegiate personality, had been hired to increase the capability of the team. He wished to return to England after four years with Union Acceptances, a South African merchant bank. At the time the export credit unit was still in Banking under Forsyth, and Robinson was rather alarmed to find that he had no interest in export credit, regarding it as a joke. Dewe Mathews arranged a meeting with Airlie to clarify whether Schroders was interested in the business or not. Airlie did not mince his words saying he was very keen on the business and wanted it expanded with no expense spared. He saw it as an important way of promoting Schroders in international markets and with new clients. Robinson felt better despite observing that Schroders had no name in the market and had nothing to show for its efforts, save for South Africa, and it was not clear how it would succeed against Lazards, Morgan Grenfell and Hill Samuel who all dominated the market. Robinson built on Egerton's work in Southern Africa and developed a thorough understanding of the facilities provided by five different European export credit and aid agencies. With the imposition of the Financial Standstill Agreement in which all commercial loans to South Africa had to be rescheduled, he turned his efforts to Singapore where Project Finance had recently set up a regional office under Peter Hargreaves-Allen to cover Thailand, Malaysia, Singapore and Indonesia.[4]

It was good timing as the Singapore government had set up a Mass Rapid Transit project to build an underground railway system and the Public Utilities Board (PUB), the state-owned electricity and water company, had plans to build a series of power stations. Both projects involved the award of large contracts to foreign companies. Robinson combined his knowledge of multinational export credits with Hargreaves-Allen's understanding of the evaluation process being used by the Singapore government to award contracts to obtain mandates from a variety of international contractors for whom Schroders had not previously acted. They were very successful and helped five of their clients to win major contracts, the fees for which more than covered the cost of the new office at the same time as building a good reputation in the region. More importantly Robinson was differentiating Schroders from its competitors by offering his clients a more comprehensive and sophisticated service.

Schroders in New York
When Wolfensohn resigned and joined Salomon Brothers, he called on his colleagues in New York and apologised for having let them down in not having carried through his vision for New York. This put a real damper on Maged's team who felt that the likelihood of building an investment bank had been severely dented. Many of the key officers decided to leave. Airlie came over on a confidence building exercise and did a good job in that people stayed but they were still leaderless. Maged was not a good administrator or a people person – everyone liked him and he had no opposition but he was never able to develop new business through his own initiative. Schrocorp was unable to compete with the best investment banks, as it had no relationships to speak of. Schroder Wagg's clients went to Morgan Stanley and Goldman Sachs and nothing much was achieved save for the venture capital business under Collinson. Petchek had left for Consolidated Goldfields, shortly after Wolfensohn's departure, and not long afterwards was tragically shot in the head while walking back home from dinner with his wife in the 70s on the East side – he never fully recovered. Gilliam left feeling that his only future would be in London to which he had no wish to go. He said of Wolfensohn,

> He was one of the most creative, original players in New York, a power house who loved his work and meeting people and attracted to Schroders a huge amount of people. New York suffered while he was in London as there was nobody there with his charisma, strength and endurance and openness to ideas. The remaining leadership was no match for what was needed. All assumed that in the event he became chairman, he would spend part of his time in New York and all were dejected by his departure. Schroders could no longer compete with the capital demands and with no leadership could not keep or attract good people. The appeal and mystique of old had disappeared.

Collinson and Hutheesing were appointed chairman and deputy chairman of Schrocorp, by then largely a venture capital business. They pottered on with Hutheesing producing further plans for the future focused on the small and medium-sized US companies and being a big fish in a small pond. The plan was recommended by New York but rejected by London. Hutheesing decided to leave in 1985 and subsequently made a lot of money carrying out his plan with some partners. Schrocorp never made any money. Hutheesing felt that individually there were many very competent people in New York but London gave no leadership and like all the other British merchant banks they did not know how to manage a US entity – 'they were too imperial!' In contrast to the deficiencies elsewhere, Schroder Real Estate, under Charlie Grossman, did very well throughout the period particularly when it became adviser to the National American Property Unit Trust (NAPUT), which was established to invest in US commercial property. This was followed by the acquisition of Sarakreek, a small Dutch quoted company through which continental European and Middle Eastern investors made substantial investments in the US. With the development of agency services Schroder Real Estate administered a portfolio of US properties valued at over $1 billion for European and Middle Eastern clients. Geoffrey Williams was heavily engaged in setting up these activities.

Airlie's real headache, however, was Schrobanco and it became the bane of his life. Wolfensohn's solution to Schrobanco's problems, which was probably ten years too late, was to increase its capital by introducing outside shareholders from the US insurance industry so that Schrobanco could expand its banking and financing business. This was achieved in 1977, by an increase in Schroders Inc's capital from $46 million to $80 million and the introduction of the Equitable Life Assurance Society of the United States, Allianz of America Inc and the Bank of Nova Scotia of Toronto, Canada as shareholders, each with a 5% stake. Wolfensohn had left before he saw the fruits of his work and it was left to Maged and Witschi to manage the expansion. Following the successful introduction of new shareholders and the increase in the capital of Schrobanco, there was an immediate expansion of deposits from $600 million to $1 billion with total assets increasing to $2 billion by 1982. Although some progress was made on the trust side of Schrobanco's business in the US, little headway was made with the lending side and therefore Schrobanco increased its banking business in Latin America based on an established presence in Argentina, Brazil, Colombia and Venezuela where opportunities had been enhanced by the recovery from the earlier oil crisis. Fred Seeley, who was responsible for the region, was surprised to find that he had to queue up with many other bankers willing to throw their money at borrowers regardless of the risk and for miniscule margins.

It was not long before Schrobanco's Latin American exposure had reached $450 million with $100 million in Mexico. Fortunately the officer responsible for Mexico under Seeley was convinced that there was a problem and so in April 1982 a programme was introduced to reduce the exposure by not renewing lines of credit and by selling some of the loans at a discount of 10%. The IMF meeting in Toronto in September brought the matter to a head with Richardson, the Governor of the Bank of England, saying the crisis had to be dealt with. Mallinckrodt with his responsibilities for the US had been travelling frequently across the Atlantic. Things continued to get worse and there was increasing alarm in London with calls for Schrobanco to be sold.

Airlie and his colleagues in London, as had those of Verey earlier, were convinced Schrobanco should be sold, being on the edge of bankruptcy due to the Latin American debts. Nobody, including Richardson and Wolfensohn, had previously succeeded in solving the problems and it was immensely time consuming and worrying and diverted everyone's attention from more important matters elsewhere. In fact Airlie went to New York every month despite his busy travelling schedule elsewhere. His instinct was to sell while there was a chance to do so but this put him into conflict with Bruno and Bayley. Despite the management's determination to sell Bruno was not convinced. He and Mallinckrodt had an emotional attachment to Schrobanco and, as the first Acceptance House to open in New York in 1923, it was a great source of pride to the family and became a religion with them. Bayley, still in New York, remained influential and was a powerful defender of the interests of New York — he was also the champion of South America, being particularly involved in the joint venture with the Monteiro Aranha family in Brazil. Maged saw the benefits of investment banking whereas Martin Witschi, the president of Schrobanco, wanted to wait until there was a relaxation to the rules for carrying on both activities with the overturning of the Glass-Steagall Act. In a way it was a repeat of the earlier confrontation over Wolfensohn but this time over the future of Schrobanco with the London directors on one side and those in New York allied to the Schroder family on the other.

Airlie arranged a meeting with Bruno at which he sought to secure the family's agreement to sell. Bruno recalls sitting on the fence and Mallinckrodt simply saying, 'the family would think about it' — a polite way of saying No. Airlie became so frustrated that he asked the chairman of First Boston, who was well known to Richardson, to find a buyer and was severely embarrassed with Bruno when it was leaked. Bruno consulted Wolfensohn who felt it was not the right time. So desperate were matters that with a capital of $120 million there was even talk of selling for $60 million. Mallinckrodt strongly argued against the fire sale, feeling that the pain had not reached sufficient level. Although he was emotionally attached to Schrobanco, because of his happy years working there in the 1950s and his frequent travelling to the States thereafter, he felt his view was not blinkered. He had doubts about the competitive position but felt strategically that a significant presence in New York was part of Schroders' heritage and should be preserved albeit in a different form. In this regard he always felt his views were independent of the Schroder family. He argued that the asset should not be discarded but a partner should be found that saw value in the bank.

Maged felt Schrobanco was not viable but this was totally unacceptable to Connor, who said that the board was answerable to the regulators and the depositors rather than to its shareholders. He was determined not to sell Schrobanco and certainly not before establishing its underlying value. At the same time he was becoming increasingly frustrated by Maged's lack of leadership and confidence in Schrobanco. He, therefore, recommended that Mallinckrodt, as a relative to the family, should take over from Maged as this would greatly boost the morale of those in New York. As Solandt had declined the request to take over Schrobanco, Airlie jumped at the opportunity to give the Schroder family the responsibility for New York and told Mallinckrodt to, 'go and deal with it'. Mallinckrodt must have been quite concerned as he had never run any of Schroders' businesses but he had no alternative having been so vocal against a sale. Despite Charmaine's reluctance, he moved to New York as chairman and chief executive officer of Schrobanco and president and chief executive officer of Schroders Inc in October 1983. What happened is described in Chapter 3 below.

Overseas Expansion

In the early 1970s, there was the feeling that life was changing and Schroders was not known for its work overseas; it needed to become an international investment bank. There were no overseas operations to speak of save for Schrobanco and Schroders AG in Zurich. Most business was done through overseas travel. Schroder Wagg had virtually no knowledge of Europe outside the United Kingdom, Richardson not being interested. In fact Schrobanco always said they knew the continent of Europe better than Schroder Wagg and at that time they were right. Verey too had little interest in anything outside the square mile and so Airlie, who was an internationalist, carried the banner on becoming chairman of Schroder Wagg, introducing the practice of people of different disciplines travelling in pairs so as to cross-sell a broad range of services. To counteract the downturn in the UK, Airlie emphasised the importance of Schroders' continued expansion abroad set in train by Richardson. He took a particular interest in Asia. To Hong Kong (see Chapter 4), was added, with the encouragement of Wolfensohn, the purchase of Crown Agent's 24.5% stake in Singapore International Merchant Bank Ltd (SIMBL) – this is described in Chapter 17. In Australia, Helbert, Wagg's earlier investment in Darling & Company, which had such promising prospects, was starting its decline but as Verey had no interest in Australia and David Murison[5], who knew the business well, had left for the Bank of New South Wales, the continuing management problems were a worry and kept Airlie quite busy. The story of Schroders in Australia is set out in Chapter 18. Airlie was a regular visitor to Japan and opened the representative office in Tokyo in 1974. He called on endless clients, which he was particularly good at, and as a result was able to introduce Yoh Kurasawa of IBJ to Mallinckrodt, which had significant consequences (see Chapter 3). The activities in Japan during his chairmanship are set out in Chapter 10. Airlie left Schroders with a powerful position in Asia and set up a Far East Committee, with representatives from across the group doing business in the region, to co-ordinate their activities. However, the individual businesses were never brought together as one regional entity, remaining largely independent of each other and therefore less effective as a regional force than Jardine Fleming. This reflected Loehnis' recommendation in his valedictory 'Wither Schroders' exercise: Stop pretending Schroders is an international bank rather than a cluster of local banks. It was one of the serious weaknesses at Schroders, which was and essentially remained a series of independently managed local fiefdoms rather than an integrated entity.

Strategic Review

In 1983, Airlie asked Ben Strickland to return from Australia (see Chapter 18) to London to take over from Bayley, the long-standing and invisible group finance director, based in New York. Strickland, a meticulous chartered accountant who had been in Corporate Finance in Schroder Wagg since 1968, had been sent by Airlie to head up Schroder Darling in 1978 after having completed the advanced management program at Harvard Business School. He was to instil some discipline into what had become a politically divided and disintegrating organisation. Having achieved a good deal of success he was ready for the challenges ahead. He considered the role of finance director to be rather boring and wanted to play a leading role in shaking Schroders up. He therefore persuaded Airlie to give him the additional responsibility for planning and allow him to take charge of a fundamental review of all Schroders' activities employing outside consultants – he was appointed the group director responsible for finance, information technology and strategic planning. Connor, in New York, had been pressing for such an activity but it was a bold step by Airlie requiring a good deal of courage, as inevitably the exercise would lead to much criticism of him as chairman and of the senior management of Schroders. He felt something had to be done about the future and 'wanted to set the ship on the right course over the next five years'.

Clearly Schroders had serious problems and needed to refocus its efforts if it was to survive and prosper against its competitors. It was therefore agreed to conduct a thorough review of the group's activities and its future direction. Strickland arranged a beauty parade of management consultants, including Booz Allen and McKinsey, the two leading international strategic consultants used by most of the largest companies in the world. He also included Management Analysis Centre (MAC), a relatively unknown Boston-based firm initiated by various professors from the Harvard Business School. The MAC team was led by James Kelly, a founding partner of MAC, who having been the president of the consultancy in Boston for five years, had set up an office in London. Although much smaller than the others it had a US presence, which was essential in view of the need to review thoroughly the business options in the US, including the future of Schrobanco. A deciding factor was Kelly's willingness to direct the assignment himself. The quiet and charismatic Kelly made a good impression and as he said, 'the underdog was chosen to advise another underdog – it was an inspired and brave decision.'

Strickland had set up a small group comprising Patrick Drayton and Richard Gordon and a team from MAC to manage the process, and this became known as the strategic review. It proved to be a highly effective team with the talents of each complimenting each other. Patrick Drayton, an economist from Nuffield College, Oxford, had joined Investment Management in 1977, after surviving an interview with Popham in which he sat through long periods of silence for which he had been forewarned. He was most impressed at receiving a job offer by telex the following morning. He had been plucked out of the struggling strategy group set up by Richard Morgan with the promise from Strickland that he would guarantee his subsequent transfer to any part of the bank chosen by Drayton. Drayton said Strickland was 'fantastic to work for as he was open, full of ideas and a good delegator.' Richard Gordon was from Banking.

Strickland was a force for change and in a hurry. He was energetic, efficient and a good organiser, pugnacious rather than reflective, more of a shaker through conflict than a persuader and good at diagnosing problems and clear on the solutions. Kelly on the other hand was smoother, more emollient, made people feel confident and had the skill of imprecision – whereas Strickland was black and white – diplomatic, a compromiser and able to get people to shift their thinking. Critically, he had the interpersonal skills to deal with Airlie and Mallinckrodt since nothing would come of the review if they were not brought on board. They made a formidable team and much credit should be given to them for the success of the strategic review.

At the time most of the businesses had away days with the directors meeting over a weekend at an exclusive hotel in the south of England to discuss the future, but there was nothing formal. Airlie formed a professional advisory panel, known as PAP, comprising Bischoff, Popham, Solandt and Strickland under his chairmanship to oversee the development of a strategic plan to take Schroders forward over the next five years. He was anxious to ensure the consultants were assisting the management rather than managing the process. Later when Mallinckrodt became chairman of Schroders Inc in New York, he also joined the panel. The panel was very ably advised by Kelly who pushed and prodded, laid seed corn and facilitated the process. It met twice a month. Solandt said PAP was 'one of the best memories I had of my 28 years at Schroders – it was a very cohesive group, all members understood Schroders' business and unreservedly gave of their best for the future of the business without any personal agendas.' Strickland set the agenda for the meetings, drove the process and drew up the conclusions. Bischoff suspected that 'Strickland and Kelly knew what they wanted to achieve from each meeting but made sure that the members of PAP felt that the solutions came from themselves. In particular Kelly was a wonderful facilitator, kept on gently pushing, bringing everyone back to the fundamentals and maintained the focus on return on capital and competitive advantage.' Mallinckrodt described Kelly as 'not wholly American, very gentle, thoughtful and sensitive. He came across well and related to everyone. He articulated his views in a simple and straight-forward manner and won a lot of sympathy and support.'

There was not a formal plan; it was more aspirational – what Schroders wanted to be rather than a plan as such. Bischoff, when asked how he proposed to plan for the investment bank in view of the unpredictable market, said perceptively, 'all you can do is shape the bank, you cannot plan it.' Looking back Kelly observed that

> prior to the Big Bang, Schroders was seen to be at a major disadvantage to its potential competitors. The US investment banks, which were entering the European markets, had more capital, stronger balance sheets and more and larger clients. Even though the

British merchant banks dominated the market, deregulation and increasing competition made things much more difficult. Schroders was in a worse position as it was losing clients almost daily. The return of Win and putting together a young team of committed enthusiasts, all experts in their own field of business and respecting each other, provided the ingredients to develop the way forward and out of the doldrums. Ben was the major catalyst – he was extremely brave, being willing to face rejection and attempted to speak the truth when others might have hidden it. He was also very tenacious and like a terrier at their heels. As a result they did a good job in avoiding the conventional wisdom of the time – they did not buy a large securities firm and stayed out of the gilts business. (It was decided not to apply for a licence to enter the gilt market, if more than 35 applications were made.) Schroders decided not to do what its main competitors were doing and did not follow the herd. It could not compete head on with Goldman Sachs and Morgan Stanley and so it pursued niche activities such as investment management, whereas Morgan Grenfell put its main emphasis on investment banking.

The future in 1983 did not look very promising – the lending business was uninteresting, Corporate Finance was doing badly, Investment Management was all right but not very profitable and Treasury was doing quite well. The family position was that it did not wish to dilute its shareholding and this created a major constraint on capital, which provided real discipline on the management and prevented the possibility of buying into the security and gilts businesses. Effectively it inhibited growth, resulting in Schroders not being able to compete with the global institutions it regarded as its potential peers. It was decided to increase non-capital intensive businesses by using brains in market related activities – investment banking rather than commercial banking. The biggest issue was the failure of Corporate Finance and the continuing loss of clients. Bischoff was seen to be critical to stabilising client relationships. Impetus was given to the investment management business and for the first time its major importance to Schroders' future was recognised. In view of the lack of capital it was decided to sell Schroder Life, the life assurance company with unitised managed funds, as to build it further required more capital and a lot of people were prepared to pay a very high price for it. It was also decided that the unit trust business should be built up over the next three years. It was agreed that Investment Management should get more involved in private banking. Schroder Ventures, which Bentley had been building up, was also to be expanded. Banking was to be downsized – 'lending on a church spire principle i.e. only to those you can see' – meaning concentrate on domestic lending and stop international.

There was a lot of focus on securities mainly at the behest of Popham, who wanted to keep the broking commissions within Investment Management, which was paying a large amount of commission on the investments it was making in Japan. The idea was not to build an investment banking business – Securities was seen to be a help to Corporate Finance rather than an integral part of an investment banking business.[6] Mallinckrodt recalls a meeting at the Stafford Hotel, when they heard the announcement of the

Warburg/Rowe & Pitman/Akroyd & Smithers/Mullins merger. There was much discussion but it was agreed to build a business from scratch rather than purchasing a top bracket broking firm like Cazenove, which in itself was wishful thinking, not least due to the Schroder family's determination not to dilute its shareholding. Solutions had to be sought which required a minimum amount of capital. Nick Roditi, who had returned from Japan and Korea, suggested that Schroders got its feet into the water by forming Schroder Asia Securities and starting to do stockbroking in Asia. He also suggested that a firm be set up in London (see Chapter 11). The strategic review did not say that the issue should be dealt with in a different way and so did not fully address the Big Bang. The responsibility for this business was placed with Solandt due to his skills as a dealer.

It was decided to change the organisation from a geographic one to a world-wide functional one with four main divisions under group managing directors – Corporate Finance under Bentley, Investment Management under Popham, Treasury and Trading (including securities) under Solandt, and Credit and Capital Markets (comprising Banking, Capital Markets and Project Finance) under a new managing director to be recruited from outside. The rationale for combining Banking and Capital Markets was that banking margins were on the decline as borrowers with a good credit were going into the bond market or commercial paper and swaps. The idea was to create a transition and to make scarce capital work harder due to being able to on-sell paper. To achieve what was effectively building a new business required exceptional skills in the new leader, not least because it required the people involved to change. The global divisional structure required breaking down the fiefdoms around the world and finding an acceptable role for the barons.

With an increasing focus on profits and remuneration based on profits associated with individuals, fee sharing was introduced in which fees earned on a transaction were shared between the businesses involved in securing and executing the transaction. The rules were badly defined by the planners and this led to continual battles between the heads of each business particularly in relation to introductions and prior relationships. To avoid these disputes it became easier not to deal with other parts of the bank and so the businesses became even more independent

The succession

The main conclusion was to sell the commercial banking activities in New York as it was making an unacceptable return but more importantly it was occupying far too much senior management time and energy instead of focusing on the clients. However, this was fought by the Schroder family, who brought in Wolfensohn to advise. His advice was ambiguous saying the timing could have been better and it could be seen in the market to be a distress sale. Schrobanco was in bad shape. Airlie was deeply upset, feeling that it was totally unacceptable for the family, with its minority shareholding, irrationally to refuse to support the management and the interests of the majority shareholders. As a man of honour how could he reasonably remain as chairman? He retired early in November 1984. Before retiring he arranged his succession by recommending to the board and receiving their agreement that Mallinckrodt, as a member of the family, should become non-executive chairman with Bischoff the chief executive. He felt that had the Schroder family been more committed to the management of Schroders, the endless problems with Schrobanco could have been avoided. He also could see that Bischoff had the character and flexibility to 'make it work with Gowi'.

During Airlie's seven years as chairman, Schroders' profits increased 4.3 times to £15.1 million, shareholders' funds 3.7 times to £164 million and market capitalisation 3.6 times to £114.3 million. During the same period the FTSE All Share index had increased by 2.8 times from 215 to 593.

Earlier in June, it was announced that Airlie had accepted the Queen's invitation to become Lord Chamberlain of HM Household. He therefore retired before seeing the results of the exercise he had so bravely initiated. He left a bank still in some trouble but he had put in place the steps to take it back to the heights it had achieved under Richardson. Perhaps his most important contribution was the arrangements he made for his succession and the senior appointments he made before he retired, all of which turned out to be successful. He was much underestimated; personally charming, he took top-class decisions on people, particularly Solandt and Bischoff. It is important not to forget the state that Schroders was in when he took it over. He was honest, straightforward, had a nice style, worked very hard and took the job very seriously – even showing nervousness on occasions. He was without doubt one of Schroders' top people and did all he could to get things back on track. He greatly enjoyed his career at Schroders but it was not the be-and-end-all of his life.

Schroders' style
One cannot complete a description of the Verey and Airlie years without mentioning the style of Schroders at that time. A picture will have come out of these two chapters. It was a very pleasant place to work in. It was sufficiently small for everyone to know each other, certainly in each of the places of work. Everyone had grown up together in the firm and knew each other's strengths and weaknesses. The directors were still referred to as partners – Bruno used to speak of fellow directors of Schroder Wagg as 'my partner so-and-so'. There was a real sense of collegiality. People had time for a chat and were pleasant to each other. Discourtesy was an unforgivable sin. There was a real sense of integrity and mutual trust among all the senior management. Unlike some of the competitors, like Morgan Grenfell and Barings, Schroders was not blue-blooded. Richardson had set the tone by developing a meritocracy in which there was little snobbery but perhaps some intellectual arrogance. He took a close personal interest in recruitment, interviewing all the executives. He believed in the best talent being employed in the best way, the right sort of people with the requisite skills. He believed in excellence, the best people, the best business and the best execution. He thought that excellence was the only thing that was interesting and that the reputation of being best was in itself a powerful draw (Richard Roberts, *Schroders, Merchants & Bankers*). There was not the same emphasis placed on being commercial and

competitive however. Nobody was fired for poor performance (hiding behind collective responsibility they were moved to another post) – only if they fiddled their expenses or told a lie would they be dismissed. At board meetings Christian names were always used, including when speaking to the chairman. These characteristics must have been passed down through the years and developed a distinctive style. So much so that if someone joined at a later date from another place, they often found it difficult to assimilate. Fisher never made the transition and Murphy remained at a distance. Bentley always remained at heart an SG Warburg man and even decorated his room in the manner of those in 30 Gresham Street.

The salaries were not much different from those in the professions and the prospects of becoming rich were remote, save for those taking advantage of inside information, but this had been firmly stamped on by Richardson. On becoming a manager, a key step towards becoming a director, one was given an interest free loan of £6000 and encouraged to invest it in the stock market. If interested, one was given the opportunity to invest in new issues not managed by the firm and there was much stagging of those issues. But this did not amount to much as everyone in revenue earning businesses outside Investment Management was far too busy to spend much time on such matters. To make money, one needed to have capital and relatively few had any. It was accepted that in view of the congenial style at Schroders people were prepared to accept salaries 15% below the norm.

Robert Whyte, an Australian property expert, who was with the firm during Verey's chairmanship found the experience fascinating – he attempted to build a fund to invest UK money in the US property market but it did not get off the ground. He came under the sponsorship of Wolfensohn for six months and stayed for nearly two years. He had an office in the 'geriatrics ward' where former directors had courtesy offices, on the seventh floor. As a result of nobody knowing what he was meant to be doing nor who he was reporting to and having a former secretary of a senior director he had access to all the benefits of a director, without being one.

> It was all very civilised but lacking the competitive cut and thrust of business I was used to – there was a good level of conversation from well-educated colleagues, mostly from Oxford or Cambridge who seemed to be trapped by either having too much money or too little. They were controlled, well-disciplined, not much loose information, discrete in handling themselves – it was clearly a good training ground.

He made good friends and was impressed by their sheer quality – by contrast he found Schroder Darling in Australia uninteresting and uninspiring. He found Murphy, who agreed to his employment, to be charming, intelligent, incisive and, with his socialist inclinations and affiliation to the Labour Party, to be totally different from the others. His sponsor Wolfensohn clearly did not fit into this polished and unworldly climate. He found Airlie, although no intellect, to be street-smart, a survivor and tenacious. After returning to Sydney he was extremely successful financially.

There was no racial or religious discrimination, only a focus on ethics, good manners and intelligence – there may have been a tendency towards intellectual arrogance in some quarters. If it is possible to categorise Schroders in those terms, one might say it was rather old style English and Protestant with strong German family values at the top. There were also very few women in the senior and middle ranks but this was to change although not significantly.

NOTES:

1. John Connor had made his career in the chemical industry with Merck and Allied Chemical Corporation, where he became chairman. In the 1960s he served as Secretary of Commerce under President Johnson and was on the board of Chase Manhattan Bank and General Motors.

2. In 1983 an agreement was reached between the Department of Trade and Industry and the Stock Exchange to drop fixed commissions and open itself to competition and this ushered in the market reforms of 1986 known as Big Bang. The run up to Big Bang saw the brokers and banks get together in a series of hastily arranged marriages (Philip Augar, *The Death of Gentlemanly Capitalism*).

3. Bernard Dewe Mathews had been introduced to Richardson by his friend Anthony Loehnis in 1969 having previously been a management consultant with Coopers & Lybrand after five years as an accountant with BP. He spent two years in the ill-fated Industrial Section under Bill Hyde (see below) and a year as the group planning manager under Sir Henry Fisher, who used the exercise to learn about the business whose future he was meant to be planning. He was then sent to the export credit unit within Banking, whose head, David Forsyth, thought it was a waste of time. The unit had virtually no business and no staff and only Alastair Forsyth to explain what they were meant to be doing. He decided he had better try and do something about it.

William Hyde was hired by Gordon Richardson in 1968 to start an Industrial Section managing direct investments in unlisted companies with a view to earning higher returns than those available from listed securities. Early members of this unit were Ronald Evans from Corporate Finance, Dewe Mathews and Richard Sadleir from Lloyds Bank International. It was not a success and was closed a few years later having disposed of most of the investments at a considerable loss. Hyde left to become the bursar of a college at Oxford.

4. Peter Hargreaves-Allen had known Win Bischoff while with Grindlays Bank in Hong Kong. He had worked in Singapore and Thailand for Haw Par, a Singapore company owned by the Slater Walker Group and so had good knowledge of the culture and business practices in South East Asia. He was hired by Bulfield in 1981 to head up a new regional office to cover project finance business in Singapore, Malaysia, Indonesia and Thailand.

5. David Murison joined Helbert Wagg in 1946, after the war, becoming a partner with Bobby Holland and Ashley Ponsonby in 1962. As a senior corporate finance director he was seconded to Darling and Company for three years in 1967 (see Chapter 18).

6. An investment bank is a financial intermediary that advises corporates, governments and investors on financial transactions including the issue and trading of securities; it is a bank that combines corporate finance advice and securities.

PART 2
MALLINCKRODT AND BISCHOFF
1985 – 1994

CHAPTER 3

GEORGE MALLINCKRODT'S EARLY LIFE AND CAREER

1930 – 1985

Early life, 1930-1960

Georg Wilhelm von Mallinckrodt was born on 19 August 1930 at Eicholz, his mother's family estate outside Köln. He was always known by his family and colleagues at Schroders as Gowi, the 'w' being pronounced as a 'v', a nickname he had acquired at school in Germany and will be referred to as such throughout this book. His father Arnold Wilhelm von Mallinckrodt had married Valentine von Joest in 1929. Both came from aristocratic German families, the Mallinckrodts being able to trace their roots back to 1250. The family, who were entrepreneurs in the textile industry, played a key role in the community and continued to be re-elected to public office until 1830, when part of the family emigrated to the United States.[1] The Mallinckrodt family in Germany had by that time become bankers, insurers and industrialists in Köln. In 1890 Wilhelm von Mallinckrodt, Gowi's grandfather moved to Antwerp where he started a bank called Wilhelm Mallinckrodt & Co and married Hortense Günther, a Belgian lady. The bank was a traditional merchant bank involved in financing trade and shipping with an extensive involvement in South America. Their son, Arnold was born in 1901 but as a result of the First World War, the family had to leave Belgium, Wilhelm having earlier not taken up an offer of Belgium citizenship, and returned to Hamburg in Germany, the bank being closed down. Arnold was educated in Germany, trained in a bank in Hamburg, where he became a friend of Helmut Schroder, and travelled to Argentina for more banking experience before returning to Frankfurt in 1928 where he joined Agfa, the photographic equipment manufacturer, wholly owned by Bayer AG and IG Farben AG, the German chemicals group. The following year he married Valentine von Joest. The Joest family were industrialists in coalmines and traded with Argentina. Valentine's father founded a glass factory and was in the steel industry, insurance and shipping. He was also granted the licence to build the first railway along the Rhine.

Arnold was appointed managing director of Agfa in Paris in 1935 and Gowi was educated at the German School, a large international school teaching in French and German. He remembers his parents being strict but caring. They led modest lives, with a concern for other people less privileged than themselves and were practising Christians going to church every Sunday. They had an attractive apartment in Paris and were members of the Jockey Club and led an active social life particularly with their French relations and the cosmopolitan community. His father, who was a good sportsman playing golf and tennis and horse riding, was a man of great charm but quite shy. Being the youngest in his family everything had been done for him but he was not spoilt. Through his Belgian mother he had a strong love of France, its language, its people and its culture. Gowi's mother by contrast, also the youngest and most adored of her family, was intelligent, forceful and ambitious and the dominant personality in the family. She was widely read, cultured and an accomplished hostess. She was stylish but not extravagant, being very careful with money.

On the declaration of war by France and Great Britain against Germany in September 1939, Arnold and his family had to move back to Germany but returned to Paris following the occupation of France in June the following year. Being fluent in French with good family connections in France and an important industrialist, he was not called up to serve in the German Army. At about the same time Gowi was sent as a boarder to Salem School, which was based on Prince Max von Baden's ancestral castle at Schloss Salem by Lake Constance on the border between Germany and Switzerland. Salem had been founded by Kurt Hahn in 1920 with Prince Max, Germany's last imperial chancellor, as its benefactor and Gowi stayed there until 1948.[2]

When Gowi arrived at Hohenfels, the junior school of Salem in 1940, it was sheltered in terms of its independence of thought and high quality teaching staff, many of whom were women, and was allowed to abide by Hahn's principles and was non-political. Although his parents were still in Paris, Gowi enjoyed school, taking an interest in practical things like managing the horses and hockey rather than academics. He was an average student with a particular interest in history and cultural things. He made a lot of friends during this very formative period which was focused heavily on character development, there being an emphasis on team spirit, tolerance of and helping others, who came from many different backgrounds, and self-discipline, standing up for people and spotting injustices. Holidays were spent at the family home in Bavaria, which was sheltered from the worst aspects of war, and in that regard he and his sisters led a privileged existence.

On 20 July 1944 the attempt by Colonel Count von Stauffenberg to assassinate Hitler with a bomb at the *Wolfsschanze* failed and was swiftly followed by the execution of von Stauffenberg and many of the heads of the elite German families, many of whose sons were at Salem with Gowi. His best friend, Clement von Stauffenberg, the colonel's nephew, was immediately and forcibly removed from Salem and sent to a concentration camp with the remainder of his family. Shortly before this dramatic event, which had a profound affect on Gowi, the *Schutzstaffel* (SS), Hitler's secret police, took control of Salem with the school having to fall into line with all the boarding schools run by the Nazis, the orientation becoming very politicised. With the strong emphasis on the doctrines of the Nazis and the SS, there was a very unpleasant environment. Arnold therefore removed Gowi from Salem until September 1945, when he returned and stayed there until July 1948. Salem was important to Gowi and the Hahn principles remained an influence on his life.

After school, Gowi started his career as an apprentice precision mechanic at Agfa, in Munich. This involved factory work using his hands. His father, who had returned to Bavaria after the Allied invasion of France, was convinced that Germany would become occupied by the Russians and felt it would be better to be a blue-collar worker rather than a white-collar worker. For his final exam he had to make an instrument that measured the elasticity of metal when bent. Two and a half years later, he became a trainee with Münchmeyer & Co, the private bankers in Hamburg, learning about trade finance that was booming due to the Korean War. During this period he attended night school pursuing his interest in foreign trade, particularly with South America, in which he learnt about its culture and traditions. In 1953 under the sponsorship of Münchmeyer, he became a trainee at Kleinwort Benson in London, his grandmother's sister having married a Kleinwort. Gowi was taken under the wing of his aunt, Mrs Sophie Renner, who was a Kleinwort and welcomed him to use her home in Hampshire as his base while he was in England.[3] It was at this time that Gowi met Charmaine, Helmut's daughter.

After fifteen months he decided to go to New York where he had been offered a traineeship in international banking by Schrobanco on the introduction of Helmut Schroder, a very close friend of his uncle Gustav, who had been the Schroder representative in Germany from 1933 to 1967. After the training programme he toured America for two months to see the country and visit steel plants in Illinois and tobacco factories in Richmond, Virginia. This gave him an exposure to the States before returning to Bavaria for three months where he had to decide whether to join Schrobanco or various private banks in Germany. Having been smitten by America with its huge horizons and freedom to trade, its dynamism and the exciting environment on Wall Street he opted for Schrobanco. Before going back to New York he spent a year with Union Bank of Switzerland in Geneva perfecting his French and gaining an understanding of banking and investment management in Switzerland followed by three months in London at J Henry Schroder under Robin Pilkington.

On joining Schrobanco in 1957, he became an assistant to Ernest Meili, a senior vice president under Gerry Beal, the president, who was responsible for foreign banking and worked on European banking visiting many companies on the East Coast and the Middle West. He found Schrobanco very international with its business in South America, Asia and Europe and full of interesting and talented Europeans and Americans invariably with wide cultural interests. Schrobanco was heavily influenced by the foreign policy interests of the US government and was much involved in Japan, South Korea and especially Taiwan. It also had very good connections in various European countries, probably better than those of Schroders in London. Ninety per cent of the Schroder group's business was conducted through New York due to all business with Germany, on which Schroders in London was largely dependent, having been frozen until 1953. For Gowi it was a formative experience from which he developed a great affection for America, which was to become an important part of his future career.

Gowi and Charmaine were married in London on 31 July 1958 and lived in New York. They had a good social life with many American and Europeans friends. Avery and Ann Rockefeller also took them under their wing, Avery Rockefeller having formed a joint venture Schroder, Rockefeller & Co Inc in 1936 to carry on investment banking business. The company was renamed Schroder Capital Corporation (Schrocorp) when Avery retired in 1968.

London, 1960 - 1985

When Gowi's and Charmaine's first child, Clare, was due to be born they returned to London for her birth in August 1960. They visited Charmaine's parents most Sundays at Englefield Green in Berkshire where Helmut and Gowi built up a close relationship. Having so much family background in common they had a lot to talk about and Helmut with his commercial flair could see that although not a great intellect Gowi had a natural commercial sense. Over the next seven years they had three more children, Philip in 1962, Edward in 1965 and Sophie in 1967. Charmaine took on the main responsibility for their upbringing and education, Gowi playing a supportive role. He was always enthusiastic, positive and gave guidance with subtle questions never exerting any pressure on results. His love of America with its freedom and opportunities played a large part in their upbringing and attendance at camps in the summer gave them exposure to the US openness. Holidays were spent on the Island of Islay in Scotland at Easter, where Gowi enjoyed the shooting and walking, and for a month in the summer at the Riegsee, the Mallinckrodt family home in Bavaria, where they were joined by many cousins. Gowi also ensured that they became familiar with the people and cultures on the Continent, particularly Germany and France.

J Henry Schroder had very recently acquired Helbert, Wagg and so Mallinckrodt was seconded to them for a year under Charles Villiers who was responsible for Europe (at that time Helbert, Wagg had no banking exposure to continental Europe) and worked closely with Meili in New York. For the next twenty years he was principally involved in the development of Schroders' business in Europe and the Middle East. Initially he joined Banking under David Forsyth looking after Germany, Switzerland, Holland and Scandinavia with many bankers from Schrobanco being seconded to London and Paris to build up the business on the Continent. His work was primarily short-term trade finance in the emerging Eurodollar market, together with some advisory work related to ventures being financed by others. In 1967 Richardson asked Martin Witschi, Fred Seeley, both from Schrobano and Mallinckrodt with the support of Cooper to look at prospects for expansion on the Continent. With severe exchange controls in London and the introduction of OFDI in the States, which removed access to dollar financing for the Group in New York, access to capital was limited to Switzerland and therefore recommendations were made to open a bank in Zurich. Ernest Ingold, the brilliant head of foreign exchange and money market operations in London, was anxious to return to Switzerland and so he and Max Zeller set up the new bank, J Henry Schroder Bank AG

(Schroders AG) in Zurich in 1967 with a capital of SF20 million (£2 million), concentrating on the Swiss money market and private placements to finance Schroders' clients. Being such a strong currency these financings proved to be very expensive for clients without a Swiss franc revenue stream to service them. Following the successful start of the bank, Erik Gasser was appointed the general manager in 1971 and expanded the banking activities and added investment management focusing on private clients, a traditional strength in Switzerland. Schroders AG went on to become a big success achieving an internal rate of return over the next 33 years of 11% in SF and 18% in sterling, the original capital increasing to SF101 million.

Elsewhere in Europe Ulf Sudeck took over from Gustav von Mallinckrodt as the representative in Frankfurt and there were discussions with a view to taking a stake in the newly merged Hamburg-based bank Schröder, Münchmeyer, Hengst & Co but they got nowhere. There was much discussion about Italy, Verey being interested, and Mallinckrodt travelled there extensively but again nothing resulted. At that time France became strategically important to Schroders, Peter Wahl being appointed the representative in Paris. In 1972 Schroders purchased a 14% stake in Société (later Banque) Privée de Gestion Financière SA (BPGF), a Parisian merchant bank, for £338,000, which was seen to be a unique opportunity to access French franc finance as the UK was about to join the EEC. Mallinckrodt became a director and Wahl moved his office into the bank. In 1981 the incoming Socialist government of President Mitterrand decided to rescue the country from economic depression by means of a programme of wholesale nationalisation and within the year he had nationalised the private banking sector including Banque Rothschild. The wily chief executive of BPGF managed to persuade the government that BPGF was foreign controlled but it was not long before it was on its knees. It was heavily involved in property investment, albeit good quality, but with interest rates escalating to just below 30%, the cost of financing the properties became prohibitive, leading to substantial losses which led to a call on the shareholders for new capital. Mallinckrodt came to the conclusion that the future losses would go well beyond those to date and that it would be better to sell the shareholding for one franc, which he recommended to the Schroder board. This was reluctantly agreed and the investment, then valued at £2.8 million, was written off. The Banque de France was livid and passed a law – Lex Schroder – stating that in future it would be an obligation of a shareholder in a bank to inject new capital when called, thereby converting the contingent liability into an unlimited liability. As a result Schroders became *persona non grata* with the Bank of France and was excluded from the boom in privatisation business in the 1990s. CSFB remained a shareholder and had to write off the new capital it injected but at the same time took a direct interest in some of the properties and when they increased in value many years later they recovered part of the new money.

In the meanwhile Mallinckrodt had moved offices and was sharing with Wolfensohn, who had recently arrived from Sydney. 'He was fantastic, a dynamo, very creative and bubbling with new ideas, he also picked up ideas very fast'. Wolfensohn drove forward the Euro-commercial paper business but the necessary critical mass of $500 million (as advised by Goldman Sachs) needed to make profits was never achieved. However, they learned a lot about the market in the process and this helped them to develop a profitable syndicated Eurodollar lending business to US companies in Europe. With the extensive travelling required across the US, they divided the country between them, Mallinckrodt concentrating on the East Coast and the Mid-West. Marion Gilliam spent a lot of time on the road with Mallinckrodt calling on the small companies, Mallinckrodt always focusing on selling the Group rather than individual services. Gilliam found Mallinckrodt Teutonic in style and intelligent. 'He made a good impression on the American customers who were puzzled by him being more Germanic than English – surprising for a British-owned bank. He had strong opinions which he voiced but had a certain modesty never showing off.'

After a fruitless investment in Rifbank SAL was disposed of, Tony Asseily agreed to the formation in 1975 of J Henry Schroder & Co. SAL (Schroder Asseily), a joint venture in Beirut in which Schroders had a 65% shareholding and the Asseily family 35%. Asseily was an impressive PhD from a prominent Lebanese family in the textile industry who had worked closely with Mallinckrodt in Banking and then with Wolfensohn in the international department. The objective was to broaden Schroders' base in the Middle East by taking advantage of money market and corporate finance business that might arise out of the oil price rises in 1973. With the outbreak of war shortly afterwards, it became impossible to continue in Beirut and so the office was moved to London. From then on Tony Asseily became the trusted person for Middle East business. However, his relationships with the rest of the bank were not easy when there was a difference of opinion as to whether Schroder Asseily was needed for a transaction. Fee splits were always difficult.

In 1976 Schroders was invited by the Saudi Arabia Monetary Authority to take a 5% shareholding in the Saudi Investment Banking Corporation (SIBC), a consortium bank to be established in Riyadh to conduct investment banking business in Saudi Arabia. The other foreign shareholders were Chase as the manager with 20% and Commerzbank and The Industrial Bank of Japan (IBJ) with 5% each. Yoh Kurasawa, the IBJ representative, had previously been managing director of IBJ (Deutschland) in which Deutsche Bank, with whom he had been a trainee after the war, had a 25% shareholding. Having spent three years in Germany he and his wife spoke better German than English. He and Mallinckrodt therefore became good friends and the relationship became more important than the investment. Mallinckrodt remained involved until Schroders sold its stake a few years later.

Schroders' Middle East activities remained rather peripheral, not least because it was very difficult to do business in the Middle East. It is doubtful if Schroders ever made more than modest profits from them.

And so in October 1983, having fought for the preservation of Schrobanco, Airlie gave Mallinckrodt the poisoned chalice and he had no alternative than to accept it. He initiated a thorough review of the business that led to the removal of 100 out of 800 staff including 19 officers, which was painful as many of them were his friends. It became clear which areas were making money and where the problems were. Schrobanco was overstaffed and trying to become a full service wholesale bank in order to balance the portfolio against the international business in Europe, Latin America and the Far East. However, it could not compete against the strength of the domestic banks and therefore had developed a lot of niche businesses some of which, like the real estate business run by Charlie Grossman, were successful.

Mallinckrodt received considerable support from Jack Connor, who came in three days a week, Martin Witschi the chief operating officer, Peter Rona and Stephen Davis, the legal counsel. In addition Solandt came over frequently from London to help Michael Magdol with ensuring that the bank was properly funded. Following the completion of the strategic review, the MAC team, led by James Kelly, advised Mallinckrodt's team on all aspects of the business. Gradually they started to turn around the business and improved the profitability. It was then that they discovered that a loan to Lapeyrouse, which was secured on a ten-year-old letter of comfort that had not been renewed, was not recognised as a guarantee by its parent, Andre & Co in Switzerland. The exposure was $19 million. Mallinckrodt took over responsibility for the loan himself leaving the management team to carry on running the business. The next month Continental Illinois Bank nearly collapsed and Senator Garn, the chairman of the Senate Banking Committee, advised Mallinckrodt that any hopes of overturning the Glass-Steagall Act were dashed and would now be delayed for ten years. The consequences for Schroders' plans to build a meaningful investment banking business were fatal and so he came to terms with the necessity to sell Schrobanco. Despite all his work he had not found a solution to the basic problems of Schrobanco. It would be better to sell the bank and provide the officers and staff with a good future while there was still the chance.

At the time he was expecting Yoh Kurasawa, his friend and now the chief executive of IBJ, and his wife to dinner. He agreed with Airlie to cast a fly over him by asking him what his plans were for New York. Having earlier heard from contacts at Schröder, Münchmeyer, Hengst, which had an investment management link with US Trust, that IBJ was considering buying an interest in US Trust, he knew he was on fertile ground. When Kurasawa said that IBJ had decided to take an interest in a US bank and that it would be wonderful if they could discuss this with Schroders, Mallinckrodt said he would have to think about it. It took nearly a year to complete the transaction with many of the earlier meetings being conducted in the Mallinckrodt's apartment. IBJ saw the benefits of acquiring a long established bank, particularly one with Schrobanco's standing in the New York banking industry. It also appreciated the potential for improving the profits from increased productivity on a larger volume of business. Much of the top-level negotiations with Kurasawa were carried out by Mallinckrodt in German. An agreement was concluded to sell a 51% shareholding in Schrobanco to IBJ for $77.4 million in June 1985 with an agreement to sell a further 24.1% on or before June 1987.

The bank was renamed IBJ Schroder Bank & Trust Company on 1 January 1986, with Alva Way as non-executive chairman and Peter Rona as president and chief executive officer. At the request of Bruno, Wolfensohn acted for Schroders in the sale but due to his weakness in execution Schroders had to park Patrick Drayton, a new corporate finance director, in his New York office to ensure the transaction was effectively executed. Mallinckrodt was particularly pleased about the price received from IBJ, which was 115% of the book value compared with David Morris' expectations of 75%.[4] With a sale value of $154 million he felt his resistance to a fire sale for $60 million had been fully vindicated. Being free of tax, the proceeds bolstered the firm's resources. Mallinckrodt had also been very conscious of the employment interests of the staff taking the view that there were a lot of good people who had not been well managed.

Late in 1984 Citibank had decided to make a provision of 30% against all its Latin American loans and this became the benchmark throughout the industry. By this time Schrobanco had sold many of its loans at various discounts. The US and Japanese banks made no bad debt provisions for sovereign debts and so Schrobanco sold its loans at par. Schroders had, however, made provisions at consolidation of its accounts and these provisions were used to offset the under-provisioning for Schroder Wagg's sovereign debts. Barham and Rock, who had recently taken over the management of Schroder Wagg's banking business, traded these debts to increase the provisions to 70% whereas before the sale to IBJ they were only 40%. Bill Slee was rather shocked by the under-provisioning when he joined the bank.[5] Schroders was now able to breath again. There can be no doubt that the credit for the successful sale of Schrobanco to IBJ should go almost entirely to Mallinckrodt. In the view of Bill Turner, who was on the board of Schroders Inc at the time and gave his advice when requested, Mallinckrodt saved Schrobanco by his actions and made it more possible to sell it. It was a good deal for Schroders and released the management from their worries in New York to focus on clients elsewhere.

NOTES:

1. The Mallinckrodts founded a tanning business to serve the leather business in St Louis processing furs from the Rocky Mountains. Later under the name Mallinckrodt Chemical Works they broadened their chemical production into fine chemicals supplying the pharmaceutical industry. Because of their proven commercial success and commitment to the United States, despite their German origins, they became prominent in the enrichment of uranium for the US government and contributed to the Manhattan project in developing the atom bomb.

2. Born in 1886, Kurt Hahn was the second of four sons in a Jewish family in Berlin and had been schooled with the conventional German rigour at Wilhelms gymnasium followed by reading classics at Oxford. He based Salem on the educational ideas of Plato, that is, the classical Greek principles of the education of the body as well as the mind and studying everything rather than simply focusing on a limited number of academic subjects, seeing this as a preferred alternative to the authoritarian, rigidly academic curriculum of the German gymnasium. As the director of Salem, which means peace, from 1920 until 1933, he placed greater emphasis on non-competitive physical activities and democratic forms of social co-operation than was the case in conventional German schools. Prince Max was particularly keen on egalitarian aims being incorporated into the design of the school. The curriculum prepared young people for higher education, but not without laying the groundwork for a life of moral and civic virtue, the chief aims of the school – the main ethos being to understand weakness in order to develop strength, to turn self-discovery into acts of compassion and everywhere to defend human decency. As the Nazis rose to power, Hahn became an outspoken opponent. In 1932, a group of fascist storm troopers kicked a leftist activist to death before the eyes of his mother, and were immediately praised by Hitler. Hahn wrote to the alumni of Salem telling them to choose between Salem and Hitler. A man who knew him at the time called it, 'the bravest deed in cold blood that I have ever witnessed'. The following year Hitler imprisoned Hahn. Fortunately he had friends in Britain and they and Ramsay MacDonald, the prime minister, were able to arrange his release and immigration to England. Within a year he started another school, Gordonstoun, in Morayshire, Scotland, carrying the Salem tradition to the new setting and bringing with him many of the staff and pupils from Salem.

3. Mrs Sophie Renner was married to a former senior German diplomat who was violently anti-Hitler and had moved to England before the war and become an advisor to Churchill. He never allowed his family to speak German and never went back becoming totally immersed in England. In this respect the Kleinworts, although great friends of the Schroders, were very different in that they had become far more anglicised and few if any of them spoke German. Lindy Renner and her future husband Anthony Leschallas became close and long-life friends with Gowi and Charmaine, including being godparents to their children.

4. David Morris was the group financial controller (see Chapter 5).

5. William Slee joined Schroders as group managing director – credit and capital markets in 1985 (see Chapter 14).

CHAPTER 4

WIN BISCHOFF'S EARLY LIFE AND CAREER IN HONG KONG

1941 - 1982

Early life, 1941 - 1970

Winfried Franz Wilhelm Bischoff was born on 10 May 1941 at Salier Allee in Aachen near Köln on the German-Belgium border. His father Paul Helmut Bischoff married his mother Hildegard Kühne in 1938. The Bischoffs were landowners from the lower Rhine who bred ponies for the mining industry. Helmut Bischoff was the last of four children and was eight years old when his father died. As he did not go to university his grandmother gave him the equivalent sum to invest in his business career. He had a business apprenticeship in Hamburg, England and in New York (with IBM) and spoke good English – he had a sense of adventure and was attracted to the new world away from Germany. Shortly after his marriage he was called up to serve in the German Army and served on the eastern front, where his brother-in-law was killed. Neither of Win's parents ever spoke about those times.

After the war, Helmut joined his friend Konrad Henkel, the well regarded industrialist and owner of Henkel, the detergents and industrial adhesives company. At about the same time, he inherited a farm from his grandmother in one of the most fertile areas of Germany. One night, while Helmut was away, the farm was attacked by the *Werwolf*, mostly former prisoners of war and former soldiers who formed gangs to plunder farms and monasteries in remote areas. Fortunately they survived and later moved to Düsseldorf in 1951.

The success of communism was of great concern in Germany and the bloody suppression of the demonstration against communism in East Berlin on 17 June 1953 made many Germans consider leaving their country. It was after this that Helmut went to Johannesburg in South Africa to set up the operations of Henkel (South Africa). Win followed him in 1954 when he was enrolled as a boarder at Marist Brothers College at Inanda outside Johannesburg. The remainder of the family including his mother, two brothers and a sister joined them the following year. Win enjoyed his time at school and had one or two close friends including Malcolm Funston with whom he competed for the top place in their class. Despite being a slow developer he did well academically but did not find it particularly demanding. He went on to the University of Witwatersrand, also in Johannesburg, where he took a bachelor of commerce degree in economics. It was here that he started to work hard and as a result was one of only 20% of those on the course who completed their degree.

His parents had a wide circle of friends, personal, business and political. Helmut Bischoff, with his brilliant blue eyes, was full of charm with beautiful manners and old-fashioned courtesy. Hildegard Bischoff was tall, elegant, spontaneous, very intelligent and ambitious for her husband. She spoke French, English and German fluently, was well read with a good memory and was an accomplished tennis player. In a world where women had no opportunities to make a career, Hildegard used her ambition and talents to enhance her husband's career and as a result they were a remarkably effective team. Win got his warmth and charm from his father and his intelligence and ambition from his mother. He greatly admired and respected his father.

Helmut was a good networker and soon decided to set up his own company, wanting the independence from corporate life, which he did not care for. His new business served the mining industry with imported goods and machinery mainly from Germany. He was very committed to his work and as he travelled a lot and had many dinner engagements the family only saw him at the weekends. They gave many dinner parties at home for business people. Helmut was the chairman of the South African-German Chamber of Commerce and so every visiting CEO and manager from Germany called at the office and from there was asked to dinner.

The Bischoffs had a nice house and led a comfortable rather than wealthy life. It was a traditional German family life. Not much fun, it was important to work at one's studies – there was plenty of time for play later. Win's parents passed on to their children a strong sense of ethics. They also learnt that appearances and form were all important and anything unpleasant such as disagreements and difficulties should always be covered up.

Win was very close to his parents, probably more so than to his brothers and sister, and was always the shining example of the parents. His brothers and sister saw him as being serious, committed, focused, difficult to get close to and to read, extremely competitive and not at all keen on losing, always having a strong will to win. He also did not like confrontation or unpleasant decisions. It is interesting to see how these early characteristics inherited and learnt from his parents were so strong throughout his career.

On leaving university Win did not have any specific plans for a career. During his many visits to Germany, Helmut got to know Hermann Volz, the head of Chase Manhattan Bank in Frankfurt. Volz, whose family had emigrated to America in the 1920s, was sent to Frankfurt in 1947 for two years but remained there until 1962, having vastly expanded Chase's banking business during the emergence of Germany as a major economic power. At the time Chase was, with Morgan Guaranty and Citibank, deeply involved in assisting the international expansion of the large American companies into the evolving markets of Europe. Its trainee programme in New York was much sought after by foreigners who wanted to get to know New York and the international banking business. Helmut, who was keen to see Win make a successful career, saw big opportunities in the growth of international banking, being one of the most powerful parts of the economy with finance at the heart of New York, and arranged through Volz, who had by then returned to New York, a place for Win on the programme. He knew that there were not the same opportunities in Germany, which was more rigid, formal and consensual with individualism being discouraged. He also saw the benefit of moving in the right circles and meeting the right people. On a broad ranging programme, Win learnt about credit in the international department followed by a year in correspondent banking. The programme allowed for the trainees to get to know the city and so Win was able to take full advantage of his time to enjoy the social scene. Volz's daughter Anita, who made a successful career herself in the financial sector, found Win to be very personable, outgoing and friendly – 'he was always reaching out for new people and new experiences, making friends very easily.' She saw his extrovert personality, love of people and action as being key assets for a successful banking career.

Having completed the programme at Chase, Win decided to enrol at the New York University School of Law but not being a serious student and lacking the discipline by going to too many parties, he did not make a success of it – he did not complete the course as he had to leave the United States to avoid the draft for the war in Vietnam. In 1964 he decided to move to London where after a period of getting to know the city, he joined Erwin Brecher & Co. Limited, the traders, who got him a work permit that was difficult for a German National. However, as he did not find the work demanding or interesting he started to look at the appointments page in the *Financial Times* and applied to Schroders who were looking for two business school graduates between 28 and 32. Although not qualified and too young at 24, he was interviewed by Cator and Murphy who seemed to be interested in him – he was impressed by the way he was interviewed and became quite keen. He was then seen by Richardson in a meeting room on a very hot day in August. They talked about the air conditioning system, neither of them knowing what they were talking about, and he left the interview convinced that the job had been lost. Much to his surprise a letter arrived a week or so later offering him a position in Corporate Finance.

Bischoff started in Corporate Finance under the tutelage of Ashton, sitting opposite him, learning on the job by going to all the meetings, writing up the minutes that were always corrected, checking schedules, doing spread sheets and working the adding machine. He kept quiet at meetings, answered the telephone and generally acted as a dogsbody. After a year and a half learning his trade he was let loose to work for the directors including Bobby Holland who gave him more responsibility than the others. After a further year he was transferred to Wolfensohn's international issues department, then run by Loehnis with Asseily, Simon Richardson, Tessa Nash and Erika Schild, which was responsible for marketing for and selling Eurobonds. Although it was difficult being behind SG Warburg, Bischoff felt they could be successful not least because of Wolfensohn's indefatigability and many contacts. Under Loehnis' direction, Bischoff did the technical prospectus work, Asseily the selling and Schild the administration – Wolfensohn was constantly travelling in America.

THE MALLINCKRODT - BISCHOFF PARTNERSHIP

In November 1970, Bischoff was asked by Wolfensohn if he would like to go to Hong Kong, where Schroders was thinking of setting up a joint venture merchant bank with The Chartered Bank and the Kadoorie family. He would answer to Airlie and Philip Robinson, a senior corporate finance director in London. Bischoff's first reaction was to reject the idea as he was enjoying his work and life in London. Expecting this response, Wolfensohn gave him a book by Hermann Kahn on the advance that he expected Japan and the rest of South East Asia to experience for the remainder of the 1970s. This changed his mind and he became very excited at the prospect, despite having made no enquiries and so was rather surprised on his arrival in Hong Kong to find that Schroders had nothing there.

Hong Kong 1970 - 1982

At the end of 1969, Peter Graham, the general manager of The Chartered Bank in Hong Kong, had benefited from a period of considerable growth following the Cultural Revolution in China in 1966 and was expanding into new areas of business, even having completed for his clients three initial public offerings (IPOs) on the Hong Kong Stock Exchange. He realised the bank did not have the merchant banking expertise necessary to take advantage of the many opportunities available and approached his chairman, George Bullen, in London to see whether he had any suggestions regarding a top-class merchant banking partner. Although The Chartered Bank had a 20% shareholding in Arbuthnot Latham, a small accepting house in London, he felt that if he was to compete with Jardine Fleming and with Wardley, the two established merchant banks in Hong Kong, he needed a more powerful partner.[1] When, after taking soundings in the City, Bullen suggested Schroders, Graham was delighted.

Bullen approached Richardson, who sent out Airlie to investigate. Having reviewed with Graham the opportunities, including the long established customer base of The Chartered Bank, Airlie agreed to a 50-50 venture, with Schroders to supply the managing director. Later, Airlie rang Graham to say that he had found the right man in whom Schroders had full confidence but he was very young. He sent him Bischoff's curriculum vitae showing that he was only 29 years old. It was agreed that they would now construct the board including an independent chairman.

Airlie was surprised when Graham suggested Lawrence Kadoorie (later Baron Kadoorie), a prominent 70-year-old business man whose operations included electricity and hotels based primarily in Kowloon, the other side of the harbour to Central on Victoria Island where all the best known companies and the banks were based. Kadoorie had even been asked to resign as a director of HSBC when it acquired the British Bank of the Middle East, due to his being Jewish. He was chairman of the Hong Kong Jewish community and worked tirelessly to secure its future in Hong Kong and as such was acknowledged as its leader. Graham explained that he had known Kadoorie for many years and that he had not only been very successful in all the businesses he owned, having lived in Hong Kong and China for nearly 70 years, but he was also a man of impeccable integrity, well respected within the business community and considered to be very astute.[2]

Philip Robinson[3], responsible in London for Schroders' operations in the Far East, went out to Hong Kong to negotiate the terms of the agreement to form Schroders & Chartered. The Kadoorie companies took a 20% shareholding, leaving Schroders and The Chartered Bank with 40% each. Kadoorie was originally offered a 10% shareholding but, at the suggestion of his son Michael, said it would be insufficient for him to devote the necessary time to the venture and so it was agreed that he should have 20%. Kadoorie and Sidney Gordon (later knighted), his deputy chairman and finance director, joined the board. Gordon, formerly senior partner of Lowe Bingham & Matthews, the leading firm of chartered accountants in Hong Kong, was a key member of Kadoorie's management as he brought a framework to the business, the skills to implement decisions and set standards thus complimenting Kadoorie's entrepreneurial talents. He was also totally trusted as well as being a formidable negotiator. Not long after the bank was set up, Airlie rang Graham to say that he had an investment manager to join Bischoff, but he had a problem – he was also called Bischof, but with only one 'f'. Ruedi joined Win almost immediately to develop an investment management business.

David Kinlock, who was working for the Kadoories at the time, was present at the meetings to set up Schroders & Chartered and attended the board meetings. He recalls the Kadoories giving Bischoff one of his first corporate finance transactions – the acquisition of the 70% shareholding in the Peak Tramways Company not already owned by the Hong Kong and Shanghai Hotels Company, which was controlled by the Kadoories. It was a relatively simple transaction due to both companies being managed by the Kadoories and Bischoff had not agreed a fee. He therefore asked Kinlock what he thought would be appropriate. When Kinlock said HK$10,000 (less than £1000), although clearly stunned, Bischoff did not dissent – he simply swallowed and accepted knowing this was the beginning of great prospects to come. He framed the fee note to show the lowest fee Schroders had ever charged for a corporate finance transaction. Kinlock recalls that Kadoorie had the highest regard for Bischoff from the beginning. 'He was highly professional and energetic, universally respected in the business community and totally trusted as well as being congenial to deal with.'

Bischoff was given a modest office – Room 206 – in The Chartered Bank building comprising an office for himself, an entrance hall for his secretary, Jendy Keung (later Lau) and a meeting room, 500 square feet in all. 'Jendy was a great hire, a wonderful person, quite good at English and very hard working' – she remained with Schroders & Chartered for the next 28 years.

Shortly after the formation of the bank Graham returned to London and was replaced by David Millar, a seasoned commercial banker who had served The Chartered Bank all over Asia. Before taking over he had spent three months meeting the management of the companies The Chartered Bank had lent to, as he had to accept responsibility for all the loans. Ninety-eight per cent of their business was with the Chinese as every major public company, including all those with expatriate links, banked with HSBC. The previously rich and successful Shanghaiese families, having escaped from communism on the mainland, were the driving force in the textile and garment industry. They created an industrial revolution in Hong Kong, turning it from an entrepôt into a major manufacturing centre bringing with them skills and enterprise and improved employment practices, but little capital. The 1970s were the heydays of Hong Kong. The Chartered Bank had a major share of this business, most of the loans being based on faith in their abilities and went beyond what was normally bankable. Millar hired BK Liu, a Shanghaiese lawyer and former advisor to South China Group, who had joined Basil Sarafis of the Ralli Group, the cotton traders, and got to know the entire textile industry. This gave The Chartered Bank access to the Chinese community who were invariably short of capital. Andrew Tuckey of Barings said 'Millar was a wonderful guy and as good a commercial banker as they come – he gave HSBC a good run for its money, having been schooled in the Colonial banking tradition. He had a big influence on Win.' Millar was delighted to have Schroders as partners as he had handled an IPO for China Engineers in a rather amateur way and needed the professionalism. He often invited Bischoff to meet his Chinese customers over lunch to discuss corporate finance and investment management business. It was useful to offer these services as they locked in his customers and prevented them going to HSBC. Until March 1973, there was a great boom in the stock market with a steady stream of new issues for The Chartered Bank's Shanghaiese customers in the textile and property sectors mostly being arranged by Bischoff. He found Bischoff had Germanic determination and great strength although he could be very moody and was prone to depression if things did not go well or his way. Once Bischoff had a bad oyster at lunch and Millar found him in his office lying on his back on the floor dictating a memorandum to Jendy. 'He simply would not give up for anything.'

During Bischoff's busy social life in London he met Rosemary Leathers, whose father Leslie was chairman of the British-South African Society and a friend of Cyril Hawker, the chairman of Standard Bank, having previously been in the family firm William Cory in London and South Africa. They were married on 8 January 1972 in St Joseph's, the Catholic Cathedral in Hong Kong, and had a reception at the Millars' house on the Peak – 'it was a wonderful wedding on a glorious day with a lovely reception from which they went off in fine fettle.'

They moved into a flat in Tregunter Mansions on Tavistock Road in midlevels, half way up to the Peak, which became the venue for frequent dinner parties for Win's clients and their friends. With such a small office Rosemary played an important supporting role in Win's business life carrying out many tasks including acting as chauffeur. Whereas most of the expatriates based their lives on being in Hong Kong for two years and counting the days to their return to England, the Bischoffs worked on the basis that they would be there for the duration and made many Chinese friends and Hong Kong their home. For the next ten years Rosemary gave dinner parties often twice a week for Win's clients and their friends with a mix of Chinese and Europeans. With the Chinese it was particularly important to entertain at home rather than at a restaurant. Lydia Dunn (later Baroness), an unofficial member of the Executive Council and a director of John Swire & Sons (HK) Limited and HSBC and a prominent Hong Kong Chinese personality, came across the Bischoffs socially. She said, 'Hong Kong was a very small community and everybody's paths crossed before long. Win and Rosemary made an immediate impact, both being outgoing and friendly and also they worked hard at it. There was a thin line between business and friendship and Win's charisma captivated all. I never heard a bad word said about him and that is a great reputation to have in Hong Kong.'

Weekends only started after noon on Saturdays and many of these were spent on the harbour and in the bays around the island and off the New Territories. Millar and Bischoff shared a 34-foot Swan sloop with No 4 registered number – 'it had been recovered from the sea after the Japanese occupation by Butterfield and Swire and been rebuilt with its lovely brass intact. It was of the traditional type, narrow-waisted and very sleek.' Airlie and Robinson often visited Hong Kong together and enjoyed a sail from Deepwater Bay to a lovely bay on the south side of Lamma Bay, where they took a swim after a picnic lunch. On one such visit Airlie and Robinson expressed to Millar their reservations about Bischoff's suitability to run Schroders & Chartered due to being too volatile and temperamental. Millar had no hesitation in saying 'Schroders will never get a better man' – although they never discussed it Millar thought Bischoff may have known he had batted for him. Time would show how right he was. Later the Bischoffs invested in a junk that was better for entertaining colleagues, clients and friends and was safer for their two young sons Christopher and Charlie.

Bischoff started by marketing for Eurobonds to the clients of The Chartered Bank converting their cash deposits into higher yielding Eurobonds. He intended to sell unit trusts until David Hunter-Johnston, a former civil servant who was a director of Investment Management in London, came out to produce the perfect trust deed for Hong Kong! The corporate finance business started after six months and there was some investment business – David Davis and Ruedi Bischof were sent out from London and Zurich.

An early deal was the placing of Ralli International's shares on the Hong Kong Stock Exchange. Alastair Goodlad and his wife Cecelia had known the Bischoffs socially in London and met them again when Goodlad became the head of Ralli International's Far East operation in Singapore. Ralli Group, the cotton trader and long-standing customer of The Chartered Bank, had earlier been acquired by a company in the Slater Walker Group and become Ralli International under the chairmanship of Malcolm Horseman. (Robinson was rather worried about the relationship with Horseman.) Goodlad[4], who was an usher at Bischoff's wedding and became a life-long friend, said

Win brought to Hong Kong a professionalism unknown there previously. He created for Schroders & Chartered an immense niche in the market and did very well for his shareholders. He and Rosemary used to entertain all the leading Chinese business people and their wives – something never seen before – and made good friends of them. He was very industrious, crossed off every name, was incredibly friendly and forthcoming to clients and up to speed on the details of every transaction – unique.

There followed a series of new issues of increasing importance. GT Management was the first new issue of an investment trust on the Hong Kong Stock Exchange, in which Sir Douglas Cleague, the chairman of Hutchison International (HIL), was a shareholder. Sung Tao Newspapers, owned by Sally Aw Sian, wanted to go public and approached The Chartered Bank. Recently the Hang Seng Bank had gone public and was hugely over-subscribed. Sally Aw Sian wanted the 'face' of an over-subscription, which rivalled the Hang Seng issue – she got it with an issue of new shares, without a significant dilution of her shareholding. IMC was the first major shipping issue – all Hong Kong shipping companies had well written down ships purchased two or three years earlier at lower prices – they were valued for the prospectus at the current prices making them a huge success – all the shipping companies wanted to follow suit and many approached Schroders & Chartered. The new issues went on for eighteen months until the Stock Market crash in March 1973. Bischoff was helped by Chris Pearce and between them they did a new issue every six weeks – 15 to 16 in all – working like slaves.

The market crash was not a good time for Bischoff personally. The market had fallen from a high of 1775 in March 1973 to 149 in December 1974 – 9% of its value. He had taken on some borrowing and suddenly faced a difficult position – he sold all his shares at 800 when the market had a long way to fall and had sufficient to buy a Porsche and a silver cup to present for the inter merchant bank golf tournament at Fanling between Wardley, Jardine Fleming and Schroders & Chartered. There was very little business and Schroders & Chartered recorded its only loss in 1974. Nick MacAndrew, who had joined Corporate Finance from Deloittes in 1971, came out to replace Pearce and found it quite quiet at first. There were a number of rights issues including one for China Light & Power Company, which regularly went to the market and was lifeblood to Schroders & Chartered during quiet periods. Wardley became more powerful after the crash due to the lending power of HSBC. Jardine Fleming was doing well because of its good stockbroking business. Schroders & Chartered did some advisory work for failing companies, one of which was Hutchison International.

During 1975, Bischoff was approached by John Richardson, a newly appointed director of HIL, one of the leading companies in Hong Kong but with severe liquidity problems, to advise the board on the efficacy of an offer by HSBC to take up new shares in the company at par – HK$1 – giving it effective control of the company with an undertaking to provide unlimited banking support on condition that the chairman stepped down. Cleague, the chairman of the company, was also deputy chairman of HSBC and chairman of the Jockey Club, and as such was probably the most prominent business leader in Hong Kong as well as being well known in England as a successful horserace owner. In Richardson's view, progress would not be made without a change to the board and the management. Cleague was opposed to the HSBC offer and supported the appointment of Bischoff, who was a friend as well as being highly regarded. Due to the prominence of the deal with its attendant local and international publicity, it became a pivotal deal to Schroders & Chartered's and Bischoff's reputation. The public fight for control of the company was very confrontational and almost unknown in Hong Kong hitherto, where things were generally arranged by consensus. Bischoff and MacAndrew were subjected to intense influence from both sides, particularly from Cleague. The board was torn between its loyalty to Cleague, its chairman, and the survival of the company. Bischoff called on Eric Udall, HSBC's legal counsel, and said that he could not put out a prospectus unless there was sufficient working capital – HSBC gave an undertaking of unlimited support. In the end Bischoff came down in favour of the HSBC offer – there were too many financial threats to the company, the economic climate was especially difficult and there was no other acceptable alternative. At an evening meeting Bischoff advised the board to accept the offer, there being no viable alternative. Cleague said the board would not take his advice and said his mandate was terminated. Bischoff said he would make his advice public. He was not fired and by a narrow majority the board agreed. 'It was a sad deal, Dougie Cleague was forced out and it was very painful as he had been a friend.' Richardson's verdict was, 'Bischoff made the correct call and after the board had accepted his advice he had to face a stormy Annual General Meeting of the shareholders to explain his views. It required a lot of guts.'

The most famous transaction Bischoff was involved with was the defence for the Hong Kong Gas Company against a bid by Hong Kong Electric. RC Lee, the chairman, had always been looked after by Wardley who, together with Jardine Fleming, were acting for Hong Kong Electric. The announcement was made over a bank holiday weekend and Bischoff who was on Lantau Island for the weekend rushed off to meet Lee, with whom he had had no previous relationship and offered to help him defend the Gas Company. There ensued a major battle, led by Bischoff and MacAndrew – it was the first defence in Hong Kong conducted as a classic London market defence with a great deal of press coverage. They won by a considerable margin beating off many increases in the bid price. David KP Li, the chairman of the Bank of East Asia, said nearly twenty years later, 'it will always be remembered as the most successful defence in Hong Kong history and will always be associated with the name Bischoff.' For Bischoff it was one of the most exciting jobs he did while in Hong Kong.

By 1976 Schroders & Chartered was, in the view of someone who worked closely with all the leading merchant banks,

well and truly established as one of the three leading merchant banks in Hong Kong, although less profitable. Wardley, originally a joint venture between HSBC and Vickers da Costa but now wholly owned by HSBC, provided the muscle but not the brains and was staffed by converted bankers, stockbrokers and second line bankers with nobody with a strong merchant banking background. Euan Launder, from Vickers da Costa, who went on to be imprisoned for corruption over the Carrion affair in which HSBC were heavily implicated, was their managing director. If a deal was dominated by HSBC the client went to Wardley knowing that it could obtain the money but would not receive particularly reliable advice. Mike Sandburg gave Wardley a lot of support as he loved deals and was an investment banker at heart. Jardine Fleming provided lots of brains but was not perceived to be independent, without any Chinese walls between it and Jardine, the other most dominant force in Hong Kong. With Peter Jamieson, who went on to become deputy chairman of Robert Fleming in London, followed by John Manser, subsequently chairman of Robert Fleming, they had superb leadership ably supported by Nick Sibley and Alan Smith. A client would receive good advice from Jardine Fleming but could never be sure that the interests of Jardine did not affect it. There were many stories of front running when shares are purchased by the house immediately before a major purchase by a client thus driving up the price and yielding a handsome profit to the house. Schroders & Chartered provided brains, independence, integrity but not the same muscle. If a client wanted independent and unbiased advice on whether or not to go ahead with a deal, he would get that at Schroders & Chartered where there was a good team under Bischoff. The other merchant banks came and went depending on the quality of the person sent out from London – they included NM Rothschild, Kleinwort, Hill Samuel, Baring and Lazard – but none of them came near the top three.

In early 1976, Bischoff alerted Dewe Mathews in London to the fact that China Light & Power Company, substantially owned by the Kadoories, together with its partner Esso Eastern, were planning to build a series of new power stations. It was hoped that power stations would be built by GEC Turbine Generators and their subcontractors and financed by loans guaranteed by the Export Credit Guarantee Department (ECGD) of the British Government. Dewe Mathews immediately rushed to Hong Kong to find out how Project Finance in London could exploit the situation. He suggested to Kadoorie and Gordon that Schroders could arrange all the financing and went back to London and informed Charles Birch at ECGD that Schroders had been asked by China Light to organise the financing. GEC, unbeknown to Dewe Mathews, had appointed Lazards, the most experienced export finance bank in London, to provide the finance. There followed a major and prolonged battle between Dewe Mathews and Lord Kindersley and David Gemmill of Lazards as to which bank would arrange the financing. At a critical point Lazards with the support of HSBC offered to finance the whole contract in Hong Kong Dollars at a fixed rate of HK$5.15 to US$1 when the current rate was HK$4.65 – a margin of 50 cents. As Schroders' offer was very much linked to a US$ financing and had no basis on which to put together a competitive Hong Kong dollar offer against HSBC, Dewe Mathews was quite exposed, particularly when, unbeknown to him, Bischoff, as advisor to China Light, was supporting the merits of Lazards' Hong Kong dollar offer. Fortunately Sir Philip Haddon-Cave, the financial secretary, when consulted by China Light, said the margin of 50 cents was outrageous and was not prepared to support it. At the same time the financial people at Esso, which owned 60% of Kowloon Electricity Supply Company (KESCO), the new power station company, were much more interested in borrowing in US$, their own currency for consolidation purposes. Dewe Mathews took advantage of this by offering to syndicate the loans mainly among their principal US bankers. The argument went Schroders' way and Schroders won the mandate much to the irritation of Lazards, GEC and the DTI. It was Project Finance's first major breakthrough in UK government guaranteed loans and due to its size, its complexity – being on a limited recourse basis – and its prestige, it put the Project Finance business in London on the map and was an additional boost to the reputation of Schroders & Chartered. It led on to a series of larger and more complex financings for other China Light and Esso power stations at Castle Peak in the New Territories over the next few years, culminating in multi-currency loans of $1514 million in 1981, with the highest fees ever earned by the Schroder Group at that time. Ten years later Project Finance arranged a $2.4 billion financing breaking once again all the records for such a financing. Over the 16 years, five financings amounting to just over $6 billion were arranged for 7400 MW of power. The key to the success of all these loans was the relationships Bischoff maintained with China Light and Dewe Mathews with the Exxon treasurers in Houston and New Jersey, who controlled the financing arrangements, and of course to GEC Turbine Generators.

At the turn of the decade, China was opening its doors to the outside world and one day, out of the blue, the Bank of China in Hong Kong called on Bischoff and asked if he would go to Peking to discuss a major petrochemical project. He rang up Dewe Mathews and asked him to come to Hong Kong prior to a visit to China. Visas, which at the time were impossible to obtain without endless delay, were made available immediately. As Dewe Mathews explained,

we set off and met the various officials in the Ministry of Chemical Industries including Vice-Minister Zhang Haorua to discover that they wanted us to put together a fully financed petrochemical complex in Shandong province including arrangements for the sale of the products in the Asian market. Having assembled a vast array of international companies and banks we found that we were in competition with a Japanese group led by Mitsui. After tortuous negotiations over many months in which I spent more time in Peking than in London we were finally informed that our group was not competitive. We received no fees for all our efforts but we learnt a lot about how to do and not to do business in China as well as establishing our credentials with the Chinese.

Bischoff's reputation in Hong Kong and his friendship with the Chinese had paid off. Bischoff received a call from John Hull in March 1982 saying he wanted to have a word about him coming back to London and to do a swap with Tyo van Marle who was head of the international issues department. Airlie had wanted to bring him back to London earlier and give him a big job but Kadoorie would not allow him to go. As Douglas Fergusson was pushing hard to get involved in foreign currency business, Bischoff felt van Marle would be helpful. At 42, it was not a bad time for him to see whether he could do well in London. It would cost him nothing as he could always come back to Hong Kong where he knew he could find a job relatively easily. Being quite superstitious he was pleased to have had the *feng shui* of having spent twelve years in Hong Kong, the full cycle of the Chinese calendar. He was born in the Chinese year of the snake, while his star sign is Taurus. 'They both go forward determinedly but the snake is more subtle.'

One of the last assignments Bischoff had in Hong Kong was advising Sir John Brembridge, the financial secretary, on the financial feasibility of building a new airport for Hong Kong. He personally led a team of his own staff under Fergusson, Project Finance and Coopers & Lybrand, in preparing a financial feasibility study. In the middle he was called back to London, but as the assignment was personal to Bischoff, he had to fly back to Hong Kong for a week each month to attend meetings with Brembridge and his staff. In the meanwhile Rosemary stayed on in Hong Kong for the next six months to see through the education of Charlie at the German-Swiss School on the Peak, Christopher having started at the Dragon School in Oxford. She took advice from the Chinese on the most auspicious day to leave Hong Kong and was advised to go between 6 and 9 January – she chose Charlie's birthday, 9 January 1983. It was very sad for her to leave especially after so long and having made so many close friends, particularly among the Chinese, but it was a convenient time to put the boys into an English preparatory school. They had had twelve happy years in Hong Kong and were ready for new challenges.

A review of Bischoff's achievements
What had Bischoff achieved in his twelve years in Hong Kong? Modestly he said

> We had established Schroders' name outside of Japan and developed a platform to expand regionally. It was not difficult to do well in an economy that grew so fast. The three leading merchant banks had helped to spread the idea of investment banking. Investment Management had done less well than expected, as Hong Kong was an institutional market based on performance and Schroders had sent the wrong people. Ruedi was a first class Swiss private banker not an institutional investor. It is important to send not only good people but also the right people.

This error was redressed later with good results.

Clients and competitors were virtually unanimous in their praise for Bischoff. Richardson of Hutchison said, 'Win established enduring relationships with the most senior Chinese businessmen. Hong Kong had never seen before or since an investment banking relationship builder of the like. When he left he was never effectively replaced as those who followed lacked his skills in strategic corporate finance advice and in deal making.' Richardson had previously got to know Bischoff on the Fanling golf course where he had noticed how fiercely competitive and canny he was. 'He always chose a long iron rather than a wood going for accuracy rather than length and was a good partner in a competition.'

Bischoff had formidable competition in Jardine Fleming and Wardley, which totally dominated the market. Neither was averse to using information on their clients to feather the nest of themselves and their shareholders – the practice of insider dealing being the norm in Hong Kong at the time. Bischoff, being a person of high ethical principles like Gordon Richardson, his mentor in London, would have nothing of this and built a reputation for Schroders & Chartered and for himself of being absolutely straight. He became known to be totally reliable and trustworthy. Nick Sibley, the managing director of Jardine Fleming at the time, said to Dewe Mathews one day on his junk almost awash with champagne and beautiful partially clad young ladies that Bischoff was 'the only person in Hong Kong that I could consult on a confidential transaction I was working on and know that he would not only give the best and most astute advice but also not use the information for his or Schroders' benefit' – unstinting praise from a competitor. Andrew Tuckey, who was running Baring Sanwa in 1974, said the same thing and that 'he was always a fierce competitor and I have had a close friendship and professional respect for him to this day.'

Sir William Purves, who was non-executive chairman of Wardley for a time, said that

Jardine Fleming had grown quicker and more successfully than Wardley as they had a large amount of good people from London. Schroders & Chartered was third concentrating on corporate finance where they were arguably the best. They had fewer clients than Jardine Fleming and Wardley but they did the business very well. I put this down to Win who was the most experienced and best leader in the market. He worked very hard, got around the clients and gave each much of his personal attention and this led to him gradually gaining more clients. He and Rosemary were a real force small but to be reckoned with. They developed a certain momentum and got a good share of the business.

Despite all this praise, it could be said that while Bischoff personally might have been the leading corporate financier in Hong Kong, there were other sectors such as investment management where Schroders & Chartered were less successful. Jardine Fleming, which commenced business shortly before Schroders & Chartered, had the full backing of the Jardine Group, which at that time was the leading 'Hong' with powerful connections around the Far East region. It therefore had a much stronger client base than Schroders & Chartered and was able to build up its corporate finance business much more quickly. It was also staffed with a number of good people from Robert Fleming in London. However, its main strength was its investment management business whose margins were far greater than those of corporate finance where local businesses, especially the Chinese, were reluctant to pay big advisory fees unless they were associated with fund raising. Under Peter Jamieson's leadership they grew this business until in 1983, when Bischoff returned to London, they had US$1.75 billion funds under management in the region. Although Schroders & Chartered had an investment management business it was seen as secondary to corporate finance as in London. Bischoff was not that interested in it and as a result Schroders & Chartered never became a serious competitor to Jardine Fleming in that field.

The Keswicks, who controlled Jardine, reckoned that as a result, Jardine Fleming, whose results covered the whole of the Far East excluding Japan whereas Schroders & Chartered's only covered Hong Kong, was ten times more profitable than Schroders, reaching HK$90 million in 1983. (S&C's profits did not reach that level until 1992, by which time Jardine Fleming's were approaching HK$1 billion.) Jardine liked Bischoff and admired his hard work and integrity and always turned to him if they needed a 'second jockey at times when Jardine Fleming was doing Jardine's more important work.' Jardine never saw Schroders as a real competitor to their merchant bank!

The Kadoories however were very satisfied. 'Schroders & Chartered was noted as the most impressive merchant bank in Hong Kong and my family was very proud to be associated with it,' said Michael Kadoorie.

> Win was a workaholic, enjoyed himself when he had time, but work came first, he was dedicated and a good leader, listening to his colleagues. He was not an inventor but collected brilliant ideas off others and took decisions on their implementation. He was also a diplomat and married the needs of London with the gung-ho fast pace of Hong Kong – he could well have been held back by London. My father was very fond of Win not least because he would always listen attentively unlike his family who kept interrupting him. He was the senior among his peers and was more able to bridge the cultural gap between the two cultures (the Chinese and the British). He was seen as independent and as more approachable to the smaller people who were happier with him.

NOTES:

1. Jardine Fleming was a joint venture between the Jardine group – one of the leading trading companies in Hong Kong ('Hongs') that was built on the back of the opium trade with China in the previous century and Robert Fleming, the well-known investment management house in London. Wardley was the merchant banking arm of the Hongkong & Shanghai Banking Corporation (HSBC).

2. Lawrence Kadoorie was comfortable being involved in merchant banking previously having been called on by most of the leaders of the major British merchant banks, including

Sir Siegmund Warburg and Evelyn de Rothschild (later knighted), and therefore knew that they all saw Hong Kong as an important market. He had always been interested in finance and enjoyed learning by meeting enthusiasts in fields other than his own. He was naturally cautious and took time before taking important decisions. For him his name was more important than money and he liked the idea of being in partnership with a family controlled company with the same conservative values. He was not interested in shortcuts and quick money. He was pleased to find Bischoff to be trustworthy, conservative and having the ability to deliver. He started by giving Ruedi an investment portfolio to manage and told him he had given a similar amount to another manager and would be comparing the two of them.

3. Philip Robinson had had a similar education to Richardson, not having gone to one of the great public schools. He had joined Schrobanco in New York from NM Rothschild's energy joint venture in Canada in 1959. In due course he came to London as a corporate finance director before becoming a strategic advisor to Airlie on Group matters. In this role he helped develop and then oversaw the growth of Schroders' businesses in Hong Kong, Japan and Singapore. He was seen by many of his subordinates in Corporate Finance as being idiosyncratic, unconventional, always looking at issues from a different angle and someone you could never pin down. He was also highly political, a rare quality at Schroders. His clients on the other hand spoke very favourably of him including Jeremy Lancaster, the chief executive of Wolsely, who said the company would not have survived without Robinson's advice. Those starting businesses in Asia had a similar the view of him. Robinson played a key support role to Bischoff's success in Hong Kong by being a wonderful foil from London. He was always keen to be involved and came out to Hong Kong frequently. He was also a great booster of Hong Kong in London. As the chief executive Bischoff needed a non-executive outside Hong Kong to chat to, particularly on matters of principle, and Robinson's brilliant analytical mind and uncanny political feel was perfect for this role. Mallinckrodt played the same role in Singapore after Robinson retired, but was more hands-on. Bischoff felt Robinson did a superb and invaluable job. Robinson had only praise for Bischoff.

4. Alastair Goodlad went on to become a Conservative MP, the Minister of State at the Foreign Office responsible for Hong Kong and China, government chief whip and then the British High Commissioner to Australia before which he was knighted.

CHAPTER 5

A WORKING PARTNERSHIP IS AGREED

1985 – 1994

Bischoff had been promoted in rapid succession after his return from Hong Kong during 1982 from deputy head to head of Corporate Finance and then to chairman of Schroder Wagg, Hull having stepped aside. He was clearly Airlie's choice to lead the bank into the future. In view of the large family shareholding, its continuing disagreements with the two previous chairmen, and the need to link its interests with the executive management, Airlie recommended to his colleagues and the board that Mallinckrodt should become the non-executive chairman leaving Bischoff to run the bank. The board, by then with a strong family support, appointed Mallinckrodt the non-executive chairman of the board and chairman of the strategic planning committee, and Bischoff the group chief executive and chairman of the executive committee. Mallinckrodt did not recall this division of roles, feeling that it had always been agreed that he was to be *pari passu* with Bischoff. He particularly remembered discussing his new role with his mother, who had a powerful influence on him throughout his life, and she advised him that to be successful he and Bischoff should be sitting on the same motor bicycle. There was a certain amount of surprise within the bank at Mallinckrodt's appointment, as he had never run a major part of the bank, even Banking which was his area of expertise. The situation in New York still had to be resolved. When asked for an explanation, Airlie said that with its controlling shareholding it would be unreasonable not to have a member of the family who was over the age of 50 and was reasonably competent as non-executive chairman.

Hull remained deputy chairman until he retired in at the end of the year. In 1987 Robin Leigh-Pemberton (later Baron Kingsdown), the Governor of the Bank of England, asked Robert Alexander (later Baron Alexander of Weedon) and Hull to become chairman and deputy chairman of the Take-over Panel which had rather lost its way in recent years. He remained the deputy chairman for very many years, at last being back in a milieu he enjoyed and excelled at and for which he was appointed a Commander of the Most Excellent Order of the British Empire (CBE).

Early on there was a row after the executive committee, under Bischoff, had agreed to support the Standard Chartered perpetual note issue in the market without Mallinckrodt being consulted. A large loss was incurred and Mallinckrodt was extremely upset. At the next board meeting Connor accused the new management team of 'betting the bank' – Bischoff justifiably was very annoyed. Mallinckrodt wanted to be chairman and chief executive. Bischoff, who was content to remain chairman of Schroder Wagg, which represented more than 80% of the business, approached his colleagues but they, strongly supported by Solandt, were adamant that he should remain the chief executive and this was confirmed by the board. The bad relationship, if continued, could clearly have a dangerous impact on Bischoff's task of turning around the bank and, in the absence of a move by Mallinckrodt, he had to reach an accommodation with Mallinckrodt to avoid future disagreements. From then on therefore, he always discussed with him any matters of contention. He only had one other major disagreement after that which was concerning whether Project Finance should be permitted to build a large book of ECGD loans fully guaranteed by the British government. Mallinckrodt, in New York at the time, took the view that these long term loans were too illiquid and should be curtailed. As a result the opportunity to make a huge amount of money and secure the future profitability of the business, as had been done earlier by Morgan Grenfell, was lost. When he finally relented it was too late, as by then Project Finance had had to syndicate all of the large loans within its control.

Bischoff reached an accommodation with Mallinckrodt over their future roles, with Mallinckrodt becoming executive chairman and chairman of the Group Executive Committee and Bischoff chief executive and chairman of the Group Management Committee. Bischoff, being brilliant at winning new business, focused on the clients and on building up the morale and enthusiasm of those involved in the revenue earning businesses, particularly in Schroder Wagg. Mallinckrodt concentrated on how to run the business as a whole. Bischoff was not particularly interested in administration and so Mallinckrodt took this on including personnel, regulatory matters and the corporate relations with the central banks and governments. Being good at networking he had excellent relationships within the US Senate including with Senator Jack Danforth, the chairman of the Senate Finance Committee. Each year he led the Schroder team participating at the annual IMF meetings in Washington and organised a dinner party of 50 people, combining foreign banks with US politicians and industrialists. This greatly enhanced Schroders' profile. In terms of geographic responsibilities for overseeing Schroders' operating companies and representative offices, they decided to divide the world between them, with Bischoff being responsible for Europe (excluding Germany and Switzerland), Japan and Hong Kong and Mallinckrodt responsible for Germany, Switzerland, the Americas, Middle East, South East Asia, The People's Republic of China and Australia. Internally Mallinckrodt had direct responsibility for strategic planning and the areas responsible to the chief financial officer and the secretarial and legal functions. Being a banker he was actively involved in risk management, particularly as it related to the balance sheet, and therefore took an interest in the treasury and banking functions under Solandt and Slee. The overall result was that, with the impending sale of Schrobanco, Bischoff was responsible for approaching 85% of the business, his main focus being the creation of revenue. Mallinckrodt was the external face in official, non-business circles and the administrator within responsible for discipline over costs with the right to say No. As Bischoff used to say at the time, 'You can only cut costs by 100% but revenue can be increased by 1000%.' It also defined their relationship with those running the businesses with Bischoff having his foot firmly on the accelerator and Mallinckrodt on the brake. You don't make many friends being the person who always says No. Someone had to do it but it must have been a lonely role. By keeping Mallinckrodt informed of new business initiatives Bischoff built up his trust and the working relationship over time became very effective. They had reached an accommodation, which took advantage of each other's strengths. It said a lot for them both that this was achieved.

The strategic review had created the future management team. They had worked well together and respected each other. Kelly of MAC said

It was a very talented team – Bischoff the corporate financier was positive, people and client oriented and a force to reverse the current weak position, he was willing to delegate the administration to others and to concentrate on the market and to support the revenue creators. Solandt had the hard-nosed financial sense to make the tough calls on gilts and securities and to build the important and profitable treasury business. Popham had the flair for investment, a business that, although overshadowed by Corporate Finance in market perception, was critical to Schroders' ability to survive in investment banking.

Mallinckrodt had reporting to him Raymond Badrock, the company secretary, and Strickland, group managing director finance, corporate planning and information technology under whom was David Morris, the group financial controller. In addition he had his seasoned deputy chairman Williams, who was a legal advisor and trouble-shooter. In 1990 with Williams' and Badrock's retirement and Strickland's departure, he had a new team with David Caruth becoming legal advisor to the Schroder group and Richard Sadleir, the compliance officer. Andrew Gaulter became company secretary and Nick MacAndrew took over from Strickland.

Mallinckrodt always found the secretarial function under Badrock and Gaulter to be very professional with their total command of the secretarial and legal issues, also playing a vital role in the link with regulatory issues. They also kept him informed of what was going on in the bank bringing his attention to matters he should be aware of as the chairman. They found him extremely demanding with his constant concern for cost cutting and his immense interest in the minutest detail on all matters. This required great dedication and endless patience, which he clearly appreciated.

Williams also had overall responsibility for compliance which was becoming ever more important with the Big Bang. Sadleir, the new group compliance officer, had had a diverse career at Schroders and therefore he had a wide knowledge of the firm and a great capacity for absorbing the complexities of the voluminous and mushrooming new regulations. He had frequent meetings with his fellow compliance officers at the other merchant banks and acquired a reputation for being as good as the best.[1]

By 1985 Williams had been at the top of the bank for over 20 years and had a very wide understanding of not only the business but also matters relating to the Schroder family. His huge wisdom, experience and authority, despite his tendency towards cynicism, provided Mallinckrodt with great support on matters of importance. He was of course kept busy with sorting out problems particularly of a legal nature as well as NAPUT and Sarakreek in New York. When Williams retired in 1990 he was succeeded by David Caruth, a senior corporate lawyer from Linklaters and Paines. Not knowing the culture or the personalities at Schroders and how they and their activities fitted into the greater whole, he found it difficult to settle in and to gain the trust of his new colleagues particularly the junior corporate finance directors who felt he had nothing to offer them. He did, however, get a lot of support from Bischoff and Strickland but had a strained relationship with Mallinckrodt to whom he reported. He found it strange coming from Linklaters to have no support, simply a small office, and came to rely on Slaughter & May, Schroders' principal corporate lawyers.

Mallinckrodt had a high regard for Strickland's ability to analyse and deal with strategic issues, his military approach being particularly appropriate. He spent a lot of time with Strickland and Kelly of MAC dealing with the group's commitment to build and expand its international investment banking business rather than commercial banking particularly in New York and whether to buy or build a securities business as well as the execution of Schroders' acquisitions and disposals. These matters are covered in the chapters that follow.

Following the departure of Strickland in 1990, MacAndrew was appointed group managing director finance, strategic planning and IT and a director of Schroders – a rather cumbersome but descriptive title for what was effectively the chief financial officer. Strickland had tried without success to become chief operating officer but Mallinckrodt would have nothing of it. He had not helped his cause by continually being at loggerheads with Mallinckrodt. MacAndrew found it mainly a finance job and rather lonely as he was kept out of everything by Mallinckrodt and Bischoff, who discussed all the main issues and simply informed the group managing directors of their decisions.

Both were served by David Morris, a chartered accountant who joined Schroder Wagg in 1966 from the Liebig Group. From then on he was involved with the increasing professionalisation of the financial control function working very closely with the tax experts. He had a total command of all the figures and introduced simple management information systems throughout the group. His main task was the preparation of the accounts. He started under Bayley, whom he liked and who despite his interest in the high life in New York had a good knowledge of the business. He appreciated Strickland's policy of extreme delegation, making sure that everyone did the work and taking decisions when needed. He and Eric Henbrey, the very able director of tax, blossomed under this regime. MacAndrew worked much harder than Strickland and was far more involved in the detail. He was very good at the deals such as the purchase of the management's shareholding in Wertheim and the sale of the investment bank being a better corporate financier than a strategist. With his extensive knowledge of the numbers Morris could see that the steadily rising profits over the years were based on the benefit of having a great diversity of businesses, many of which could be volatile, one balancing against the others, exceptional profits on different activities being the key to the growth in profits. Tax played a significant role in certain transactions that enhanced profits, such as setting up the offshore tax haven in Bermuda, and the renegotiation of the lease and subsequent sale of the head lease of the Cheapside office. He had much to do with Mallinckrodt and, like others, found him painstaking in the amount of time he spent on the detail, perhaps at the expense of the big picture and with a great interest in the running of the organisation.

Mallinckrodt, being very interested in people, totally revamped the personnel function, which at the time was rudimentary, and totally lacking in professionalism. He appointed Desmond Boyle as the group personnel director with responsibility for building a personnel function and servicing the board in respect to personnel matters. In 1987 Bischoff hired Sue Cox, who had been with The BOC Group for 15 years, the last five as the international personnel manager, as the personnel director of Schroder Wagg. She set about moving the staff department from administration to a fully participating personnel function including the development of statistical information on staff, the introduction of procedures for staff appraisals, job descriptions, training and recruitment, including a broadening of the base for graduate recruitment beyond Oxford and Cambridge. They then turned to remuneration structures, which are described in Chapter 19.

Following the Wolfensohn affair and the departure of Verey, the Schroder family had ensured that they would never be out-voted again by appointing non-executive directors who could be counted on to support the Schroder family. Baron Daniel Janssen, chairman of the executive committee of Solvay & Co SA, had been brought on to the board by Bruno after Airlie became chairman. On Lord Franks' retirement in 1984, he was replaced by William Turner Jr, chairman and chief executive officer of Consolidated-Bathurst and Alva O Way, a director of Travelers Corporation, the following year. These three non-executive directors together with Bruno and Mallinckrodt, gave the family at least five votes. Gaulter as the company secretary was made responsible for making sure that the overseas non-executive directors and their wives were well looked after, always staying at the very best hotels with attractive side trips to European countries and as a result he became affectionately known as 'the shepherd'.

Bill Turner, from a Scottish engineering background, was a big player in Montreal with a powerful intellect and very shrewd. Having spent virtually all his career at Consolidated-Bathurst, he had built up a substantial personal stake in the company, which he sold in 1989 when everybody sold out and had become independently wealthy. Like the best North American directors, he was superb at delivering courteously the toughest and most searching questions. Most of all he was clearly genuinely interested in the bank.

He had been appointed to the advisory board of Schrobanco Inc by Wolfensohn in the mid-1970s. He had met Wolfensohn earlier when he was president of Power Corporation with Maurice Strong and they had asked him to run Travelodge in Australia after he had received his MBA from Harvard. Wolfensohn had greater ambitions but they kept in touch. Turner regularly visited New York on business and came across Wolfensohn in the street after he took over Schroders Inc in 1970 and shortly afterwards was asked to join his board. Wolfensohn introduced him to Bruno and Mallinckrodt and they became friends. Having considerable experience of family-owned companies – the Desmarais family at Power Corporation and the Bombardier family in Canada and the Johnson family in Sweden – he became close to the Schroder family understanding their interests and knowing how to deal with them. He bought Airlie's shares when he retired feeling he should have an interest in the companies he was associated with and so when Bruno asked him if he could help place some of John Schroder's shares which were critical to the Schroder family's control of the bank in 1989, he bought 100,000 shares at the same time as the Kadoorie family (see Chapter 1). He saw Schroders as a safe investment but it turned out to be a marvellous investment being one of if not the best performing shares on the London Stock Exchange between 1985 and 1995. He therefore had a good knowledge of Schroders when Mallinckrodt asked him to join the Schroders Plc board. Mallinckrodt said of him, 'having been an effective chief executive, a director on many other boards and with much international experience and a wide spread of interests, he brought to the board a great depth of experience. He was very perceptive, had superb and balanced judgement of people and businesses, together with clarity of mind and impeccable integrity.'

Al Way had originally met Mallinckrodt when he was restructuring Bull, the computer company, in Paris for General Electric in 1967. Having exhausted French sources of finance he came to London and called on Schroders where he met Mallinckrodt. This was the start of a lifelong friendship and was maintained during Mallinckrodt's visits to New York up to the time he took over Schrobanco in 1983. In the meanwhile Way had become the chief financial officer of General Electric and he often sought Mallinckrodt's advice as one of his two confidential advisers. The roles were reversed when Mallinckrodt had to save Schrobanco with Way giving much strategic advice concerning the sale to IBJ, following which he was asked by IBJ to become chairman of IBJ Schroders taking over from Jack Connor. Having been the chief financial officer of GE and president of American Express before becoming the chairman of Travelers' finance committee, Way had a thorough understanding of finance, regulatory and audit matters. His other directorships, including McGraw Hill and Eli Lilly, as well as being the chancellor of Brown University, meant he was well informed with a strong global input and good insights. He was also known for his excellent strategic thinking. Mallinckrodt, with his long-standing and close friendship, was enormously influenced by him and there was nothing he would not share with him. He greatly valued his judgement particularly on strategic issues and having earlier nominated him as chairman of IBJ Schroders, invited him on to the executive committee of Wertheim Schroder, where he attended all the meetings. He played a key role on the Schroders Plc committees especially on compensation issues. His relationship with Mallinckrodt was seen by many of the other directors as being 'unhealthy'. There was a certain rivalry between Turner and Way.

Sir Ralph Robins and Charles Sinclair, both of whom joined the board in 1990, were probably the first directors to be appointed through a formal process using head hunters, in this case Anna Mann of Whitehead Mann, rather than the usual old boy net customarily used in the City. Robins had spent his entire career in Rolls-Royce, becoming the chief executive and then chairman. He was also on the board of Cable and Wireless, Standard Chartered and Marks & Spencer. Mallinckrodt was very pleased to have him on the board saying,

> He was an outstanding industrialist with great human qualities, and courageous having taken tough decisions on the restructuring of Rolls-Royce involving closing down factories and shrinking the work force. Having travelled widely he had a great knowledge of the international markets, particularly in Asia where his contacts were immense. With this experience he made a major contribution to Schroders, bringing a clear strategic vision and a focus on the key issues although he had less time than the others, due to his many other commitments, to devote to Schroders.

Charles Sinclair had recently been appointed the chief executive of Daily Mail and General Trust plc, the parent company of the Associated Newspapers Group, which had come into the public eye following the effective family privatisation of part publicly owned assets whereby value was released to all parties and especially to the Northcliffe family. Sinclair had met Bruno, whom he found, 'charming and affable and able to discuss surprisingly interesting subjects', over lunch at Schroders, and had explained what he had achieved for the family at DMGT as well as introducing debt which was used as leverage to improve and expand the business without increasing the equity. This was clearly attractive to Bruno as the principal shareholder of a family controlled company. When approached by Anna Mann he therefore had some knowledge of Schroders as well as knowing Nick Ferguson, a contemporary of his at Winchester. He also knew Turner as DMGT had an 18% interest in Consolidated-Bathurst and with Desmarais owning 34% they controlled the company between them. And so in March 1990 at the age of 41, he and Robins became non-executive directors of Schroders. Mallinckrodt said of Sinclair, 'he was a clear strategic thinker, having been a first class chief executive of DMGT, and conversant with family companies. A man of few words with impeccable manners, he was very analytical, a real professional and hard working.'

The view of others was that there were rarely any disagreements or great debates at the board under Mallinckrodt's chairmanship as all the issues had been discussed in private beforehand. The board was therefore for approvals rather than debate. Mallinckrodt effectively had three boards: one with Way with whom he had a formidably close relationship; the second the Group Compensation Committee chaired by Turner and comprising Way, Bruno, Mallinckrodt and Bischoff, in which Mallinckrodt tested out his ideas on any important issue with Turner and Way and either adjusted his views or secured their support for his position in advance of the board meetings; and finally the board itself. Mallinckrodt also regularly had long telephone conversations with Turner and Way outside the meetings. This meant that not all non-executive directors were similarly briefed and in this respect these inner boards were not ideal. The other non-executive directors were not comfortable with this approach. More importantly it meant that little of any substance, other than securities and acquisitions, was fully discussed at the board. Robins, who was desperately busy with Rolls-Royce and his many other directorships, and had little time available for Schroders, generally supported them. The only truly independent director was Sinclair, who had the uncanny knack of being able to put forward an independent view and getting it accepted or at least seriously considered. Turner thought Sinclair was outstanding.

Bruno did not play a large role at the board and was regularly briefed on all matters by the management beforehand in private so that his very detailed concerns could be fully satisfied. Invariably he supported the judgement of the management. Mallinckrodt said he never allowed the family's interests to influence his thinking on the running of the bank. In Turner's view Mallinckrodt felt that if the bank was properly run it was in the best interest of the shareholders and the family.

Within the firm Bruno was seen by those who had no dealings with him to be extremely polite and a concerned and paternalistic proprietor who was deeply interested in the firm and those who worked for it. For those who had to persuade him to accept change he was seen to be immensely obstinate and, although no intellect, extraordinarily shrewd and he used these characteristics to ensure that the family maintained its control. Being surrounded by highly intelligent people he was concerned that they might try to pull a fast one on him and so he made sure that everything was documented in the most minute detail. With his strong retentive memory the management had to be sure of their facts. He felt Schroders had a wonderful business and people and if there was a fault it was the people rather than the business model.

Nobody was conscious of the family abusing its position as a proprietor and being willing to have such an enormous chunk of their wealth in one basket required remarkable boldness. With their negative powers to veto any acquisitions and the issue of new shares, the only way to expand was internal but this was restricted by the maintenance of a generous dividend policy that was the only way the family could diversify its wealth. Although this probably suited the other shareholders, it meant that there were no spare funds in the business for the management to invest and to expand and this had a major impact on all the strategic decisions related to the development of the investment banking business.

This way of working carried on after Mallinckrodt stepped down from the chairmanship in 1994 into 1995 and 1996. Bischoff was honoured to be chairman but was not particularly interested in corporate governance and happy to leave it to Mallinckrodt and others so that he could concentrate his efforts on helping the people running the business, which he did supremely well. Therefore nothing changed. The board meetings themselves were therefore somewhat anodyne focusing on historical financial results. Often the directors were asked for contacts and Robins, who knew everyone on the international scene, was always very helpful.

Mallinckrodt greatly valued his non-executive directors, saying, 'there was a lot of inter-reaction between us. It was a fantastic partnership.' Schroders was clearly very fortunate to be served so well and for so long (over ten years) by a remarkably able group of non-executives, although perhaps an input from fresh outside minds might have been beneficial.

Schroders, with its ownership of Schrobanco in New York, had had the benefit of having been subjected to the banking laws and disciplines of the Federal Reserve as well as the New York State banking laws and was therefore familiar with North American disciplines. Connor and Turner being used to American board practices proposed the formation of a Group Audit Committee and this was set up in 1987 under the chairmanship of Turner, who handed over to Sinclair, a chartered accountant, in 1994 at the time of the Baring crisis. This involved a huge amount of painstaking work. In 1987 such a committee was virtually unheard of in the United Kingdom. The committee systematically talked to the auditors, saw all their reports and ensured they received answers to all their questions and instituted separate meetings with them without the presence of the management. Turner was particularly concerned about the treasury area especially the structured products. He approached a friend at the Federal Reserve, with whom he had been at Harvard, and asked him how he dealt with such complicated transactions. He said he had hired a professor from MIT to review them, the golden rule being not to do anything you do not understand. Solandt was assiduous in ensuring the non-executive directors were properly briefed. Schroders' good record was a testament to the success of this due diligence.

In the same year a Group Compensation Committee was formed and chaired by Woodroofe until he retired in 1989 and then by Turner. It was after Way became a member of this committee that it widened its role to being used as sounding board for Mallinckrodt to test his views privately before the board. The only other non-executive director on both committees was Bruno. Compensation became the most important and controversial issue and the one that totally transformed the style of Schroders from being collegiate to divisive (see Chapter 19).

Mallinckrodt was very interested in corporate governance and made sure that Schroders kept ahead of others in this area. There were other committees such as the Market Risk Committee, which set and monitored market risk exposure limits, and the Liquidity Risk Committee that monitored the Group's overall liquidity position but these were chaired by and comprised of the management.

The board was never involved in the businesses themselves although it did take an interest in Schroder Ventures, particularly concerning shareholder lawsuit issues. The key management decisions therefore were debated at the Group Executive Committee (GEC), which met monthly. It approved new projects such as opening new offices, capital expenditure on IT systems, new capital for subsidiaries and whether Schroders should be operating or doing business in country X. To ensure that the bank's capital was put to good use, all projects had to reach certain high hurdle rates of return on capital. It also dealt with the approval of limits, risk parameters and contingent liabilities. There was virtually no discussion regarding the operating businesses which were run very smoothly by their heads and their directors and it was rare that anything came up to the GEC let alone the board. Most matters were discussed and agreed with Bischoff beforehand so that anything unacceptable was not tabled. The papers, however, were quite voluminous and involved a considerable amount of reading. Mallinckrodt used to read them all and from the discussion he knew who had read them. He handed over the chairmanship of the GEC to Bischoff in 1992.

In the meanwhile Bischoff spent all the hours of every day on improving the reputation of the firm, developing client relationships, recruiting key people and encouraging and motivating everyone by sheer example. He concentrated on Corporate Finance and never interfered in Investment Management or Treasury, having total confidence in Sedgwick and Solandt. He hired a new managing director of Credit and Capital Markets and gave Dewe Mathews his full support in turning round Project Finance. He also travelled regularly to Hong Kong and Japan to develop the businesses in Asia.

NOTES:

1. Richard Sadleir joined Bill Hyde's Industrial Section from Lloyds Bank International in 1970 where he looked for new acquisitions but when the business folded a year later, he went to the international department under Loehnis. From 1978 he was Airlie's personal assistant for two years and then spent two years working on project finance opportunities in Latin America for Bulfield. This came to a halt with the debt crisis and the collapse of the economies in the region. He then returned to the ill-fated international department now briefly under Bischoff.

CHAPTER 6

DITCHING THE GENTS

1983 - 1989

Following his return to London during 1982, Bischoff was made deputy head of Corporate Finance and within a month or two he took over from Ashton, his former teacher, who the following year left to join the board of his client Hanson. Within a year Bischoff replaced Hull as chairman of Schroder Wagg, Hull remaining deputy chairman of Schroders. He found Corporate Finance demoralised, lacking in any passion for the business and in gentle decline. He knew if he was to turn it round he had to lead by personal example and get closer to the clients. However, his most important task was to choose the head of Corporate Finance. John Bushell, who had done a lot of work with Williams, was favoured by Williams but Bischoff opted for Adam Broadbent who was 46 at the time and recently back from the Stanford Executive Program and thinking of a new job. It was unfortunate that the delay in his appointment until 1984 left the impression in some of his colleagues' minds that he had been selected only after Schroders had failed to find a more suitable candidate from outside the bank and that therefore he was a second choice.

Broadbent had joined Schroders in 1968, aged 32. While considering a job in the City following an introduction from Gervase Buxton, of the Barclays dynasty, who was in Banking, he was recommended to Richardson by Loehnis who became a life long friend thereafter. It was not clear who was interviewing whom but Broadbent was hugely impressed. He accepted an offer without any idea of what job he would do. Not being thought suitable for Corporate Finance, as he was not an accountant or a lawyer, he was sent to the research department in Investment Management under Colin Leach. When he was interviewed by Airlie, Airlie glancing at his suede shoes said, 'we do not employ shits at Schroders.' He spent two years under Leach and found it a good way into the bank. He learnt how to price new issues under Ponsonby but more generally found the investment management business rather boring. He therefore transferred to Corporate Finance in 1970 under Williams. Apart from Richardson, who as chairman was somewhat remote, Broadbent most admired Williams and Murphy.

One of the deals that he worked on with Williams was acting jointly with Goldman Sachs for CT Bowring in 1979 in its defence of a hostile bid from Marsh McLennan. The manner in which the US investment banks organised and conducted themselves as well as their aggression was a rude awakening and made a strong impression. He had always seen Schroders as having been divided between the gents and the players. He was now being introduced to the real players for the first time in a market he had not seen before. SG Warburg was a player in a way that Schroders had ceased to be. This transaction also taught him of the internationalisation of the business and was his introduction to the Concorde and 747s, a faster moving world unfamiliar to Cator and Ashton. The US investment banks had entered the market and the mood had changed. At the time he was not at all comfortable flying and he had to grit his teeth before each flight, but knew he could not avoid it if he was to survive as a corporate financier.

It was time to make a change – the gents had to be replaced. The curious thing was that after the departure of Richardson, who was a real player, the control of Schroders had reverted to the gents against the tide of the market. They did not study the competition and were not interested in making money. The players needed money; the gents didn't, having their private means – after all it was vulgar to talk about money. During Bischoff's year as head of Corporate Finance he had done very little internally. He had spent a lot of time with Airlie and was distracted by the strategic review. He did however achieve the beginnings of a new attitude. Broadbent had arranged for him to meet the chief executive of English China Clays in Cornwall. Bischoff missed the scheduled flight because the road to Heathrow had been closed without notice and so he hired a private aeroplane arriving at the meeting rather late. The client was most impressed. Bischoff led by sheer personal example, clearly wanting to win, and was a doer. He instituted dinners at the office for the chairman, chief executive and finance director of clients to discuss strategy, taking great care beforehand to prepare with his colleagues the agenda for the meeting. This was the perfect role for him. It is probable that he would not have had the stomach for the revolution necessary within Corporate Finance. A number of people could have managed the division but none could have done what he did.

Broadbent found they were losing clients every week. All the directors dreaded picking up the telephone. Every week he reported to the board on clients lost and held back good news until it became public. Occasionally they were able to pull back a client. He addressed himself to the organisation and the people. He found that clients were being charged fees based on time spent, as with accountants, and therefore the division had lost the incentive to create business – they were reactive rather than pro-active. He studied the competition and saw that they had defined their target market – Morgan Grenfell was focusing on growth companies on the acquisition track whereas Kleinwort Benson went for the government and privatisation. He knew that if he was to re-establish Schroders' position in the market he had to be clear about the target market, put the right quality people in the market and support them. He had acquired about 40 people including 15 from a strategy group under Richard Morgan, following the strategy review. Morgan had built a strategic consultancy that could not successfully compete with the likes of McKinsey and, apart from making no money, added no value to Schroders' main businesses. Broadbent had a ratio of one director to two staff whereas SG Warburg had 1 to 3 and Morgan Grenfell 1 to 4. None of the directors were held responsible for their clients.

Broadbent knew exactly what he had to do. The average age of the directors was 48 – within a year it was 38. The whole of the strategy group disappeared save for Will Samuel and Patrick Drayton, both of whom were outstanding. The gents were discarded leaving the players, of whom there were some top-class operators – Nicholas Jones, Nick MacAndrew, David Challen and Derek Netherton, the latter two being particularly supportive in the organisational changes being introduced. (Bushell had departed to a client shortly after Broadbent's appointment.) All of them, together with Nigel Saxby-Soffe, were strongly motivated by their experience of the failure of Schroders and were determined to reverse the position. There was a backs-to-the-wall feeling and camaraderie developed amongst them which itself reflected a team spirit as well. Bill Harrison had the year before been hired by Bischoff from the oil industry to set up an energy team.[1] Robert Swannell had also returned when he saw the new broom.[2] This was a good nucleus on which to rebuild the business.

The problem was recruiting junior staff because Corporate Finance's reputation did not stand up to the competition, particularly that of SG Warburg, Morgan Grenfell and Kleinwort Benson. The removal of second-rate people boosted the morale of those who remained but it took a good year or more before they were able to hire the people below director level they really wanted. Fortunately, as SG Warburg and Morgan Grenfell did not appear to employ women in corporate finance, Schroders was able to attract a number of first rate women including Alison Carnwath and Karen Cook to name only two, and made it a policy thereafter to have a regular female intake. There followed many years of hard work and long days trying to rebuild the business and its reputation, involving a lot of marketing for new business. The transactions which are described below are simply a few of the many successful public deals, albeit some of the major ones, and are centred around the key directors involved in the transformation of Corporate Finance's fortunes over the next six years.

Fresh air from the Midlands

At Harrison's first Monday morning meeting of the corporate finance directors, it was reported that P&O had decided to discard Schroders as a client and move to Morgan Grenfell. 'There was little response and no post mortem let alone recriminations,' recalled Harrison. 'At Lehmans the director responsible would have tried to jump out of the window.' That was the problem. It was never clear who was responsible, Williams or Bushell. However, this was the turning point that galvanised the young directors into action. The reaction to John Maltby, the chairman of Burmah, another long-standing client telephoning Broadbent to say he was moving to Lazards, was entirely different. Broadbent did 'a deathbed repentance' and persuaded him to give Schroders another chance. Bischoff, who was on holiday in Bali with his family, was asked in the middle of the night to return for a meeting with Maltby and Lawrence Urquart, the chief executive. His immediate response was to ask for his secretary to arrange his return by the next available flight and fix the meeting saying he was on his way. A team of Bischoff,

Broadbent, Samuel and Drayton made the presentation and the client was saved – with Bischoff clients came first even before the family.

In view of the earlier loss of clients, one of Broadbent's first actions was to introduce a relationship management and senior statesman system for dealing with clients and establishing clear lines of responsibility for them. Accountability lay with the relationship managers but the so-called senior statesmen, particularly Bischoff but also Broadbent and others, would maintain contact with the clients' senior management and act as a back-stop. Broadbent passed over all his own clients to others to give himself more flexibility to manage the division.

In the meanwhile Harrison set up his oil team focusing on companies in that industry. It was almost unknown in the City at that time to have an industry group. He was a fantastic marketer and brought in many excellent clients, largely through entertaining them in the evening and was known to have said, 'dinner at home with the wife is a lost business opportunity.' Broadbent was delighted to see him entertaining so many clients as, when he took over Corporate Finance, he had sent round a note to the directors showing that the average entertaining expense per director worked out at about the cost of two Chinese take-aways per client and this was going to have to change.

Schroders lost most of the defences for its clients until in 1984 it acted for Premier Oil against a bid from Carless Capel. It was the first successful defence since Schroders had started losing clients. It was only a small transaction but had a high profile since it was also the first deal in which Boesky, the well-known raider, had tried to 'greenmail' the company by buying 15% of Premier Oil's shares in the market in anticipation of being able to sell them to the bidder at a higher price. He lost money on the shares when he disposed of them as the shares immediately fell after the bid had failed. More importantly for Schroders it was the beginning of the resurrection.

In 1986, Harrison left for Lehman Brothers KuhnLoeb, his former employers, which had recently been acquired by Shearson. Schroders had just lost the mandate for a convertible issue and he felt Schroders would not be able to compete in the face of the onslaught of the US investment banks. He felt Schroders was strong in corporate finance advice but was nowhere in debt or equity and would never be a factor in underwriting. Hopefully it would survive in its traditional role of being close to the CEOs of its clients, whom it had now learnt how to service proactively. He was also concerned at Schroders huge weakness in New York. He left Schroders after four years with a good reputation in the energy sector, a strong client base and good people to carry on after him. He was sorry to leave so many friends and was greatly missed.

In parallel with putting the key people in place, Broadbent was working on the organisation. He set up a separate IPO team under Robert Swannell, demonstrating that marketing and new business mattered – it raised the profile with new clients and in the market generally. IPOs were arranged for, to name only a few, Menvier Swain, an electric wholesaler, Wilson Bowden, a house builder, and RAMCO, an oil services company. The IPO team was extremely successful as it went after business not sought by others and they learnt how to do presentations. Corporate Finance had never previously given a truly professional presentation and had to learn from scratch and from endless mistakes. The team did particularly well in the computer software market acting for many companies including Hoskyns, probably the most broadly spread computer services business in Britain (*Sunday Times,* November 1986).

Broadbent also created an M&A and marketing team under Nick MacAndrew to develop ideas for business – including looking for vulnerable companies to propose as bid targets or to advise as had been done so successfully by Morgan Grenfell. Through this they got to know the market better as well as opening new doors. He then turned to making money – the main business of investment banking, in the view of the then chairman of Morgan Stanley. He circulated lists throughout the division of the entertaining expenses, the fees earned by each director and the monthly profitability. The setting of fees was discussed by all the directors thus forcing each director to be tougher with his favourite clients – there was a big drive to increase fees. It was impressed on all that there was a need to make money, i.e. profits.

In the meanwhile Bischoff was working in tandem with Broadbent, leading by example. He worked hard, showed total commitment and never said no to a client (which sometimes had to be unscrambled). He held the ring and, with no axe to grind, was completely trusted and had a passion to get into the market. He was always on the lookout for new people and took a keen interest in hiring senior people. Broadbent supplied him with the machine to create business. In an interview by Heather Farmbrough of the *Financial Weekly* in March 1987, Bischoff described his philosophy towards clients and the services provided by Schroders,

> If you have a strong client base, goodwill exists; the first thing is to make sure the client is happy. The client needs to see that the bank is confident and committed. It's no good saying on a Friday night that you decided to spend your weekend with the family if the client is being bid for. But you also have to go after new clients. We believe the kind of activities we do best are those which are specialised and complicated, where the skills are at a premium …We like to be in a business where the competition is in dozens rather than in thousands.

Bischoff clearly made a good impression on his interviewer too, as she described him, 'clear blue Germanic eyes suggest an iron will behind a courteous exterior'.

A new client from South Wales

Before Bischoff and Broadbent took charge of the business, the clients were expected to be of reasonable size and market capitalisation before being considered. This changed with the decision that size was irrelevant – what mattered was prospective size. You made money by being associated with growth. It was equally important that the clients had to be of quality – trustworthy and straight. The Schroder Wagg Executive Committee, known as the 9.45 Committee, had to approve all new clients and was a good discipline in avoiding taking on clients who were in any way doubtful. It proved to be an extremely efficient and effective body, which, because of its judgements, saved the embarrassment and loss of reputation of some of the competition. An example of a growth company was Williams Holdings.

Early on Bischoff was visited by two young men of 35 from South Wales. They ran a metal-bashing business called Williams with a market capitalisation of under £1 million. Their share price was on the rise and they were ambitious with lots of ideas of how to build the business. Nigel Rudd (later knighted) and Brian McGowan, respectively chairman and chief executive, found Bischoff very polite but did not think he would take them on due to their size and so were very surprised to receive a call a few days later, after a due diligence check, inviting them to come back and meet some colleagues.

They were introduced to David Challen, whom they found bright but down to earth, and Andrew Shaw, one of the cleverest young investment bankers of his generation but rather lacking in charisma to say the least. Their first acquisition was J&HB Jackson, a metal-basher in the Midlands, for £22 million. By 1997, twelve years later, when they acquired Chubb Security for £1 billion, they had completed over 20 deals with the assistance of Schroders and their market capitalisation had risen to over £3 billion. Schroders too had done well having received substantial fees. Rudd spoke well of the relationship that was one of absolute trust. He always felt he was getting good advice with Schroders' main concern being for Williams rather than its own fees – often he was advised not to go ahead with an acquisition. Rudd said,

> I felt I could call on Bischoff at any time to discuss important issues regarding a deal as well as the composition of the team supporting us, if there was someone who did not fit – he was good at listening. He was extremely good at critical times of a deal, making appearances when needed. He was a good client man and made you feel important.

Taking the fight to Morgan Grenfell

Nicholas Jones was one of Broadbent's stars – a strategist of star quality (*Sunday Times*, November 1986).[3] One of his responsibilities was taking care of Lord Aberconway's companies, including John Brown and English China Clays. One afternoon, after a particularly good lunch at the National Westminster Bank, his lordship came in to discuss his chairman's statement and was greeted by Jones together with his assistant, Gina Scheck. 'Many of Gina's family had been eliminated at Auschwitz. She was very bright and tough – although she could barely add up, she spoke seven languages fluently'. She was the first female executive in Corporate Finance and as a result of her abilities, many others were to follow. Aberconway leaned back and started dictating, looking at Scheck who immediately folded her arms. In a mild panic, Jones quickly stretched across the table for a pencil and pad of paper to write down his lordship's 'pearls'. Aberconway clearly did not expect to see a woman in a merchant bank except in a secretarial position.

Jones took a major part in Schroders' recovery as a corporate finance house, including earlier having helped Ashton advise Hanson on its successful bid for United Drapery Stores. However, in 1984 Schroders was still on the back foot with Morgan Grenfell carrying all before it. In 1985, Scottish & Newcastle, a former Schroder client now advised by Morgan Grenfell, bid for Matthew Brown and Jones led the defence with an historic victory – Morgan Grenfell had bought S&N shares after the bid was closed and declared victory. Jones said they had committed a foul and appealed to the Take-over Panel who, after a hearing from both sides, overturned the victory as Morgan Grenfell had been proved to have breached the rules. Jones received a huge amount of faxes and letters saying, 'thank God that someone has, at last, stopped Morgan Grenfell driving a coach and horses through every rule in the book.'

Shortly afterwards in October 1986, Challen successfully defended LCP Holdings against a bid by Ward White, a conglomerate with highly rated paper seeking to purchase an ordinary company on the cheap. Philip Birch, the chairman, was supported by an ever-confident Morgan Grenfell, who had created an image and reputation that it could deliver whatever its client wanted. In this case LCP and Schroders were able to reverse the tables by not only querying with the Stock Exchange a suspicious purchase of 25,000 LCP shares the day ahead of the announcement of the bid, but also demonstrating the emptiness of the Morgan Grenfell arguments. Schroders punctured Morgan Grenfell's position by showing that its techniques were not so admirable. It was to use similar arguments in other defences such as for Pilkington against BTR (Dominic Hobson, *Pride of Lucifer*).

An uneasy joint role with Goldman Sachs

At about the same time, Lloyds Bank made a bid for Standard Chartered at a price that was regarded in the market as being virtually a *fait accompli*. It was immediately rejected by Michael McWilliam, the general manager, as being unwelcome. Schroders, led by Bischoff and Jones, put together a defence with a revised profit forecast seeking to push up the bid price, which was seen by the institutions to be a full price. McWilliam, who was determined to see off the bid almost at any price, rather than accepting a higher price, was at the same time being courted by John Thornton, a 31-year-old executive from Goldman Sachs who advised him that he should fight the bid and showed how it could be defeated. McWilliam's found young Thornton to be a phenomenon who never slept and always had another new idea, using his New York office to work through the night so as to have on McWilliam's desk at 8.30 am a 15-page facsimile full of numbers showing that the sum of the parts of the bank was far greater than the whole. These arguments were then presented to the public. Thornton found McWilliam far more receptive to his ideas than Thomas Tilling had been three years earlier. The fact that his ideas were acted upon was maybe because Bischoff was always receptive to ideas that would help the client irrespective of where they came from. Thornton was impressed to see that Bischoff was always present at every important meeting, unlike Scholey at SG Warburg.

Despite all this the bid looked set to win and so McWilliam sought some 'white knights' willing to purchase Standard Chartered shares in the market to prevent a majority acceptance by the public of the Lloyds bid. He approached Robert Holmes A'Court in Australia, YK Pao in Hong Kong and Tan Sri Koo Tee Phuat in Singapore, all major customers of the bank. They all came to London and each bought 15% of the shares for £200 million with David Mayhew of Cazenoves, who knew who all the shaky shareholders were, acting for YK Pao. It was essentially a classic market operation with Cazenove and the other brokers undoing the acceptance list by paying cash for non-assented stock. Following allegations of impropriety, there was a Bank of England enquiry into whether there were any illegal support operations involving considerations being received as an inducement to purchase shares. Mayhew had to go before the inspectors and was challenged on co-ordinating the other brokers in buying unaccented stock for the institutions supporting Standard Chartered but was able to explain that this was not the case. The enquiry found no evidence of complicity against any party. It was a close run thing however. 'The City was at a point of real change having moved from good behaviour to observance of the law, which was not that clearly defined, the Panel rules being constantly contested.'

Not long afterwards, after much solicitation, Jones left Schroders to become a partner of Lazards with a direct share of the profits, this being better than being an employee of a Plc with 'one's remuneration being at the discretion of the Germans'. It was a tough decision as he got on so well with Bischoff and Broadbent, both of whom made a great effort to keep him. He felt Mallinckrodt was too tight with the bonuses – many directors had lobbied about remuneration compared with the competition. He also liked the people at Lazards, which had a strong advisory arm in New York that Schroders lacked – 'Wertheim was a second XI player with no prospects of becoming a premier investment bank.' Schroders was now at its peak in London as a corporate finance advisor – the *Financial Times* had recently reported that Schroders had come top of a league table for bid advice in the first half of 1987. Schroders could only go down whereas Lazard was number ten. Jones' departure was a serious blow to Schroders. Broadbent had a high regard for Jones, 'he had the great strength of not saying too much. He played successfully the role of an M&A star, being naturally good with the press, never saying too much and photographing well. He was quite lazy.'

Following Jones' departure, his clients had to be allocated to the remaining directors who were already suffering from the strain of the pressure of work with long hours and little time at home. One of the directors felt that Broadbent's Jesuitical approach to work, acquired from his Spartan education at Stonyhurst in the fells of Lancashire, with the families getting such a raw deal, was perhaps excessive. This view was not shared by everyone but it demonstrates the pressure under which they all were and their distorted priorities. Broadbent took the view that to beat the competition you needed, almost literally, to be up before them and to go to bed later — 'the late as well as the early bird caught the worm!'

Schroders fights for industry against the City

Challen made his name as a pre-eminent corporate finance advisor while acting in two major national defences that caught the public imagination, that is for Pilkington and Rowntree. In 1987 BTR, a conglomerate run by Sir Owen Green, decided that Pilkington would make a good picking and put in a bid. BTR had grown by using highly rated paper to acquire mundane companies, with the help of its friends at Morgan Grenfell. Pilkington represented the best of British industry with all its manufacturing plants in the North. It was one of the leading glass manufacturers in the world, having invented float glass and licensed it on good terms to all its international competitors. It was also a family controlled company with huge loyalty from its work force, particularly in its home town, St Helens in Lancashire. BTR, on the other hand, was one of the fast growing new companies by acquisition and subsequent sale of surplus assets. Its plans for Pilkington were anathema to the Pilkington staff who had worked for the company for generations. A huge press campaign, including calling out all the MPs in industrial constituencies, was initiated by Antony Pilkington (later knighted), the chairman and Challen arguing for long-term industrial interests and the creation of wealth rather than City short-term financial returns. Pilkington made it clear that it did not need BTR. This put BTR on to the defensive and, following a barrage of attacks with the press puncturing its reputation as a predator, it withdrew badly wounded. It was a very visible victory and Schroders' reputation was enhanced.

Not long afterwards another long-standing client of Schroders with a major national reputation, Rowntree, the Quaker chocolate maker in York, received a dawn raid on its shares. Jacob Suchard, the Swiss chocolate manufacturer, picked up 29.9% of the shares in the market valuing Rowntree at £2.1 billion. Schroders, led by Challen, made an appeal for a reference to the Monopolies Commission arguing that such a merger would lead to Suchard having too large a share of the UK market — this was a good way to defeat a bid. A major press campaign was orchestrated to argue the case that this national asset should be saved. Schroders was flooded with chocolate bars! Nestlé, also of Switzerland, did not like the prospect of Rowntree being acquired by its young and rapidly rising competitor and entered into discussions with Rowntree. Nestlé's style was much more compatible to Ken Dixon, the chairman of Rowntree, although he continued to argue for independence. However, the government saw no reason to intervene and the reference was refused. Nestlé made a bid of £2.55 billion and this was agreed. This was another very visible transaction and Schroders came out well in the press. Schroders had at last restored its reputation as one of the leading corporate finance houses. It had also fought off bad practice, avoided sinking to those levels and had shown that you can still win for your client by integrity, professionalism and honesty.

BP reviews its merchant banks

Schroders was acquiring a strong reputation in the market and this was noticed by David Simon (later Baron Simon of Highbury), the finance director of British Petroleum. As a commercial person largely involved in marketing, he had no knowledge of accounting and finance and so he decided to visit all the traditional merchant banking relationships of BP including JP Morgan, SG Warburg and Lazards among others. He asked them all what they were going to do about the Big Bang and received 15 different answers. Nobody could explain the Big Bang and none of them, save for Cazenove, remained in sole ownership 15 years later. He had not visited Schroders as it was not a relationship bank.

BP was involved in three major transactions at the time. The first was the buyout of the Standard Oil's minority interests for $7 billion in 1986 – the largest acquisition in the US to date. The second was the sale of the British government's 30% shareholding in BP, which was part of a £7.24 billion issue that went disastrously wrong following the stock market crash on Black Monday on 19 October 1987 and resulted in the Kuwaitis acquiring most of the stock. (The BP issue was a truly major event as the US banks simply could not believe they would be held by the Treasury to their underwriting commitment.) The third was BP's acquisition of Britoil, including the government's special (golden) share, in 1988 from the government for £2.77 billion. Following the first two transactions Simon had met more people giving advice than any other finance director in London. His conclusion was there were not many people he could trust to give totally objective advice. He had earlier met BP's traditional investment banks in New York including JP Morgan, Morgan Stanley and First Boston, the three leading investment banks on Wall Street at the time. Goldman Sachs was big in the US but not in international markets and so he saw them despite them not being a relationship bank of BP. He was more impressed with John Weinberg, Peter Sachs and Geoff Boisi than the others and so he took them on for the BP issue – 'John Weinberg nearly throttled me when he found Goldman Sachs had incurred a heavy underwriting loss of £100 million on the government sale but stood up to the plate and never complained.'

After the first two deals Simon said to his colleagues that he was not happy with the advice he was receiving and said he wanted to talk to others.

I met Win, and his assistant Will Samuel. I was incredibly impressed by Win and how straightforward, objective and competent he was. I liked the people and the way they talked as with Weinberg, Sachs and Boisi at Goldman Sachs. They were more direct than anyone else I had dealt with, the quality of the relationship was of intellectual equals – I did not like being thought to be total gold or told that it was all far too complicated and leave it to us. Win was very good at breaking down complexities and was very good with Samuel treating him as a grown up, which gave him the confidence to deliver. I liked to see that good relationship. The Brit Oil take-over went well – it combined a larger political element than many other large transactions due to the government's golden share, but the financial issues were crucial – although we paid too much because of our exploration people being over ambitious over the future prospects. It was our fault not Schroders. I was very happy realising I had a good relationship combined with extreme technical competence. Schroders had both whereas most others had one or the other but rarely both.

The relationship continued under John Browne (later Lord Browne of Madingley), who followed him as finance director and then chairman and chief executive, with much corporate finance and a string of project finance advisory assignments in Asia and Europe.

A record fee is earned

Harrison's desk was taken by Gerry Grimstone from HM Treasury where he had run the privatisation unit.[5] On his first day, John Reynolds walked into his office for a chat and recommended that he stop tucking the back of his tie into his shirt – 'one of the most useful tips I received!' Initially he teamed up with Swannell who taught him how to do public offerings including one for Hoskyns. Swannell was known as the 'Vicar' as he always looked as if he had just come from church – 'the politest man you could meet and one of the best and most attentive client men'. Grimstone's breakthrough was when he acquired from MacAndrew responsibility for Consolidated Goldfields. Although historically a major client Schroders had progressively lost out to SG Warburg. The company, one of the premier mining houses, was personified in its chairman Rudolf Agnew (later knighted), one of the great City buccaneers.

After Consolidated Goldfields had received an unwelcome bid from Minorco, a badly disguised front for Anglo-American, SG Warburg had, much to its disappointment, to withdraw as advisers to Goldfields as its broking arm had a prior relationship with the Oppenheimers. Agnew and Antony Hichens, the finance director, turned to Schroders, whom they had observed had turned over a new leaf under the leadership of Bischoff and said they would appoint Schroders if Bischoff provided a suitable director. Hichens found Grimstone 'had real brilliance and great and unexpected insights. Win and Gerry were an excellent team.' Agnew checked progress with Bischoff occasionally. 'Being a former soldier, he was very forceful and set the tone for the battle by giving clear guidance – to fight on the beaches and in the hills, with no compromises and to take no prisoners.' Schroders accepted the instructions and developed a strategy for defeating the bid. During the next eight months they were living in each other's pockets meeting daily and 'Win and Gerry gave their best and we got the best. I do not remember other than us being of one mind and Schroders having everything under control.'

In September 1988, shortly after Minorco's bid, the Mergers and Monopolies Commission stepped in to examine the bid for competition. It was Europe's largest take-over defence and the first public bid run by Grimstone, who received much help from Challen. In Grimstone's words, 'There followed eight months of trench warfare with the No 1 gold miner trying to take over the No 2 and it was the bloodiest and most vicious take-over ever.' Anglo was forced to increase its bid which was supported by the shareholders but not recommended by the management. During the progress of the battle going on in London, Goldfields fought many court cases around the world including in the United States where a judge, who was very concerned about Anglo cornering the gold market, ruled in April that Anglo could not acquire any mining assets in the United States and Minorco withdrew its bid.

Minorco sold its Goldfields shares, which had increased by 28%, to Hanson Trust, which finally matched Minorco's bid of £3.5 billion, the highest price bid for a British company at the time. Schroders' success fee of £15 million was the largest fee ever received. It was the making of Grimstone who shot into prominence with the huge publicity – he greatly enjoyed the experience and realised he had found the right career. He really was a star and such faults as he had were more than compensated by his enormous talent. He made a lot of money for Corporate Finance and developed fantastic relationships – he had everything going for him.

Helping to sell Britain's natural assets

Not only was Corporate Finance making a success of its work in the corporate world, it also made a major impact with government and the general public in its four years' advice to the Department of the Environment on the privatisation and the £5.2 billion offer for sale of the ten water companies of England and Wales. Kleinwort and Rothschild had the lion's share of the government's major privatisation business, such as BP, Telecoms and Gas, and Schroders needed to make an impact. It had been involved in a few less prestigious privatisations for the government, such as National Freight, Associated British Ports and Jaguar cars and had impressed the Treasury with its work on the sale of the government's third tranche of the Cable and Wireless shares raising £993 million – the government being advised by Kleinwort Benson and SG Warburg for the first and second tranches respectively. It had also advised British Airports Authority in 1987 on its privatisation in which £1.28 billion was raised. Schroders was therefore well placed when it competed for the role of advising the government on water under the leadership of Saxby-Soffe. Although not hugely profitable due to the nature of its time related fees, privatisation work got Schroders' name into the public arena and gave confidence when the mandate was won always against stiff competition – Netherton did particularly well in this area.

Challen led the Schroder team for the second phase of the water privatisation (Saxby-Soffe having left – see below), including Netherton, Drayton and Shaw, which grew by the month as the government's demands for resources became greater and greater. It was the first occasion on which ten simultaneous flotations had been attempted and one of the largest privatisations and certainly the most complex to date. Challen said,

> it was a very successful privatisation despite being very political and most unpopular at the time. It was a ghastly experience as everyone said it could not be done. It took four years and only in the last six months did people start to feel it might work. We

all had to endure a lot of personal vilification from those violently against the principle of selling our natural assets. We received £10 million in fees but it involved nearly half the staff in the division. In terms of reputation, it finally restored Schroders' position.

Netherton recalls, 'walking back with David after having heard we had got the job we asked ourselves do we really want it? It was an absolute nightmare and a big job to keep David's spirits up.' It was difficult for Corporate Finance to sustain the effort in view of it being during the peak of the market for corporate finance fees and it turned Schroders off advice to government on large privatisations.

So when electricity came up not long afterwards, Schroders could have won the mandate without any difficulty. However, despite the pleadings of the Department of Energy, Schroders did not bid. It was to regret this bitterly later when the M&A market dried up and the electricity privatisation unfolded. Kleinwort had been appointed to act for the industry – Rothschild for the government – but many of the companies felt they should be separately advised. With Grimstone's help, Schroders acted for three of the electricity distribution companies and this led to much work in the sector including acting for National Power (see next chapter). Grimstone felt 'Schroders had no strategy for privatisation as nobody liked doing this work finding M&A more exciting and glamorous and so privatisation was opportunistic and ad hoc, whereas at Rothschild and Kleinwort it was pursued with great intensity and to great effect.' Despite this they did fairly well and were not far behind the main competition.

Seeking a foothold on the Continent

The business, however, was almost entirely a UK business with nothing to speak of on the continent of Europe. Broadbent set up a team for Europe under Saxby-Soffe – Challen and Netherton were surprised that Broadbent should feel it warranted the full time of a director. Saxby-Soffe, who had higher ideals than the City, left to become finance director of Actionaid – a few years later he amusingly sent a letter asking all his colleagues for a donation just after they had received their six figure bonuses – hopefully they were all in a generous mood. Swannell, speaking no foreign languages, took over the European mantle and made a fist of it. Earlier there had been some fraught discussions with Solandt and Slee regarding the restructuring of the Eurobond activity, which had never come up to expectations (see Chapter 14). Slee had recently hired Michael Wellman, an American Eurobond salesman and they had hired Panfilo Tarantelli and a team of Italians from SG Warburg. This team was acquired by Corporate Finance with its new responsibilities for Eurobonds in 1987 in recognition of the internationalisation of the markets. Tarantelli had been hired by Slee to introduce an international dimension to capital markets. Instead of competing with the big Japanese institutions on low margin Eurobond business, he focused on the embryonic Euro-equity market and achieved, with Ron Liss, two immediate and very lucrative issues for RAS, the Italian subsidiary of Allianz, and Banesto, the Spanish bank. Hitherto all equity issues had been arranged in their domestic markets. These transactions were therefore novel apart from being highly profitable with commissions of 4-5%. As Schroders had no placing power, external brokers like Hoare Govett had to be hired. Tarantelli was noticed and in conjunction with developing the Euro-equity market he started on international M&A, which was very exciting as this too had been previously mainly domestic.

By sitting among the corporate financiers, Tarantelli began to acquire the skills of a corporate financier and was able to import UK skills into Italy. He moved to an office in Milan in Italy while his team remained in London. Broadbent enjoyed walking down the corridors of the sixth floor in Cheapside hearing people speaking Italian. Once the team had become established they were gradually moved to Italy. Two major transactions brought them great credibility in London. The first was a three-way merger involving the £2.9 billion sale of the controlling interests in Banco di Roma and Nuova Banco di Santo Spirito into Cassa di Risparmio di Roma group (later Capitalia), creating Italy's largest banking group. This was one of many mergers in the consolidation of the Italian banking industry. The other landmark deal was Credit Lyonnais' acquisition of Credito Bergamasco, the first large cross-border transaction between France and Italy, which started initially as a hostile bid but became friendly. Credito Bergamasco was owned by the Catholic Church, a speculator, and some prominent local families. The negotiations with the Archbishop of Bergamo on behalf of the Church were conducted by Tarantelli and the self-professed atheist John Andrew on behalf of Credit Lyonnais. They took place in a church and were half to do with the financials and half to do with the religious credentials of Credit Lyonnais and its commitment to maintain certain local church interests. They managed to achieve a breakthrough by getting all the parties, each of which had different sets of shareholders and different agendas, to sit down together around a table and to agree a deal. It was the first time that the majority and minority shareholders had ever received the same price for their shares in Italy and became the model on which the new take-over law was developed. Schroders was in the lead and highly visible in bringing Anglo-Saxon work practices to the Latin markets of Italy, Spain and France. Developing a business in Italy and Spain where they were more open to ideas was clearly going to be easier than in France and Germany where they were not interested in outside ideas. The teams in Paris and Frankfurt were handicapped by never having the right people and development took much longer coming. Fortunately with profits rising there was never a problem in investing back in the business.

Looking after the administration.

While advising a number of clients Netherton became interested in the recruitment market and in administration and organisation and composed a paper on remuneration showing what was going on in the market.[6] Thereafter he took on the management of these issues for Broadbent. They accelerated the recruitment of women with Linda Cribb and Alison Carnwath among others and went out of their way to woo young graduates, arranging for them to lunch with people in Corporate Finance who were a bit older. The last interview was always with Broadbent. Netherton also oversaw the introduction of a staff appraisal system and training programmes for presentation and interviewing skills. He and Nigel Pantling, a new director, worked on a video to show how to do presentations but the one he did with John Reynolds, showing how not to do it, was so good that they rejected the other. He worked on team structures, co-ordinating the decisions on who should work with whom. His main task, however, was remuneration. The US investment banks were changing the attitude to pay and it was plain to see that their employees were taking a significant share of the profits. The process that was developed with the help of Elizabeth Warren, one of a new breed of highly professional personnel managers hired by Sue Cox, the new personnel director, to determine salaries and bonuses is described in Chapter 19.

Although Mallinckrodt had no involvement in or indeed knowledge of corporate finance, he used his contacts to help get new business. A case in point was acting for Siemens in its joint bid with GEC for Plessey in 1989. Netherton, who was responsible for advising Siemens, recalls John Walker-Howarth of SG Warburg being unmercifully bullied by his client, Lord Weinstock. 'Gowi did all that could be expected of him. He delivered the client, kept him sweet at the senior level and did not interfere with the conduct of the bid' – high praise indeed.

A review of Broadbent's achievements

By 1989, the sixth successive record year, Bischoff and Broadbent and their colleagues had arrested the process of decline and restored Schroders to its former glory to become one of the premier corporate finance houses in the UK. In the words of Andrew Tuckey, a formidable competitor at the time, 'Win was the architect with the vision, energy, commitment and dedication and the natural ability to develop clients.' If Bischoff was the architect, Broadbent was the builder, who supplied the tools and the equipment and a phenomenally well-run and polished organisation, which was so critical for success to be achieved.

Having spent six years of long days and short nights in the process, Broadbent handed over the mantle to Challen, the most senior director in the division. Broadbent became group managing director responsible for corporate finance world-wide and moved with his wife Sara to New York, where he found that all the decisions were taken in London without reference to him. He was unable to do anything, as Steven Kotler, the chief executive of Wertheim, was very hands-on with the loyalty of his staff and the full support of James Harmon, his chairman. It was an unpressurised job without any involvement in running people day-to-day. He did not enjoy all the travelling across the Atlantic. Challen, who had been trained by Broadbent and was a close personal friend, said, 'he worked to a frazzle (in London) and needed the opportunity to recapture his *joie de vivre*. He should really have left Schroders then (in 1990), as he did not have a role in New York or the energy to create one.' He returned to London in 1992 to be handed the poisoned chalice of the securities business (see Chapter 11) before it was amalgamated with Corporate Finance in 1994 to become Investment Banking. Following the purchase of the Wertheim shares held by the management in 1994, he returned to New York as group managing director, investment banking. Throughout the book those who became group managing directors tend to disappear from the story as their role was detached from the running of the businesses and therefore less visible. The key role at Schroders was being head of one of the major businesses.

Broadbent's colleagues were unanimous in their praise for him saying he and Bischoff were a brilliant partnership with complementary skills. He was much stronger and determined than his predecessors and very courageous. He was also very caring and always had time and listened. He was seen to be a first class manager, who was good with people and decisive. He may have had an easier model mainly to do with UK advisory work whereas later it had the added complication of equity, distribution, capital risks and international – a much more complicated mix. However, unlike them, he had very little to start with. Bischoff captures much of his colleagues views in saying,

> he had a very good intellect and a good strategic sense, he was loyal and trusted, very calm in a crisis and gave the impression of being older than he was and had seen it all before. He was modest and did not take credit away from others, was good at handling the prima donnas and did not dominate by personality. He was also very amusing.

David Mayhew, of Cazenove, said 'he was very considered in his advice, thoughtful, perceptive and careful of the 1980s.' Perhaps the nicest appreciation was from his old friend Loehnis, who said, 'he was a nice sardonic fellow, much valued by the clients and had a lovely wife, Sara.'

NOTES:

1. After having completed his MSc degree with a distinction at the London School of Economics – as had Broadbent – Bill Harrison's tutor suggested that he look for a job in the City. Harrison's response, with its strong nasal twang from Birmingham, was, 'with my accent they will think I have come to clean the windows.' After four years at Manufacturers Hanover working for Minos Zombanakis on Eurobonds and infrastructure finance, seven years in the oil industry, three years with the fledgling British National Oil Corporation and finally with Tricentrol, a car distribution company which found itself with a stake in the Thistle field in the North Sea, he was sent to Hong Kong to see whether he could raise capital to finance an oil concession in China. He called each time on Bischoff who in the end said, ' Bill, I have told you ten times that the Chinese would prefer to invest in racehorses rather than in oil and gas.' On his return to London, Bischoff contacted Harrison, then 34, and said, 'we are changing Schroders, we have lost too many clients and need new blood and industry knowledge' and persuaded him to head up a new energy team as a corporate finance director. With his strong Birmingham accent, his phenomenal energy and working habits he was a very welcome breath of fresh air. He felt very comfortable with his new colleagues and had a lot of laughs with them. They were welcoming, likeable, open-minded and meritocratic but incredibly uncommercial. A few days after his arrival, Harrison was in the lift with a senior director who, noticing the leather patches on the elbows of the coat of his suit, asked who he was. Harrison said he was a new director of Corporate Finance and was told he should go home and change – it was not a good start and he felt very humiliated.

2. Robert Swannell, a chartered accountant and barrister, had joined Corporate Finance in 1977 under Cator and then Ashton. The division, which had endless directors and only three assistant directors, was busy but progressively poorly managed, so much so that he put his views on paper to Ashton but, as they were not well received, he decided to leave in 1983 to join others in setting up a small investment bank financed with Middle East money. As he was leaving he saw Bischoff, who was exceptionally nice to him, saying he understood his reasons for leaving and in the event that the venture did not suit him he was welcome to return. The venture was a disappointment and Swannell missed being at the heart of life. He called Bischoff who invited him back and he joined Nick Roditi in the early stages of setting up Schroder Securities (see Chapter 11). Although Roditi was clearly exceptionally talented he found the operation misconceived as it was divorced from Corporate Finance and so he transferred to Corporate Finance under Broadbent as the director responsible for the new IPO team.

3. Nicholas Jones, a Wykehamist, of whom there were relatively few at Schroders, and a chartered accountant, had completed an MBA at the London Business School, specialising in finance and the relationship between government and industry. He interviewed at a number of merchant banks in 1975 but was impressed by Hull whose description of the big picture and left of centre politics appealed to him. He survived an interview mainly comprised of long pauses between frequent intakes of tobacco by Cator. Not one for unnecessarily filling in gaps in conversations, Jones recalls, 'long periods of silence and clouds of smoke'. He received an offer of £5000 a year but his wife was particularly taken by the Christmas hamper from Harrods and that 'swung the day'.

4. David Challen joined Corporate Finance in 1972 at the age of 29, after having spent eight years with J Walter Thompson, the advertising agency. Despite being a gold medallist in mathematics, he knew nothing of finance but was inspired by the teaching of John MacArthur while doing an MBA at Harvard. MacArthur, who later became Dean of Harvard Business School, introduced him to Bruno, which led to various interviews with Wolfensohn and Richardson. He found Schroders astonishingly different from the world he had come from where the people were very bright, broadly educated, stimulating and creative. Schroders in contrast was cast in a mould of gentrification, mostly accountants and very grey – it was a terrible come down but the real world. Everything was done to a high quality. He was struck and pleased by the insistence on standards of behaviour and accuracy.

> Everything said had to be fully justified and backed up. All work was checked and double checked, in stark contrast to the casual atmosphere in advertising. On the other hand, there was a degree of self-confidence, which bordered on self-satisfaction, in riding high and having a good client list. The work was a long way from the theoretical optimum and there was no thinking of new ways of doing things. Mind you there was no deep thinking elsewhere and no challenge to current ways. The US investment banks had not yet brought in their different approaches.

Challen found himself working under Broadbent – both were anomalies not being of the classic accounting mould.

5. Gerry Grimstone had been a civil servant for 14 years and the youngest assistant secretary at the age of 33. As head of the Private Policy and Public Enterprise Group of the Treasury under Nigel Lawson and John Moore in the Thatcher government, he came across Schroders in 1985, when it was acting for the government in selling the third tranche of Cable and Wireless shares owned by the government. Schroders was thought to have done well on this privatisation, which was the largest privatisation after the record-breaking British Telecom issue, as Netherton and Samuel had come up with new ways of making pricing more friendly to the sellers, i.e. the government, and also ways of reducing the underwriting fees. Netherton was of the view that all these clever ideas were initiated by Grimstone and Schroders was given the credit for them! As the Treasury did not allow him to become the principal private secretary to Lawson and as his father had recently died, he decided to privatise himself and called Broadbent. He thought the Schroder people were nice, particularly Broadbent and Bischoff – 'two of the finest people you could work with' – and accepted an offer of a directorship in Corporate Finance with responsibility, after his 18 month immunity period with government had expired, for building on Schroders' privatisation business. The advantage of the Treasury having banned him from contacting the government for 18 months was that he had the opportunity to develop a new career rather than having to beg for government business.

6. Derek Netherton, an actuary, had joined Investment Management in 1969 as a financial analyst in the research department under David Walters and then moved to new issues under Ponsonby learning when to take up an issue and how to price it. He was then transferred to Corporate Finance. He was not impressed with Cator but found Ashton 'a really nice bloke'. It was not a good time for Corporate Finance, which was in decline, the attitude being that clients should visit Schroders. There was no recruitment of good people and much living in the past and on previous successes.

CHAPTER 7

DO WE WANT TO BECOME INVESTMENT BANKERS?

1990 – 1994

C hallen took over from Broadbent as head of Corporate Finance with Netherton his deputy. Broadbent had left for New York exhausted. Bischoff had many other matters to look after in the Group, not least the Far East to which he travelled frequently. Challen felt bereft of senior colleagues and found there was insufficient capacity to expand and take advantage of Schroders' improved reputation in the market. 1990 however saw a general decline in investment banking activity around the world and a collapse of the M&A market in the UK to a fraction of what it had been two years earlier and finally there was a credit squeeze. Challen was reluctant to cut less regarded staff, feeling they should be kept for the upturn. He tried to supplement the work with company reconstructions for GPA and the Rosehaugh-Stanhope joint venture for Broadgate office development in the City and an increasing number of disposals but it was a difficult period for the next four and a half years.

GPA, a major aircraft leasing company based in Ireland, had to be restructured following a failed IPO and involved a team under Swannell having to renegotiate all the debts and aircraft orders of $20 billion, most of which had not been financed. There were hundreds of separate finance agreements with an array of different banks involved. It was incredibly complex and at the end there were 50 yards of documentation to be signed. To survive it was necessary to sell a lot of GPA's assets to GE Capital but in the end nobody lost a penny, including the banks. This lead to the establishment of a specialist service for disposals, the largest being the sale of British Sugar for £880 million. There were other sales for Swedish Match, Bass, the Post Office and ICI in respect to its 25% stake in Enterprise Oil.

An unsatisfactory fee

Schroders had always been the merchant bank to the bankers and this was reconfirmed in the early 1990s when Schroders acted for virtually all its peers in their hour of need. Although the corporate finance market remained depressed for a third year in 1992, it was in that year that Schroders acted for HSBC Holdings in its £3.7 billion acquisition of Midland Bank. Bischoff, who knew its chairman, Sir William Purves, from his many years in Hong Kong, asked Netherton to represent Schroders. He and Alison Carnwath went out to Hong Kong to be briefed by HSBC. They stayed at The Peninsula Hotel in Kowloon and travelled daily on the Star Ferry to visit HSBC's imposing and progressive office building, designed by Foster & Partners in the early 1980s, to avoid being seen by their colleagues at Schroders Asia. HSBC already had a stake in Midland and had been talking for some time about a merger. Little progress was made, as Midland was seeking too high a price. Two years later HSBC decided to make a bid rather than to seek a merger. Midland was difficult but in the end a price was agreed. There was a disagreement over the content of the press release in which it was normal in the City to disclose profits and how and by whom the merged company was to be managed. This was anathema to Purves, who was not used to this amount of disclosure and Netherton found himself on the side of Midland – 'getting Purves to agree was like extracting teeth.' Having spent virtually his entire career in Asia, Purves was unfamiliar with the ways of the City and unused to providing information for what he regarded as spin doctoring, which was never the practice in the East. He felt Netherton at times showed undue deference to City attitudes. Obtaining the agreement of the Midland shareholders was not easy as the history of cross-border bank mergers had not been good, many having failed. To maintain the value of HSBC's offer, Schroders had to close the gap between HSBC's perception that its shares were like gold compared to Midland's and that of the City institutions who regarded Midland as being reliable and HSBC as racy. It was then that Lloyds Bank intervened with a bid for Midland. It was far easier for Lloyds to sell the merits of its bid on the grounds of cost savings than HSBC's case for revenue growth. Midland withdrew its agreement to sell to HSBC. HSBC and Schroders managed to argue for the Lloyds bid to be referred to the Monopolies Commission but not HSBC's. Lloyds withdrew, leaving the field to HSBC. Schroders' task was very difficult, not least because Purves was not easy to deal with, the issues were complex and Sir Brian Pitman, the chief executive of Lloyds, generally accepted to be the most successful commercial banker in Britain, was on his own turf. HSBC also dealt with many of the issues, particularly those in Asia, independently from Schroders. It was the job that Netherton was most proud of, not least because the acquisition has been such a success.

Schroders' relationship with HSBC is reflected in the views of Purves who recalled the position as being rather different. When HSBC decided to bid for Midland, Purves needed a London merchant bank. In an earlier unsuccessful attempt to buy The Royal Bank of Scotland, HSBC had used Hambros but by 1992 its reputation had declined and it was no longer sufficiently significant in the market for this transaction. SG Warburg, the biggest, was already committed to Midland so Purves approached Bischoff, whom he liked and held in high regard. Generally he was not very impressed with the London merchant banks, finding them slow and unresponsive. Their performance was dependent on the quality of the individual you were dealing with and his willingness to devote his time to you. Unfortunately Bischoff was the chief executive and only had so much of his time available. He was always there for the major problems but he left the main work to Netherton and Carnwath, who in Purves' opinion were not in the same league. This view may have been coloured by Purves not being used to authoritative and confident women standing up to him. There was a great deal of work and he put together a big team of his own people and from Wardley – whom he found to be just as good as Schroders but quicker – in Hong Kong and London, with Frank Frame, formerly deputy chairman in Hong Kong, holding the fort in London with Bernard Asher, the head of investment banking. It was not helpful that Schroders was in London and its responses were generally very slow. In fact he became quite irritated and set a tough deadline for the bid that Netherton said could not be met. Purves told him it would be. He was used to Hong Kong-style work practices in which everything was done on the run and there was no beginning or end to the working day. The others involved at HSBC, however, 'were impressed by how Netherton, in his quiet and patient way, held the disparate group of an ever moving cast together under a lot of pressure'.

Once the bid was accepted, Purves saw something of the SG Warburg people and was equally unimpressed. He said, 'the support from Schroders was good, they did a lot of leg work but did not earn a huge fee. Win was unhappy thinking they deserved more and that we were a bit mean. I checked with my deputy chairman and we increased the fee by a modest amount'. Earlier Frame, who had respected the work done by Netherton, had had 'a spirited discussion with Bischoff on the final sharpening of the pencil regarding the fee'. There was clearly a difference of opinion. Schroders was seeking a fee which related to market practice for a transaction of this scale, whereas HSBC felt that all Schroders had done was to document and process a transaction which HSBC had initiated and thought through, with Schroders adding very little. Also HSBC was not used to using advisors and, like most companies in Asia, did not believe in paying for advice. Having been involved in major acquisitions elsewhere, HSBC only needed knowledge of the market and the ways of the City. The fact that it became known later that SG Warburg acting for Midland was paid a fee of £12 million which HSBC would have had to pay indirectly could not have pleased Purves or indeed Schroders.

Despite the downturn in business, Schroders' reputation continued to improve with new clients being secured. Not long after the privatisation of National Power, John Baker, its forthright and highly intelligent chairman, and his colleagues came to the conclusion that they needed better advice than they were receiving from Lazards. He therefore arranged a beauty parade between three merchant banks and Lazards and chose Schroders because its team had the most forward-looking view of where National Power should be going. It was the first time that Schroders had combined its domestic corporate finance skills and its international power industry skills within Project Finance. It was to repeat this later when securing a major appointment from British Gas. Baker was particularly impressed by the leadership of the team – Challen and Swannell.

Both were top class performers and we rapidly found we could have a full and frank and wholly constructive debate with Swannell and his team knowing that we were receiving bespoke advice totally focused on the needs of National Power rather than

Schroders' earning potential. Swannell was always personable, hard working, understanding, well prepared and easy to work with. Challen was incredibly insightful with Bischoff hovering in the background. We could not have been better served.

Much work followed, including the response to the approach by Southern Electric Inc of the USA and the agreed acquisition of Southern Electricity Board, both of which were blocked by the regulator, the sale of Drax power station to AES for £1.8 billion – a phenomenally prescient transaction – and the subsequent return to the shareholders of £1 billion, the sale of two other generating plants and the demerger of the company into International Power and Innogy. All of the work related to the sale of Drax and the other generating plants was done harmoniously by a joint Corporate Finance and Project Finance team. At the same time Project Finance was advising National Power on the development and financing of a number of independent private power station projects and the acquisition of power assets around the world.

The gathering strength of the US investment banks

Throughout Challen's period in charge of Corporate Finance, the challenge to the British merchant banks' position in London by the integrated banks from America that had started in the early 1980s was gathering momentum with many joining Goldman Sachs in the chase. Schroders had the predicament of having no equivalent corporate finance capability in New York, Wertheim Schroder being primarily a securities house with a very small corporate finance department specialising in the small to medium sized companies rather than the large ones focused on by Schroders (see Chapter 8). For any transaction involving a client with assets in the States or wishing to make an acquisition there, Schroders had to work jointly with a major US investment bank. This involved effectively giving away the client relationship and creating a bridgehead for future international business. This entrée together with a willingness to invest over a long period enabled the US banks, with their powerful base in New York, to build a competitive position in London by sheer persistence and professionalism. Goldman Sachs in particular had put in people of real quality under the leadership of Thornton and as a result did significantly better than its competitors including Morgan Stanley, whose people were far less effective. With predators like BTR and Hanson breathing down the neck of less aggressive British companies, they felt threatened and were receptive to the arguments of Goldman Sachs and others that they had significantly more experience of defending their clients with techniques not used by the British merchant banks. Although persuasive this was not strictly true as the M&A rules in the US were not as investor friendly, particularly for the minorities. They did, however, have good ideas on the recapitalisation of companies which created more value to shareholders and their private equity businesses, as demonstrated by KKR, were far more developed in their thinking. They were also very willing to be brought in as a junior advisor. It all sounded like magic to the vulnerable British companies. Once involved they were ruthless in their attempt to supplant the British merchant banks. Even though there was an agreed split in the work the US banks duplicated the work being done by the merchant bank, always trying to trip up the merchant bank in the eyes of the client. They were not interested in acting within a team and were extremely difficult to work with. Finally they were far more sophisticated in their dealings with the press, knowing how to conduct a transaction, which would have traditionally been dealt with privately, in the full glare of the media. Although Schroders more than held its own in the UK, it had no real answer to this international challenge other than developing a serious capability in New York. Its disappointing and ineffective response is described in the next chapter.

The competitive threat described above was in respect to Schroders M&A activities. They were also totally dominant in the capital markets, a major weakness at Schroders. A far more serious issue was having a totally ineffective securities business that was managed independently of Corporate Finance (see Chapter 11). Schroders could not decide what to do. It could see that it would not survive if it did nothing but could not afford to do anything dramatic after two failed attempts at building a securities business from scratch. It clearly needed an experienced partner but with the Schroder family not being willing to dilute its equity interest this was unaffordable. Anyway everyone had made their dispositions and the best partners had all gone, Schroders having rejected the prospect at the time of the Big Bang. Could Schroders face a third attempt? With the increasing threat from the States did it want to be an integrated investment bank or not? Challen had always been and remained a sceptic. By his own admission he was wrong in feeling that Schroders would fail if it tried a third time, as he had not bargained on getting top class people. He was right in thinking that the Schroder family would not fund the amounts needed to make a success, which looked very scary. The alternative strategy of sliding back to being a top class advisory bank like Lazard made little sense as Schroders had proclaimed to all that it was a global bank, whereas in fact there was no integration between any of the units which were essentially local with very different businesses. This self-delusion was difficult to turn back on. With this indecision and total lack of leadership at the top on the integration issue (Corporate Finance and Securities), people started to leave. Challen was openly criticised by his colleagues. The continual process of trying to stop people leaving took its toll. There was always a key person about to leave. They were always struggling to keep up the pay supposedly provided by the competitors. 1992 had not been a good year and bonuses were lower. Challen was surprised to have to go before the Group Compensation Committee to argue the case for Corporate Finance – he felt this should have been done by Bischoff who had ducked it. Colleagues continued to snipe and there was a breakdown in team spirit. In 1990 Corporate Finance profits were 51% of the Group's profits; in 1994 they were 14%, having been overtaken by Investment Management and Treasury. The absolute amounts involved had not, however, significantly changed.

Despite the internal problems, the transactions continued to flow and to maintain the reputation and profits, including advising ICI on its defence against Hanson and

Westland on the hostile bid from GKN. On the Continent, the Italian team, under Tarantelli's leadership, was going from strength-to-strength, continuing to play a leading role in the consolidation of the banking industry, including acting in 1993 on the first public defence as a result of which it was able to secure significantly improved terms for the shareholders of Banco di San Geminiano e San Prospero. It also advised Grand Metropolitan on its successful bid for Buton, the Italian drinks company, having initiated it from scratch. In 1995 the Italian government instituted a privatisation programme in which the Italian team with Grimstone's help was appointed to arrange the sale of the Treasury's shares in INA, the national insurance company, involving three tranches over the next few years. This was followed by a privatisation appointment by Italimpianti. Sir Patrick Fairweather, the British ambassador to Italy at the time, said Tarantelli was head and shoulders over his British competitors. He had good reason to have an opinion as, unusually for a diplomat, he had a good commercial sense and had taken a keen interest in the privatisation programme of the government and made it his business to get to know all the investment bankers. Despite not being very well organised Tarantelli was full of imagination and innovation. After Fairweather retired from the FCO in 1996 he became a valued advisor to Schroders in its Italian business activities. Elsewhere on the Continent particularly in Germany and France, little progress was made largely due to the markets being more difficult to penetrate and the lack of stature and quality of those involved.

Challen creates a new role for himself

Challen was replaced by the joint leadership of Samuel and Netherton in 1994 – Netherton, as explained earlier, had a great appetite for team structures and compensation packages and was liked by his clients, was too senior to lose. Challen decided to give his full support to Samuel who was seen to be *primus inter pares*. This was difficult, as Schroders' management structures did not lend themselves to accommodating senior directors who were not managing a business. Challen had to create his own position including taking a senior role with many of the clients as Bischoff had done. He did this with remarkable skill, not being a threat to anyone, and provided wise counsel to his colleagues. He kept up the long established culture within Corporate Finance of people being willing to discuss with others their problems – in some respects he recreated, in a different form, Williams' earlier role.

He needed to regain his confidence and did this in 1994, by leading the defence of LASMO against a hostile £1.6 billion bid from Enterprise Oil. Lasmo's chairman, Rudolf Agnew, who regarded 'merchant bankers as the whores of the western world', had a higher regard for Challen, 'I think he is terrific. He is very unassuming, very cool in action and not a panicker. I have always listened to his advice. It is sound and impartial,' (*Daily Telegraph* 14 February 1998). In time he was able to re-establish himself as a leading advisor to some of the most important companies in the land as well as to the government. Arguably he became the most highly regarded corporate finance advisor in the City in the late 1990s.[1] In 2002 he was appointed a Commander of the Order of the British Empire (CBE) for his work in the City, a rare distinction.

Something of the reasons for Challen's failure as a head of Corporate Finance but his pre-eminent success as an advisor to clients is seen in the views of his colleagues and clients, which are summarised and amalgamated below.

He was seen to be uncomfortable in the role of head of Corporate Finance, lacking in charisma and finding it hard to relate to people. Not being a natural leader, he was a poor manager, a poor delegater, far too consensual and insufficiently forceful and a poor judge of people – not really a businessman, being far too nice and intellectual. People-pressure turned him into a different person and he had the disadvantage of having a difficult business climate to contend with while doing a job he clearly loathed. The view of him as a professional advisor was the opposite. His clients regarded him very highly, finding him very wise and with a good intellect, thinking through problems comprehensively, cool and calm under attack and difficult to out-smart. One client was more critical saying, 'he had the same professional attributes as Bischoff but not the same self-confidence, being somewhat diffident. On the other hand he had integrity, commitment among the best, was thoughtful and reflective and made a good team with Bischoff.' Mayhew, the leading broker of his day, said, 'he is a broad chap who does not throw his weight about.' His colleagues said he had a first class mind, tremendous judgement, was a natural client man, always thinking things through carefully and more highly admired as an adviser than any of his other colleagues. He was also greatly admired for having taken on the role of a senior advisor to clients and colleagues after the humiliation of his failure as head of Corporate Finance.

Challen illustrated the lack of Schroders' ability to differentiate properly between the relative importance of the manager, the leader and the business generator. Being head (manager) of a business led to being a member of an important management committee and these people were paid more than anyone else irrespective of whether they were making as much contribution to the business as the business generators. This forced brilliant people like Challen and others who followed into doing management roles for which they were unsuited. Leadership also did not necessarily come with management skills and this was well illustrated by Bischoff who was universally accepted as a brilliant leader (as well as a business generator) but not a particularly good manager (or administrator). He was fortunate in being able to leave to others the management/administration role while maintaining his leadership position but this was not duplicated below. This lack of understanding of the difference between the three roles and the qualities required of each may have been one of the reasons why Schroders did not seem to grow leaders from within its ranks. It was not helped by the business generators having very little respect or interest in management/administration. Having said that none of the status conscious British competitors seemed to have found a solution to these problems, unlike the Americans who, probably through their business school training, separated the roles and those that were most suitable to carry them out and avoided them being mixed up. At Goldman Sachs for example, the most highly rewarded people were the business generators not the managers.

NOTES:

1. With David Challen's increasing stature within Schroders he was appointed chairman of Schroder Wagg in succession to Solandt who retired during 1996. The role of the chairman of Schroder Wagg had significantly changed, as with all the businesses coming under the functional managing directors there was no direct management role. As the chairman of Schroder Wagg was the person within Schroders to whom the Financial Services Authority looked to for compliance with regulations, he had to make sure that the businesses were being conducted properly. Being the guardian of reputation he was in effect a sort of non-executive chairman. Its status had dropped to below that of the functional heads and so it did not carry a place on the Group Executive Committee, although outside the bank this distinction was not understood. One of the main responsibilities was to chair the 9.45 Committee which met every morning at that time to discuss new business, involving matters of principle, risk, conflicts of interest and new clients, which needed approval before being pursued. Challen's breadth of knowledge and experience and pleasant manner made him an ideal chairman.

CHAPTER 8

A MISTAKE IN NEW YORK[1]

1986 - 1994

Wertheim Inc was a medium-sized investment bank in New York, principally in the securities business. In 1982 Frederick Klingenstein, its chairman and 60% shareholder, decided that he had had enough of managing prima donnas and wished to sell his shares in the company. He therefore sought a partner in London to purchase his shareholding. An agreement to sell the whole company was reached with David Scholey of SG Warburg and preparations were made to sign the agreement at the Ritz Hotel in London in June 1984. Between reaching agreement and the signing ceremony, SG Warburg, following advice, had requested a minor change to the convertible that upset Klingenstein who, being a man of considerable integrity, felt he could not do a deal with a party who made changes at the last minute, however small. He left for New York, despite the arguments of his partner Jim Harmon who had negotiated the agreement for Wertheim. At the same time there was a revolt within SG Warburg by the partners of Rowe & Pitman against the consequences of the merger on their business and concern about the amount of time Scholey would have to spend in New York when he already had his hands full preparing for the Big Bang in London. Scholey was also upset to hear that Bob Shapiro, the partner who ran Wertheim on a day-to-day basis, was proposing to retire since he saw Shapiro as being the key to a successful merger. The agreement therefore failed. Harmon always hoped the merger might be resurrected but this proved to be forlorn.

In November 1985 many months after the Wertheim/SG Warburg merger had failed, Al Way met Harmon, a fellow trustee of Brown University, on a flight to New York. Harmon was still depressed by the failure of the merger and recounted the events to Way who in turn explained the situation to Mallinckrodt. Having just sold Schrobanco, Schroders was ready to build up its investment banking capability in New York and Mallinckrodt saw Wertheim as a heaven-sent opportunity for Schroders to get into investment banking in New York in a big way. Klingenstein had been advised that his shareholding was worth $125 million but to support his partners was prepared to accept less if the sale was agreed in principle in six weeks. Unusually for an investment banker Klingenstein was not excessively interested in money. He simply wanted to get his partnership funds out of the firm; he was not out to make a huge profit. The offer made to Schroders by Harmon and Steve Kotler, the fourth senior partner, was totally different from the agreement with SG Warburg. Schroders was offered a 50% minority interest with management control remaining in the hands of the Wertheim partners. The transaction was effected through a management buy-out by the non-Klingenstein partners with Schroders purchasing 50% of Wertheim for $101 million and a $90 million nominal subordinated note issue by the new company, being a heavy premium over the net asset value. Wertheim, described ambitiously in the Chairman's Statement to the 1986 Annual Report as, 'one of the major bracket Wall Street investment banking and securities firms' was renamed Wertheim Schroder & Co Inc. (Throughout the book Wertheim Schroder is referred to as simply Wertheim as everyone on both sides of the Atlantic always spoke of Wertheim, not Wertheim Schroder, even when it had been fully acquired in 1994.) The Wertheim partners were to have management independence providing they kept the profits to an agreed level. In 1985 there were 600 employees and revenues of $180 million. For Schroders to become investment bankers in New York it had to reduce its shareholding in Schrobanco to 5%. With the sale of Schroders' 75.1% share of Schrobanco for $100 million and Schroder Life for £100 million, Schroders had more than enough money to close the deal. Klingenstein, Shapiro and Harmon, the co-chairmen of Wertheim Schroder, became directors of Schroders and members of the Group Executive Committee. Within two years Harmon became sole chairman and the chief executive officer. Kotler was appointed the president of Wertheim Schroder.

In an interview shortly afterwards Bischoff expressed his admiration for Wertheim, 'it's superb, like all American investment banks, at welding together operations like market-making, sales and research and corporate finance. The advantage of the partnership is that we can see how it all works, how each side feeds off each other. Wertheim has been able to keep its end up by earning high returns because it has focused on certain things.' (*Financial Weekly,* March 1987). The Wertheim business was essentially one-third research, another third risk arbitrage and various other businesses including corporate finance, most of the profits coming from the arbitrage operations. The rationale was to build a major trans-Atlantic corporate finance business and to achieve a reverse technological transfer of securities. The trouble was it was very small and had no access to the Fortune 100 companies.

The 20 remaining partners of Wertheim thought the deal was wonderful – they got all their money out of the firm while maintaining their interest and also retained control, including the right to sell their share. They could not understand why Schroders agreed to the terms offered, which they regarded as being 'not very smart'. Mallinckrodt clearly wanted to do the deal and the management most affected and having the responsibility to make it work – the heads of Corporate Finance and Securities – were not consulted. Strickland, the finance director who negotiated the details of the transaction with Kotler, expressed grave reservations about leaving management control to the management but was overruled. The purchase of Wertheim was therefore a board decision with Mallinckrodt and Way being the prime advocates. Bischoff let himself be persuaded, having taken comfort from the mistaken understanding that SG Warburg had been keen to sign the same deal. It was all done on the rebound and Bischoff had not appreciated that if you were not in the top ten on Wall Street you were nothing.

Way, then chairman of IBJ Schroders, having previously been a non-executive director of Schroders between 1985 and 1986 and the prime instigator of the deal, was highly regarded by Harmon and Kotler. They found him very thoughtful, a shrewd strategic thinker with good judgement and great experience of the US way of doing things and therefore uniquely well-positioned to advise Mallinckrodt, who totally trusted him. Harmon was surprised that Way had such an unusual influence over Mallinckrodt.

Harmon, the new chief executive officer, had been in corporate finance for 13 years with another investment bank before joining Wertheim in 1974, bringing with him all the staff and clients. He was smooth and extraordinarily articulate with virtually all the main client relationships, which he had largely built up himself. He had played a major part in building up Wertheim's business and Kotler was his protégé. He felt that a cross-border alliance would offer Wertheim an international presence without a significant capital investment, while enabling the firm to maintain its independence. Kotler became, 'the thirteenth member of a twelve-man corporate finance team at Wertheim in 1974, sitting with the secretaries, previously having been a partner in a medium-sized investment bank that went bust.' By 1978 he was the youngest non-family partner, aged 30, and in 1981 became head of Corporate Finance, responsible for M&A, IPOs and advisory work. At the time of the Schroder merger, strongly allied to Harmon, he was one of the four senior partners and did the detailed negotiations with Strickland. He did not know much about Schroders, but saw it as an interesting partner with a global reach, plenty of capital and clients. Wertheim could have sold the whole firm as proposed to SG Warburg but the deal agreed was very attractive to him and to his other partners. Harmon and Kotler were a strong team, Harmon being the outside man with his client relationship skills and Kotler the insider, being a good and tough operator who lacked client skills.

Wertheim did reasonably well until the stock market crash in 1987, which exposed the volatility of the securities business and demonstrated its vulnerability to the market. All the investment banks took huge losses but did not necessarily lose money. It recovered in 1988 with the boom in M&A and arbitrage did well but equities did poorly. Wertheim needed to expand if it was to progress but this could be dangerous in view of the volatility of the markets and the huge overheads involved. Since Schroders was unwilling to put up the money, in 1989 Harmon increased the capital by introducing three new institutional shareholders (Bank of Boston, Massachusetts Mutual Life and The Mitsubishi Trust & Banking Corporation) with a 4.9% non-voting interest each, for a price based on a 4.5 multiple of the book value. Regrettably 1990 was a very bad year for Wall Street and for Wertheim as reported in an unusually strong statement in the Schroders' Annual Report.

In the USA, Wertheim Schroder experienced a major set back that had a significant impact on the Group's earnings in the form of substantial losses in its risk arbitrage activities, which in previous years had made a meaningful contribution. Also, the need to close the Government securities department, following continuing trading losses and a re-assessment of the prospects for this market, resulted in the absorption of considerable closure and redundancy costs.

As a result of Wertheim's arbitrage losses, following the collapse of United Airlines, Wertheim was in considerable difficulties and Harmon rang Mallinckrodt saying they needed $25 million to survive. Mallinckrodt immediately agreed to Schroders providing a one-year loan on very generous terms. Strangely he did not take the opportunity to gain more control. He was not best pleased when Wertheim did not want to repay the loan when the crisis was over. The following year Kotler broached the idea of a full merger but it was not taken up despite it being clear to Schroders that if it was to get anywhere in New York, it would have to take full control of Wertheim. Mallinckrodt was cautious and worried about the risks involved in the business and so it was deferred until 1994 when it was almost too late.

In December 1992, Ames Department Stores, recently emerged from Chapter 11 protection from its creditors, demanded damages of $375 million from Wertheim in relation to its $1.3 billion purchase of the discount division of Zayre Corp. Ames had earlier been advised by Wertheim, whose chairman Harmon was the non-executive chairman of Ames. In addition Wertheim acted as adviser to Zayre. Wertheim was effectively acting on both sides of the transaction, something totally unacceptable in London. In an out-of-court settlement it was agreed that Wertheim would pay $19 million to Ames, the value of its fees. Relationships with London were further soured. However, once the settlement was reached Schroders moved ahead with its negotiations to buy out the Wertheim partners.

Mallinckrodt and Way were hugely protective of the Wertheim management and told the Schroder management to keep their hands off, saying they did not understand the New York market. Alison Carnwath, a junior but well respected corporate finance director, was seconded to Wertheim to assist with the integration and marketing processes of London and New York but nobody senior from London put their career on the line to cement the merger. She was amazed that Mallinckrodt, as a commercial banker with no experience of investment banking, should be responsible for the investment. Extraordinarily Bischoff appeared to have no interest in the largest investment banking market in the world. 'It was a bad division of labour.' Early in 1987 Kotler offered to take over the whole of Schroders' securities business but Schroders rejected this, as there was a worry that if there was a divorce Schroders would have nothing. This was the end of any discussion of integration as far as Kotler was concerned.

There were two inter-related businesses that were the key to a successful merger; corporate finance and securities. Schroders was strong in corporate finance in Europe but weak in securities. Wertheim was selectively strong in securities in New York but weak in corporate finance. Both parties needed to help each other but their views were at odds. Quite an effort was made to build a successful trans-Atlantic corporate finance business and this lead to some successes, in particular Pilkington's acquisition of Vision Care, Revlon's ophthalmic business, for £574 million in 1987 and four privately placed senior note offerings for Rank Organisation totalling $800 million by 1992. This led in time to many cross-border private placements of long-term fixed rate dollar finance arranged by Steve Schechter, who operated out of London, for large UK companies, many of them not being Schroder clients.

Carnwath quickly discovered that the style and methods of working of the two organisations were very different. Whereas Schroders was institutionalised, focusing on providing an outstanding overall service to its clients by client relationship teams with complete written records and little quantitative analysis, Wertheim was individualistic – relationships being personal to the partners rather than corporate – entrepreneurial and transaction-orientated with ideas being generated by generalists, virtually no written records and used to complex quantitative analysis. With Broadbent's move to New York in 1990 to promote international business, Schroders' techniques in relationship management were introduced and Wertheim became more structured and more professional with a greater emphasis on client service. At the same time Schroders was becoming more open in terms of entrepreneurial activity. To respond to the need for greater co-operation, an integration committee was formed at the end of 1991 with Broadbent, Challen, Carnwath and Richard Broadbent (not related to Adam) from Schroders and Arthur Rebell, Ken Siegel and Schechter from Wertheim. The committee reviewed transactions that had arisen from the alliance and how to increase them. It helped to root out hidden misunderstandings and to focus on ways to improve the alliance. Training programmes were arranged in Wertheim and in Schroders for the newly hired from across the Atlantic. Despite all this, however, there was no change to the fundamental fact that Wertheim dealt with small companies not the large ones Schroders was used to. Carnwath in a liaison role tried quite hard to make a difference. She got on well with Harmon but found Kotler unpleasant to deal with. The problem as she saw it was that Schroders had failed to educate the leaders of Wertheim about what they wanted done.

Wertheim lacked the skill set and determination necessary to turn Wertheim into the US office of Schroders, which had to be done in 18 months. All they needed to do was to hire four or five top investment bankers on which to build a quality corporate finance capability with Kotler being replaced. There were within Wertheim three or four people who were as capable as the best on Wall Street including Ilan Kauftal, Mark Shapiro, Peter Bacon and Steve Schechter. These were the base on which they could have succeeded. Their problem was they did not understand relationship banking and could not see the route to the loot. On the other hand Schroders made no effort to understand Wertheim's products such as arbitrage. It was one of the great missed opportunities.

A MISTAKE IN NEW YORK

Arthur Rebell acted as a liaison between Corporate Finance in New York and London and developed good relationships. As a young lawyer he had joined Wertheim in 1968 and progressed through most of the departments of the firm to become head of Corporate Finance. He soon saw that London did not understand what it took to become a successful investment bank on the US model. In an honest statement without rancour he said, 'the corporate finance people in London thought the corporate finance people in Wertheim were second rate and made no attempt to disguise their disdain. This arrogance combined with a lack of knowledge of Wertheim and the New York market did not help.' There were endless acrimonious disputes over fee splits for joint work, which were temporarily avoided by Challen and Rebell having one meeting at the end of each year to agree an overall split in which none of those involved in the transactions had a say. They tried global industry groups for chemicals and energy led from New York and London respectively but this did not work. Despite all the troubles the Wertheim people liked their London colleagues and had a high respect for their abilities and intentions. The problem was that neither party was speaking the same language. Schroders wanted to use Wertheim to carry out trans-Atlantic M&A transactions and could not understand why Wertheim was unable to get business from the largest US companies and indeed did not even know them, as was the case in London. When Schroders were advising the British government on the privatisation of Jaguar Cars, they were frustrated by the fact that Wertheim did not know General Motors. In Harmon's view, 'they always hoped they could convert Wertheim into a "bulge bracket" firm but this was an unrealistic expectation as Wertheim had always specialised and done well out of medium and small companies.[2] Schroders never really understood Wertheim's business.' In London's view, 'Wertheim was essentially a research, sales and trading firm with which Schroders was not familiar. The business was mainly opportunistic based on the friends of Harmon. They were not high quality companies as in London. They were generalists and had no industry knowledge to speak of. They had excellent research but no corporate finance capability.'

In the area of Securities, where Wertheim was the more experienced partner, co-operation was much more difficult to achieve than in Corporate Finance as an economic tie was necessary. Lack of control of Wertheim made Schroders reluctant to invest in the creation of the necessary strategic resources. At the same time Wertheim had no economic incentive to enhance Schroders' performance and had the same reluctance about investing in strategic resources it would not control. Whereas Securities was a strategic necessity to Wertheim, in London there was still a debate about whether Schroders needed a securities business at all. Schroders therefore did not receive the support it had hoped for. With the Big Bang, Schroders wanted to be in securities and thought Wertheim could help and that Fred Sapirstein, the group head of Equities, could transfer the technology and knowledge to London but it did not happen. As Bud Morten, the head of Equity Services in Wertheim, observed, 'What was needed was for Wertheim and Schroders to share a common view of the type of securities business they wanted to create. Then we needed to be globally integrated and functionally managed with a single person overseeing all security functions and the geographic and departmental heads reporting to that person.' Wertheim needed international capabilities and global sophistication if it was to compete as a major player in the international markets. At the same time there was growing pressure in London with the American firms bringing in their superior industrial expertise within the US model offering a full range of services including financial advice, underwriting, brokerage, and market making – what became known as a fully integrated investment bank.

According to Barry Tarasoff, the head of Research, 'the prospect of Schroders becoming a significant force in New York and building a premier investment bank that would survive the ferocious competition was a most unlikely outcome'. Tarasoff had joined Wertheim in 1983 after four years at Goldman Sachs. In 1989 he took over from Morten as head of Research of Wertheim Schroder and in 1994 he became global head of research for the Schroder group. With Wertheim under the control of Harmon and Kotler he saw no incentive for Wertheim to expand resources to generate revenue for Schroders and no basis on which Schroders could create revenue for Wertheim. He could not understand why Schroders had purchased 50% of Wertheim without any control, with the partners retaining the right to sell. London understood that the valuable part of Wertheim was the brokerage business but did not understand the business. He visited London regularly to help them understand the research product but was too busy in New York to make an impact. This was only rectified in 1995 when Philip Augar arrived (see Chapter 22). Tarasoff liked the Schroder people and found them bright and well meaning and enjoyed the inter-reaction.

The culture and style of the two firms could not have been more different. Schroders, although equally competitive and aggressive when necessary, was essentially pleasant, considerate and consensual with a strong emphasis on teamwork. By contrast Wertheim was individualistic, money-driven and consisted of many personal franchises – the research analysts could at any time take their business with them to a competitor. The firm Rebell joined under Klingenstein was very collegiate with people staying for many years.[3] In the view of many of the partners the firm totally changed after Klingenstein left, Harmon and Kotler engineering the exit of his closest colleague, Shapiro. Harmon and Kotler had voting control over all the other Wertheim partners and treated the firm as their personal fiefdom. Mallinckrodt clearly felt he could make a success of the merger but he did not know Harmon and Kotler. Kotler's partners said he had no intention of achieving a merger and did everything he could to stop it, always being protective of the interests of the Wertheim partners. He agreed to a job for Broadbent that he knew could not be done. This was confirmed by Broadbent who said having been given no authority he was unable to do anything, as Kotler was a very hands-on chief executive with the loyalty of his staff and the full support of Harmon, his chairman. He managed the firm with a rod of iron, dividing and ruling. When Ivan Sedgwick, who was not related to Peter, arrived in New York to help in improving working relationships on the securities side in 1993, he was told by Bud Morten, the head of Equities, that he was welcome socially but not for business. He found the place racked with guerrilla warfare, most of the departments not speaking to each other. Kotler and Morten did not talk and Morten did not carry the support of the equity traders who were close to Kotler who played them off against each other. The other partners were amazed that Schroders allowed Kotler to get away with it, expecting him to be fired. He was regarded by many of them as being completely self-centred, 'Jim's boy', an intellectual bully, exceptionally bright but a short-term tactician. He could be charming and knew how to play his colleagues off against each other. He was seen by those who knew him in London to be a street fighter, uncultured, not a natural executer, very black and white, with an ability to frighten people and to sack without compassion. Such a person would not have lasted two minutes at Schroders. With such a diverse approach to management, an effective integration was never going to work until Schroders owned 100% of Wertheim and was willing to enforce its views.

Harmon could not see Schroders succeeding against Goldman Sachs and Morgan Stanley and felt it was better for Schroders to sell, but they were not willing to do so. Kotler had a similar view saying, 'The problem was that it was a strategic misfit. Schroders had large clients, Wertheim small. Schroders wanted to compete with Goldman Sachs and Morgan Stanley which made no sense to Wertheim who knew it took generations to build such firms and they could not be built overnight.' The fact that Morgan Stanley's profits increased from $400 million in 1986 to $4 billion in 1995 whereas Wertheim's profits remained static at $50 million must have had something to do with the attitude and competence of the management of the two firms, particularly Schroders' lack of willingness to take the measures necessary to make Wertheim as successful. In Carnwath's view,

> a more interesting comparison was DLJ, which was the same size as Wertheim in 1986 and had similar skills, being a research broker with a money market activity. Unlike Wertheim they added a formidable investment banking product by hiring a half a dozen good people to add to the top management. Unlike Schroders they had no qualms about firing low-grade people. It was extremely well managed by Joe Roby and Tony James, the CEO of investment banking, and was sold to CSFB in 2000 for over $10 billion.'

Schroders received virtually nothing for Wertheim (see Chapter 27).

In 1994 Schroders increased its shareholding in Wertheim Schroder from 42.5% (carrying 50% of the votes) to 100% for $92 million – $24 million for the 15% non-voting equity interest of the three institutional shareholders and $68 million for the 42.5% equity interest (carrying 50% of the votes) held by the management of Wertheim Schroder. This brought Schroders' total investment to $255 million. Shareholders' funds at the date of acquisition were $122 million and Wertheim made a loss of $1.5 million that year. Once again Schroders paid a heavy premium this time for control. Effectively Schroders paid two times the book value, paying $255 million for $150 million business. The decision to buy out the Wertheim partners was by no means unanimous, with Sedgwick and Solandt said to be against. Harmon reckoned that between 1986 and 1994 Wertheim Schroder had made a 10% – 12% return on capital but this was not the view of the people in London.[4] In his final Chairman's Statement Mallinckrodt said,

> Over the eight years since our original investment in 1986 a close working relationship has been developed between the two organisations and full ownership was the logical next step, enhancing opportunities and synergies. Since the merger we have been working hard on the integration of various functions, with the main aims of ensuring that our securities operations provide a firm support to investment banking as a whole and earn a proper return over the economic cycle.

This is so far from the truth that it beggars belief but chairmen's public statements can often be pious hopes and rarely stand up to the test of time.

When interviewed by the *Wall Street Journal* in November 1994, before handing over as chairman to Bischoff, Mallinckrodt said his business philosophy could be encapsulated in two phrases: 'Protect your capital. Never succumb to the vagaries of fashion.' In considering purchasing the remaining 50% of Wertheim he said, 'the forces of globalisation make you realise that you should ideally work as one firm that has its own business plans rather than as two linked – but still largely autonomous – companies as now.' The lack of a placement capacity for big share issues was now seen as a drawback. With corporate customers increasingly looking for financial advisers that could both organise a share issue and place the shares with investors, insiders admitted that Schroders was leaving money on the table. By acquiring Wertheim Schroder, Schroders hoped to bridge the gap. 'Schroders is very strong in the origination of business in the capital markets area and we are quite strong in the distribution side,' said Harmon.

NOTES:

1. Extensive reference is made in this chapter to a Harvard Business School case study, Wertheim Schroder/Schroders, that was prepared in 1993, analysing the attempts of the two firms to achieve some integration prior to the decision by Schroders to buy out the Wertheim partners in 1994.

2. The bulge bracket firms were a handful of US investment banks that were the principal underwriters of the largest issues – this capital raising capability requiring strong capitalisation.

3. Fred Klingenstein was highly regarded by his partners as a man of complete integrity, totally trustworthy, honest and straight and primarily interested in the success of the firm he had built up. Ken Siegel, who had joined Wertheim after receiving a Harvard MBA in 1982, described the company environment at that time,

> Wertheim had a family feel about it. The firm was run by Klingenstein who was soft spoken and not interested in the limelight. When new partners were admitted to the firm he supplied the majority of their capital. He was very philanthropic, conservative, did not tolerate yellers and screamers and was not a big risk taker. The firm had a reputation of being a conservatively run, highly profitable, closely held partnership.

4. Unfortunately the author was not given access to information within Schroders and so was unable to make a judgement on the conflicting views of Wertheim Schroders' financial performance.

CHAPTER 9

MAKING MONEY

1984 – 1995

Following the strategic review Jean Solandt was appointed group managing director of Treasury and Trading. Although he had ambitions to become chairman of Schroder Wagg, he accepted that Bischoff was the man for the moment and was fully supportive of his appointment. In view of his success as a banker, he was asked to take over Schrobanco but because of his children's education he declined the offer. He did, however, help in repairing its weak treasury operations in which he found no understanding of interest rate risks. After many visits to New York, he managed to turn around the treasury operation, much to the relief of Mallinckrodt who was full of praise for his contribution in this area. The strategic review recognised the importance of the treasury function being a separate division from Banking. As Solandt was the only dealer at a senior level he was also asked to take on the securities function together with Eurobond trading and swaps. He was absolutely determined to make the treasury function the third leg of Schroders' business in terms of profitability. Unlike most of Schroders' activities, the treasury business was all about making money. There was little talk at that time of providing a service and client relationships, although these had some importance; it was simply about making more and more money.

The main activities of Treasury had traditionally been foreign exchange transactions and the management of the Group's balance sheet – most importantly its liquidity and solvency. Solandt transformed the business from spot and forward foreign exchange dealing and balance sheet management to cover an increasing number of instruments. In addition to own account risk taking, he introduced customer-driven services, the most sophisticated of which involved the design of custom-made structures for both investing and capital-using clients. In managing the balance sheet he became less reliant on the inter-bank market and cash instruments using derivative instruments, such as futures, forward-rate agreements and options to enhance yield or to protect the balance sheet against loss. Having worked under Mallinckrodt on the German banking desk for many years, Solandt was trusted by Mallinckrodt and so never had any trouble getting his limits approved – without this support he would never have been able to build the business as successfully as he did.

Solandt's two most senior lieutenants were Richard Bown and Andrew Sykes. Bown, the chief dealer, was responsible for treasury, interest view-taking and foreign exchange. He had joined Schroders from school and always modestly stayed in the background.

He was the most committed executive in Treasury, rising at 4.30 am each day, so that he could read all the papers and agency reports in the office before any of his colleagues arrived. He then gave them a full economic and market briefing before trading began. He also travelled a great deal, particularly to the States where he had good contacts at the Federal Reserve. By inclination he was a market man rather than a manager but still commanded great loyalty from his team. He was an exceptionally good dealer, foreseeing future interest rate movements with enormous prescience. He was quiet, a good and consistent money maker and pivotal to the resolution of the CD crisis in 1973 (see Chapter 1). He also shared Solandt's determination to build Treasury into a major activity. As the financial markets grew with more and more sophisticated products the dealing activities became relatively less important although still very profitable. One of Bown's more colourful figures was Rupert Birch who joined him in London and later in Paris, after spells in Banking, New York and Capital Markets. He was a great personality, an excellent salesman and an extrovert. He did not fit in with the self-effacing and modest ethos within Treasury initially but it was a risk that succeeded, since with his outgoing and friendly disposition there were no conflicts.

Sykes was responsible for swaps. He also started derivatives trading – largely client driven – which had previously been successfully developed by Mark Hopkinson in Australia and by Greg Bone in Tokyo (see Chapters 10 and 18). Sykes was the first graduate to be taken on by Treasury. He joined Solandt's German team in Banking in 1978 under Michael Ladenburg and Bernd Marenbach. Not long after he joined Schroders, his father, a senior diplomat, was killed when the IRA blew up his car. He was incredibly brave and mature in coping with this appalling tragedy. A few years later, he asked Solandt for a year off to help Beasley, the publisher, to set up a commercial side to the Royal College of Art. As this was not a success he asked Solandt if he could return. With the formation of Treasury and Trading in 1984, Solandt advised him that the lion's share of the profits in Banking came from the treasury activities and therefore he should join his new division. Although by then Solandt had recruited many graduates in Banking, none were willing to join Treasury, wishing to remain lenders. Later with the development of new products by Treasury the situation was reversed. Sykes started as assistant to Solandt and was tried out as a spot foreign exchange dealer but within six months he had lost £100,000 – he was terrified but Solandt took it on the chin and agreed it was not his thing. He was moved on to building the business of selling treasury services to customers and this grew into a good business. He found that interest rate derivatives were more his metier and he remained in this area until jointly taking over Financial Markets in 1995. 'He had a considerable intellect, probity and was trustworthy as well as being a good organiser. On the other hand he could be cold and was not naturally a team person – his seeking of profit was driven intellectually rather than commercially. Maybe he was more like St Paul who never preached against money itself only the love of money!'[1]

Sykes enjoyed the intellectual challenge of interest rate derivatives, which can be interest rate swaps or interest rate caps. Swaps involve a contract between two parties to exchange a stream of fixed interest rate payments from one party for a stream of floating rate payments from the other party on an agreed underlying principal amount. The party arranging the swap, i.e. Schroders, hedges itself in the market at the same time giving itself a margin in the transaction generally reflected in the fixed rate. An interest rate cap is effectively a guarantee of interest rate payments being no higher than an agreed amount. It is an insurance in which protection is purchased against having to pay more than an agreed level of interest and is secured through the payment of a premium in advance. Foreign exchange options are arranged on the same principle.[2]

Essentially his team, including his successor Nigel Harris, was seeking to minimise the risk of its corporate customers while creating risk for its investors. This could be arranged through a basket of equities, the relative value of two currencies, the future level of interest rates, one stock market against another or the index. The aim was to improve the risk/reward ratio for the customers as well as for Schroders. The swaps team in Capital Markets was incorporated within Treasury, and together they became even more professional. However, as markets became more competitive, more transparent and more liquid, the ability to make substantial margins when dealing with customers was eroded. To make the same profits the team had to make markets and warehouse transactions involving greater risk and complexity and the development and use of new systems. The team was supplemented by a number of exceptionally bright young mathematicians, theoretical physicists and classicists, all with double firsts or doctorates and mostly with no financial training. They were all very serious individuals glued to their computers all day and into the night, the brightest of whom, Mike Hodgson appeared never to go home. They could write the software as well as operating in the market and many highly sophisticated and highly profitable transactions were concluded. Whereas originally there were no graduates in Treasury, by the 1990s over half the 120 executives in Treasury worldwide were graduates, since the new activities demanded people with the kind of mental ability possessed by those from universities.

In fact, these young graduates soon out-numbered the old guard who became known affectionately as the dinosaurs, Bown being the arch dinosaur. But he had the last laugh on them during the ERM crisis in 1992 in which there was a major run on sterling, as with his vast experience he managed the firm's books with consummate skill, both protecting its liquidity and building up extremely profitable positions for the future. He never sat down throughout the day and was constantly bombarded with questions from the new bloods when he was not actually trading. They greatly admired him.

A major blow was when in 1987 the House of Lords ruled that the local authorities were not empowered to enter into swap transactions. This meant that all such deals were null and void and the banks at the other end of them had to unwind them in the market. Collectively the banks in the City made huge losses and Treasury took a significant cut in its profitability that year.

During the early 1990s there was enormous volatility in interest rates and currencies, which created great opportunities but at considerable risk. With the Wall coming down in Berlin in 1989 and West Germany taking on the East German economy, interest rates shot up as people worried about the cost of financing the East German economy and the inflationary pressure of exchanging one deutsche mark for one ostmark. In 1992, sterling dropped out of the ERM and in 1993, there was a bull market in bonds with yields falling by 2.5% and the Federal Reserve and the other central banks pushed up interest rates so that short-term rates doubled in the year. Schroders took advantage of these unstable conditions to make substantial profits.

In the meanwhile Greg Bone wished to return to London and to join Solandt who had recruited him. Reporting directly to Solandt he ran structured products, an even more complicated set of transactions – the creation of customised investments. Bone was a complicated person, the son of a meat porter and with an excellent brain he was the first pupil from his school to go to Oxford. He had the rare ability of combining a tremendous intellect with an acute commercial flair. He was also a great money maker and was very loyal to his teams in London and Tokyo, which he managed well. He had the ability to see and think through business opportunities with Japanese clients and to persuade them to do the transaction, being a very effective salesman. The Japanese insurance companies were obliged to separate their income from capital. They had a lot of unrealised capital gains on their share portfolio and insufficient income to service the cash flow of their businesses. Bone was able to convert their capital into income within the law and on a large scale, which resulted in huge margins for Schroders and a large increase in its profits. He dealt with the big banks and used other people's balance sheets to develop appropriate structures for his clients, invariably leading to a web of interrelated but independent transactions, often too intricate and complex to be understood by many of his colleagues outside his team. This large and highly sophisticated derivatives business with the Japanese institutions was the most successful development within Treasury and its greatest single success. It also had a major beneficial effect on Schroders' standing in Japan. However, like most of these exceptionally clever people, Bone was difficult to manage and was very demanding on remuneration – in fact a special bonus scheme had to be developed to suit his business. Being a fanatical supporter of Charlton Athletic Football Club he used his first bonus to buy the shareholding required for him to become a director of the club.

A real issue and a constant source of complaint was the cost of the back office. As the years went by nothing was done and the costs grew and grew, much to the irritation of the revenue earners. In 1987 Lester Gray, a 26-year-old New Zealander, with a degree in mechanical engineering, was introduced by a mutual friend to Solandt, who took an immediate liking to him. Shortly afterwards he joined as a generalist helping with the budgets, risk measures and other administrative tasks, later taking over the back office. Initially Solandt and Gray explored a joint venture back office with Morgan Grenfell and Barings but when this got nowhere they reached an agreement with a number of banks to hire jointly a management consultant to conduct a survey of each firm's cost of processing its treasury transactions. This provided a benchmark for introducing a system of internal transfer pricing. In the first year the back office lost £1.5 million, the next year it broke even thanks to Gray's management. Outside the office he was a serious mountain climber.[3,4.]

The heads of Treasury in Zurich, Hong Kong, Singapore and Australia reported to Solandt and their market liquidity and credit limits were controlled and approved through the Group Market Risk Committee. When things went well Solandt left them alone but if not he had to intervene. Tommy Lee, head of Financial Markets in Hong Kong, was very good and made a lot of money but was difficult to manage. He was an out-and-out market man with great loyalty from his team. He did not like being put under Hopkinson when he was appointed regional head of Financial Markets but this was eventually diffused by Solandt, to whom Lee was very loyal.

One of the reasons for the success of Treasury (and later Financial Markets) was that they reacted quickly to the introduction of new products and therefore made profits when the margins were high. An example of this was arbitraging the cash market in dollar interest rates in London with the futures market in Chicago — very attractive spreads were earned with very little risk. The other main reason was the quality of the executives and the low staff turnover.

Solandt was one of the first directors in the bank to arrange international conferences for all his senior colleagues at country house hotels near London and did this every year throughout the 1990s with 30 to 40 colleagues from Australia, Japan, Hong Kong, Singapore, Zurich, New York and London. It developed a good team spirit among the regions. As the Chinese influence increased, the London dealing room installed a large fish tank, which soon became covered with Chinese good fortune signs. There was good *feng shui* thereafter.

The problem with the business Solandt, Bown, Sykes and Bone had created was that it was so complicated that few of their colleagues outside Treasury understood it. Unlike the other businesses that were largely advisory and fee earning, Treasury earned its profits both as a principal and on customer business in the form of a margin or spread between what could be dealt with in the market and what could be charged to its customers. This gave rise to a different culture than that prevailing in the rest of the bank. As chairman of the Group Market Risk Committee, Solandt tried to rectify this by reporting annually on the methods applied to market risk and the limits set for market risk taking on the various activities of the Group. He also gave periodic teach-ins to his colleagues and members of the board. One wonders if the same practice had been adopted by Barings, its collapse through the activities of the rogue trader Nick Leeson would have been avoided.

In 1995, Solandt was appointed chairman of Schroder Wagg and handed over what had become Financial Markets to Hopkinson and Sykes. This did not suit Bone who had become more conscious of his status in the company than the business and demanded a new division — he wanted his business totally separated from the remainder of Financial Markets. This might have worked at the beginning when it was quite small but as it grew it needed to build relationships across the Group if it was to thrive. He became so difficult that his people revolted against him, and such a destructive influence that he was asked to resign. Schroders had made great compromises to accommodate Bone in view of his huge talents but this was a step too far. However, after he left the profits from structured products were never as good and this had an adverse effect on the profits of Financial Markets.

Solandt was highly regarded by his colleagues. He was an excellent judge of the markets and had an ability to think through and to see what was important. He was good with people and knew how to get the best out of them, particularly if they were traders. He really cared about those who worked for him. He was straight, happy in his role and did very well. He handed over a business which, including a small contribution from Banking and leasing, had become Schroders' second most profitable activity earning on average 39% of the profits in the five years to 1995 compared with 43% by Investment Management and Ventures and 18% by Investment Banking and Project Finance.

NOTES:

1. The first letter from Paul to Timothy, 6:10. – 'The love of money is the root of all evils'.

2. In a currency swap, a US company wishing to borrow in yen begins by borrowing in dollars and then swaps its dollar debt for yen debt. The swap intermediary (i.e. the bank) pays the company the dollars necessary to service the dollar debt while the company pays the bank the cost of servicing the yen loan.

3. Lester Gray successfully scaled Pumori, which at 7,500 metres is close to Everest in the Himalayas, after having been forced down from Annapurna I by bad weather. He was one of a number people at Schroders interested in mountaineering including Mark Warham of Corporate Finance who successfully climbed Everest on his second attempt. Charles Arthur another colleague in structured products climbed Cho Oyo which is over 8000 metres in Tibet.

4. After the sale of the investment bank Gray later progressed to became the chief operating officer of the Group taking control of all the computer systems and administration.

CHAPTER 10

JAPAN

1970 – 1983

Jeremy Hill had joined Schroders from Consolidated Goldfields, where he was a mining analyst during the Australian mining boom – Poseidon and all that. De Havilland had introduced him to Ponsonby and Popham offered him a job at the end of 1970. He was concerned that the Australian market would go caput and so told Airlie that everything in Australia should be sold and as a result he was out of a job. He read an article in the *Financial Times* by Henry Scott-Stokes on Japan and said to Airlie that he would like to go to Japan. He went to the Berlitz Schools of Languages in Oxford Street and learnt very little. With his wife and two small children, he set off for Tokyo and travelled the length and breadth of Japan over the next six months working for periods in some of the securities houses and the Industrial Bank of Japan (IBJ). He became fascinated by the country and wrote notes on all the companies he visited but no notice was taken of them by London. Robinson, who was thought to be the most qualified director to oversee Japan, because he had learnt some Japanese as a young man when interrogating prisoners of war, came out occasionally but no one came from Investment Management. With nobody showing any interest the market started to rise. The problem was that Richardson was dead against Japan.

Schroders in fact had impeccable credentials in Japan, since through the introduction of Horatio Nelson Lay, the impecunious son of an English vicar, Schroders arranged a ten-year £1 million customs loan for the Imperial Government of Japan in April 1870 to finance part of the first railway in Japan between Shimbashi and Yokohama. It was promptly repaid but the Japanese never forgot it. In 1954, Sumitomo Bank opened its London Representative Office in Schroders' offices in Leadenhall Street. In the 1960s Schroders had done a number of issues for Mitsui and Komatsu, two world-ranking companies, and they could not understand why Schroders never visited them. Schroders' name was therefore well known but the enthusiasm of the Japanese was not reciprocated.

In 1971 Schroders was approached by the Sanwa Bank with a proposal that Schroders, Sanwa and Nomura Securities establish a joint venture to undertake investment banking business in Japan. Following a thorough review by Murphy and Wolfensohn with Burgis Coates, a seasoned Pacific banker being called in from New York, and a visit to Tokyo, the invitation was rejected 'due to disparity of size'.

Hill, having returned to London with no interest in his findings, had to wait until 1972 when Richardson visited his son in Tokyo following a posting there by his company.

When Hill heard he immediately wrote him a paper setting out the reasons for Schroders to open an office in Tokyo. Having been summoned by the great man to explain his paper, he stammered away with Richardson remaining silent. There was a long gap before he was, unexpectedly and without notice, called to make a presentation to the board where again he was able, despite being totally unprepared, to go through his party piece. The board agreed to go ahead and as Hill was thought to be too young at 33, Coates, who had tasted the fruits of the Japanese nightlife as a bachelor after the war, took his wife to Tokyo. She took one look and said, 'No way'. In the absence of anyone else, Hill and his family returned to Tokyo as the Schroder Representative.

Following the oil shock in 1973 and the three-day week in England, things looked pretty bleak but Hill still received full support and opened the Representative Office in Room 404 of the Imperial Hotel in February the following year. Nick Roditi, who had spent three months in Hong Kong and South East Asia, came out shortly before the opening and stayed for six months getting to know Japan. One of his jobs was to write up the books of account for the office. Hill also hired Ed Merner, an ex-peace corps worker, as an analyst. He had worked for a broker and had the best nose for a company that Hill had ever met. He was the best investor in Japan and was the reason for many years of success of the Japanese Smaller Companies fund. At first, however, there was no investment business. Mitsubishi lent Schroders £50 million to buy a tanker for them in Panama. As it was in Schroders' name, it took a margin for virtually doing nothing and these margins covered all the costs of the office. Slowly Schroders began to invest in companies and got to know their managements. Daiwa asked Schroders to manage a Eurobond convertible issue for Sanyo Electric and this was followed by regular invitations for companies such as Ito Yokado, a small supermarket whose owner became one of the richest men in the world and produced business for the next 20 years. Hill had some difficulty in persuading London to deal with such a small company. The issuing business grew as well as banking transactions with huge margins of 3%.

A fashion at the time was for foreign banks to enter into joint ventures with the Japanese commercial banks. Hill took the view that Schroders would do better with the Trust banks as they had access to vast investment funds. Bulfield, who had the most impressive connections with the Japanese banks, having lent them money over many years, suggested Mitsubishi Trust and Banking Corporation (MTBC) and arranged an introduction through the Bank of Japan. As the Mitsubishi group already had a joint venture with Orion Bank in London it was decided to set up the 50/50 joint venture in Brussels in 1976 to undertake syndicated loans and to provide corporate finance services. When in 1981 MTBC wished to expand the lending activities and Schroders had received none of the Mitsubishi's investment funds and was less interested in the lending business, it sold its shares to MTBC for a profit of £1 and withdrew its name.

Hill returned to London in 1976 to be replaced by David Pain, a former naval officer in Banking. Speaking about those he had most to do with while involved in Japan, Hill said,

Airlie came out a lot and could charm the management of the companies in three minutes. He was wonderful to take around and never put a foot wrong. He was the ideal chairman and never interfered. Verey on the other hand, although he could not have been more helpful, did not like abroad and so never appeared. Van Marle was very popular with the Japanese and, despite not having total command of English, he knew his business and so was very effective – he was completely without prejudice and gave the impression he genuinely liked the Japanese unlike Robinson, who clearly did not. Robinson was immensely entertaining, not a businessman but a good head office man. Bulfield was very competent, well connected and one could not have had a better person to travel with. Popham was completely inarticulate but a brilliant investor – as he hated abroad he gave me my head. De Havilland was also a brilliant investor and carried Investment Management for all the years from 1970 to 1980. The business during those years entirely depended on de Havilland and Popham. De Havilland made £8 million alone in one year dealing in Japanese warrants for Schroders' book.

On his return to London, Hill attended a planning weekend at the Bell Inn at Aston Clinton at which it was agreed to set up SCMI in London with extensive travel to the US – looking around the table he saw that they were all looking at him. He took a rest from Japan for a period and turned his mind to the new world (see Chapter 12).

Roditi, who was Hill's back stop in London, was an enthusiastic tennis player at a club in Hampstead, where one day he was asked by a Japanese if he would play tennis with him. The following Saturday Mr Miyasaka turned up in impeccable whites together with a new tennis racquet and they set off for Number One Court where it soon became apparent that Miyasaka was a very inexperienced player. Foreseeing a potential embarrassment, Roditi quickly arranged a mixed doubles match asking his friend, the club's ladies champion, to play with Miyasaka. Miyasaka went away very happy having won the match but was not seen again at the club. In the meanwhile Pain was doing a good job in Japan being a man of painstaking detail and hard work. Roditi, who had been identified as his successor, was sent around the departments starting with Banking which, like many, he found excruciatingly boring and importantly did not get on with Solandt. He learnt about bonds from van Marle and was sent on a well-organised training course at IBJ where he met a Texan banker who, lacking any finesse, suggested that he go to Korea. After a discussion with Bulfield he was allowed to go to Korea where he was able to assist build up a small loan book.

In September Pain returned to London and was replaced by Roditi who travelled straight from Seoul. Within the month Mr Park, the president of South Korea, was shot by his driver and Roditi had to rush back to ensure the loans were safe. While there he was given the mandate to raise $20 million for Daewoo Shipping and Engineering Company, which was the most difficult transaction he ever arranged. It had various tax wrinkles and a margin of 20% – on a participation of $1 Schroders received $200,000 each year for five years. Back at the office, which had moved to the Shin Yuraka-Cho Building with three rooms within 1200 square feet, there were four people: Roditi, Merner, Miss Tsuda and another secretary. The main business of the office was a small investment portfolio being run by Merner, looking for Eurobond business and what one might call quasi-banking – in reality it was helping Japanese companies get around exchange control and other domestic regulations. The Japanese banks wanted to lend to their customers three-year loans but could not do so without being able to show they could borrow for three years. If they received two letters from a UK bank one saying it would lend for three years and another revoking the first they would pay a margin of one-eighth. Things were done and expected to be done by the foreign banks that would not be permitted today.

At about the same time, some two years after their last meeting on the tennis court, Roditi came across Miyasaka who, after a period of re-education in Japanese behaviour in Hiroshima to eradicate his Western ways, was now head of the bond department of Nippon Kangyo Kakumaru Securities (NKK Securities). Miyasaka explained that none of the top four securities houses that controlled 98% of the market could be seen to sell government securities as this would be regarded as dishonourable and would impact on their selection to manage future issues. He suggested that as a foreigner this would not apply to Roditi. So he bought Y1 billion stock from Nomura and sold it to NKK adding a margin. Every day Roditi bought from one security house and sold to another, neither party knowing of the other and often very large sums were involved. Despite an intensive international investigation Nomura was never able to discover how Schroders had become the largest buyer of Japanese government securities. It came to an end when physical trading was replaced by electronic dealing in 1983 but in the meanwhile the office costs were more than covered with no risk.

When Roditi went out to Japan and then to Korea in 1979, exchange controls were lifted and investment into Japan really took off. The Schroder Tokyo fund was set up and from $2 million in 1977 was built up to $1 billion by the end of the 1980s. The Japanese Smaller Companies fund was set up in the early 1980s. As a result Schroders held a big position in a lot of the large Japanese companies and was able to go into the front door for issuing business. Stephen Brisby succeeded Roditi in 1982 but was only in Tokyo for just over a year during which he took advantage of the market in building up a good convertibles and warrants business which was being processed in London by Paul Sauvary, who took over from him in 1983 when he returned to Capital Markets in London.

Sauvary found the investment management business being competently run by Merner and concentrated on the solicitation of capital market bond issues for Japanese companies issued in London and Swiss franc bonds issued in Zurich. With Hopkinson in Australia, he originated the structured products business, which under Greg Bone was to become one of Schroders' most profitable businesses in the late 1980s (see Chapter 9). He persuaded Japanese companies to issue fixed rate bonds in unusual currencies, which Hopkinson swapped into US dollars. Having been previously in RAMP, based in Singapore, Hopkinson had many clients in the region that wanted to hedge their currency exposures. Sauvary was pleased to have Bone working on these innovative deals finding him 'a clever bright lad'. Curiously at the time there was no swaps business in London. He returned to London in 1986 to run syndicate bond trading and was replaced by Ladenburg in a new and elevated post of managing director of the new Schroder Japan branch, which was responsible for all Schroders' investment banking businesses in Japan including its new securities business.

NOTES:

1. Paul Sauvary joined Corporate Finance in 1980 as an assistant to Nick MacAndrew, having previously been with Orion Bank under Andrew Large (later knighted and also deputy governor of the Bank of England) dealing with international bond issues. He found Corporate Finance under Ashton to be in another age. He worked on Japanese bond issues and convertibles and Eurobond issues in London for small and medium-sized US oil companies, there being nobody else in Corporate Finance who could document these issues. This involved much time in Houston.

CHAPTER 11

DITHERING ABOUT SECURITIES

1983 – 1994

Nick Roditi, who had become Asia weary, returned from Japan and Korea to London in late 1981 and was asked by Airlie to come up with some ideas. He suggested gold trading but this was rejected. He also looked at swaps but could not understand them and so suggested stockbroking. In Japan there were fixed commissions for securities with rebates for brokers. In order for Schroders to secure these rebates on the extensive business it was doing it had to be a stockbroker. Schroder Securities was therefore started as a means of getting a share of Japanese commissions payable on investment management business. Hill and Roditi decided to start in Asia with Roditi applying for membership of the Hong Kong Stock Exchange but he was black-balled by Jardine Fleming, which was already a member of the Exchange. (This proved to be a continual personal embarrassment to him throughout his business life when filling out formal documents.) After Airlie had spoken to Robert Fleming in London, Jardine Fleming withdrew its objection and Schroders was accepted. Offices were set up in Hong Kong to deal in Hong Kong, Japanese and Australian securities with ten staff and in Tokyo for Japanese securities with four people. It was not an easy period with markets bad as a result of the abrasive discussions between Margaret Thatcher and the People's Republic of China over the future of Hong Kong after 1997.

Back in London, Hill and Roditi decided to convert the Schroder Asia Securities office in London into a London stockbroking business and to re-activate the old name Helbert, Wagg, which had formerly been a member of the London Stock Exchange prior to 1912. It was said that at the time Geoffrey Williams remarked wryly that, 'Big Bang would leave the City with only two independent brokers in the London market, Cazenove and Helbert Wagg!' Roditi knew John Anderson of Panmure Gordon and explained Schroders' stockbroking plans saying he needed three members to apply. Anderson persuaded his two partners Donald Bryce and Alastair Villiers to join him in starting a new stockbroking business and in July 1984 a licence for membership of the Stock Exchange was applied for in the name of Helbert Wagg & Co, Anderson Bryce Villiers. Schroders' shareholding was 29.9%, the largest amount permitted, until 1986 when Schroders took complete control and renamed the firm Schroder Securities. This was a minimalist and low risk approach to the Big Bang and as such was supremely successful save for the huge costs involved! Schroders completely misunderstood what the Big Bang was all about, that is raising capital for its clients through a combination of sales/research/trading/syndication, despite the example of Morgan Stanley in New York, which had built a highly successful business from scratch. Morgan Stanley had thought through the issues and knew what had to be done. They had the benefit of being surrounded by competitors who understood the business, unlike in London where it was emerging. Equally importantly they appreciated the importance of integration as well as securities itself.

Offices were initially set up in London Wall with Hill as chairman and Roditi as managing director. It was at this point in 1985 that the strategic review group, in the absence of any interest by Corporate Finance, decided that as Solandt knew about dealing he should take charge of Schroder Securities under his new fiefdom Treasury and Trading. Solandt who had been known to say that he had 'never owned an equity and never wanted to' took over. Roditi, who did not get on with Solandt, left the bank[1] and Hill, who saw he had a tiger by the tail, decided to go back to concentrating on Investment Management in Asia. He was never consulted on securities matters thereafter, despite all the efforts he had put into its creation.

In attempting to build a new business, Anderson and his colleagues had taken over expensive offices in Devonshire Square and spent a lot of money hiring new staff. They had also set up a European office in Paris with many analysts. Unfortunately with all the banks trying to get into stockbroking at the same time there was a huge demand for a limited supply of brokers, most of whom were grossly overrated. As a result Schroders had to pay vast amounts for second-rate people. To Solandt it appeared to be totally out of control and he saw no prospects of the costs ever being recovered by revenues. He therefore closed the European office and fired Anderson, Bryce and Villiers. At about the same time Schroders had acquired a 50% stake in Wertheim, a well regarded but small securities house in New York (see Chapter 8). With its depth of experience of stockbroking and its good analysts, dealers and a sales force under Fred Sapirstein, Sapirstein was appointed joint head of securities. However, as explained in Chapter 8, Sapirstein did not have the time or commitment to Europe to be able to make much of a difference.

Europe was not the only problem facing Solandt. In Asia things were going no better. The heads of the Hong Kong and Tokyo offices, who had also not been effectively managed by Hill and Roditi, had to be replaced as well. Earlier there had been great embarrassment when the Japanese authorities granted stock exchange licences to SG Warburg and Kleinwort Benson and not to Schroders during Airlie's farewell visit to Japan – nobody had bothered to apply. In fact such licences were only available for firms with significantly larger offices than Schroders had in Japan. Solandt had to make many humiliating visits to Tokyo involving him having to sit outside the offices of officials before a licence was finally secured. At about the same time Mrs Thatcher was very exercised by the unfair playing field for British financial institutions in Tokyo compared with the treatment of the Japanese in London and she took a strong line about opening the membership of the Tokyo Stock Exchange to British banks. She put some pressure on

Schroders to apply saying it would receive her full backing – so Schroders was pushed into making an application and agreed to do so after Bischoff's blessing in early 1987. Rupert Caldecott was sent out to prepare the ground. Caldecott had joined Schroders in 1974 on the recommendation of his father, who was deputy chairman of Kleinwort Benson, and worked in Banking under Chris Cairns and Bernard Barham in what was known as the AAA team.[2] After nine years he transferred to Schroder Asia Securities under Roditi. Solandt, who saw no way through the problems and had become quite ill through the worry, asked to be relieved of his duties. It was not his finest hour. He was more than delighted to hand the poisoned chalice temporarily to Strickland, who immediately appointed head hunters to find a new managing director of Securities.

Ladenburg, who had been well thought of by Solandt when working in his German banking team and been the first graduate recruited by Banking, had earlier been sent out to Tokyo to take charge of the new securities branch, which oversaw all Schroders' business in Japan excluding Investment Management. Unfortunately he proved to be an unfortunate choice. He was an experienced banker but had no knowledge of the broking business, little of the capital markets business built up by Sauvary and more importantly no experience of Japan. The people involved in broking, which was seen by many in Schroders to be a rather racy business, were not of a kind he was used to working with and when combined with his apparent dislike of the Japanese, it was a recipe for disaster. The fact that he lived in a grander style than any of his predecessors had done did not help his relationship with his colleagues. He therefore lost the respect of Caldecott, Gordon and the prickly Bone. Greg Bone, who was running a highly complicated treasury operation, clashed with Ladenburg, whose style was completely different from his – Bone loathed Ladenburg and did not mince his words. It was a shambles and there was a complete lack of harmony. Things got so bad for Richard Gordon, who was responsible for capital markets and under a lot of pressure, that he led a revolt against Ladenburg. During a trip to Japan, Bischoff and Solandt addressed the issue with Solandt having the unpleasant task of having to relieve Ladenburg of his position leaving Caldecott and Gordon jointly in charge. Caldecott, who managed to survive the situation, was in the meanwhile building up the stockbroking team from 20 to 120 staff with a view to conducting a domestic brokerage business. The application for membership of the Tokyo Stock Exchange was accepted at the end of 1987 and trading commenced in June 1988. It was a boom market and the business managed to more than cover its costs until 1990 when the bear market started. Caldecott handed over to Tak Murakami and returned to London where he remained in charge of the Japanese business. Gordon and Bone were still in Tokyo running capital markets and structured products. In the meanwhile on his return to London with no managerial position open to him Ladenburg was asked to prepare a paper on Schroders' strategy for France. As this did not lead to him being put in charge of its implementation he left the bank. It was a sad end to what had initially been a sparkling career.

In early 1988 Strickland employed a head hunter to find a new chief executive for

Schroder Securities. Richard Watkins, who had spent seven years at Kleinwort Benson doing project finance in South America and Australia followed by five years stockbroking in New York with Phillips & Drew and then with Hoare Govett, was interviewed by Strickland, Mallinckrodt and Bischoff and then hired. The fact that he had been to Wellington apparently was an asset. He did not meet anyone in Schroder Securities or Solandt. He was asked to prepare a business plan to show how the business could be made profitable, including a plan concerning the tolerance of losses. There was indecision regarding the relationship with Wertheim under Harmon in New York, Capital Markets under Slee and Corporate Finance under Broadbent and no interest by these parties to integrate as Schroder Securities was felt to lack professionalism. He found a well developed and well structured business under the management of Caldecott and Gordon in Japan with a seat on the Tokyo Stock Exchange – it was ambitious, expensive and the core part of the business. The Asian team under Richard Witts had offices in Hong Kong and Singapore but had a confused relationship with a spectacularly successful business in Seoul under YT Kim. The European team had no leader and the UK team was the weakest of all. There was no securities culture and no linking strategy between the four units which were all acting independently. Watkins was particularly shocked by this. The biggest flaw was that the Japanese and Asian businesses which represented 80% of the business were operating in markets which were about to enter the most severe bear market that anyone had ever seen and would continue so for the next 13 years – the Nikkei 225 index fell from 38,916 at the end of 1989 to 8579 in 2002. At the same time there were bull markets in Europe and the UK but no real capability to exploit them.

Watkins saw his main task as being to bring together all the parties – Securities, Corporate Finance and Capital Markets – into an integrated whole and to develop the weak areas in the UK. He found Strickland to be the only person with a far-sighted view of the business, anticipating that it would be developed on the New York model, and was the most supportive. Bischoff was keen to see the business functional but Watkins was not sure if he saw it as an insurance policy or a real strategy. Mallinckrodt clearly saw the business as necessary but was constantly nervous of its potential downside. Slee, although initially reluctant to give up his improving and stronger capital markets business, when he saw how essential it was to the future success of Securities he was very supportive. The investment management directors were extremely friendly, with Sedgwick and Hill going out of their way to use Schroder Securities whenever it was competitive. Corporate Finance were less ready to see a joint role, seeing themselves as being one of the top three in the UK whereas Schroder Securities were struggling to be in the top 15. Schroders was also slow to move from a relationship to a transaction culture.

The biggest weakness was the inability to integrate with Wertheim. In Watkins' view, Wertheim never had any intention of integrating, as the partners would have undermined the value of their shareholding in Wertheim Schroder. He found them good on their own patch with very able people but totally incompatible with Schroders in London. They were chiefly interested in the middle markets including the 'rust belt', i.e. traditional manufacturing industries including metal bashing and engineering companies. They had the capability to move upmarket but were not interested. Watkins therefore put a foreign team into Wertheim's offices in New York, Paris and Geneva. The latter two offices and the Wertheim offices in London were effectively franchises with the heads, Hugues Lamotte, Pierre Bottinelli and Paul Ruddock getting 45% of the revenues as commissions and as a result making vast sums of money for themselves.

By the end of 1990 a more organised structure was put in place for Securities, including a very effective capital markets team under Sauvary and Williams, a good syndicate team under Conor Killeen and a good European research team under Sarah Lavers. The losses of £9 million in 1987 and 1988 had been reversed into a profit of £500,000 in 1990. Staff including the acquisition of 32 from Capital Markets had increased from 203 to 303. When the Iraqis invaded Kuwait, the markets stopped trading and business became extremely difficult. A few staff were laid off and there was much concern whether Schroders could compete. Watkins felt this was the time to move from the third tier to the second tier through an acquisition or major expansion seeing it as a great opportunity if people were prepared to hold their nerve. The problem was that Corporate Finance did not know how to deal with Europe, how much resource to put in or how to manage it. Schroder Securities was stronger in Europe than in the UK.

At the same time the Japanese business was becoming a drag, having peaked in 1989. The high cost base in Europe became a problem and the lack of integration with Corporate Finance made life very complicated. Things were not helped by Bischoff having no involvement in New York, which was Mallinckrodt's responsibility. The business was going nowhere and Watkins, although delightful, was a poor manager and not a market man – clearly he had insufficient experience to develop and manage the business and had not brought in good people. There were also two underwritings of Spanish construction companies, which went sour and proved expensive. He therefore lost the confidence of Schroders and his colleagues. Watkins, who probably saw the writing on the wall, felt very pressurised and decided to quit in March 1992 to set up his own brokerage business. Sauvary and Caldecott were put jointly in charge under an executive committee chaired by Broadbent with MacAndrew, Barry Tarasoff and Bud Morten, respectively head of research and head of US equities at Wertheim. The securities business chugged along with Asia becoming weaker, the markets being too small to support the costs. The main issues to be addressed were: Would the Japanese market recover and become viable? With the Wertheim relationship not working should Schroders take full control by buying the remaining 50%? How would Corporate Finance deal with distribution with the UK securities business being so small?

Ivan Sedgwick had joined Schroder Securities in 1989 from Morgan Stanley, where he was doing stockbroking in Japanese securities. He was hired to sell Japanese equities to UK institutions in London. The Japanese market was booming and it was Schroders' biggest and most profitable market. Sedgwick had met Bischoff before joining and had asked him if he was committed to the idea of integrated investment banking. 'He looked at me with those steely blue eyes and said he was. What he failed to mention was that the rest of the management did not share his vision.' In 1992 he was moved to the European business and asked by Broadbent to develop a viable plan. Following a very detailed and exhaustive review of the plan with Broadbent, it was presented to the GEC for approval. At the same time Tarantelli had found that most of the money earned on privatisation business in Italy was going to the distributors rather than the advisors. If he was to succeed he needed a distribution capability. Sedgwick's plan was therefore adopted for Italy but rejected for the rest of Europe, for which there appeared to be no commitment or acceptable management.

With nothing to do in Europe, Sedgwick was sent to New York to help in improving the working relationship. His reception by Morten and his views of the atmosphere there was described in Chapter 8. He observed that no investment had been made in the business and so Wertheim totally missed out on the highly lucrative and booming IPO market in the 1980s and 1990s. Schroders' understanding of the position at Wertheim was clearly non-existent in London. At the same time Schroders was wrestling with the decision whether to buy out the Wertheim partners and take complete control. Terms were delayed due to the Ames litigation.

The cost of Schroders' abortive efforts to develop a securities business in Europe and Asia up to 1994 has been estimated by those involved to have been of the order of £100 million and there was virtually nothing to show for it.

NOTES:

1. After successfully managing funds for Jacob Rothschild, Nick Roditi went on to manage the Quota fund for George Soros. This hedge fund was aimed at achieving absolute as opposed to relative returns and could go long as well as short and also be leveraged with debt. Through the brilliance of his management Roditi established an enormous personal reputation for making vast sums of money for his clients and for himself. He learnt a lot at Schroders and made many friends whom he still sees. He said Hill was a wonderful man manager and a fine investor, de Havilland the best trader Schroders ever had with 'balls of brass' and Merner the master of the small Japanese companies with an encyclopaedic knowledge of Japanese equities. Hill said Roditi was a tremendous wheeler-dealer but a bad picker of stocks and best when trading in currencies and interest rates with nerves of steel.

2. The banking team responsible for lending to America, Australia and Japan (Asia) as well as the UK christened itself the AAA team.

CHAPTER 12

CREATING SHAREHOLDER VALUE

1985 – 1995

Peter Sedgwick, the new head of Investment Management, had joined Schroders in 1969 at the age of 34. The annual profit of Investment Management that year was only £1 million. Generally it barely broke even relying heavily on the skills of John de Havilland, who in one year had made £2 million by buying gilts in large volumes for Schrovest with money borrowed at 3.6% net of tax and selling them at 4.5%, thereby making a tax free capital gain of 0.9%. After ten years as a commercial banker with the Ottoman Bank in Southern Rhodesia, Sudan and Cyprus, it was taken over by Grindlays who sent Sedgwick to manage the Gulf States. He found himself in danger of becoming a permanent expatriate – with young children and not liking the people at Grindlays, he decided to resign and with no job was out in the cold. He answered an advertisement from Schroders and was seen by Airlie who said, 'We don't know what we are going to do with you but think we should offer you something.' Having a commercial banking background, he was given a low salary and a low level job in Investment Management. On his first day he went to see Lord Chelsea, the adminis-trative manager, who remained on the telephone to his racing trainer for the next 15 minutes before sending him down to the third floor to see Colin Leach, the head of the research department. Not knowing where to go he asked where he should hang his coat and in due course found Leach, who sat him in the corner of the research depart-ment for three months. He was then transferred to John White and sat opposite David Mumford, who over the next eight years taught him how to manage pension funds, gradually handing over some of the clients. One of his clients was IBM with £20 million under management. In November 1974, Popham told him to put it all into equities. Within two months the market had doubled and Sedgwick's name was made. In 1982 he was fortunate to be appointed a director, as there was a split vote among the direc-tors with Popham casting his vote for Sedgwick.

In late 1984 with the business taking off, Mercury Asset Management (MAM) was floated on the London Stock Exchange and established a very large market value. Investment Management was not even incorporated, unlike most of its competitors – Govett had raised the matter earlier in the year with Popham but had been rejected. Sedgwick and his colleagues saw the need for the investment management business to be incorporated and separated from Schroder Wagg if it was to expand in the market. The main arguments were: to avoid growing potential conflicts of interest with stockbroking, market making and new issues; the need to appoint many new directors to take on the extra work and the management of clients; and to follow the practice of the main competitors. Sedgwick had considerable opposition from the board, particularly from Solandt, who was worried about the adverse impact on Schroder Wagg's balance sheet with a loss of the substantial client cash deposits held in Investment Management. Sedgwick fought his corner with considerable strength of purpose and it took him two years to gain the agreement of the board. He also argued that if Investment Management was an independent and a stand-alone business it would be far easier to sell, should Schroders wish to do so without an adverse impact on the remainder of the business. His hand was considerably strengthened by his having been appointed head of Investment Management through the intervention of his colleagues, since this gave him an extremely secure power base. Had he not secured this agreement he could well have sought independence through a form of UDI and would have received the support of his colleagues. Schroder Investment Management Ltd (SIM) was incorporated in 1987, moving to new premises in Old Jewry and then to Gutter Lane. At the same time John Govett was appointed deputy chief executive of SIM in charge of investment policy.

Sedgwick ran SIM as a business with a tight control on costs with no opulence and the minimum amount of space. Remuneration was improved but contained and everyone knew exactly where he or she stood. The struggle to achieve competitive rewards for SIM employees took a lot of effort and time. Eventual success was vital to keep together the excellent team of fund managers that had been built up. Govett was heavily involved in this process, often having to make the case to Bischoff and others. This was a constant problem involving periodic battles over the next ten years (see below). Sedgwick had a strong management team: Govett, his deputy, responsible for investment policy and research; Hill for Japan and the Pacific; Josiane Pain for Europe; Niven for UK pensions; and Roger Hills for private clients. They were supported by Ponsonby, Baker Wilbraham and Mumford with their strong client relationships. All these directors were completely trusted and given a good deal of freedom of action and knowing exactly where they stood there were no misunderstandings between them. They were all hungry to succeed and as a result built an institution, which created great value for the Schroder group. Whereas investment banking businesses were valued at a multiple of 7 to 8 times earnings, investment management was valued at 20 times earnings or 2% to 3% of its funds under management. (The greater multiple was due to the stability and reliability of the earnings compared with investment banking where profits were highly volatile.) SIM was therefore quickly able to establish an independent value from the remainder of the bank from which it became clear that it was the most valuable asset in the Group. With funds under management growing from £10 billion in the mid-1980s to £75 billion in the mid-1990s they fuelled the huge rise in the share price, supported the cost of Corporate Finance and provided extra liquidity to the Treasury operations. By 1996 SIM was a very similar size to MAM in terms of funds under management, and its profitability on a properly adjusted basis steadily increased until it was also comparable. The market capitalisation of MAM thus gave valuable evidence both to the directors of SIM and to Schroders of how important SIM had become. It could be, and indeed was, argued that SIM alone accounted for all the £2 billion goodwill within the £3 billion market capitalisation of Schroders. During this period SIM together with MAM drew away from their peer group of merchant banks such as NM Rothschild, Morgan Grenfell and Hill Samuel and dominated the market.

Sedgwick had become a sound investor. He had good common sense and was popular with his colleagues and staff and the clients. He could also take tough decisions when needed. In October 1987, when the market fell by 40%, Sedgwick came down, like Popham before him, and addressed all the senior management of SIM with instructions to buy as many good quality stocks as were available. It was a brave decision although it could not be fully exploited as there was very little liquidity. 1987 was an extraordinary year for UK equities. The market rose nearly 20% in the first five or six weeks, and at this stage it was already looking quite expensive. Suggestions that liquidity was gradually built up as the market continued to rise so as to have money to put back in on a meaningful setback, were rejected and so when the crash came SIM had very little cash to invest. Despite this, with the reversal of the market, Schroders' performance went through the roof and helped to cement the long and good track record from the mid-1970s to the late 1980s. SIM's performance had been fairly average between 1983 and 1987 and funds under management were fairly static, with the boutiques, like MIM, Britannia and Henderson Administration, gaining market share. After the crash they were seen to be a bit too go-go and too risky which led to the pension funds reverting to the traditional virtues of SIM, which had made a big thing about the importance of the value of stocks. 1988 was a brilliant year and, after not having secured any new accounts for some time, SIM started to win new clients again, commencing with £15 million from Llanelli Radiators. Thereafter new accounts were won every month. Over a 20-year period performance was below the median in only two years and the rolling three- and five-year records were consistently above median and often in the upper quartile. Funds under management steadily grew and took off in the early 1990s. The pension fund market became a big business and many pension funds became larger than the companies' capitalisation. This lead to greater competition with pension fund managers being prepared to change their investment managers on the advice of the consultants. Due to Schroders' formidable track record it was at an advantage in securing more business. Funds under management grew almost exponentially and, combined with a roaring bull market, the profits of SIM rose in 1995 to just under £100 million.

Govett was responsible for investment policy, and for the UK pension fund clients this was set by the Asset Allocation Committee under his chairmanship – policy for other clients was required to be consistent with this. In UK equities, which represented as much as 60% of the UK pension fund portfolios – which in turn represented 70% of SIM's funds under management – policy from 1986 onwards was set by the Green Committee (so called because its minutes were printed on green paper) chaired by

Govett. As SIM's UK equity performance had fallen in 1984 and 1985 largely through the collapse of a small number of holdings that had previously soared and had been allowed to stay in the portfolio with much too high a weighting, Govett formed the committee to set a much more disciplined framework for UK equity selection. BSR, a small electronics company, was an example having risen by 300% and represented over 4% of the UK equities holdings in some portfolios before collapsing and later going bust. Govett chose for the Green Committee what he saw to be the best UK fund managers including particularly Jim Cox, Ronnie Eyres, Jim Horsburgh and Humphry van der Klugt with Nicola Ralston representing the research department. They introduced a whole range of portfolio risk controls, prescribed stock weightings and separate focus on large, medium and small stocks, that today are commonplace but which at the time were groundbreaking. Govett also introduced bases of stock comparison such as enterprise value to sales, which are now mainstream, but were then entirely new.

> These new approaches and disciplines had the desired result of both improving investment performance and avoiding maverick bad performance. It went down well with the consultants, giving them peace of mind that Schroders would never have a really bad year and, when we had a good year, all our client portfolios would participate in that success. This was the principal building block for the large market share of new business achieved through the late 1980s and early 1990s.

> This structure, with a number of further refinements over the years, worked remarkably well. It still gave scope for individual managers to use their own judgement, but it reduced the risk of anyone performing really badly. The style of management, with small groups fully accountable for their decisions, was very effective for pension fund management. It was before a more disciplined approach became the norm in the City. Schroders led the way in the UK in introducing professional disciplines to portfolio management and this played a key part in the rapid subsequent accumulation of new business. 'Good performance had always been a *sine qua non* of a successful investment management house, but from the mid-1980s consultants played an increasingly important role in fund manager selection and they came to realise that the way performance was achieved mattered. They looked to see whether performance was volatile and whether there was a wide dispersion of performance within a house.'

Cox, whose Enterprise Fund was one of the most successful in the City, chaired the Green Committee in Govett's absence and said,

> We met weekly and agreed and issued instructions regarding the weightings in the largest companies. Keith and Nicola focused on the process looking at large, medium and small companies. These instructions were not to be rigidly applied but used as guidance. John's basic policy was that the fundamentals of a business will always come out in the share price and so stocks were picked which appeared to be undervalued

in this respect, no differentiation being made between growth and value stocks. We appear to have made the right decisions on the big stocks and the big sectors. Sometimes mistakes were made. John felt that British Telecom at its privatisation was over valued and SIM did not buy a lot. The market however saw it differently and SIM suffered, despite John being right!

Cox had joined SIM from Prudential in 1986, following Mick Newmarch becoming the chief executive. He had been recommended by Jim Findlay, his boss, who had discussed joining Schroders with Sedgwick but had decided to accept a partnership at Cazenoves instead. He was the only fund manager taken on under Sedgwick to have a beard – another candidate had been offered a job if he shaved off his beard which he accepted and duly arrived clean shaven. Sedgwick clearly could not risk a rejection from Cox! Commenting on the Pru under Newmarch, Cox said, 'there was too much nemesis following hubris – Schroders avoided the hubris.' Initially he worked as a UK pensions fund manager under Niven and did high-level investment research for Govett identifying recovery stocks. Before his arrival, SIM had had a few years of indifferent performance and he became associated with the turnaround. He was given £100,000 to start a unit trust fund and in twelve years the Enterprise Fund grew to £2 billion to become the largest fund in the country, with a good performance in ten of the twelve years. Another very successful fund manager was Andy Brough, a talented young accountant hired from Price Waterhouse, who ran the UK Smaller Companies Fund.

SIM became very successful and this transformed the morale. More and more money came pouring in. New people had to be hired and trained and others promoted to cope with the growth. SIM had grown organically from managing 1.2% of the UK equity market to 2.8%. Problems arose in managing this growth, as it was not appreciated that running a large business is not the same as running a small one. Although SIM took on larger and larger numbers of bright trainees from university they were increasingly wooed by competitors, as Schroders was known to provide an excellent grounding in fund management. As SIM became larger and more investment disciplines had to be imposed, the prospect of moving on to a smaller, more informal organisation became more appealing to the fund managers. To some extent in this type of business success has a tendency to sow the seeds of eventual failure. There was also an under-investment in technology in the quest for greater and greater profits. It was difficult to turn money away. Performance in the UK, Japan and South East Asia remained good until 1996. Europe and America were not so good. The problem was that Schroders became too big to change its positions quickly. Having a fund of £2 billion with 40 holdings meant that each was an average of £50 million, making it difficult to get out. There was a tendency not to deal.

Elsewhere, particularly in Japan, great strides were also being made. The SCMI business, which managed the overseas investments for US funds and had been set up in 1979, grew into a business of $40 billion by 1998. Sedgwick handed over its management to David Salisbury in 1984. The team comprising Richard Foulkes and Charles Tallents had the advantage of being one of the first companies into the market and within five years they achieved a fantastic performance and were able to demonstrate that in the middle and late 1980s their performance was always in the first quartile over every 1,2,3,4 and 5-year period. As a result there was an avalanche of clients. They managed the portfolio using the wider experience of SIM in London and around the world. In the end it became too much for Foulkes, Tallents having sadly died in the meanwhile, and David Salisbury was put in charge of the administration to the great relief of Foulkes.[1] In 1993 SIM, as the largest manager of foreign equities for US institutions, was given the Queen's Award for Export Achievement, the first ever to an institutional investment manager.

Hill's job in SIM after handing over SCMI to Sedgwick in 1982 was to oversee the investment management business in Japan and the Pacific with offices in most of the countries in the region. Most important of all was building a domestic fund management business in Japan and following receipt of a licence to establish an investment trust company the business grew enormously over the next 15 years. With the setting up of the Schroder Asia Securities, the representative office had been split in 1985 between investment management and securities, investment management being managed directly by SIM in London. As the rules changed Schroders secured a licence in 1987 to manage discretionary money in Japan – with Uyji Kudo being appointed president of SIM Japan – and this became a big business. Six years later, Peter Wolton, aged 35, was sent to Tokyo by Hill as head of the investment management business.[2]

As Kudo was in his fifties and had been president of SIM Japan for six years, Wolton had to develop an effective and harmonious working relationship. They agreed that Kudo would be the external face to the Japanese clients and Wolton the face to the foreigners. Wolton would run the overall business, which included a separate unit trust company, behind the scenes, giving Kudo the appropriate 'face'. Hill had seen the enormous potential of the Japanese pension fund market and the benefit of bringing in head office experience and importing best practice to Japan. SIM did particularly well as Wolton was the only foreign asset manager with head office experience running such a business in Tokyo, the competitors relying solely on Japanese. Of course to be successful one had to be good and SIM had the advantage of considerable experience in investing in Japanese equities, established over a long period. The key investors were Merner, who had joined Hill 20 years earlier, Denis Clough, 'the real hero', and Hiromi Fukuda, both of whom were good team players. Merner, by instinct a small company man was finding it increasingly difficult to work in an ever-expanding company – SIM had decided to be a large manager of funds – and therefore decided to part company amicably in 1995. It was the right decision for both parties although a sad one. Wolton returned to London in 1998 having seen the business mushroom, pension assets managed on a discretionary basis having increased from 40 billion yen in 1993 to 1032 billion yen in 1998 and Schroders' position rising from seventeenth to fourth below IBJ, Nomura and Nissay.

Bruno Schroder

Win Bischoff

Gowi Mallinckrodt

Gordon Richardson

Michael Verey

John Hull

Jim Wolfensohn

David and Ginny Airlie at Cortachy Castle

John Bayley

Leslie Murphy

THE CORPORATE FINANCIERS

Geoffrey Williams

Francis Cator

Philip Robinson, Schroder's mandarin

Hugh Ashton

Adam and Sara Broadbent

David Challen

Nicholas Jones leading in a mare and foal at Newmarket

THE CORPORATE FINANCIERS

Nigel Saxby-Soffe in Co. Mayo, Ireland

Gerry Grimstone

Derek Netherton

Bill Harrison

THE CORPORATE FINANCIERS

Gina Scheck

Alison Carnwath

Patrick Drayton

Guy Harington

THE MALLINCKRODT TEAM

Ben Strickland

Nick MacAndrew

Raymond Badrock

Andrew Gaulter and the Company Secretary's team

THE MALLINCKRODT TEAM

David Morris

David Caruth at Ascot

Richard Sadleir

Sue Cox

SCHROBANCO

Jack Connor

Mark Maged

SCHRODER WERTHEIM

Jim Harmon

Steve Kotler

THE MONEY MAKERS

Jean Solandt

Andrew Sykes

Richard Bown

Lester Gray

SCHRODERS JAPAN

Jeremy Hill

Nick Roditi at Pansanjan Falls
in the Philippines

The opening of the Tokyo office in 1974 with Ed Merner, Matt Snyder, David Airlie, Peter Bulfield,
Jeremy Hill, Win Bischoff, Michael Verey, Jim Wolfensohn and Burgis Coates

THE INVESTMENT MANAGERS

Gordon Popham

John de Havilland at Bisley retaining the long range
rifle championship, 1981

The Happy Hookahs: Tony Asseily and Richard Foulkes having a quiet smoke
in Beirut before the war, 1975

THE INVESTMENT MANAGERS

Peter Sedgwick

Rosalind and John Govett at Goodwood Races

THE INVESTMENT MANAGERS

David Salisbury

Keith Niven

Hugh Bolland, Brian Wood and Josiane Pain with Bryn Tyfel, the Welsh bass
baritone, whom SIM sponsored for a season before he became internationally known

Bill Slee

Anthony Loehnis

Tyo van Marle

Stephen Brisby

THE CAPITAL MARKETEERS

Paul Sauvary

Andrew Williams

SCHRODER SECURITIES

Richard Watkins

Rupert Caldecott

THE LENDERS

David Forsyth

Tony Lesser

Michael Ladenburg

Bernard Barham

John Rock

SCHRODERS A.G. ZURICH

Erik Gasser

Ernest Ingold

Max Zeller

THE PROJECT FINANCIERS

Bernard Dewe Mathews cooking at Ballymaloe

George Wadia among his books

Philip Robinson

John Burnham

THE PROJECT FINANCIERS

DIRECTORS AND SPOUSES PLANNING MEETING 1996

Read Gomm, Michael Sutcliffe, Philip Robinson, Diana Wadia, Lyn Robinson, Annie Sutcliffe, John Burnham, Titine Freely, Chris Houston, Jean Burnham, Chris Ewbank (hidden), Andrew Brandler, Dominic Freely, Bernard Dewe Mathews, George Wadia, Jill Houston

THE VENTURE CAPITALISTS

Michael Bentley

Nick Ferguson

The Managing Directors of Schroder Ventures, (*from left*) Thomas Matzen, (Michael Drew), Nobuo
Matsuki, Gordon Bryn, Jon Moulton, Nick Ferguson, Jeff Collinson

SCHRODERS IN ASIA

ASIA PACIFIC EXECUTIVE CONFERENCE
(*clockwise from near left*) Ian Boyce, Peter Mason, Arthur Charles, Nick MacAndrew, Torquil McAlpine,
Adam Broadbent, Tony Tanaka, Anil Thadani, Khoo Siew Bee, Robin Tomlin

Mark Hopkinson   Jenny Lau   Nifty Lim

Retirement after 28 years service, both joined
Schroders in 1970 as secretaries to the Managing Directors
of Schroders & Chartered and SIMBL

SCHRODERS AUSTRALIA

Michael Gleeson-White

Richard Griffin

Peter Mason and Arthur Charles

THE INVESTMENT BANKERS

Will Samuel

Richard Broadbent

Robert Swannell

Panfilo Tarantelli

THE INVESTMENT BANKERS

Philip Augar

Barry Tarasoff

Ruth Sack

Gowi and Charmaine Mallinckrodt with their family, including
Bruno Schroder, his daughter Leonie and his mother Marga Schroder

Win, Rosemary, Christopher and Charlie Bischoff outside Buckingham Palace
after Win received his knighthood from HM the Queen

During his five years in Japan, Wolton had received superb support from London. 'Jeremy was a terrific man manager who backed his staff and gave the freedom to operate but knew that they would come to him if they had a problem and receive wise counsel.' He found Bischoff,

> the most charismatic person to work for. The Japanese clients just loved seeing him. Being one of only two foreign members of the exclusive 300 Club reserved for the three hundred most eminent Japanese golfers, needless-to-say he went down very well. He flew out for a day to give a speech on the Britannia which enormously impressed the Japanese.

Towards the end of the 1980s de Havilland was spending an increasing amount of his time on Fuel Tech, a venture in California, and decided to retire at the beginning of 1990. Thinking he was now free after 30 years he was persuaded to become chairman of the National Rifle Association. He had been in the National VIII for each of the last thirty years, never accomplished by anyone else since – it required shooting for a place each year and he made top score into the bargain. He was passionately keen on shooting and, 'by a Wednesday it was a black week which was not brightened by the prospect of shooting somewhere or other on the Saturday whether with a gun or rifle.' His extraordinary abilities with a rifle must have had something to do with Schroders as he said, 'after I retired I never shot straight again (with a rifle).' He was not alone in Investment Management in being a good shot. Bruno, in memory of his father who had died the year previously, gave a Silver Pheasant as a trophy to be presented to the winner of a shooting competition to be held annually from 1970 between the members of the Acceptance Houses Committee. De Havilland organised the competition every year, at which between ten and thirteen banks competed. Schroders was represented by a four-man team comprising Baker Wilbraham, Hill, de Havilland and someone from Corporate Finance. Having won the trophy three years in succession they decided it would look better if they tried to win it only every other year!

On Hugh Bolland's return from Sydney in 1990 (see Chapter 18) he was made chairman of Schroder Unit Trusts in which Clive Boothman and Rod Duncan were the managing and marketing directors. In 1989, the year the unit trusts were relaunched, they received the accolade of 'Unit Trust Manager of the Decade' from Micropal, the leading statistical authority to the unit trust industry. Within three years they were making large profits not least because they had the right products to sell on the back of the good performance of the fund managers. Earlier Bolland had been asked to make presentations to the mounting list of new clients wishing to get SIM to manage their pension funds, as everyone else was so busy. With the successes he was well placed to take over the pension fund business in 1993 when Niven became ill through pressure of work. There followed four golden years in which the institutional business expanded with ever increasing profits. Although Niven later recovered to play an important role as chairman of the Unit Trusts business, sadly his very considerable talent was never used as fully as had once seemed likely.

In July 1992, The Wellcome Trust sold a third of its shareholding in Wellcome plc for £2.3 billion – the largest ever non-government international share sale. Sir Roger Gibbs, the chairman, asked Schroders to look after the entire sum until the end of 1992. This was following a lengthy conversation he had had earlier with his first cousin, Sir Ashley Ponsonby, about every detail of Schroders' short- and long-term track record as well as about the key people in the investment side of Schroders. Gibbs had similar conversations with other investment houses both inside and outside the City. He came to the conclusion that Schroders and in particular Govett should advise The Wellcome Trust. Today he says that was one of the best investment decisions he ever made.

Gibbs hardly knew Bischoff but he telephoned him to formalise the arrangement. Bischoff made himself available within the hour. 'He was friendly not effusive, decisive and helpful. He delegated to his colleagues and ensured that everything went smoothly from that moment on – an ace professional'.

Gibbs went to see Govett and with his detailed knowledge of the fixed interest market, and on this occasion being exceptionally bullish, he suggested to Govett that, in the immediate term, a substantial amount of one year CDs and a broad spread of gilts should be purchased. Govett wholeheartedly agreed that the fixed interest market was going to move much higher but persuaded Gibbs that if this was to happen, equities would do even better – maybe spectacularly well. In the summer of 1992, the FTSE 100 index moved between 2180 and 2320. By 15 September Govett had invested 94% of the £2.3 billion for the long term. On 15 September interest rates were raised by 2% on no less than three occasions during the day. These decisions completely failed to convince the market place. The interest rate rises were reversed and sterling fell sharply as the UK withdrew from the European Monetary Union. Within a week, equities had gone through the roof and by the end of December (FTSE 100 index 2847), the Wellcome funds invested by Govett had risen by 25%. Gibbs, and indeed all the Governors of The Wellcome Trust, say they owe a great debt of gratitude to Govett.

With a total portfolio now valued at almost £4 billion, Schroders helped The Wellcome Trust interview potential investment managers. The Wellcome share sale had attracted worldwide publicity and, as a result, 245 investment firms approached the Trust to look after their funds. Schroders and the Trust narrowed this field down to 50, then Schroders reduced it further to 30 – all of these were interviewed over a period of five days. The panel consisted of Gibbs, his co-lay governor, Sir Peter Cazalet, two brilliant scientific governors – the deputy chairman, Sir Stanley Peart and Sir Julian Jack, and Ian MacGregor, the key financial man at the Trust. When it came to Govett being interviewed,

the debate was lively but obviously friendly. He should not have been, but being the modest fellow he is, John was very anxious about the outcome. He was particularly so after Peart asked him how large his immediate team was and how long they had been working together. John said there were eight of them and they had been working together for 14 years. 'My God, you must be so bored with each other!' retorted Stanley. John was hoping against hope that Schroders would be allocated as much as £750 million of the Trust's portfolio. In fact they were given £1 billion and performed exceptionally well until John retired in 1996.

Apart from the redevelopment of the unit trust business and the development of a fund management business in Japan, most of the initiatives for new business had been set in place under Popham (see Chapter 2). Sedgwick's main achievement was to build on the heritage left by Popham and through Govett introduce a new professionalism to the business. He did not make many changes and resisted pressure following the 1995 strategic review to build a private banking business. Bill Slee, with the support of Boston Consulting Group, prepared a feasibility study setting out the merits of setting up a new division to target high net worth individuals around the world bringing together the expertise of the private clients team under Hills in SIM for equity portfolio management and the private bankers in Zurich and London for banking services. To succeed it required a new head as Hills was felt to be too junior. Slee felt it should come under von Elten, a former private banker, who was the chairman of the board of management of Schroders AG based in Zurich. Sedgwick rejected the proposal, arguing that private banking was meaningless and the private clients business of SIM was very successful making profits of £10 million a year. Hills and John Henderson were happy to continue to develop their essentially UK business with much of the new business coming from introductions from accountants and solicitors. Being very protective of SIM and fiercely independent and loyal to his colleagues, Sedgwick probably did not want to find himself losing control of such an expanded business to others. As private clients was a minor business, entirely dependent on SIM for its systems and services, and as SIM was focused on institutional business, SIM did not adapt its systems or invest in new systems more appropriate to private clients and so the business was not able to respond to the rapidly changing private banking market.

One of the most important initiatives of Sedgwick and Govett was to develop for SIM a more competitive remuneration structure. They were keen to retain good staff and attract new staff by finding ways of giving key employees, at both director and below director level, remuneration that was both competitive and linked to profitability, but which also had an element of deferral to discourage departure. Explaining the actions they took Govett said

The senior executive share option scheme of 1986 was confined in SIM's case to a handful of senior directors (see Chapter 19). By 1992 a Long Term Incentive Plan (LTIP) was introduced for SIM, but again initially it was restricted to only 15 people, rising fairly quickly to 25. The LTIP set aside a proportion of the amount by which each year's profit exceeded a base target for release to the participants on a rolling five-year cycle. Due to the strong bull market, combined with good performance, the scheme yielded much higher rewards than had been anticipated, albeit way below the equivalent rewards going to SIM's main competitor MAM. Mallinckrodt was very unhappy and quickly started to tinker with the base profit hurdle, which caused widespread resentment. Once people's trust had been lost, it became virtually impossible to regain it. As the GCC was now not prepared to extend the LTIP across a sufficiently wide number of executives, a simpler system of partial deferral of the annual bonus was by 1996 extended to 109 people. Together with the then 57 members of the LTIP, 166 people out of a combined UK and overseas staff at SIM of 1163 had some form of deferred remuneration, still well behind the 300 staff MAM had achieved.

The irony was that, whereas in many organisations the top directors are guilty of retaining too much of the rewards to themselves, within SIM the senior directors were fighting to spread rewards wider, an essential strategy if the business was to continue to grow. A further irony was the fact that in Corporate Finance, where share options continued to form a major part of the remuneration package, the full undiluted rewards of SIM's success flowed through to the employees from the rising share price, without the GCC being able to tinker with the terms.

Sedgwick was seen by all his directors to be a good chairman, letting them all do their own thing. He was robust in the support of his directors and staff and prevented any interference by the board members. He was a strong leader and never in doubt of what he wanted and was often heard to say, 'if I have to choose between intelligence and common sense, give me common sense any time'. However, when he handed over to his loyal and brilliant deputy Govett in 1996 and relocated to Cheapside, his former colleagues were disappointed to see him switch his allegiances away from SIM to Mallinckrodt.

Those leading Corporate Finance, with whom there had been a certain amount of friction, felt he was very straightforward although not reflective, with a common-sense approach to business, and had kept SIM simple and very disciplined and done a first-class job. He had ruled with a rod of iron and was a slight bully. He had made good decisions, many of them being intuitive but had made no serious changes to the business. They also found him very defensive of his business, becoming increasingly divorced from the rest of the Group. Some found it difficult to have a rational conversation with him, particularly concerning people he had made up his mind about. Maybe their views were coloured by his exceptionally successful performance and irritation at complaints he often made that their increasing demands for bonuses were having to be funded by SIM's superior profitability (see Chapter 19).

Whatever was said against him, when he left SIM it was one of the largest and most respected investment houses in the City, by far the most profitable part of the Group and more than half Schroders' stock market value. The funds under management had risen seven-fold from £10 billion in 1984 to £74 billion in 1995 and profits before tax nine-fold from under £10 million to £93 million. During the same period the FTSE All Share index had increased three-fold from 593 to 1803.

NOTES:

1. Richard Foulkes spent the remainder of his career on the SCMI business but gave up when Salisbury became chief executive of SIM in 1996. He kept a foot in the market while running Europe and finally went back to managing the funds of his largest client Vanguard, which by that time amounted to $10 billion (from an initial fund of $25 million 1982). Looking back Hill said Foulkes was one of Schroders' most successful investors, along with Popham, de Havilland, Govett, Merner, and Ronnie Eyres – modestly omitting his own name.

2. Peter Wolton had joined SIM ten years earlier having spent five years at Savills buying commercial property for pension funds. He worked under Niven, 'the coming man with a terrific reputation for looking after clients and gaining new clients', dealing with the institutions. He noticed that there might be an opportunity for Schroders to become the largest charity fund manager and therefore set up two dedicated funds – one common investment fund for fixed interest and another for equities. As the Charity Commission regulated these funds, outside trustees were appointed. The business grew fast and was a great success. It was probably because of this that he was noticed and sent to Japan.

CHAPTER 13

NOTHING VENTURED ---

1984 - 1993

M ichael Bentley might not have come up to original expectations as a potential successor to Airlie but he left Schroders with the beginnings of a major new business – venture capital, or what was to become known as private equity. It was he who decided that Schroders should get into venture capital and he received encouragement from Bischoff to do so. Venture capital had had a poor record at Schroders in the early 1970s under Bill Hyde, chiefly because it was staffed and managed by people without industrial experience (see Chapter 2). Bentley did not repeat this mistake. He turned to Nicholas Ferguson to help.[1]

Having done well in Singapore putting SIMBL on the map of South East Asia (see Chapter 17), Ferguson returned to London where he was been given responsibility for co-ordinating group marketing under Bentley. After a short period he said he wanted to build something that involved making profits. Bentley therefore asked Ferguson to explore the opportunities and discover what venture capital was all about and come up with a plan.

Ferguson was a great fan of Bentley finding him, despite his lack of diplomacy, to be bright and entrepreneurial, with the ability to see opportunities early and to make things happen. He also understood how to give someone his head but was always there to listen and to help and to give unequivocal help. He had already brought a US perspective to Schroders by introducing the concept of managing money through limited partnerships in the oil and gas and real estate businesses and had turned his mind to venture capital. David Walters, then with SIM, had invested successfully in the high tech boom in California in the early 1980s and it was agreed that he move there to work on private equity transactions for Schroders. Bentley suggested that Schroders set up a fund of funds limited partnership and find the best managers and funds to invest in – he was well ahead of the market. Unfortunately this was frustrated by Collinson, who was running a life sciences fund in New York. He said he was responsible for private equity in the States and that the fund of funds idea was crazy as it was far better to invest in deals directly. How misguided he was. As a result a trust was set up with Collinson responsible for the east coast and Walters the west. The Schroder Ventures Trust was set up at the end of 1983 with a fund of $58 million. The relationship between Collinson and Walters did not work out and Walters left.

In the meanwhile, Corporate Finance was occasionally coming up with investment ideas like Cullens and Edgely Aircraft and so Ferguson suggested that there might be opportunities in the UK and was given Michael Gwinnell, formerly from the Strategy Group, who had suggested Edgely Aircraft, as his assistant. Venture capital was in its infancy in the UK with very few participants: 3i, Electra, Candover and Citicorp Venture Capital (CVC). Ferguson went to see them all, asking whom they respected most outside their firm, and was pointed towards Jon Moulton, the head of CVC. Following a discussion with Moulton about Schroders' plans he suggested that he come and run the new business and shortly afterwards, having been interviewed by everyone, was hired as the managing partner in the middle of 1984. It was agreed that he would receive a salary and bonus like everyone else at Schroders and a proportion of the managers' share of the carried interest in the funds, with Schroders receiving all the management fees and responsibility for all the costs.

Moulton had run CVC for five years in the United States and London and therefore knew what the business was all about and how to manage it, including setting up all the accounting and control systems. Bentley encouraged him saying he was prepared to invest in success and provide the seed capital. After having considered and rejected many other more complicated alternatives, the name Schroder Ventures Advisers was adopted as the name of the UK partnership. The team was increased with Moulton hiring Andrew Marchant from Prudential Venture Managers, the private equity arm of Prudential, and then Charles Sherwood, the son of James Sherwood, a well known entrepreneur who owned Sea Containers and was a friend of Bischoff. Sherwood, who had been with Boston Consulting Group prior to receiving an MBA from Harvard, wrote in at the suggestion of Bischoff and was interviewed by Moulton and Marchant over lunch at the Savoy. That evening he received a job offer to join the partnership to make three. As his term at Harvard was finishing on a Friday, Moulton suggested he took some time off and start the following Monday. All his class friends at Harvard set off on a well-earned holiday but he had no regrets – none of them had been offered a partnership in an exciting, new, well-backed business.

Moulton had found a small office in Groveland Court behind Cheapside – its front door could be differentiated from the others by being the only one that was not a public house. Another early recruit was Veronica Eng from SIMBL (see Chapter 17) who, at 33, rejected Corporate Finance, Securities and the Far East desk of Investment Management for her old boss Ferguson. She was deeply impressed by Moulton, finding him different, very quick and entrepreneurial. He clearly knew the business and came from a very different background to the other people at Schroders. Peter Smitham completed the early team having been found through Whitehead Mann and interviewed by Moulton, Ferguson, Bentley, Govett and Bischoff. He had been with Jermyn, an electronics company, for the previous twelve years and was on the board of Murray Johnston. He therefore had an understanding of growing young businesses, technology and finance. During the 15 minutes Moulton gave him (longer than usual he said), they sat on a table, the room having no chairs. Smitham was impressed by his mixture of brilliance and wackiness. He was the key to Smitham's decision whether or not to join

Schroder Ventures. Ferguson was very young, enthusiastic and naïve – very much from a textbook clearly with no experience of venture capital. Bentley was direct, down-to-earth and penetrating in his highly relevant questions. Govett was charming, very smart and low key, questioning him on how he invested his own money.

By April 1985 Ferguson and Moulton had raised a UK Venture fund of £25 million, practically all of which came from the funds managed by SIM. Not long afterwards the Japan Venture Fund of Y315 billion was raised with Nobuo Matsuki, a friend of Ed Merner, Schroders' brilliant American investor in small Japanese companies, as the managing partner with Gartmore, SIM and its clients as the investors. Towards the end of the year, the deputy chairman of Prudential, who was a good friend of Bentley, said he wanted to invest in management buy-outs in the UK and would put up £25 million if Schroders could find £50 million. And so the first UK Buy-out fund of £75 million was closed in January 1986. In just over a year Schroders had four funds in three countries with $215 million of committed funds making it among the biggest private equity management groups in the world, the total amount being not much more than $2.5 billion. Having achieved this remarkable feat, Bentley decided to join Michael Stoddart at Electra as deputy chairman with a view to taking over from him. He realised that his prospects of becoming chairman of Schroders or Schroder Wagg had by then disappeared.

Before joining, Moulton sent Smitham his business plan and various investment proposals. He was impressed by Eng who was very quiet and found Marchant and Sherwood like young boys. The UK partnership was in two businesses: smaller ventures comprising start-ups, development capital and small buy-outs; and management buy-outs (MBO) comprising larger buy-outs and turnarounds. Smitham ran the ventures with Henry Simon, Sherwood, Marchant and Carl Parker and Moulton ran the MBOs with Eric Walters, Richard Winkles, Eng and Pam Scholes. Ferguson and Gwinnell as part of the Schroder Ventures Holdings (SVH) team never worked on deals, concentrating on the relationship with Schroders that they managed well. Their main concern was to grow the business, investor relations and new entities. They never focused on the performance of the funds.

The UK business took off and all deals were submitted to an Investment Committee, chaired by Ferguson and comprising Govett and the UK partners – Govett with his feel for the stock market made an important contribution to investment decisions. He did not speak much but when he did everyone stopped to listen.

Another important member of the Schroder Ventures team was Gordon Byrn, an old classroom friend of Ferguson from Harvard, who was from a prominent family in Vancouver in Canada.[2] Not long after Ferguson took on Schroder Ventures in 1985 he asked Byrn to become a consultant to him and Moulton and he started the Canadian fund, raising C$80 million which after ten years returned two and a half times its capital to its investors, one of the successes of Schroder Ventures. Of the 20 or so investments, fortunately the small ones failed rather than the big ones, most of which were successful. One of those was the Mitel Corporation, which was listed on the Toronto and London

Stock Exchanges with 51% of the shares owned by British Telecom that had for some time virtually ignored it as it withered. Byrn purchased BT's 40 million shares for C$1 each in 1987 and they were split between the UK and Canadian funds. Mitel was a manufacturer of telecommunications equipment and silicon chips for the telecommunications industry. Henry Simon, another partner of Moulton, had received a doctorate in telecommunications and been trained by Harold Geneen, the famous chairman of ITT, for 30 years before becoming a partner of Moulton in his fifties. He was responsible for a lot of the UK profits and was in the words of Byrn, 'highly respected, strong, independent-minded and charming but tough'. With Byrn becoming chairman of the Mitel board and devoting 30% of his time to the company and Simon becoming chairman of the executive committee, they changed the board and the senior management and introduced new management, a new strategy and new disciplines which led to a major turnaround enabling Schroders to sell its shares in stages at C$6 and C$8 per share in 1991. The shares later rose to C$49 at the height of the tech bubble in 1999 before falling back when it burst shortly afterwards.

As a managing partner Byrn was on the executive committee of SVH with Moulton and the other managing partners with Ferguson in the chair and so he had a good knowledge of the overall business and an ability to see things from the perspective of a successful managing partner of Canada as well as that of Schroders. With the complete trust and friendship of Ferguson, he was importantly able to act as a confidant of Ferguson.

Ivor O'Mahony, who had been in group financial control since 1973, becoming deputy financial controller of the Group under David Morris, joined SVH as finance director in 1988 and set up numerous funds starting with the first Italian venture fund of £50 million. Moulton was enormously helpful to O'Mahony in teaching him about the structuring of funds. 'He was the cleverest person I ever came across at Schroders with a very low boredom threshold – you had to get your point across very quickly.' Schroder Ventures had a highly complicated structure. SVH was owned by Schroders and it arranged a variety of funds which were financed by a number of limited partnerships established for tax purposes in Bermuda, Guernsey and Delaware in which a Schroder Venture management company, such as Schroder Ventures Managers Limited, was the general partner. Ferguson together with the country managing partner went to the investors to raise money that was to be invested by the advisors, on terms which included an annual management fee on the funds drawn down and a carried interest in the profits of investments sold. The country partnerships identified, evaluated and recommended investments to their investment committee, which was chaired by Ferguson and comprised the partners and these were recommended to the management committee which approved them on behalf of the relevant fund which drew down the money from the investors for the advisors to invest in the recommended investment. The investors originally paid an annual management fee of 2% and a carried interest of 20% on a deal-by-deal basis thereby carrying all losses but only 80% of all gains. Bell South Pension Fund, which invested in a whole succession of funds, gradually tightened up the commercial terms and was ever more demanding. By 1990 carries on a deal-by-deal basis were replaced by carries only being paid out after a hurdle rate, which could be as high as 8%, had been achieved on the total amount invested. The main investors at that time were Prudential of America, Wellcome Trust, Bell South Pension Fund and IBM. Other investors to follow included the California Public Employees Retirement Scheme (Calpers), the California State Teachers Retirement Scheme (Calstrs), General Motors Pension Fund and Metropolitan Life. All investments were financed by a combination of £1 of equity from the LBO fund and £2 of debt from a consortium of banks, principally the Bank of Scotland, NatWest Bank and Bankers Trust.

The UK partnership was well differentiated from the other venture capitalists in its market in that it never joined the venture capital club of Apax, Advent and Causeway Capital, all of whom participated in each others' deals and were members of the British Venture Capital Committee. This was primarily due to Moulton's personality who, apart from being like a bull in a china shop, thought such committees were a waste of time.

Most of the industry was dominated by accountants, many of whom had started at 3i and become disenchanted with their pay. Moulton, on the other hand, built up a team with people drawn from a variety of skills including: experienced industrialists such as Smitham, electronics, Richard Winckles from Laskys, part of Ladbrokes, Eric Walters from Grand Metropolitan, Henry Simon from ITT and Stewart Binnie from Hatchards; consultants adding Damon Buffini and Graham Wrigley to Marchant and Sherwood; and financiers adding Pam Scholes and Diana Noble to Eng. The industrialists had the ability to assess and run businesses, to develop plans on how to improve them and to grow the revenue and cut costs and generally sat on the boards of the companies invested in. The consultants knew how the industry worked within its market place and how the company was positioned in relation to its competitors. The financial people knew all about projections of sales and purchases and the legal and banking aspects. Ferguson was keen on hiring bright young graduates with first-class degrees but this was resisted by Moulton and Smitham who felt the partnership was too small to be able to afford to carry them while they learnt and favoured people in their late twenties with some relevant business experience.

Another characteristic which differentiated the UK partners was their strong streak of independence from Schroders and from each of the other country partnerships again because of Moulton's personality but also due to the nature of the business and that the other offices were in cities where there was little if any Schroder presence. Each partnership was motivated by its own performance and was entirely domestic. The only glue was the common name and Ferguson, who continually struggled to create a collegiate feeling.

The final differentiator was that the partners all worked on deals irrespective of type (start up or MBO) or industry (restaurants, biotech or newspapers) as generalists rather than specialists. Over time there was a shift from the generalist and one man team to teams of six with multi-skills, all understanding the deal overall but each partner having great depth of expertise in his or her own area. There was also an increasing focus on a narrower set of industries, venture capital concentrating on technology and healthcare with MBOs being pursued opportunistically in any industry. In the end venture capital was dropped entirely with more focus on sectors and types of business particularly MBOs and MBIs. The other change in business practice was seeking to change the business through value creation rather than simply changing the balance sheet by financial arbitraging. The two key transactions that led to this were Parker Pen and Glass Glover.

The most spectacular success of Moulton and his partners was the purchase of The Parker Pen Company in 1985 from Manpower when it was losing £20 million a year and selling it to Gillette seven years later when it was making profits of £43 million a year. They made a profit on the sale of £90 million on an investment of £10 million. The turnaround was accomplished by reducing the head office in America from 110 people to 2, closing it down and transferring the management to its UK subsidiary under Jacque Margry, the European sales director, who was appointed the chief executive officer, and increasing the profit margins on the pens by 2% each year in seven consecutive years, all achieved by superior marketing.

The most spectacular failure was Glass Glover, which was incredibly difficult and involved investing too much and twice and resulted in great tensions with Schroders. Glass Glover was acquired as a public company and turned into a private company. It had two businesses, a strong food distribution business and an horrific food growing business, affected by endless adverse factors over which there was no control. The UK partnership had underestimated the difficulties of managing the food growing business and also discovered that the £10 million cash supposedly at the bank turned out to be an overdraft, making a huge hole. Finally the existing management was much worse than anticipated. It proved to be a tough learning experience but the team stuck with it, Walters working full-time for a whole year as the chief executive of the company. Gradually two thirds of the investment was recovered and the banks were repaid all their loans, together with interest. It was a great achievement, which impressed the investors. Fortunately the returns on the fund involved were strong enough to sustain this bad deal. Following this deal there were no more public to private deals for the next ten years and there was an increasing emphasis on impact investment, that is, the impact that could be made on a business. With Parker Pen money was made; with Glass Glover money was saved.

Another interesting investment, for political as well as commercial reasons, was the Sheffield Forgemasters MBO, an offshoot from British Steel prior to its privatisation. This steel castings and steel tubes manufacturer was another turnaround. Prior to its purchase, it had forged eight steel tubes to be used as oil pipes in Iraq not knowing that they were to be used as part of the barrel of a supergun known as Project Babylon that could fire one-tonne anthrax shells on Tel Aviv. The tubes were seized by Customs on Teeside in April 1990. There was a great political outcry during the Arms-to-Iraq scandal and most of the board were arrested but no charges were ever brought (*The Times*, 5

September 2003). During the furore Schroder Ventures received some bad press. The company was subsequently sold for an amount that was nine times its cost.

In the meanwhile, Ferguson, highly respected for his intelligence, vigour and ability as a salesman, was building up a network of independent country funds, all with different partnerships with Schroders. He was the visionary rather than being involved in the operations of the different businesses. Effectively he replicated in the other countries what he had achieved in the UK. Having put together the UK Buy-out fund he turned to the Continent. Robert Osterreith of RHO, a German friend, felt that there were good opportunities for MBOs in Germany and agreed to set up a fund 40/60 with Schroders. Having made extensive enquiries, Ferguson persuaded Thomas Matzen, currently commercial director of FM, the German subsidiary of Mars of the USA, to become the managing partner. A fund of DM140 million was raised with the backing of the Prudential, Argos and SIM and an office opened in Hamburg in 1986 with Thomas Krent joining shortly afterwards. Two years later Ferguson set up a partnership in Milan based on two Italians who had been at Harvard Business School at the same time as Ferguson and Byrn. Mario Ferrario was suave, well connected, and a lawyer and dealmaker who negotiated with the banks and oversaw the tax and legal matters. Paulo Colonna was an ex-McKinsey consultant with manufacturing process experience. Setting up the fund was not easy in view of concerns about the Mafia and whether one paid tax in Italy. Moulton was rather suspicious of their business practices, not appreciating that much was done on trust rather than in legal documents in Latin countries.[3] Ferrario and Colonna were a great combination and their second fund did very well, not least due to the turnaround of Riva Cantieri, the luxury boats builder that was sold to Vickers plc in 1990 at a considerable profit. They finally had a falling out and Ferrario left but that was in the late 1990s. Italy was followed by an office in Paris with Gerard Tardy as the managing partner and a French Buy-Out fund. To complete the Continental businesses Jaime Grego became the managing partner of a business in Spain opening an office in Madrid in 1990. Schroder Ventures was now established in eight countries with $1.3 billion committed capital and 100 people.

Ferguson made sure that all the managing directors not only knew how to do buy and sell businesses but also how to supervise and build a management team and to run a number of companies. Over 150 companies were controlled by Schroder Venture funds. Moulton had been a receiver, Smitham had run an electronics company and Matzen many parts of Mars in Germany. Friedrich von der Groeben, who took over from Matzen, had run his family bottling company, Ferrario and Colonna had bought and owned a series of operating companies in their own right, and Grego had owned a pharmaceutical company in Spain. Finally Byrn had owned and run a big drinks company. They were an impressive and independent minded group.

All these businesses were domestic and came under a management structure chaired by Ferguson. The executive committee, which met twice a year, comprised the managing partner from each country and Ferguson. It considered issues that affected all the countries, common standards, cross-border transactions, new countries, the co-ordination of fund raising programmes and budgets. The best performances came from the UK and Germany, followed by Italy, Canada and life sciences, which was set up later under Simon. The rest, that is, Japan, Asia (see below), France and Spain largely failed, although Japan improved in the late 1990s. Germany's big success was Vögele, a family owned retailing business with 400 outlets in Switzerland, Germany and Austria, which the German partners under von der Groeben restructured with its good management and introduced a new strategy and this resulted in an exit three years later in 1993 at a price that was seven times the purchase price. Italy's most successful transaction was Ferretti, a luxury yacht company that purchased nine other leading boat companies with well known brand names and grew fast to make annual revenues of $600 million before being taken public. It carried on growing and a few years later Schroder Ventures bought it back into private ownership. Collinson built up a steady life sciences business in the US, including Insyt, which started as an idea on his desk with an initial investment of $25,000, but when it was decided to create a unified and global life sciences business under Simon, he decided to leave. France, on the other hand, did badly losing 40% of its capital.[4] The business in Japan managed not to lose too much against a rapidly falling market helped by Xymax, a property management company that expanded from 100 to 250 buildings under management before being sold at a multiple of nine times the purchase price. Ferguson's overall achievement was to build a very profitable business from nothing. The UK partners saw him as being very entrepreneurial, a real creator, good at getting things going, a projector of opportunism, but not as good at managing and controlling after the event, his key skills being ideas and finding the people to develop them.

Having been successful in Europe and the Americas, Ferguson looked at South America and got close to acquiring the ventures team of ING but this came to nothing. He had met Anil Thadani of Arral & Partners while running SIMBL in Singapore and been impressed by his abilities – Byrn said he was perhaps as smart as Moulton but not as good at the business. Arral & Partners was well known in the region having four equal shareholders – Ronald Arculli, Adriann Zecha and the two co-managing directors, Thadani and Lewis Bowen. Ferguson was therefore very pleased to be able to attract Thadani and part of his team to form SV(Asia). Unbeknown to Ferguson, Thadani had been recently fired having been accused with Zecha of self-dealing by Bowen. Shortly after Schroders announced the formation of SV(Asia) with Thadani as the managing partner, the problems were spread across all the Asian business magazines and the *Asian Wall Street Journal*. After the Arral people told Ferguson he should have nothing to do with Thadani, he instructed Allen & Overy and Coopers & Lybrand to carry out another due diligence exercise which cleared Thadani.

Moulton did not trust Thadani and Mallinckrodt was worried about the bad publicity and they were relieved that Byrn was willing to go out to Hong Kong as vice-chairman of North America and Asia Pacific of Schroder Ventures to oversee the business in Asia. Byrn focused on ensuring that all the deals and contracts were properly documented, as

Schroders was accustomed to. Ferguson, Byrn and Thadani then made a presentation to the investors in the fund previously run by Thadani for Arral to get them to switch to SV(Asia) in competition with Bowen of Arral and another. SV(Asia) won with the smaller amount of $125 million and a lower management fee than previously awarded to Arral. The advisory board to the fund, which included Roddy Swire and Kevin Delbridge of Hancock, insisted that Byrn stay in Hong Kong and that they pay him a separate fee for doing so. This fund regrettably took 15 years to return its capital to the investors. Its best known investment was Silverlink, which owned the Āmanresorts with a string of exclusive hotels throughout South East Asia. Another Asian fund of $225 million was raised a few years later, $100 million of which was provided by Byrn's associates including Ontario Teachers. It has not done much better than the first fund but has time to improve.

The economics of the Schroder Ventures business was based on the receipt of annual management fees of 1.5% to 2% on the committed capital within each fund and a carried interest of 20% of the profits on each completed transaction. Initially Schroders took half of the management fees and 60% of the carried interest, Ferguson's personal share being a carry of 0.75% that came out of the partners' share of 8%. Matzen, the managing partner in Hamburg, had done very well with the first German fund with a number of good deals – including the purchase in 1987 of Ex-Cell, the largest-ever MBO in Germany – and was second only to Moulton in terms of return on investments. He pioneered venture capital in Germany being involved in what Moulton called the 'rape and pillage' stage as had the UK partnership a few years earlier. He was, however, a prima-donna of the first order and became very difficult for Ferguson to deal with. He also wanted to build a holding company rather than exiting his investments. He therefore forced a change in the division of the management fees and carried interest with Schroders, saying he could raise his own funds without Schroders' involvement. In 1988 a deal was struck with him in which Schroders' take was dramatically reduced to 10% of the management fees and a quarter of the 20% carry, the remainder going to the German partners. This split was also applied to the new funds in the UK. Ferguson could see that over time unless Schroders provided all the funding, the power would move to the management. As the investors were paying handsome management fees over the life of each fund, the economic risk to the management was low and there was no longer the need for a large sponsor like Schroders. He therefore explained to the Schroder board that it could either be flexible over the carries and hold on to the business, although not forever, or the management would break away. The board therefore agreed to the new financial arrangements with Schroders continuing to put up small amounts of money to support the management. The investors expected the management to invest alongside them and so Schroder Ventures Investment Ltd had been set up with Schroders putting up half the funds. These arrangements were to last for the next twelve years and enabled new partners to be attracted to the group.

It was stated in the 1988 agreement that this split would be reviewed in five years, that is in 1993. In 1991 Matzen decided to leave to set up his own fund and Friedrich von der Groeben became the managing partner in Germany, setting up a partnership in Frankfurt rather than in Hamburg. He was joined by Thomas Krent through the effective persuasion of Ferguson. The highly profitable UK partnership had eleven partners participating in 90% of the management fees and the 14.25% carry, with Moulton having a 20% share of the partnership. In terms of voting on major changes to the constitution of Schroder Ventures, Schroders and the non-UK country heads had 49% with the UK partners having 51%. To achieve a change against the wishes of the UK partners, Schroders therefore had to get one of the UK partners to support them against the other partners.

By the time the agreement was due to be reviewed in 1993, many of the investors in the funds were complaining about the size of the cake being taken by the umbrella companies such as Schroders. The investors felt that they were making little if any contribution to the business other than having been the founders and were pressing for a reduction in their percentage of the management fees and the carry. With the Americans coming to Europe, investors were asking the UK partners, 'how are you going to compete with one of your hands tied behind your back?' They wanted more of their money to be used to meet the running costs of the partnerships and to motivate the staff directly involved in the business. This view was also shared by the partners who saw little contribution coming from Schroders. None of the partners fully appreciated the merit of the Schroders' name as did Ferguson and Byrn. Both sides also exaggerated their side's contribution to the business.

Moulton wanted independence from Schroders and asked Ian Sellers, the in-house lawyer, to sound out the UK partners regarding their views on the future of the partnership arrangements. There was near unanimity that they should set up independently of Schroders. The situation was not helped by Ferguson not being seen to be a good people manager. Some shared Moulton's concern about the impact on the UK partnership's reputation with their investor base of being linked to country businesses over which they had no control and which, in their view, had questionable business practices, particularly Italy, Spain and Asia. Moulton forced the issue and submitted an ultimatum to Ferguson including the fact that in future Ferguson would have to work under Moulton. Prior to them meeting Byrn advised Ferguson to simply listen and not to argue and said he would offer him a cookie every time he thought he should have kept quiet. 'I was impressed that I only had to offer him a cookie once.' Moulton underestimated Ferguson and Schroders' resolve in not being prepared to have what they regarded as their business taken away from them. Simon was the only UK partner who fully recognised the importance of Schroders' involvement. He had a high regard for Moulton and his ability to put together such a diverse and talented team and also to hold them together but he felt Moulton lacked social graces and that this weakness needed to be counter-balanced by the weight of Schroders' reputation. It did not help that Moulton had once been extremely rude to Simon who was many years older and more experienced than him. Ferguson, the consensus builder, was in an impossible position as he was taking part of the partners' earnings and also acting for Schroders. Most of the partners resented the amounts being paid to Ferguson but only Moulton voiced their views. Ferguson had to negotiate each reduction in Schroders' take with Mallinckrodt, who was always concerned at what the partnerships were doing which might adversely impact on Schroders' reputation.

At the time Mrs Thatcher was in Paris during the challenge to her leadership of the Conservative Party and having won the first round decisively was advised to resign. This might not have happened had she remained in London. Moulton was planning to go to Puerto Rico on business at this crucial stage and Smitham warned him not to and to take heed of what happened to Thatcher. Bischoff and Ferguson moved fast with legal advice from Slaughter & May and threatened to liquidate the UK partnership. Crucially they secured the support of Simon who crossed the floor thereby giving Schroders a majority against the other partners. Simon, who was at odds with the other partners regarding the importance of Schroders' name, was at the time arranging to leave the partnership with the life sciences business and needed a continuing relationship with Schroders. Ferguson said that he had received indications from a number of the partners saying they wished to remain with Schroders but wanted this to be kept private to him and that without this he would not have forced the dissolution of the partnership.

Moulton was informed by telephone at 5am while in Puerto Rico that Schroders had combined with Simon to vote for the liquidation of the partnership. He promptly resigned saying that Schroders had acted against the interests of the partnership. Instead of negotiating he gave Schroders an ultimatum, which it was not prepared to accept. He even took legal advice and was confident that he could have won in the courts but fortunately it did not come to that. The other partners felt he should have apologised and stayed. He was too important to the business to be fired and they wanted him to stay. It had, however, passed the point of apology, the personal chemistry with Ferguson being well beyond repair. Many in the office cried. But he was intransigent and Smitham and Sellers negotiated a very generous settlement, which had the full backing of the partners, reflecting that the success of the business was largely due to him. Moulton had enjoyed himself enormously and was genuinely sad to go. He had been part of a very impressive team: 'Peter was good at everything; Carl was good at ventures; Damon was very gritty and determined; Charles, an all-rounder could see everyone's point of view; and Veronica was brilliant at deal execution.' When a few years later he set up his own business, Alchemy, Moulton adopted the friendly and open culture that had been so successfully developed by Schroder Ventures.

Moulton's departure was very upsetting for his partners who greatly admired his exceptional abilities. They also enjoyed his company and were inspired by him. He was a great salesman who could see opportunities others could not and could smell deals and do brilliant negotiations. He achieved more than most in his day being very clever and exceptionally fast. At the same time he was a straight-talker, much loved by the Americans, and tough – not suffering fools or taking any prisoners. Although he gave the impression of being a hard man, below he had a soft and loyal side – his main recreations were fishing and chess. Eng said of Moulton, 'he was the most interesting person I ever met in my business career and I learnt more from Jon than anyone else.' Smitham said, 'Jon was a star and brought more to the business than anyone. He was without doubt the best venture capitalist in the UK.' Affectionately Smitham recalled a difficult trip with Moulton to Tokyo in which visits to Japanese institutions had been arranged by Ladenburg.

After the first day, Ladenburg asked to see us at the Imperial Hotel. He suggested to Jon that he should refrain from using slang, as the Japanese did not understand it. Jon asked for an example to which Ladenburg said he had answered, 'No way' at a meeting with Mitsubishi Bank. Seeing nothing wrong Jon asked for another example. When Ladenburg said he had said, 'Not a snowballs', Jon said he should have said 'Not a f****** snowballs chance in hell' followed by another expletive. At another of the meetings Jon was giving a presentation to a senior Japanese who promptly fell asleep. He carried on and I suggested that he stop. Jon told me to kick him. I nudged his feet to which the Japanese woke up and asked Jon, 'What are you doing here?' Jon gave him an earful and we left.

At the time Moulton left the UK partnership, consisting of 25 professionals, had five funds with £400 million under management. He recalled the business being very profitable in 1993 with a £200 million gain being made from sales of investments and flotations of investments that had cost £200 million.

Moulton's departure was seen by many of the partners to be the honourable thing to do. He had sacrificed himself for the greater good. This enabled the relationship with Schroders to be restored, although it would never fully recover. The partners' gratitude was reflected in the settlement in which Moulton received a share of their carried interest for over 18 months after he had left as this was seen by the partners to be the right thing to do. It also enabled the business to develop further. They could remain a strong small and cohesive team or become bigger by merger to become a pan-European business conducting large cross-border transactions. Moulton was best with small teams doing domestic business like Alchemy, not managing large numbers of people. They opted for the latter.

It was the end of an era but the UK partnership had to carry on, being in the middle of a major fund raising for its third buy-out fund. Smitham took over as the managing partner and had to explain to the investors that Moulton had left. Although the investors were legally committed he decided to repay to them all the funds invested and to make a new presentation to them. Fortunately by that time they had built up such a good team that they were able to retain the goodwill of the investors all of whom came back into the fund. Thereafter the relationship with Schroders changed and the partnership acted independently. Ferguson felt he had been justified in his actions, as witnessed by the investors remaining and none of the partners joining Moulton. He also needed to keep the UK business.

NOTES:

1. Nick Ferguson had joined the research department of Investment Management under de Havilland in 1971 before being sponsored by Schroders on the MBA program at the Harvard Business School, where he became a Baker Scholar. During the summer of 1974 he worked for Jeff Collinson, who was responsible for venture capital at Schrocorp in New York. On his return to London he spent 18 months in Project Finance before leaving in 1976 to become the managing director of MEFCA, a joint venture based in Munich between Brown Brothers Harriman, the exclusive New York bank, and Prince Mohamed bin Faisal Al Saud, the second son of King Faisal of Saudi Arabia. MEFCA provided advice to US companies wishing to invest in the Middle East. Airlie was disappointed at Ferguson's departure and asked Dewe Mathews to keep in touch with him. Having a high regard for Ferguson's energy, enthusiasm and intelligence, Dewe Mathews maintained contact with Ferguson when he visited London. Airlie and Mallinckrodt called on him in Munich and persuaded him to return to Schroders in 1980 and he joined Richard Morgan's strategy group (see Chapter 6) where he reviewed the merits of purchasing Continental Illinois' 24.5% stake in SIMBL, in which Schroders had earlier acquired a 24.5% shareholding from Crown Agents (see Chapter 17). He was then appointed managing director of SIMBL.

2. Gordon Byrn and Ferguson, of a similar age, were in the same section at Harvard Business School in 1973 and became good friends as well as Baker scholars – coming in the top five of their class. Ferguson persuaded Byrn to apply to join Schroder Wagg in London but in view of the four-day week and working by candlelight in 1974, he was directed towards Schrobanco where Wolfensohn hired him to build a business for Schroders in Canada. It was not long before Wolfensohn rang to say he would not be staying at Schroders and that Schroders was more interested in investing in Asia than in Canada and so Byrn returned home to buy into a financial business.

3. Having set up the partnership and raised the first venture fund, Ferguson found he had overlooked obtaining approval from the Group Executive Committee and so with cap in hand he made a presentation to find that Mallinckrodt had major reservations about doing business in Italy in view of a bad family experience there in the 1930s. His mother had visited Venice and on her return to Munich, had stopped for lunch at the Austrian border, near Bolzano in the Dolomite Mountains, while her chauffeur had filled up her car with petrol. On arriving back home she found that the luggage in the boot of her car had been replaced with a dead body. There was so much laughter that the meeting moved on to the next item on the agenda, the secretary noting that the Italian venture had been approved.

4. Ferguson recalls being in Paris with his mother when a sock manufacturing company owned by Schroder Ventures was in the middle of an advertising campaign with large posters at every bus stop of naked men and women showing off the socks.

CHAPTER 14

THE PERENNIAL PROBLEM OF CAPITAL MARKETS

1984 - 1995

In 1983 van Marle and Bischoff did a swap, with Bischoff becoming head of the international issue business. However, as he was only head for a few months he barely got to grips with it and not being a capital markets man concentrated on what he was good at – fronting up presentations. He sought to build up the team and Sauvary recommended Andrew Williams, a friend from Oxford who was currently at European Banking Company (EBC). However, due to Schroders' reluctance to match his salary, which was considerably higher than that paid to the capital markets people in Schroders, he did not join the team for nearly a year. Williams joined a good team comprising on the buy side: Brisby, head of the Japanese issuing business; Pearce, who had returned from a few years running the office in Rio de Janeiro, head of UK issues; Sadleir, syndications manager; Ron Liss; and Gert Reiff-Winterhelt and Gerard Colignon who did the trading. Williams had always been puzzled by Schroders never leading its own issues rather than simply participating in issues led by others with much lower commissions. In fact it had always lost out to its competitors on the lead role for major UK issues as it had always bid less well than the competition. As he knew a lot about the margins on floating rate notes (FRNs), Williams with Brisby and Pearce pulled in a number of good mandates that went well for Schroders' clients like Standard Chartered Bank. This was followed by an 8% convertible bond for ICI, with an innovative put option, which secured for them new investors – high coupon bonds had not been seen before. Following these and other equity linked issues for Rowntree, Land Securities and Schroders' first swap for Consolidated Goldfields, Schroders' UK clients were being well served with good profits also being made. There was also a lot of Japanese business, which was mostly good and profitable, followed by a horror, which wiped out much of the previous gains.

With all this successful business, there was a new spirit in the team. Unfortunately Brisby wanted to become head of Capital Markets and brought all his internal political skills to the task resulting in Pearce feeling marginalized. He therefore left in 1984 for County Bank and then became finance director of Rentokil, which over the next 15 years he helped become one of the most successful companies in Britain. Williams then made the mistake of taking over coverage for North America from Pearce as well as France with Guy Harington, leaving him with no time for product creation – he and Liss were the only technicians in the team. It was as this stage that Capital Markets was combined with Banking under a new managing director, William Slee, a former colleague of Williams at EBC.

One of the decisions made during the strategic review was to cut back on the banking activities which effectively became wholly domestic. Banking was broken up with the treasury activity being moved to Treasury and Trading under Solandt with the remainder coming under Ladenburg. Problem debt was separated from Banking under Bulfield who also reported to Ladenburg. Banking came within a new division – Credit and Capital Markets – together with Capital Markets nominally under Brisby and Project Finance, which Dewe Mathews had been running for a year. Ladenburg and Brisby decided to merge and re-organise on a geographic basis with teams of bankers and capital markets people on the basis that they could sell all their products to the same customers.[1] With targets set to reduce radically the lending business, many of the banking staff were diverted to work on capital markets, which was being expanded by active recruitment. Ladenburg presented his proposals to Dewe Mathews, showing how Project Finance would be broken up between the geographical teams under a troika. Dewe Mathews promptly dismissed the proposals as unworkable for Project Finance, principally due to the difference between the provision of advisory services and the sale of products, the greater specialisation required and the nature of the clients involved. He told Ladenburg that Project Finance would remain independent.

Shortly after its formation, Bill Slee, aged 43, was appointed group managing director of Credit and Capital Markets. Slee had been recruited from EBC, a small consortium bank where he was deputy managing director under Stanislas Yassukovich. Previously he had been the vice president in charge of Citibank's oil and gas business in London where he arranged and led the limited recourse financing of the Ekofisk field in the North Sea for Phillips and Norsk Hydro – 'It was the best job I ever had.' He therefore came with real knowledge of project finance, which was to be of great benefit to Project Finance when dealing with his less knowledgeable senior colleagues in the future. He did not have an enviable job not least because all those who reported to him were independent minded and difficult to manage and considered themselves to be more experienced in their respective fields than him. Ladenburg, on hearing of his appointment, called on him at EBC and suggested that he be appointed his deputy. This was the last thing Slee wanted knowing that he would never get to the bottom of what was going on. Having had a preview of the naked ambition in Ladenburg, he then met the supremely confident Brisby and finally Dewe Mathews, 'an awkward chap to deal with, running a barely profitable business whose elimination Strickland was actively seeking.'

He found the banking business to be well run with good standards and the appropriate risk and credit controls, but very old fashioned. It was a low margin business, save for Schroder Leasing, which had high margins and a brilliant team of people. Project Finance, which is covered more fully in Chapter 15, he found to be in good hands but without anyone in the bank having any understanding of it. He spent much of his efforts defending its existence particularly against Strickland who appeared to have a vendetta against it and Mallinckrodt who felt good people were being wasted. By keeping these people off Dewe Mathews' back he gave Project Finance the breathing space it needed to develop into a more successful business.

With the opening of the new Schroder Japan branch in Tokyo in 1986, Ladenburg was appointed the head of investment banking incorporating capital markets and securities. Being an experienced banker with little if any knowledge of capital markets or securities and more importantly no knowledge of Asia and its cultures he was a curious appointment but a person much trusted by Solandt and Mallinckrodt.

Banking

With Ladenburg going to Tokyo Bernard Barham and John Rock were appointed respectively head of Banking and chairman of the Credit Committee. Both were long-standing and seasoned bankers who had joined Schroders from school at the age of sixteen.[2] Not long after Ladenburg's departure, it became clear that the merger of the activities of Banking and Capital Markets was not working as the customers for their products were completely different, and therefore Banking was separated from Capital Markets, but remained under Slee.[3] In a climate of tight budgets, Barham prepared a plan to rebuild the banking business in the face of huge competition from the clearers and the international banks. With the margins on loans to international markets and to the large UK companies at levels where Schroders could not compete, the international business faded away. Each of the banking directors was required to prepare details on five new UK names each Friday and from these a new customer list was developed. Costs were reduced by not having to serve international customers. Gradually the lending book was reduced and focused on smaller companies with productivity being improved with smaller teams. Lending was directed by Barham, Rock and Chris Cairns, the son of Alec Cairns, the head of Banking in J Henry Schroder in the 1950s. An attempt was made at invoice discounting but this was closed down when it failed due to being started during the wrong cycle in the market. A big ticket leasing business was developed successfully by Robin Corner, who had previously been with Schroder Leasing – this business had the added benefit of being able to shelter group tax arising from Schroders' increasing profits. Debt restructuring for existing and new customers, following the recession in the early 1990s, created opportunities to become banking advisors yielding good fee income and these were developed by Corner with the support of James Brent, a former Army officer without a degree who did very well like Barham and Rock. Essentially these were well secured workout loans syndicated to other banks.

A very profitable private lending business to individuals was also developed by Bernd Marenbach, which was fully secured and at significantly higher margins, and this also served many of SIM's clients. By the time Barham retired in 1993, he, Rock and Corner had refocused the banking business, putting it on to a sound and profitable basis and created the springboard on which a successful advisory business was later developed.

They fully used the little capital they were allocated. It was not easy to make profits when they had to borrow and match all their funding from Treasury, which alone was allowed to make profits by mismatching. Barham rarely saw Slee except during the annual salary review, which showed how much trust Slee had in his capabilities.

He was succeeded by Rock who combined both roles of head of Banking and the Credit Committee. Rock had worked very closely with Barham for over 30 years from their time together doing Eurodollar lending to the UK and Australian markets in the 1960s and 1970s. 'He was a very nice man, who got on well and was liked by his staff and colleagues. He was always laid back and cool in a crisis.' Barham repaid the compliment finding Rock 'relaxed, very competent and sound as a bell, although perhaps less of a driving force than he could have been.'

Rock was also chairman of Schroder Leasing, which steadily grew. A number of approaches were made to acquire it but these were resisted as it was a reliable and trouble-free earner whose capital value was increasing. Finally it was sold to the Siemens Group in 2000 for a cash consideration of £97.5 million, having earned profits before tax of £8.7 million in 1999 with shareholders funds of £36.3 million. It was sold through the intervention of Mallinckrodt, who had yet again demonstrated that he was a good seller of businesses. Mallinckrodt sent Morris and Henbrey to see Siemens about the sale of Schroder Leasing, which was not included in the investment banking business sold to Citigroup at the same time. They were impressed by how protective Mallinckrodt had been of the staff ensuring that they were well looked after by Siemens following the sale.

Bulfield had put in hand a programme of asset sales and loan swaps for the Latin American debts to achieve a better spread of risks and a reduction of the exposure. Schroders' exposure had originally been fairly modest with corporate lenders on a short-term basis but these had been extended to up to five years during the expansion of the book under Lesser and Ladenburg. Most of these debts had become government liabilities – risks Schroders had previously avoided – prior to default and their values became heavily discounted. The swap programme resulted in a spread in the liabilities to a diverse set of countries including Yugoslavia, which proved to be a mistake. After Bulfield retired in 1986 to become a director of Yamaichi International, he handed over to Barham who, with the support of Alastair Forsyth, accelerated the programme. Slee played an active role in this work having been rather shocked on his arrival to see the state of affairs. In the absence of a decision from the GEC, Barham liquidated the total portfolio resulting in a final loss of about £40 million, which would have been considerably greater but for the write back of the bad debts released following the sale of Schrobanco to IBJ in 1985 (see Chapter 2). It was a great relief to be finally clear of these liabilities, which had originally stood at nearly £100 million, at what was a significantly lower loss than that incurred by many of the competitors. Apart from the Latin American debts, Schroder Wagg had incurred virtually no bad debts compared with those in New York and Asia.

As chairman of the Group Credit Risk Committee, Rock managed the Group's risk exposure in the trading, lending and capital markets businesses – higher exposures were referred to London. Generally the overseas operating companies were permitted to take risks up to a quarter of their capital before reference to London. After that they were considered by the Group Credit Risk Committee and approved by the GEC.

An area of difficulty with Mallinckrodt was lending to the property sector where he had previously been badly burnt over the failure of BPGF in 1982 (see Chapter 3). Schroders' lending experience in this sector, including the property crisis in the early 1970s, had been patchy. The exposure had been modest and if well managed it could make good profits. Inevitably some losses were incurred on property loans, particularly in situations where in hindsight they could have been avoided. The banking directors had had a rethink of their position in 1987 and agreed that it was reasonable to have some exposure if the risks were well considered and conservatively managed. They agreed specific limits for different types of property and these were submitted to the GEC for approval. When Mallinckrodt became aware of this, he challenged Rock asking him to produce historical information on the lending experience. With Morris' help he found that, after deducting the cost of capital, the net benefits over the past 20 years were nil, the improved performance in recent years having been out-weighed by the past particularly in New York. In these circumstances he was advocating continuing in the sector. There were long and tortuous discussions with Mallinckrodt who felt the cycle would turn and recent profits would be wiped out. Rock and his directors felt they could and had learnt the lessons of the past and had achieved good improvements in performance. Every time he sought an increase in the limits, he had to go through the same arguments. Mallinckrodt would never give up and maybe because of this added caution, Banking did well in the sector.

Capital Markets

With Banking in good hands Slee concentrated on the weakest area of his empire. Capital Markets had a reasonably well developed and staffed buy side to get new mandates but absolutely no capability in distribution, trading and research and nobody realised the need for these critical elements of the business. As the liaison director with the Bank of England Slee had to face the bemusement at the Bank that Schroders clearly had no strategy for dealing with the Big Bang, being the only leading merchant bank that had not bought an established stockbroking company. Brisby wanted to be put in charge of Capital Markets and kept going behind Slee's back to see Bischoff. Slee felt he did not have the trust and confidence of those in Capital Markets to be made their head. They hired people at a considerable cost, having to pay 'golden hellos' to get them and 'handcuffs' to retain them – everyone was after the same people to develop and run a business they had no knowledge of. Schroders committed insufficient capital to the business to put in place what was needed. It built some distribution strongly focused on equity-linked securities, particularly Japanese issuers. It could not afford to build a research business without having a securities business. They took the brave decision to get out of the debt issuance business in the Euro currencies capital markets because of its requirement for huge capital to sustain a low margin commodity business that lacked the benefit of the big domestic government bond trading activity available to the US, Japanese and German banks, to support it. Schroders decided not to apply for a licence from the Bank of England to trade in gilts, when it understood how many licences were to be granted and how much capital would have to be committed to the business for such low returns. This was the last straw for Brisby, who decided to leave, having already lost Schroders a good deal of money on the sterling perpetual for Standard Chartered Bank, which is described below.

Earlier Brisby had persuaded Standard Chartered Bank, Schroders' ever loyal client, to issue a sterling perpetual floating rate note. Slee and Bischoff were not present at the meeting to fix the terms. Investors generally received a higher yield for sterling than for the dollar. Brisby proposed five basis points below the dollar in sterling. With nobody willing to stand up to Brisby, the issue went ahead and was a flop. Despite great efforts by Brisby and others it could not be sold. It had been priced on the wrong data and Schroders had to buy the notes back in the market to maintain its credibility and as a result built up a holding of £80 million at 98.5. However, as bonds held by banks had to be deducted in full from their capital, with a capital of only £100 million at the time, Schroders had to sell. Mallinckrodt insisted on the position being closed taking a loss of a few million pounds but significantly less than had been feared. There was very little sympathy for Brisby from his colleagues. Brisby was a highly effective marketer, being particularly good at getting the attention of clients but he needed to be supported by a much more professional and disciplined team of technicians who controlled the pricing of issues. A colleague who worked closely with him said of him, 'he was clever and hard working but self-confident to the point of disaster, never thinking that anything could go wrong until it did.' With his failing reputation and Schroders' decision not to trade in gilts he left shortly afterwards for Salomon Brothers International Ltd for a significantly enhanced remuneration package.

Sadleir, who had never been comfortable in the role of syndication manager, handed over to Liss, who was even less suitable, since he lacked the necessary charisma. Sadleir was appointed the group compliance officer where he could bring to bear his good brain to master the complexities of the emerging and voluminous regulations being imposed on the financial services industry following the Big Bang. Slee in the meanwhile was struggling with the integration and retraining of the banking and capital markets people and became temporarily ill under the intense pressure. The morale of the capital markets people reached rock bottom as most of the best people had left. Schroders' reputation in the market was near to being a laughing stock.

Sauvary, who had been the representative in Tokyo before Ladenburg's elevated appointment, returned to London to take over the buy side from Brisby, having previously succeeded him in Japan. He found the bond-trading book to be in a complete mess. Most of the business was rubbish, nobody having thought what they could issue and sell. He cleared out the book taking losses and persuaded Slee to fire the salesmen and the traders as they could only do fixed rate and floating bonds. He needed equity salesmen as Schroders could only originate equity based issues and so he replaced the salesmen with young graduates who worked with Conor Killeen, the syndicate manager, and Rupert Birch, Sauvary becoming director of syndication and sales. He proved to be a great benefit to Slee, being a good marketer and having a good knowledge of the securities business. In the meanwhile the Japanese warrant business for Japanese clients and convertible bonds for major UK issuers continued with Richard Gordon, being in Tokyo. A few good years followed until 1990 when the capital markets business was split up, Sauvary's international business going into Securities under Watkins (see Chapter 11).

There was a constant battle between Corporate Finance and Slee regarding who should control Capital Markets. Broadbent and Slee went into battle to resolve the matter, with Solandt appointed by Bischoff as the adjudicator. Broadbent wanted control of UK capital markets buy side so that he could serve his clients better but was not willing to take on the rest. In the end, it was split between Corporate Finance, Securities and Credit and Capital Markets' successor, international finance division known as IFD (see below) and fell between the stools thus ensuring its continuing demise. Looking back on the disappointing performance of Schroders' capital markets activity, Bischoff said,

> To be successful in capital markets one needed people with flair and a willingness to take risks with a large amount of capital combined with a good securities business with trading of equities. We had nothing for bonds as we had decided not apply to the Bank of England to trade gilts in June 1985. We were considered a small house despite being profitable.

International Finance Advisory Department (IFAD)

Grimstone was asked by Bischoff in 1992 to take over Schroders' equity capital markets and international corporate finance activities within a new group called IFAD under Slee. (Slee continued to oversee Project Finance, both activities confusingly being called IFD.) Capital Markets, which was important to Schroders' overall capability as an investment bank, continued to be in the doldrums. It was a refugee camp with poor relations with Corporate Finance and very little business – in fact to be truthful it had always been a disaster but Schroders had to be in it. It was one of the poisoned chalices that was passed from one division to the other as they all complained about the effect its poor performance was having on their businesses. Broadbent, who earlier had taken over responsibility for the domestic capital markets business, had no interest in promoting international capital markets business. He felt Schroders did not have the competence to lead domestic let alone international issues not having the combination of sales, research, trading and syndication skills necessary to be successful. Schroders could underwrite but nothing more. Secondly he could extract more money and more quickly from his UK clients but had insufficient staff. Sauvary felt this was a serious error of judgement with its focus on short-term profits rather than growth that required an investment in people. In view of the history of this business Broadbent's view as a UK corporate financier is understandable.

Sauvary had long conversations with Grimstone, finding him clever and capable of thinking through serious issues that went to the heart of the business. 'If he had been used better he could have made a significant and positive effect on the way the whole investment banking business was developed. The senior corporate finance directors however were scared of his abilities.' The corporate finance directors may not have agreed with this view of course. With government privatisation business picking up in international markets following the successes in the UK, Grimstone and Sauvary pooled their different experiences to try and capture some of the market occupied by Kleinwort Benson and NM Rothschild. It was extremely competitive and they came to the conclusion that it would be better to get half the cake than none. They identified markets where they had some competitive advantage in securities or special market knowledge and in other markets, teamed up with banks with distribution skills. Using Grimstone's formidable marketing skills they were successful in securing a number of IPO mandates in the peripheral countries of Europe against strong competition such as Tofac, the national car manufacturer in Turkey with CSFB, OFE the telephone company in Greece with CSFB and various Hungarian business with Creditanstalt. This led to IPOs for DSM, the Dutch chemicals company, and Fred Olson, the Norwegian shipping company, a long-standing client of Banking. Finally the team assisted in securing the privatisation mandate for INA, the Italian insurance company, where Corporate Finance had a good and well connected office in Milan under Tarantelli, who also understood the capital markets business. Much privatisation business followed arising from the restructure of the banking sector following the Amato law, which forced charitable foundations to sell their controlling shareholdings in the banks.

Another member of the team recruited in 1994 by Slee and Grimstone was Philip Mallinckrodt, Gowi's eldest son, aged 31, who had spent eight years at CSFB finishing as co-head of equity capital markets for Europe. CSFB was one of the big five international equity underwriters and so he came with a strong and proven record in this field. He found Schroders to have corporate finance as its core discipline but with an undeveloped securities capability and little strength in equities and no capability in debt. He therefore became part of the team, seeking to put together an integrated corporate finance, capital markets and securities business in Europe. He saw capital markets as being the bridging function between corporate finance and securities. His first task was assisting with the INA issue following the completion of the corporate finance work undertaken by Tarantelli's team and worked closely with Sauvary and Maurizio Tassi and was surprised to see the head-to-head competition between Schroders and Goldman Sachs in corporate finance when in capital market issues it was necessary to co-operate to achieve success. He therefore set about building the required good working relationship. Over the next three years he worked on issues in Italy, France, Germany, Greece and Hungary.

Also within IFAD came the Central and East European team led by Guy Harington that was developing from scratch the markets of Poland, Czechoslovakia and Hungary.[4] Harington's career, which looked and felt rather fragile within Corporate Finance, was rescued by the fall of the wall in Berlin and the collapse of the communist empire. The Schroder family had had business interests in the region before the war and there was a strong feeling, particularly among Germans, that they should participate in the redevelopment of the region. Mallinckrodt was therefore very supportive of Schroders' involvement. Harington was asked to have a look at the region and identified Poland, Hungary and Czechoslovakia to be the key markets.

An important contributor to the early success of the team was the Know-How Fund set-up by the British government to finance consultancy work to assist in developing the economies of these former communist countries. Harington said,

> It was a very imaginative and efficient system implemented by the Foreign Office with individuals from the private sector, such as Richard Wilson from Hoare Govett, being responsible for each project. They ran a simple straightforward tender process, which resulted in appointments being made within a few weeks. As a result the UK stole the march on other European countries in winning many privatisation mandates, much to irritation of France in particular.

The first success was the privatisation of the Krosno glassworks, one of the four flagship privatisations of the new reformist Polish government. As the management spoke no English, communication was in French. The team was not too happy to be housed in the company's hostel with blankets rather than curtains to cover the windows and given very indifferent food, particularly when they heard later that the company owned a fine chateau up the road. Insult was added to injury when they were each billed $50 per night. This was the first flotation on the Warsaw Stock Exchange for 45 years and was not made easier for the prospectus being in Polish, as verification presented a few problems. Wielkopolski Bank Kreditowy, the first major commercial bank to be privatised, and Bank Haldlowy followed this. In Hungary they brought Gedeon Richter, the pharmaceutical company, and OTP, the savings bank, to the market. When asked to develop a privatisation strategy by the Hungarian government, the minister was not satisfied with Schroders' straightforward practical scheme, saying it was too simple. Harington redrafted the same scheme overnight into a more convoluted proposal, which he presented the following morning much to the delight of the minister who said, 'it is now suitably complex.' Harington received good support from Challen and Netherton in securing experienced corporate finance staff to manage each privatisation, including Giles Elliott and Andrew Whitehouse among others. His own team included Sriram Chari who had previously been in Project Finance and William Wells, both particularly hard workers. The fees were not particularly good but they managed to cover their costs. He was also helped by unstinting encouragement from Mallinckrodt, Bischoff and Slee. The formation of IFD with its many international-minded and entrepreneurial people interested in doing new things within international finance, made his life easier and also enjoyable.

Grimstone said 'Guy worked like a dog for 15 to 20 hours a day, gave everything he had but could not turn these Herculean efforts into money. His tenacity was fuelled by having been mugged in Moscow and seen his fine suits destroyed by Polish factory machinery.' Grimstone with his flair for marketing sought to help him convert his relationships into money. He was involved in advising the Czech government on its mass privatisation programme with vouchers distributed to the population. Vouchers were issued to all citizens between 18 and 65 enabling them to apply for shares in the privatised companies as they became available on the principle that as the people owned the state they too owned the assets and so were entitled to own the companies. A secondary market was also created to enable the people to sell the shares they had acquired through their vouchers. It was a highly innovative scheme devised by Vaclav Klaus, the minister of finance (and subsequently president of the country) and very well-regarded by outside observers. Schroders was worried about the dangers of unregulated funds but Klaus wanted a totally free market – he lived to regret not taking Schroders' advice.

Following the successes in privatisations, the team used its knowledge of the region to assist foreign companies in purchasing the assets being privatised. Although much more speculative, the fees were greater and led to working for Schroders' clients, such as Solvay, Siemens and Conoco as well as clients of its competitors such as BAT, Cadbury Schweppes and United Biscuits. Harington acted for BAT in its attempts to acquire the tobacco industries in seven different countries, four of which were successful, all yielding good fees. He spent many months in Uzbekistan. 'It was like reliving the great game. We had to run an endurance course before they were prepared to deal with us. Our 12-man team had to work out of a two bed-roomed dacha in shifts around the clock.' It was hard work travelling to these god-forsaken places with poor hotels and bad food dealing with irate ministers and inefficient and often corrupt officials.

Wadia had a high regard for Harington, 'he knew project finance and had worked in many parts of the bank. He went after very ambitious mandates and always forcibly pulled in Project Finance, which resulted in Project Finance doing well in East Europe.'

The biggest and by far the most profitable privatisation was advising the Government of Hungary on the privatisation of MVM, the state electricity company. This assignment was won in the face of fierce international competition and was managed by Wadia and Dominic Freely from Project Finance and Chari, the leader of the Hungarian team. The assignment involved the full privatisation of Hungary's electricity industry breaking it up into individual power stations and distribution companies and auctioning them off to international consortia. Regular disputes with the inefficient Hungarian government team, as well as the murky practices of the Hungarian government and business generally made the assignment all the more difficult.[5] Freely moved his large young family to Budapest and worked 16-hour days every day of the week for six months. He co-ordinated all the advisors and by brute determination he forced through the process to success. [6]

Harington set up Schroder Polska a merchant bank in Warsaw in 1993. Originally he thought it might be necessary to have a joint venture with a Polish bank but having failed to agree terms, he became increasingly comfortable with Matthew Olex, a Pole who had been educated in England and wanted to go back to Poland now that it was free, and decided to go it alone. He received great support from Mallinckrodt and Bischoff and Schroder Polska became the clear market leader. It flourished and became the employer of choice, building up to 20 staff including secondments from London and made acceptable profits. A representative office was set up in Budapest to serve the Hungarian business but only a working office was used in Prague, as there was less work there, the Czechs being more difficult to deal with. In addition the team had 15 in London including Chari, Whitehouse, Wells and Jonathan Warbuton. It is interesting to contrast the nomadic existence of Harington's East European team with that of the Corporate Finance teams in Western Europe where there was a sufficient volume of profitable business to invest in permanent offices. Schroders was fortunate in having in Harington such a dedicated person who was also remarkably nice. A mark of his success was that the business continued to thrive, albeit in a smaller guise, when the investment bank was sold to Citigroup five years later.

Having once again made his mark Grimstone was asked by Bischoff to become head of Corporate Finance in Asia based in Hong Kong. He was told that it was an opportunity to demonstrate his skills in running an important business and if successful he would be considered among others for Bischoff's future succession. It suited his personal circumstances but as he wanted to maintain a base in London to see his children it was agreed that he should remain temporarily head of IFAD spending a week in London each month.

Slee decided to leave Schroders in 1995 and become a part-time advisor. He was fed up with all the administration and the continued policy of running Wertheim as a satellite operation. Slee felt that Wertheim had a good research and distribution capability on which Schroders could have developed a trans-Atlantic business but Mallinckrodt and Way had prevented any interference and change to Wertheim saying the people from London did not understand the culture. They were also not prepared to see an experienced American brought in to ensure the necessary changes.

Slee had an extraordinarily difficult job being in a bank where technical skill in a business was all-important. Although he had direct experience of each of the areas under him he was not an expert in any of them as he had moved on to general management, an area of expertise Schroders badly lacked. Nobody at Schroders had previously been asked to work under someone who did not have similar or better expertise to them. Unlike them however, he had a good understanding of each of the businesses and let them blossom independently by managing with a light touch. The fact that he made a success of his job was due to the respect he achieved through his being a remarkably nice person and a good administrator. Sauvary spoke for many in saying, 'he was always exceptionally honourable having the courage to say what he thought was right. Schroders owed him a huge debt for managing the run down of the firm's Latin American bad debts. He was much liked but not a good politician.'

In addition to being group managing director of Credit and Capital Markets, Slee was put in charge of a large part of Schroders' infrastructure or, as it was known, 'the back office' and appointed chairman of the Staff and Admin Committee, which was renamed the Schroder London Group of Companies Management Committee, in short SLOGMAC. This committee was staffed by the heads of each of the divisions, with Dewe Mathews representing Credit and Capital Markets since Slee was chairman, with the heads of various back office functions such as personnel in attendance. It dealt with all non-business issues such as space. When Slee joined Schroders he was amazed to see that each of the businesses had different furniture from different suppliers and that 'the decoration and furnishing of directors' private offices varied between being like an Oxfam shop and a Mayfair drawing room.' Each of the divisions fought its corner, some more aggressively than others, on the issues that affected them most. The most heated debates concerned the allocation of what was known as attributable costs, that is the cost of non-business activities. This led to significant cost savings when the business units challenged the need for certain back office activities. Space planning was a biannual issue. Taking on a few floors of the new Senator House building at £10 a square foot for five years, in the face of a threat from Mallinckrodt, was to save Schroders considerable costs. Everybody agreed that Slee did a top-class job, being patient and good at developing a consensus and willing to take on achieving greater efficiency and cost savings in activities of no interest to the revenue earners.

With Slee's departure and Grimstone's transfer to Hong Kong, IFD disappeared, its capital markets activities being incorporated into Securities within the new investment banking business, and the Central and East European team under Harington being subsumed within a UK-dominated corporate finance business both under Richard Broadbent, the new head of European Corporate Finance. Project Finance, which by that time was making significant profits, carried on as an independent global business within investment banking.

NOTES:

1. Michael Ladenburg set out the thinking behind the merger of Banking and Capital Markets in the 1984 edition of the *Schroder Wagtail*:

At a time of major upheaval in the Financial Markets, when it seems that bankers are trying to become stockbrokers, discount houses seem to feel that they should become money brokers, and just about everybody wants to make markets, the cynic might level at Schroders the accusation that we are jumping on a bandwagon by trying to turn bankers into bond salesmen and bond salesmen into bankers. Why therefore have we made this move?

It is in response to the changing financial world, certainly. But is more than this. In particular, it is a response to the blurring of the distinctions between the bond market and the loan market. The combined division gives us the ability to provide a better service to clients, and to market more effectively. Our structure enables us to offer, through integrated teams, a wide range of fund raising possibilities in a number of different markets. Not least, it involves the members of the new division in direct exposure to different market products, which they will be responsible for selling on behalf of Schroders... The new structure will give us a greater awareness of opportunities, because we cannot only succeed by individual effort, but by team work within the division, the firm, and the Group. The challenge which lies ahead will involve everybody in developing a greater awareness of a wider range of markets, whilst retaining professionalism.

2. Bernard Barham, armed with his school certificate, was advised by the youth employment agency in the City to approach Schroders. He arrived at Leadenhall Street for an interview in 1949 to find that nobody had been recruited for ten years. It was the same year that Ted Schroeder had won the men's singles at Wimbledon. He was taken on straight after his interview and spent the rest of the afternoon at the office. In due course, he was selected with six others, including Lesser, to move around each of the banking departments learning on the job, finally finishing up in the cash department. In 1961 he was sent to Sydney and built up a money book from scratch before returning to London in 1963 from which he was sent to Edinburgh where he built up another money book which made as much as its capital in one year. He then joined the exclusive AAA team under Bulfield where he worked on lending opportunities in Australia, America, Japan (Asia) and the UK that represented the lion's share of the banking business. Like everyone else he found Bulfield to be a very competent banker who was fair and focused and a nice man.

John Rock had joined Schroders in 1959 as a promising youngster and risen through most of the clerical jobs to become an assistant to the chief cashier of the sterling money book in 1965 which led him to foreign exchange dealing under Cooper and then lending under Bulfield. He, like Barham before him, therefore received as good a training in banking as anyone. When Solandt was appointed head of Banking in 1977, he was made a director and with Barham became responsible for UK lending.

3. It is interesting to compare the announcements regarding the merger and separation of Banking and Capital Markets:

Strategic Review, January 1984

For our principal banking divisions, their merger with capital markets' operations will represent a logical extension of policies pursued in recent years, which have concentrated on increasing banking revenues from sources other than conventional credit extension, such as transactions relating to leasing, tax and securities.

JHSW Staff Notice, June 1986
During the Strategic Review... it was decided to combine the marketing of both banking and capital markets products through integrated geographic marketing teams. Since that decision was taken both markets and client requirements have changed very dramatically, to a large extent negating the potential for cross-marketing banking and capital market services.

4. Guy Harington had joined Banking in 1971 under Solandt and joined Egerton and Forsyth in the Nigerian venture which was aborted by two coups in 1977: 'the removal of General Gown as president; and the departure of Wolfensohn from Schroders' (see Chapter 1). Wolfensohn was the driving force behind such international ventures and with his departure Harington and the team were recalled by Hull, who had taken charge of Nigeria. After a period in Brussels under Bulfield working at Mitsubishi Trust & Banking Company he returned to London as a bridge between Banking and Corporate Finance trying to get bond business from European companies. As a member of Credit and Capital Markets under Slee he was part of the unhappy and constantly changing capital markets team. It was a turbulent time. With the break up of Capital Markets, Harington found himself in a European team headed by Corporate Finance people who had only been abroad on holidays and had no idea of how things worked in Europe let alone spoke the languages.

5. Thomas Suckermann the Hungarian Minister for Privatisation came with two of his government colleagues to lunch at Schroders and before raising his fork attacked the Schroder team for its incompetence and threatened to dismiss it. Dewe Mathews responded with equal vigour in defence of his team accusing one of Suckermann's colleagues, who was present, of causing all the problems. Suckermann, who clearly enjoyed being stood up to, rose from the table and slammed Dewe Mathews on the back saying, 'I like you Dewe. I am simply an old Bolshevik at heart and each morning as I get up I feel as if I am in a large tank armed with a full magazine of shells to fire at my enemies.' Thereafter he was always available to Dewe Mathews and any problems were resolved immediately.

6. When interviewed by George Wadia, Dominic Freely asked, 'Why should I join Project Finance?' Wadia's response, 'because it is the most intellectually exciting thing to do' seemed to convince him. He started by working on the Barking power station – described in the next chapter – with Read Gomm. Both played a leading role in developing Project Finance's tailor-made mathematical models, which differentiated it from its competitors. It was a prickly alliance with both having different skills and Gomm being quieter and far less demonstrative than Freely. Wadia held them together and brought out the best in them through five exhausting years. Freely then turned his talents and linguistic skills to East

Europe. Wadia spoke for his colleagues all of whom had a high regard for Freely's commitment and sense of duty,

He had a pugnacious attitude to life and no matter what the odds he always came out fighting. He brought to the team the assets of an accounting training which was invaluable for privatisation. Being half Bavarian and married to an Austrian, he wanted to re-conquer the Hapsburg Empire and, with his fluent German, was very much at home in Germany and East Europe. He was a strongly committed Catholic and was prepared to wear it on his sleeve with pride. He came to be admired by all his competitors.

CHAPTER 15

BUILDING A GLOBAL BUSINESS

1983 - 1994

Early in 1983 Airlie asked Dewe Mathews to take charge of Schroders' project finance business. It was agreed that Bulfield would return to Banking to oversee the recovery of the bad debts that had arisen out of the Latin American debt crisis. The business Dewe Mathews took over, principally the arrangement of UK export credits, was barely profitable, highly volatile and largely dependent on one market, Hong Kong. Schroders was well behind its main competitors – Lazards, Hill Samuel and the ever-aggressive Morgan Grenfell. It could have been significantly more profitable – in fact it could have started each year with all its costs covered – had it been permitted to partic-ipate in the loans it arranged for its clients with the full guarantee of the British govern-ment. Export credit business provided fees for the arrangers of the loans, which due to their size were invariably syndicated to other banks at the request of the client. These loans had unusually high margins bearing in mind that they were wholly guaranteed by the British government and were therefore very popular with the banks who could not understand why Schroders was not permitted to participate in them. Effectively Project Finance was giving away most of the profits it earned from its work. Unfortunately Mallinckrodt was alarmed by the length of these loans, which could be up to 20 years, having an aversion to any loans over seven years. The fact that they earned margins of 1% and were risk free, requiring no allocation of risk capital, was dismissed. Regrettably by the time he reluctantly agreed Project Finance had lost the opportunities and a steady annual income of £2 million. Life became a major struggle over the next five years and Dewe Mathews made sure that in future Project Finance never undertook any business that was dependent on Schroders' capital. He set it on a course of independence.

Relying on one product and scarcely making a profit – in 1983 Project Finance made a loss of £240,000 – it faced extinction. To survive it needed to be in a growing and profitable business. Attempts had been made at developing a project finance business and this was still peripheral, but in Dewe Mathews' view critical to its survival. What he needed was some expertise and credibility in this area. Slee had the answer. He advised Dewe Mathews to hire George Wadia and David Cockburn from European Banking. It was a stroke of genius as Wadia was the start of a brilliant business. Wadia had been in Shell for twelve years before becoming number two in EBC's successful project finance business under Slee. Slee's call was opportune as Wadia felt the consortium banks had had their day. Although he knew of Schroders' reputation it was not in project finance and he saw this as an opportunity. He was a very cultured person, widely read and interested in all the arts. He was extremely intelligent and articulate and with his relaxed and authoritative manner he impressed all the clients and gave them confidence in Schroders' abilities. He became Dewe Mathews' right arm as far as growing the project finance business in the same way that Robinson was the rock on which the export credit business fed steady albeit modest profits to finance it.

Although the businesses ran in parallel with the contractor finance business – the new name adopted for export credit – being gradually replaced by the new project and international corporate financing businesses, it is easier to explain their developments separately which is how they have been dealt with below. The contractor finance story follows straight on from the project finance section in Chapter 2.

Export credit

In 1984, NEI Parsons appointed Project Finance to support its bid to supply turbines to Public Utilities Board (PUB) in Singapore for the first phase of its 750MW power station at Pulau Seraya. NEI was desperate to get back into the Far East market where it had lost out to fierce competition from Japanese companies, which had been able to offer significantly lower prices. Robinson discovered that the Monetary Authority of Singapore (MAS) took over the foreign exchange risks on loans incurred by public sector bodies such as PUB, charging them 1% per annum. As there was no differentiation between the currencies it meant that loans with the lowest interest rate would evaluate best. Robinson therefore decided to try and arrange a UK export credit in Swiss francs despite it never having been done before and so not only ECGD and the Bank of England but also MAS and the National Bank of Switzerland and the Swiss banks had to be persuaded to agree. After extensive negotiations with the authorities and the banks, UBS agreed to provide a SF152 million loan guaranteed by ECGD and NEI won the contract. A decade later, after NEI had lost the second phase of the power station to the Japanese due to an uncompetitive price, Robinson had to support them for the third phase. He and Thomas See (see below) discovered that the MAS had changed its foreign currency policy and that PUB now had to bear its own currency risks. They therefore arranged a UK export credit in Singapore dollars and went through the same arguments with the authorities. The successful S$225 million loan enabled NEI to win the contract. Both loans were firsts and earned Schroders great credit for innovation.

Robinson had converted a conventional export credit business into a sophisticated one involving funding overseas contracts in many different foreign currencies, in which Schroders was unable to participate as lenders. At the same time the export credit agencies were steadily increasing the fixed interest rates they were willing to support – that is closer to commercial rates – so that for the emerging countries, in which Project Finance was most active, export credit became increasingly less competitive and Project Finance's role became less relevant. Robinson was essentially running a dying business. However, the profits made by his able team, particularly Sasha Chamberlain[1] and Mark Davis, from the export credit transactions enabled the project finance business to develop without the profit pressures it would have faced in the early days had it not been supported.[2]

Decline in oil and gas

Almost immediately on joining Project Finance Wadia, who had a good knowledge of and client contacts in the oil and gas sector, and Cockburn started to advise on a number of North Sea projects including one for Thompson with the help of Bill Harrison's oil and gas team in Corporate Finance and thereby added credibility to the team. It was not long, however, before the oil price dropped from $30 a barrel to $10 and all new investment, particularly in the North Sea, was cut back – this effectively killed off the project finance business in the hydrocarbons sector for the next three or four years. It was also the beginning of a worldwide recession, which was ominous for project financing. However, there were signs of new business stirring in other unknown sectors. The UK government's privatisation programme was in full swing with the beginnings of the privatisation of the utilities – telecoms and gas having been privatised and announcements made of the forthcoming privatisation of electricity. The Cross Channel tunnel, on which Schroders was advising the Department of Transport, was being evaluated by the private sector and there was talk of bridges, tunnels, roads and rail being carried out in the private sector too. Through its contractor finance business, Project Finance had a good knowledge of and contacts in the power and transport sectors and therefore an opportunity to diversify into a new business.

The emergence of power

Having been involved in many competitive international tenders for mega power stations in Asia, it occurred to Dewe Mathews that this could be repeated in the UK with a view to obtaining cheaper electricity. However, it would require the breakdown of the monopolies of British Coal to supply coal – involving a fight with the militant miners under Arthur Scargill – and of GEC and NEI to supply the plant as well as changing the way in which contracts were awarded by the Central Electricity Generating Board (CEGB). Dewe Mathews therefore approached Ivor Manley, the under secretary at the Department of Energy responsible for the privatisation of the electricity industry, who had had a short secondment to Schroders under Adam Broadbent, and said Schroders would be willing to develop a privately financed independent power station based on international tendering at fixed prices, which would sell its electricity to CEGB. He suggested that Dewe Mathews discuss his proposals with John Baker, then the secretary of CEGB, and later the chief executive of National Power. Baker saw this as a good opportunity for someone outside CEGB to break the monopolies including that of Barnwood, the all powerful in-house project development group responsible for the design and construction of all CEGB's power stations. He therefore offered Schroders an option on a site and with the help of the leading consulting engineers, Ewbank Preece,

Barking was chosen. Later Baker, who had wanted an equity role in the project, told Dewe Mathews that he had had his wrists slapped by Nigel Lawson, the Chancellor of the Exchequer, for encouraging such ventures. This was the beginning of Project Finance's attempt to diversify its business into an area where it could earn fees in the millions of pounds rather than the thousands.

For the project (eventually called Barking Power) conceived with the help of Ewbank Preece, Project Finance brought in BICC and Canadian Utilities as the developers. It was the first private sector power station to be developed in the UK but was overtaken by two others, both of which Project Finance was involved in as an advisor rather than a developer. The delay was principally due to local planning difficulties over the site but the project took off once Gary Bauer of Canadian Utilities took over its management and three regional electricity companies were brought in as shareholders and off takers of the electricity. Wadia was responsible for all the work, with Read Gomm and Dominic Freely in support. Project Finance's role was to optimise the after tax return to the shareholders by developing the financial structure and the debt financing based on the cash flow arising from the interrelationship between all of the contractual arrangements, which was projected on specially designed computer models. Seven years after its initial conception, the project was finally financed and earned a fee, which transformed Project Finance's profitability as well as its reputation within the bank.

For this work a totally different group of professionals was required. A major recruitment drive was initiated from which a new team was built with diverse skills, including Read Gomm from London Business School and the Canadian oil industry, Dominic Freely, an accountant, Chris Ewbank, a lawyer, and Kathie Painter, a PhD economist from Exxon. With Wadia, Cockburn regrettably having been poached by Harrison at Lehman Brothers, overseeing their training, Project Finance was able to develop a formidable team. When added to the contractor finance team of Robinson, John Burnham, Chamberlain and Chris Houston, the next step was to find some profitable business. Freely, Gomm and Painter and later Alasdair Cleghorn developed a strong capability in mathematical modelling to analyse and control the projects advised on. By controlling the models they became central to the management of their clients' projects and the only people who fully understood the financial impact on the project of each of the commercial issues being negotiated. This gave Project Finance an advantage over its competitors. Everyone was encouraged to specialise in the industries Project Finance focused on – oil and gas, power, transport, water and petrochemicals. The next parallel task was to build up the profits and so Dewe Mathews took the unusual step of seeking to drive up the success fees by refusing to work for clients who were not prepared to pay the fees sought. This led to clients only appointing Project Finance for their most difficult business. It was also very selective about the work it took on, only accepting work for projects it felt had a reasonable chance of success. It was quite proactive about projects approaching clients unknown to it or to the bank, if it felt they had a real commitment to success. It proved to be a winning strategy but only after five rather worrying years.

THE MALLINCKRODT - BISCHOFF PARTNERSHIP

South East Asia

With little further business in Singapore after the contracts for the MRT and Pulau Seraya projects had been awarded in 1984, Hargreaves-Allen turned his attention to the remainder of the region, particularly Malaysia, which was entering into a substantial privatisation programme. He secured an advisory role for the privatisation of the container terminal at Port Klang in Malaysia, which was awarded to P&O Australia, giving Project Finance an entrée to a major Malaysian company backed by Prime Minister Mahathir. He also set up an arrangement to pursue joint work with Ferdaus Siddik, a friend of Michael Kadoorie, in Indonesia, which lead to advising Bakrie Brothers, a prominent pri-bumi group, on the development of a seamless steel pipe project to supply the huge off-shore oil and gas industry. After seven years of frustration, a fee was paid for the work but more importantly Project Finance learnt a lot about how to do business in Indonesia. This helped it to secure many major advisory appointments from foreign companies that were so much easier to work with. By the time Hargreaves-Allen left for London in 1985 he had put Project Finance on the map and created a good platform on which his successors could build. He returned to London where he started to develop a telecom and media business. He had begun to make quite good progress including advising the BBC on the financing of its international television news service when tragically he died of leukaemia, with which he had been bravely struggling for some years.

When John Burnham[3] succeeded Hargreaves-Allen, South East Asia had entered a recession and he advised that there would not be any export credit business for the foreseeable future. Realising that export credit was a dying business and that the future lay in project financing, his move to Singapore enabled him to make this transition. He therefore set about building a new business based on Malaysia's wish to privatise its state-owned assets. IPCO, a Singapore-based construction company, had appointed Schroders to arrange the finance for its bid to supply a water pipeline between Sabah and the island of Labuan. With the new government policy to privatise, the project had to be rearranged with equity and debt based on IPCO and its friends owning the pipeline. This led to the first private sector infrastructure project in South East Asia. It was quickly followed by an electricity transmission line project in Labuan by IPCO again financed by Burnham and his team.

Burnham built up the office by recruiting well-educated Singaporeans, often president scholars, like Thomas See, whose education at Cambridge had been paid for on condition that he worked for the government for a number of years. Four other outstanding staff, Chan Kok Pun, Chan Wing Leong, YK Hiew and Mark Yeo, were also hired and they bore the brunt of the highly successful work in Malaysia, where a satellite office in KL was set up. The office became progressively more self-sufficient.

Privatisation opportunities multiplied in the infrastructure field and Burnham was inundated with work: the KL toll roads project, a feasibility study for the privatisation of the National Electricity Board of Malaysia (NEB) and the privatisation of the assets of Port Klang not previously sold to P&O of Australia. Taking advantage of the Mahathir government's strong commitment to privatisation, Burnham persuaded the prime minister's office to take Schroders on as advisors for a privatisation master plan, a highly prestigious and visible assignment. When it came to the agreement being signed by the Ministry of Finance various inducements were sought which were refused. Thanks to Burnham's tenacity and his superior presentation to that of the competitors then introduced by the Ministry of Finance, he was ultimately awarded the contract. Schroders' intransigence against bribery, despite the ambivalence of some of its competitors, played into its hands over the years to come as Schroders was seen throughout government to be incorruptible.

Having secured this important assignment, which gave access to every government department at the highest level, Burnham returned to London in 1988 leaving Gavin Anderson with the task of seeing it through. Anderson had joined Project Finance from the Foreign Office where he had been bored by the lack of a policy-making role, seeing the FCO as being subordinate to the home departments. He was highly intelligent and found the work of project financing interesting, despite his preference for playing the piano, which he did for many hours in the evening. He gave the impression of finding little difficulty in advising the Malaysian government despite his limited experience of privatisation matters. Anderson did Project Finance proud in Asia and also back in London but his love of the piano and his lack of materialism led to his departure for a more fulfilling life.

Transport sector

In the meanwhile in London Project Finance was adding to its emerging power business by expanding its transport business with the hiring of Nicholas Lethbridge, a brilliant but mercurial transport economist. He worked with Derek Netherton of Corporate Finance in 1985 on the Channel Fixed Link project advising the government on the merits of three bids to construct, operate, finance and own a fixed link across the English Channel. Eurotunnel was the only bid that could be financed and then only with difficulty. Unfortunately the government were not persuaded of the risks implicit in a cost plus contract rather than a fixed price contract and this ultimately lead to serious problems with the loans. Lethbridge, being a great expert on transport, brought in and managed a lot of good business, including the second cross-harbour road and rail tunnel in Hong Kong, the concession to build and operate the Queen Elizabeth bridge across the Thames at Dartford and endless light railway projects in the provinces, few of which came to fruition. He was highly respected by the officials he dealt with in the Department of Transport and his clients and he also had a good following of bright people within Project Finance. Although this business never made much money in comparison with power it was important in reducing Project Finance's dependence on the energy sector.

Unfortunately Lethbridge was very dismissive of the contractor finance team whom he regarded as being of a lower order of intelligence, despite the fact that they were providing the profits to pay his salary. This was extremely divisive and Dewe Mathews had a running battle to stop it – in the end Lethbridge had to go but that was for trying to unseat Dewe Mathews. He took advantage of Dewe Mathews being away from the office for a month, having taken a holiday straight after a business trip, to organise a coup and tried to get Robinson, Burnham and Wadia to join him in making representations to Slee. He also had a group of followers among the young. Having been so rude about Robinson and so difficult about Burnham's re-entry he did not get as far as he might have done. Following Dewe Mathews discussing the issue with Bischoff and Slee, it was agreed that Lethbridge would have to go and Dewe Mathews was told that his management style was too authoritative. After Lethbridge left harmony returned. During the 15 years Dewe Mathews ran Project Finance it was the only internal discord. There were also no other departures from the strong team. Speaking of Lethbridge, Wadia said,

> Nicholas had a highly original mind and was always challenging but extremely averse to any direction or supervision. He had a good eye for spotting opportunities and pursuing original concepts although many of them failed. He was particularly strong on transport, which reinforced our credentials. He was always shaking trees, had a slightly conspiratorial attitude and was the king of the wine bars and great fun. He engendered great loyalty.

Dewe Mathews said, 'I always enjoyed Nicholas' company but found him impossibly erratic in his many changes of mood and his need for praise and attention. Despite this he played an invaluable part in building our transport credentials.'

Lethbridge recruited Michael Dunne, who was his opposite. A construction engineer and MBA from Manchester, where he had been at school and university, he was blunt and direct, well organised, very hard working and in the office every morning at 7am. He filled in the gap when Lethbridge departed in taking on the transport sector. In all his work he was highly efficient. He was not as brilliant or entertaining as Lethbridge but more reliable and less emotional and a better team player. He made a considerable contribution to the business not least in advising Abittibi Price of Canada on the extraordinarily frustrating Orinoco Pulp and Paper project in Venezuela. He also did a great job on the East European fund of Robert Maxwell that Schroders inadvisably got involved with, through Merrill Lynch, as an independent adviser.[4] However, he was never altogether happy at Schroders and was better in a smaller team preferably led by himself, which he achieved in joining Westdeutsche Landesbank Merchant Bank.

Private Power
Burnham found his re-entry to London in 1988 rather difficult largely due to Lethbridge, who may have seen him as a threat. He had handed over to Anderson a wonderful portfolio in Asia and now had to fight for survival. Since he had left London three years before, the export credit business had shrunk, particularly as compared with the growth

of private power. He was appointed the co-ordinator of the private power business world-wide and while Wadia was battling away with Barking he romped away with a 350MW combined cycle gas turbine (CCGT) station at Corby for East Midlands Electricity Board which was in negotiation with a consortium led by Hawker Siddley. He also advised four of the regional electricity companies on the terms of their electricity purchase agreement and the price to acquire a 50% equity share in the 1875 MW Teeside power station from ICI and Enron Corporation, an emerging international force in private power from Houston, Texas, who were the promoters of the power station.

At the same time in Malaysia, following the feasibility study for the privatisation of the NEB, Burnham supported by See advised on the bid by YTL, a medium-sized construction company owned by the family of Tan Sri Yeoh Tiong Lay (Francis Yeoh) — one of Malaysia's most prominent ethnic Chinese business families which enjoyed close ties with Mahathir, to develop two private sector CCGT power stations, Paka and Pasir Gudang. They were based on two critical contracts with the government to purchase gas from Petronas, the national oil company and to sell electricity to NEB. The key to the success of the bid was the economics of the project and the interrelationship between the pricing of the two contracts and the expected return to the shareholders, which was significantly enhanced by the high leverage of the financing. These were important fee earners and contributed to Project Finance's emerging reputation for the financing of private power around the world.

Burnham was ambitious and having seen the writing on the wall for the export credit business developed into a fully-fledged project financier. He always had goals and was very courageous in going barefaced for mandates, often succeeding. He had a first-class mind and the ability and confidence to take on the switch to Project Finance. He was Wadia's principal partner over many years, supporting each other with a good working relationship. Burnham thought Wadia was 'a wonderful man, who was enormously talented. He was not interested in management or administration and therefore left it to others. Although not a self starter he was a wonderful mentor to the young and created a culture of excellence and co-operation.' The reason for Wadia not being mentioned much in regard to individual projects was that he oversaw all of them acting as a quality controller and internal adviser to all.

Continental Europe

Having established a leading position in the UK power and transport sectors, Project Finance needed to develop a position on the Continent. It decided to start with the Iberian peninsular as it had a less developed merchant banking sector. Rosamund Blomfield-Smith spearheaded this work.[5] Her linguistic skills made her particularly effective in opening new markets and she set off for Lisbon and got to know the government departments, the banks and the utilities. This led to three major financings in Portugal: acting for Trafalgar House on the Second Tagus Bridge Crossing; for Siemens on the Tapada Power Station; and for National Power on the $1 billion refinancing of

Pego Power Station. This was followed by the financing of a Steel Mill in Spain. Not having been made a director she accepted a directorship from NM Rothschild. Wadia said of her,

> Rosamund was one of the most rounded people with her talents as a pianist and a linguist, as well as being cultured and having considerable social flair. Not being a natural project financier, she did a phenomenal job in Portugal on the Second Tagus Crossing facing unacceptable treatment from an extremely difficult client. She was a remarkably good marketer and picked up many new mandates.

There was however a culture within Project Finance that, as well as securing business, directors had to be responsible for the detailed implementation of their own mandates – she did not have the confidence of the directors in this and Dewe Mathews felt he could not overrule them, 'much to my discredit'.

The increasing volume of work in the power sector, particularly in Europe meant that more experienced staff had to be recruited. Burnham recommended that Michael Sutcliffe who had impressed him while working for the other side on the Corby transaction. Following a protracted negotiation in 1993, Dewe Mathews found himself with a team of three from the London office of Fieldstone, a New York based project finance boutique. These three were Sutcliffe, Andrew Brandler and Alasdair Cleghorn, all of whom were first class and added considerably to Project Finance's capability to take on and to carry out top level advisory work. Sutcliffe was a very strong marketer of new business and maintained strong relationships with his clients. Being very gregarious and warm he knew most of the people in the power industry and was never afraid to go straight to the top of the companies he knew. His weakness was that he was not as skilled in execution and did not develop a good rapport with some of his most able colleagues. Brandler was a real star. He had a first class mind beneath a very genial exterior. He was one of the most balanced of his colleagues and fitted in like a glove immediately. He could perhaps have been more assertive. Always courteous he was strong in banking and corporate finance and clients swore by him. Cleghorn was the behind-the-scenes technician, brilliant on the computer and indispensable to Sutcliffe's ability to execute transactions – they made a powerful team. Cleghorn made a big contribution to developing the computer modelling skills, which were a key to the strength of the team's work and differentiated it from the competition. Although greatly valued by the clients, he always seemed to be more comfortable in the background and this held him back in a group that gave a premium to the business getters.

International corporate finance

With the completion of the financing of the Barking Power project and Project Finance's largest fee of £5 million in 1992, the profits had jumped up to £6 million from £750,000 the year before. Project Finance was now well established as a leading project financier throughout Europe and Asia and initiated a move into areas of international corporate finance of no interest to Corporate Finance. Dewe Mathews deliberately avoided Project Finance duplicating Corporate Finance's areas of expertise, which were largely related to the rules governing take-overs and the stock market, of which Project Finance had no knowledge. It therefore concentrated on acquisitions arising from trade sales in the industries with which it was familiar, particularly power, whose values were often based on their projected cash flows. Initially British Gas was advised on its purchase of Ballylumford power station in Northern Ireland and this was completed in 1992.

At the same time Project Finance extended its activities to advising on privatisation, which was becoming increasingly popular internationally especially in South America. The countries in this region had thrown out their disastrous import substitution policies and embraced democracy and the market economy, initiating programmes for the sale of state owned utilities – telecommunications, gas, electricity and water. By combining its knowledge of these industries and the large private sector utilities in Europe and the USA with its earlier experience of working, albeit somewhat unsuccessfully, in these countries, Project Finance was unusually well qualified to advise potential clients. Initially it sought to act for the governments of Argentina, Brazil, Chile, Colombia and Bolivia and advise them on how to conduct their privatisations and trade sales, thereby giving it increased credibility with overseas buyers. Through Schroders' representative offices in Buenos Aires, Sao Paulo and Bogotá it got to know the leading local investment groups and banks with strong government connections and as a result was able to assist in putting together bidding consortia comprising international and local companies and advising them on their bids and their financing. This led to a substantial volume of business that was masterminded by Chris Ewbank, who, as a former solicitor from Clifford Chance, had the documentation skills that were critical to the effectiveness of this government privatisation work. A bachelor, he spent his weekends climbing Munros – hills over 3000 feet – with his climbing friends from Cambridge. This led to much government work in the gas and electricity sectors including acting for National Grid and their partners in purchasing Transener, the Argentine electricity transmission system, and for the Bolivian government on the privatisation of its electricity industry.[6]

Having become one of the leaders in advising overseas governments on the privatisation of their energy industries, Project Finance became increasingly involved in advising on the acquisition and sale of power plants and distribution facilities for National Power in the UK and for the large US and European utilities in many parts of the world. It had become a highly successful and well-regarded world player in the electricity and gas sectors.

Following the successes in the 'southern cone' of South America with extensive work in Argentina, Chile and Bolivia with the help of Rupert Sword, the Schroder representative in Buenos Aires, Project Finance decided to repeat the process by sending John Rutherford to Bogotá in Colombia to cover the 'northern cone'. Being Anglo-Venezuelan he was ideal for the job and helped to secure the prestigious role of acting jointly with Salomon Brothers in New York for the Colombian government in the sale of their 1900MW of generating plant. Regrettably after the successful conclusion of this assignment, he was accosted in his car by two armed thugs and deposited without clothes, money or papers on the side of the road many miles from his home. Dewe Mathews felt it was unsafe for him to continue in Bogotá and he moved to Caracas. It also put off Dewe Mathews' plans to repeat on a smaller scale what had been done in Asia by sending Ewbank out to Latin America to run the business throughout Latin America. To be successful in Latin America it was essential to have international credibility in the capital markets as well as knowledge of the privatisation process and capital markets was not one of Schroders' strengths. This deficiency was offset by always acting jointly with a major US investment bank who invariably did as little detailed work as was possible after having agreed their share of the fees.

At the same time, with the encouragement of Guy Harington's East Europe team, Project Finance became advisors to the Hungarian government in 1994 on the privatisation of its electricity industry, as described earlier in Chapter 14. With the introduction of a major privatisation programme in Australia, Richard Beales was sent to Sydney from Hong Kong where the team had many successes in helping international clients to buy electricity assets and for a period a project finance office was set up. It did less well in transport where Macquarie Bank was dominant.

In Asia the project financing business continued to boom with Gomm taking over from Houston in Hong Kong (see Chapter 16) and Brandler and Houston in Singapore and KL, all under Burnham as director of Project Finance in Asia, based in Hong Kong between 1993 and 1995. In South East Asia advice was being given on a petrochemical project in the Philippines for BP, power stations for Eximbank and another for BP in Indonesia, the long spun out Thai Aromatics project for Exxon Chemicals and the privatisation of the Selangor water supply in Malaysia.

In view of the increasing need for export credit agencies to guarantee limited recourse loans arising out of privatisation of public utilities around the world and in view of Project Finance's reputation for arranging complicated limited recourse loans particularly those for Castle Peak in Hong Kong which were mainly guaranteed by ECGD, Malcolm Stephens, the chief executive of ECGD, asked Dewe Mathews to give a paper on the subject to a conference in Montreal. All members of the Berne Union, the heads of all the export credit agencies from around the world, would be present. It was an ideal opportunity to make an impression and Robinson gave a speech. Out of it arose a decision by the Export-Import Bank of the United States (Eximbank) to set up a special unit to deal with limited recourse projects. It was also decided to hire a pool of advisors so that appointments could be made to advise on different projects. A public invitation was made in 1993 for qualified banks to submit their credentials. From the 45 responses, five banks were selected: Morgan Stanley; JP Morgan; two boutiques; and Schroders, the only foreign owned bank. It was a great coup for the team of Robinson, Wadia and Davis. The flow of work, which followed was phenomenal, covering projects all over the world including LNG projects in Qatar and Oman, an oil pipeline in Cameroon, a power station in Indonesia and a telecommunications system in Mexico. An experienced director like Kathie Painter managed each Eximbank assignment.[7] The contract with Eximbank was renewed, giving Project Finance good exposure to many new companies and governments and this led to much new business.

One of the key members of Project Finance was Chris Houston, who spent a lot of time in the Far East working in and then running the project offices in Hong Kong and Singapore. Like Burnham he was one of the very few graduates who was retained and made the transition to project finance with ease. He combined his love of the Far East with his work. He had a dry sense of humour and never had to bully or dominate. Clients swore by him. He was very sound and thought through issues carefully. He was economical with his time and went home when he had finished his work, doing only what was necessary – difficult to do nowadays. He was a superior jack-of-all-trades with the ability to handle any task, be it the clients or managing his staff, most of whom were Chinese. He had a good appreciation of the many different cultures and treated everyone with great sensitivity. He carried through everything with apparent ease and without panic and commanded all his colleagues' respect and affection. His industry skill was transport, much of which he learnt from Lethbridge who remained a close friend. On returning to London he took over the transport work from Dunne and also led the Private Finance Initiative (PFI) work in the health sector advising on the ownership and financing of many private sector hospitals in the UK, including arranging the first bond financing under the PFI. He also managed major project financings in other fields including a very difficult petrochemical project in Thailand over many years. He was clearly a future leader of Project Finance.

By 1994 Project Finance's annual revenue had increased to £11 million with profits of £6 million. By pursuing a policy of never accepting second best it had become a world player and established itself as a reliable albeit modest contributor to the Group bottom line. It was valued far more highly within the Group in terms of its international reputation than its profits.

NOTES:

1. Sasha Chamberlain was an expert in export credit documentation and managed all the loans. Robinson was always surprised that someone who appeared to be so disorganised was in fact totally in control and better than others at the thought process. She had a great amount of admirers in ECGD and among the clients, especially in Hong Kong, where most of her largest and most complicated loans were.

2. One of the controversial pieces of business completed by the contractor finance team was acting for Balfour Beatty and Trafalgar House (with GEC having a sub contracting role) in 1991 in respect of their negotiated contract to construct the Pergau hydro power station for

Tenaga National Berhad, the new name for NEB. Robinson and Chamberlain had organised an attractive mixed credit combining export credit and aid at the same time that GEC was leading a group in negotiating a very large defence equipment contract with the Malaysian government. Endless problems were caused by a series of articles by the Andrew Neil in the *Sunday Times* saying that aid was being given to Malaysia to secure defence sales. Robinson had to go before a parliamentary committee to give evidence that the two contracts and especially the finance had been independently arranged. The damage caused by the press articles, which were particularly critical of Mahathir, the prime minister, was long lasting in that he imposed a buy British last policy. It was many years before Britain won another major contract in Malaysia and that was only after extensive diplomatic work by the British High Commissioners. The work on the Pergau project led to advising Trafalgar House, Costain and Mitsui on their contract to build the Tsing Ma Bridge to link Hong Kong to its new airport on Lantau Island in 1992. And this was followed by the $2.4 billion multi-currency financing for GEC Alsthom and General Electric of the USA's contract to build China Light and Exxon's Black Point Power Station in 1993. These proved to be the last major contractor financings arranged.

3. John Burnham, a graduate with a first in geography from Cambridge, had joined the export credit department in Banking in 1976 despite the disapproval of David Forsyth, the head of Banking, and had as a result become an assistant to Dewe Mathews. He was to have no other boss for the next twenty years. When he joined the team there was very little business and was kept busy doing various studies, which he completed far too quickly. Burnham was very bright and ambitious and helped with the Castle Peak financings in Hong Kong and later arranged the export credits for GEC's contracts for the Keephills and Genesee power stations in Canada with barely any supervision.

4. At the height of the euphoria over the fall of the Berlin wall in 1991, the infamous Robert Maxwell decided to set up a fund to invest in the new business opportunities likely to arise in the east European countries. After he had appointed Merrill Lynch to raise a $500 million fund to be managed by himself, Merrill Lynch said the funds could not be raised without a blue chip house being appointed as the financial advisor to review all the investments proposed by Maxwell. Mallinckrodt, being very committed to the east European adventure, persuaded his rather reluctant colleagues to bid for the appointment and Dewe Mathews was asked to assemble a team. Much to his surprise, having put in very large fees to avoid being selected, Schroders was appointed. There followed a series of unpleasant confrontations between Maxwell and Dewe Mathews before Merrill Lynch said the funds could not be raised. Not long afterwards Maxwell's empire collapsed and he disappeared over the side of his yacht near the Canaries before being exposed for having stolen the pension funds from his companies.

5. Rosamund Blomfield-Smith had joined the export credit department from Morgan Grenfell, having in the interim tried to establish herself as a concert pianist and been a financial journalist. She initially concentrated on the Middle East having earlier been the

private secretary to the British Ambassador in Jordan. These markets were not easy particularly for a woman but she would not accept defeat.

6. Kleinwort Benson and NM Rothschild with their strong privatisation credentials in the UK particularly in the energy sector were powerful competitors. Like Schroders they always worked alongside a US investment bank as their capital markets' capabilities were not sufficiently strong.

7. Kathie Painter came from Exxon where her boss Chris Potter, whom Dewe Mathews knew well through the Castle Peak financings, said if she had a fault it was that she was too fast. Painter having already received a PhD, Dewe Mathews was irritated when after only a year she decided to go to Cranfield Business School. He kept closely in touch giving her well-paid consultancy assignments to help her pay her way. 'Needless-to-say she came top of her year and rejoined Project Finance. She was arguably the brightest person in Project Finance and fitted in well with her peer group of Gomm, Freely and Ewbank, none of whom were short of brains. She had a very direct approach to life and did not suffer fools gladly.' Once she asked Dewe Mathews why the clients were so stupid and he responded, 'why do you think they pay such high fees – they also have other skills we lack.' She was very economical with her time and being so well organised packed a huge amount of work into her day running a number of mandates in parallel. Clients had great trust in her work. Generally she returned home at 6.30pm to feed her three children and put them to bed. Not long afterwards her laptop computer was switched on for a few hours before going to bed. She anchored much of the work for the oil companies including many oil and gas pipeline and petrochemical projects.

CHAPTER 16

HONG KONG AFTER BISCHOFF

1983 – 1994

Bischoff directly swapped his job as managing director of Schroders & Chartered in June 1982 with van Marle, the head of the international issues department in London. Having no experience of the main activities of Schroders & Chartered and not being British, van Marle was to some extent – despite being good with clients – like a fish out of water with nothing to offer, there being no prospects for Euro issues in Hong Kong. John Reynolds, an acolyte of Bischoff, was in charge of Corporate Finance and well plugged into the social and business scene having been handed over all Bischoff's clients. With the Hang Seng Index down from its peak of 1600 in early 1981 to 800 by the end of 1982 and remaining just above that level until mid 1984, there was not much corporate finance business. The collapse of the market was associated with concern over the future of Hong Kong following an abrasive meeting between Mrs Thatcher and Deng Xiaoping in Beijing in September 1982 when Deng rejected Thatcher's proposal for continued British administration of Hong Kong after 1997. This combined with Thatcher, heavy with a cold, losing her footing on the steps of the Great Hall of the People leading down into Tiananmen Square and tumbling to her knees and seeming to kow-tow towards the mausoleum of Chairman Mao, were bad omens for the future of the Colony to the superstitious Hong Kong Chinese (Robert Cottrell, *The End of Hong Kong*). This was shortly followed by the collapse of Carrian, the 'glamour stock' of the 1979 to 1981 property boom, managed by the larger than life George Tan who had entered into a series of property deals in a booming market with the assistance of a number of unscrupulous bankers. Carrian's bankruptcy was to cost its bankers and shareholders more than US$2 billion.

The huge volatility in the stock market and the collapse of the property market resulted in a secondary banking crisis caused by fraud and reckless lending during the property boom. Schroders & Chartered became involved in virtually all the attempts to rescue the banks as Wardley was invariably unable to advise them due to its parent HSBC being the bank of last resort. With Schroders & Chartered's leading reputation for high quality independent advice, it was approached for help by the Government and also by the owners of the banks. Giles Elliott, who had come out from London to assist Reynolds, was soon up to his ears in bank reconstructions for Hang Leung, OTB, HIBC and Ka Wah to name but a few.

1983 and 1984 were difficult years for Hong Kong in view of the negotiations between the governments of Great Britain and China regarding the terms under which sovereignty would be passed to China in 1997. Lydia Dunn (later Baroness), as one of three unofficial members of the Executive Council, was much involved behind the scenes with Sir SY Chung in representing the interests of the Hong Kong people in informal discussions with the British and Chinese governments at the time, said,

> The results of the negotiations were kept confidential but there were deadlocks and when they became known to the community they created a crisis of confidence resulting in a run on the Hong Kong dollar in September 1983 with the exchange rate falling to HK$9.50/US$1. This was resolved by an announcement by Sir John Bremridge, the financial secretary, on 15 October 1983 linking the HK dollar to the US dollar at a target rate of HK$7.80 and this has stood the test of time, the rate not having been changed since despite the massive swings in the economic cycle.

The signing at the end of 1984 of the Sino-British Joint Declaration on the Question of Hong Kong, in which the Chinese guaranteed to allow two systems within one country, effectively promising no change to the way of life of the people in Hong Kong for 50 years, brought political and economic stability and the market took off with the Hang Seng Index rising steadily from 800 to 4000 in October 1987. This brought a big flow of issuance business but Schroders & Chartered, with its lack of distribution capability, had always lagged behind its competitors, notably Jardine Fleming and Wardley, and also the powerful brokers Baring Securities, Vickers da Costa and Hoare Govett. Whereas Bischoff had done a remarkable job carving out a name for Schroders in the traditional relationship-based advisory business he had not gone into the securities business that was to be the big money spinner in Hong Kong over the next few years. Schroders Asia Securities, which had opened for business at the end of 1982, was mainly focused on securing rebates on the fixed commissions SIM in London was paying on its Japanese investment business (see Chapter 11). The Hong Kong brokerage business was very modest by comparison. Schroders & Chartered was effectively a high quality advisory house as in London. Jardine Fleming on the other hand had built a substantial pan-Asian investment bank with stockbroking businesses throughout the region. In fact this business was so strong, making profits of up to US$100 million a year, that the corporate finance advisory business in Hong Kong was virtually closed. With the advisory business being relatively small, Schroders & Chartered found it difficult to maintain its position in the market. By contrast with Jardine Fleming, with its fully integrated investment banking business across the region being managed out of Hong Kong, Schroders had four totally separate businesses in Hong Kong, Japan, Singapore and Australia which barely did any business together, all having differing capabilities. Schroders & Chartered was deceived into thinking it was a continuing success by increasing profits that were in decline relative to the competition which had radically changed their businesses in response to the opportunities in the market.

It was not therefore a particularly easy time for Corporate Finance. Despite the political and economic uncertainties van Marle started a banking business under Douglas Fergusson initially concentrating on the money market and participation in the CD and commercial paper markets. This grew in time to become very profitable.

Earlier in March 1982 shortly before Bischoff left Hong Kong, Hugh Bolland had been sent out from Investment Management in London to take over from Ruedi Bischof, who decided to join Swiss Bank Corporation.[1] Bolland, who was from a highly professional pension fund management organisation with good systems, was surprised to find no institutional clients, simply Swiss private clients – Ruedi was a private banker from Switzerland and had developed essentially a private client business. Bolland installed some new systems and went out to find new clients. Things went well over the next two years and together with Schroders' good investment record in London, he started to receive appointments from some big names and Investment Management became the largest profit maker of Schroders & Chartered.

Bolland returned to London in 1984 to discuss a new job only to hear that Airlie wanted to speak to him. He was amazed to be asked to go back to Hong Kong as managing director of Schroders & Chartered as van Marle had accepted an offer from CSFB to run its business in the Netherlands, much to the relief of his wife Christine who never really cared for Hong Kong. After some careful thought Bolland told Airlie he was in no way qualified to run Schroders & Chartered as he knew nothing about corporate finance and banking. Airlie dismissed his arguments and thereby did him a great favour. He returned to Hong Kong where John Reynolds, who was running Corporate Finance, gave him great support despite his disappointment at not having been made managing director. Reynolds returned to London shortly afterwards[2] and was succeeded by Paul Banner who, shortly afterwards, resigned to join a bank that was being restructured by the government with the advice of Schroders & Chartered. Apart from the blow to Bolland, the government was not too pleased. He was succeeded by Giles Elliott.[3] Not long after Fergusson, who had also expected to be made managing director, left to run Prudential Asia, leaving the banking business in the capable hands of Tommy Lee. Investment Management remained under Frank Heath and continued to thrive with funds under management increasing by 50% during the year, due to the very high success rate in presentations for new business. This was followed the next year with a further 60% rise, reflecting favourable market conditions.

In view of the number of major infrastructure projects being supported by the government, Project Finance decided to transfer Sriram Chari from Singapore to Hong Kong in 1985 to set up a project office to provide project finance advise in the Colony, China, Taiwan and the Philippines. Not long afterwards the government appointed Schroders to advise on the bids it was receiving to construct and finance its second cross-harbour road and rail tunnel between Victoria Island and Kowloon. Lethbridge from Project Finance in London, who had helped win the assignment, came out to Hong Kong to help and guide Chari with the advice. This and other projects were highly prestigious and had Project Finance been more generous with its fee splits it could have become an important fourth leg of Schroders & Chartered's business.

To compound Bolland's difficulty not long into his reign, Bill Brown, the general manager of the Chartered Bank, who had taken over from Millar, informed Bolland that he was setting up his own merchant banking business a few floors below Schroders & Chartered. Standard Chartered was at this time building a small merchant banking business in London to include Eurocurrency lending and project finance and wished to expand into Hong Kong. Standard Chartered's earlier move into syndicated loans in Hong Kong in direct competition with Schroders & Chartered was the result of Standard Chartered feeling that Schroders & Chartered, due to its limited capital would not be able to take full advantage of the Eurocurrency lending market in Hong Kong – this inevitably led to the parting of the ways. Bolland got on to Philip Robinson, who was still very helpfully fulfilling the role of the senior director in London responsible for Asia, and he came out to negotiate the break up of the 16-year partnership (see Chapter 4). Standard Chartered's 40% shareholding was purchased for book value and the company was renamed Schroders Asia with Schroders having 75% of the shares and the Kadoories 25%. Michael Kadoorie and Willie Mocatta joined Lord Kadoorie and Sir Sidney Gordon on the board. This coincided with the signing of the Joint Declaration on the future of Hong Kong, which had restored confidence to the Colony, and the outlook for further increases in profitability looked bright.

Towards the end of his three-year secondment in 1987, Bolland was asked to take over Schroders Australia from Brian Gatfield who had decided to leave (see Chapter 18) and handed over Schroders Asia to MacAndrew, one of Corporate Finance's senior directors.[4] Bolland left a business with Corporate Finance breaking even, Investment Management making good profits from a good set of institutional pension funds with an emerging unit trust business, and a successful banking business based on being a major issuer of CDs.

When MacAndrew arrived Elliott, then head of Corporate Finance, was acting for Hong Kong and Shanghai Hotels Company in which the Kadoorie and the Liang families each owned 30% of the shares. David Liang sold his shares to Joseph Lau, a new property magnate from Kowloon, who immediately bid for the company proposing to pull down The Peninsula Hotel to redevelop the site. This was anathema to the Kadoories and became a battle between old and new money. It was agreed that the Laus would be bought out and this would be paid for by an international share offering arranged by Schroders Asia. Schroders Asia only managed to place two-thirds of the US$250 million issue by the 13 October with the sub-underwriting running out on Monday 17 October. On the Saturday morning Robert Ng of Sino Land agreed to take the balance at the issue price on a hand shake, agreeing to bring round his cheque on the Monday morning. With the collapse of the stock market in New York on the Friday after the markets had closed in Hong Kong and London, there was a good deal of nervousness over the weekend until Ng came in at 10am with his cheque which was cleared by HSBC at noon with the underwriters being let off the hook. It was 'Black Monday' and the Hang Seng Index dropped like a stone from 4000 to 2000. In fact the stock exchange never opened on Black Monday nor on any day that week.[5]

There was a little improvement in market conditions during 1988 and then the market plunged back to the same level following the massacre of students in Tiananmen Square by the People's Liberation Army on the night of 3/4 June 1989.[6] Corporate Finance made losses in 1988 and 1989, not being helped by the emergence of a number of corporate finance boutiques. Fortunately Bolland had left a good legacy in Investment Management under the good management of Heath, who having been passed over as managing director, left for the Bank of Bermuda and was replaced by Richard Haw, who was to stay for many years. Another good earner was Financial Markets under the brilliant Lee. Banking, following the setting up of Standard Chartered Merchant Bankers in competition, was virtually non-existent and Lee's business was concentrated on principal trading of HK$ CDs and commercial paper where he and his team were very effective in the market. The other business was Project Finance where Chari was running a satellite project office within Schroders Asia – a very prestigious assignment was advising the government on the feasibility of the financing and institutional aspects of a replacement airport and of future port facilities. MacAndrew wanted Chari to report directly to him rather than to London and this was the beginnings of a struggle between geographic and functional control of the businesses. It was only later that Schroders decided to go functional with the local barons not being at all happy to lose control of their fiefdoms. Project Finance, which had always developed as a global business controlled from London, never had a problem save in Hong Kong and that was only temporary.

At the end of MacAndrew's three-year secondment, with Heath having left, there was no obvious successor. Following the Joint Declaration agreement business prospects in Hong Kong looked less rosy. London was concerned about its financial exposure and felt caution was needed with the foot on the brake rather than on the accelerator. None of the business heads in London, who were all doing well, was prepared to release anyone of any quality and so it was agreed to look outside. Ian Boyce, the managing director of East Asia Warburg, a joint venture between SG Warburg and Bank of East Asia, was known to the Kadoories as he had acted for the family in transactions when they needed independent advice including on the take-over bid for the Hong Kong and Shanghai Hotels Company. At the time SG Warburg and the Bank of East Asia were acting independently of each other in Investment Management and Treasury and Boyce saw little future for himself and agreed to return to SG Warburg in London where he had been from 1972 to 1984 before going out to Hong Kong. Preferring to remain in Hong Kong he approached MacAndrew to see whether he could join Schroders Asia knowing that MacAndrew's wife Vicky did not like the life in Hong Kong and found a receptive ear. As the Kadoories had been impressed with Boyce and liked him they recommended him to Schroders. MacAndrew as a competitor had seen Boyce and felt he would do a good job in the changed circumstances. He was seen as a safe pair of hands. It would not be easy for him to come into Schroders from the outside.

MacAndrew therefore left Hong Kong in 1990 before he could make any real impact on Schroders Asia, which in terms of reputation, although not in profits, was on the slide since Bischoff had left. Many clients, competitors and professional advisors felt that Bischoff had never been effectively replaced. The corporate financiers who followed were nice people and good technicians but they lacked a strategic sense for corporate finance. In reviewing those who followed Bischoff as managing director of Schroders & Chartered and Schroders Asia, Michael Kadoorie said,

> Win was a hard act to follow not least because all those who followed him were there for shorter periods and so never established themselves. Tyo was very nice but not a corporate financier, Hugh was dedicated but did not have the same presence, Nick, a delightful friend, was less aggressive, not as clever or as astute as Win – being very much the gentleman from the land, maybe he did not have to make his way as Bischoff had had to.

Purves said Schroders Asia did not grow after Bischoff left as it did not have the same leadership and there was more competition.

It was during MacAndrew's time that Schroders Asia was acting for a rather dubious Chinese company in a very complicated and messy take over of a New Zealand company listed on the Hong Kong Stock Exchange, which became known as the Paladin case. Following the take-over the company failed and Schroders Asia, as advisors, was sued by the Chinese who were unhappy with what they found. The Take-over Panel ruled against Schroders Asia because the long form report on Paladin prepared by the auditors was in final draft form rather than confirmed by them – in fact they changed it subsequently. David Caruth, the group legal adviser, was called in to assist in resolving the problem. His findings were not very palatable to Schroders, particularly MacAndrew who was then participating in an advanced management program at Harvard Business School. Christopher Clarke, Schroders' counsel, felt Schroders had a 60% chance of winning and advised against an offer to settle for HK$25 million. Boyce was worried about his bottom line and reluctant to settle, particularly with Sir Sidney Gordon, his deputy chairman, being strongly opposed to any settlement with the Chinese for whom he had no respect. Caruth and Boyce sought a meeting with the Chinese who insisted on it being in Beijing. They made such a derisory offer that it was rejected by the Chinese who realised Schroders Asia was on its back foot. On the eve of the trial Schroders Asia's new counsel, who was far more negative than Clarke, who was not available to continue the case, advised that Schroders Asia should settle for HK$100 million plus costs (£8.4 million). The Take-over Panel reprimanded Schroders Asia for its conduct, a censure, a much more serious offence, being avoided. The lesson for Schroders was that if in litigation with the verdict in doubt it is important to settle early – it forgot this lesson ten years later when sued by an employee for unfair discrimination and paid a heavy price. MacAndrew was dumbstruck by the settlement and deeply upset by the whole issue. Having been the managing director at the time the work was being done in 1989 by Francis Jackson and Paul Campion he offered his resignation, a typically honourable move, but this was rejected. Jackson having left in 1991 Campion was left with the task of clearing up the mess, which occupied over half his time.

Apart from the Paladin saga, Boyce found the business in good shape. The profits in 1989 were only marginally lower than those in 1988 despite the adverse impact of the Tiananmen Square massacre on the market with the Hang Seng Index falling from 3400 to 2000. Schroders Asia was still a leading M&A house being the top rated arranger in Asia in 1991 and 1992 which included acting for Hang Chong Investments in their HK$7 billion sale to a consortium led by CITIC, the leading Chinese investment corporation from Beijing and for HSBC in its take-over of Midland Bank. Most of the local Chinese banks were listed by Schroders Asia including Wing Hang. Schroders Asia also had a strong position in the Hong Kong capital market arranging many CD issues for the banks and was one of the two most active arrangers in Hong Kong. Treasury was also a leading trader of Hong Kong government bonds and Exchange Fund bonds. Investment Management had a particularly powerful position in the pension fund sector as evidenced by the Wyatt Survey that showed that Schroders Asia managed 52 of the 212 funds managed by 36 managers followed by Jardine Fleming and HSBC with 47 and 30 respectively. As these funds increased to 304 over the next decade Schroders Asia's share increased – managing 76 compared with 52 by HSBC and 35 by Jardine Fleming. The returns on these retirement schemes were reported to be above the median for the seventh successive year in 1989 and this continued for the next five years. Throughout the period Schroders Asia's unit trusts remained in the top quartile as measured by the Hong Kong Investment Funds Association. So on all fronts Schroders Asia was a top performer and this was reflected in its profits and shareholders funds which doubled between 1990 and 1994 to HK$97 million and HK$400 million. Jardine Fleming's profits, which covered the whole of the Far East, were at the same time US$200 million, that is 15 times greater.

China

There was much concern in Hong Kong about whether the reforms in China would be sustained and how far it would go in introducing a capitalist free market. In the early 1990s a momentum was developed with the manufacturing industry moving from Hong Kong to Guangdong to take advantage of the cheap labour leaving Hong Kong to be largely a marketing centre. Once the Shanghaiese in Hong Kong moved their businesses to Guangdong everyone knew that the reforms would not be reversed. The Chinese economy was too strong to ignore and Hong Kong's business became entirely dependent on it. [7] All the banks, particularly those from America, set up new offices in Hong Kong to exploit this new market.

Mallinckrodt was highly committed to supporting Boyce's efforts in China that led to the opening of a representative office in Shanghai in 1994 directed by Ivan Chan, formerly of Arthur Anderson, from Hong Kong. They built up a good quality advisory business, but of course the Chinese do not like paying advisory fees and so they were totally dependent on international companies, like Bass, who were looking to set up joint ventures. It barely covered its costs. This work, however, was completely overtaken by the listing business where Schroders Asia was at a major competitive disadvantage having very little distribution capacity. It found itself squeezed out by the large US investment banks, which, despite their lack of knowledge of the market, had considerable name recognition, capital and placing power, and Peregrine, which picked up most of the smaller issues.[8]

Mallinckrodt visited Hong Kong and China at least twice a year mainly concentrating on the government and the Bank of China. As always he was keen to ensure that costs were kept to a minimum. On one occasion Tim Williams, a Chinese-speaking Australian former journalist who advised Schroders on its business in China, arranged a trip for Mallinckrodt and Boyce to visit Shanghai and hired an old car as a cost saving measure to transport them between meetings. On leaving one of the largest and most prestigious banks with its chairman and his colleagues standing on the top of the steps, the car failed to start and Boyce and Williams were seen ignominiously pushing the car down the street as the bank officials looked on. Bischoff, who was responsible for Hong Kong, visited it frequently invariably combining it with his calls in Japan. He maintained all his old contacts and was a good ambassador always having access to the highest levels including the governor and the financial secretary.

The major area of activity in China in which Schroders was a leader was project finance. Read Gomm was moved from London to run the North East Asia project office in Hong Kong in March 1993 having spent the last few months travelling there to work on Wing Merrill private power projects in China.[9] He arrived in Hong Kong at the beginning of the power boom in China with the Chinese inviting all and sundry to present proposals for the construction, operation and financing of private sector power stations. The Chinese economy was booming and investment of foreign capital was being encouraged particularly in greenfield power generation projects due to the scarcity of electricity to support the rapid growth in their industry. Every province wanted more power but no overall policy had been agreed with Beijing. There was a great scramble with every international power company supported by all the lawyers, accountants and banks wanting to be in on the potential gravy train. On the back of the Wing Project in Henan Province, Gomm and his able team worked on some eight to ten such projects over the next three years, always having to cope with the conflicting demands of Dewe Mathews and their chairman. Burnham, who was heading the project business in Asia, bore the brunt of being caught between Mallinckrodt, who wanted him to devote all his resources to pursuing business in China, and Dewe Mathews, the ultimate sceptic, who sought to limit the efforts in China, having had considerable experience of the frustrations of negotiating with the Chinese and needing to make profits to secure a reasonable bonus pool for the division.

Inevitably it ended in tears with Beijing cancelling most of the programme. It was an incredible waste of time although it helped to raise Schroders' profile in China.[10] Gomm visited China over 90 times during his period in Hong Kong between 1993 and 1995. Ultimately Schroders was only involved in one successful power project when it advised ECGD on financing a 3000MW coal fired power station in Shandong Province. Fortunately there was project work concerned with the improvement of Hong Kong's ever expanding infrastructure – including the HK$15 billion sewerage project for the Hong Kong government, the Tsing Ma suspension bridge for an Anglo-Japanese consortium and the Black Point power station for GEC Alsthom and GE – which more than paid for the office and the losses on the work in China.

1994 saw a significant fall in the markets throughout the region the Hang Seng Index falling from 12000 to 7000. There was also a good deal of nervousness over Patten's patronising attitude towards the Chinese. Fortunately the Chinese were quite pragmatic when it came to business. Endless arguments with the Chinese in Beijing over contracts being placed for the new airport and much suspicion regarding the Hong Kong government's intentions regarding the preservation of its large reserves continued the uncertainty, but gradually things settled down and the economy stabilised.

In the previous year Lord Kadoorie died. Up to two weeks before he was still chairing the board meetings of Schroders Asia and Sir Elly Kadoorie in his wheelchair. It was the end of an era. One of the great men of Hong Kong and a good friend and partner of Schroders had gone. Over the previous decade he had played an influential role behind the scenes regarding the British government's dealings with China. His great wish to shake hands with Deng Xiaoping at the handover in June 1997 was denied. Deng died in February 1997 four months before the handover and thus saved the British government the embarrassment of their greatest adversary taking the spoils. Kadoorie was succeeded as chairman by his long serving deputy chairman, the formidable Sir Sidney Gordon.

NOTES:

1. Hugh Bolland had joined Schroders in October 1970 after a series of interviews, which culminated in one with Airlie who was rather surprised as neither he nor his father knew anyone at Schroders and he had applied by letter. After a period under Leach and White, where he learnt a lot during the bad bear market, his career was going very well but he was always broke and never knew if he would have sufficient to buy his wife a present at Christmas. He was then offered a partnership by Rowe & Pitman, one of the leading stockbrokers, to run its investment management business with a considerable increase in salary with bonuses also being mentioned. He had no alternative but to accept and to inform Popham, who had shown an interest in him, that he could not afford to stay. Popham said if he wanted to earn more money he could go to Hong Kong, to which he and his wife were rapidly sent to survey the scene and job. They were well looked after by Win and Rosemary Bischoff and agreed to a two-year secondment.

2. John Reynolds having played an important role in Hong Kong returned to Corporate Finance in London where he acted for many clients on major M&A deals. Bischoff said he was one of the best fee negotiators in the firm. He left in 1996 to become chairman of ABN-Amro Bank's corporate finance business in London. Sadly he died in his sleep at the early age of 50 in 1999.

3. Being an expatriate in Hong Kong in the early to mid-1980s was very attractive with a net disposable income considerably greater than that of colleagues in London with their high taxes, mortgage payments and school fees. In Hong Kong, they only paid 16% tax, they let their houses in London for rents, which more than compensated for the cost of the mortgage, their school fees were paid as well as all their accommodation costs, including utilities, the debenture for a sporting and dining club was paid and most entertaining costs were corporate. Finally an annual travel allowance for the family to return to the UK was granted and mainly used to fund local holidays. With these financial rewards and Bischoff and others having returned to London to more senior positions, such postings were popular. This was to change in the 1990s.

4. Nick MacAndrew had spent three years in Hong Kong under Bischoff ten years previously and so he knew many of the key people and the manner of doing business. Since then he had been in Banking in London, in Houston as president of Schroders Energy and in Corporate Finance. Being one of Broadbent's key directors in leading the transformation of Corporate Finance in London, with his strengths in building client relationships and in finding new business, Broadbent was disappointed to see him go. He had been involved in a number of the transactions that brought Schroders back into prominence including defending Haden against a bid from Trafalgar House which resulted in the incumbent management successfully negotiating a pioneering management buy-out at a higher price than Trafalgar was willing to pay. With such good prospects in Corporate Finance it was curious that he agreed to go to Hong Kong. He saw it as a chance to run a business, which if successful, could enhance his career. Schroders Asia had also had a poor record in Corporate Finance since Bischoff left five years earlier. Finally he saw no prospect of running Corporate Finance in London for some years.

5. Ronald Lee, the chairman of the Hong Kong Stock Exchange, who was later found guilty and imprisoned for fraud, had rung Sir Piers Jacobs, the financial secretary, early in the morning saying that the market should not be opened. Instead of saying he would see him in his office at 8.30am Jacobs agreed and Lee announced that it had been agreed to keep the market closed. This turned out to be a blessing in disguise as the Futures Exchange was in a complete mess, although it did great damage to the Hong Kong Stock Exchange in the eyes of the world. Many punters had accumulated huge short positions betting against the market with Robert Ng having an exceptionally long position on the other side and unable to meet his commitments. Following a week of frantic discussions, including an investigation by a brilliant lawyer and his team from Hambros in London, the complexities were unravelled and found to be even worse than had been forecast by Purves of HSBC. A lifeboat operation was put together with the support of the banks including the Bank of China, and the Hong Kong government and the Bank of England which included a future levy of 1% commission on every future stock market and futures exchange transaction. Schroders Asia was called on to participate in the lifeboat despite not having been involved in the futures business. The only people not willing to assist were the American financial institutions. Ng reached a settlement with the futures exchange to pay 80% of his liabilities paying what he could at the time and the balance in instalments over the next few years. He was thereafter seen as a person who had not paid his debts. Being in such a difficult financial position Schroders Asia was lucky to have received Ng's cheque and had it cleared. The following Monday the market opened and the shorts made a fortune although they too had to support the lifeboat. Amazingly the supporters of the lifeboat were repaid in full by 1992.

6. In the weeks before the Tiananmen Square massacre Hong Kong had been caught up in the innocence and the optimism of the Beijing protesters with a million people marching to show support and to collect money for the Beijing movement. The unofficial members of the Executive and Legislative Councils even unanimously agreed to support an acceleration of democratisation within Hong Kong. When the massacre followed, the effect on Hong Kong was convulsive. A million marched once more but in the black silence of mourning. It was a great shock to confidence in Hong Kong – Is this what they will do to us after the handover? However, the will to keep alive its public anger soon died.

7. At the same time in mid 1992, Chris Patten, the last Governor of Hong Kong, was determined on introducing some democratic government into Hong Kong before the handover despite the British government having run a benign dictatorship for 95 years. His proposals brought heated debates with the Chinese in Beijing and much uncertainty in Hong Kong. Although Patten was greatly respected by the people, most of the business community rose up against him siding with their new masters. Baroness Dunn, who Patten described in his book *East and West* as a business woman of legendarily adroit instincts, said when interviewed by the author,

> you have to appreciate that the Hong Kong people are mainly refugees struggling to make a better life for their families and wanting to survive in peace in the future. In these circumstances when you find you have a new sovereign it is natural to take his side. Their faith has been rewarded in that all the doubts about the promises made to allow two systems within one country have proved groundless as the Chinese have kept their hands off Hong Kong leaving it to the management of the Hong Kong officials.

8. Philip Tose, the godson of Ralph Vickers, the former senior partner of Vickers da Costa which had been purchased by Citicorp at the time of the Big Bang, got fed up with the failure of the Citicorp management and decided to set up his own company, which he named Peregrine. It was backed by a number of major Chinese business people including Li Ka-shing, the owner of Hutchison Whampoa. Tose was a hustler and a good networker. He undercut the competition, particularly Wardley and also cut corners. It did not take him long to become the largest merchant bank in Hong Kong but eventually he got too big for his boots, over-extending himself in bonds and trying to become a banker. He got into a huge mess in Indonesia that led to the collapse of the firm. It was such firms that made life more difficult for Schroders Asia.

9. While at the London Business School, following having worked in the oil industry, Read Gomm answered a project finance staff advertisement in 1988 and made a good impression. Project Finance was at the beginnings of its innovative work in the electricity sector and he spent the next few years with Wadia working on the Barking project for Thames Power. This project, which tested everybody's patience, was the making of many of them not least Gomm whose dedication, thoroughness, understated manner and courtesy impressed everyone. Wadia said of Gomm, 'he worked for long hours over many years and knew every aspect of his projects to his fingertips. Beneath his self-deprecating presence, he had a first-class mind and was extremely popular with his colleagues and clients. He did not appear to have an enemy in the world, a very rare quality.' There was a lot at stake working on a success-only-basis for the largest fee ever agreed and so there was much relief when the project was finally signed up in 1992, it having been a lean period and was the beginning of a massive hike in the profits. It was at this time that Gomm became ill with cancer. Dewe Mathews told him to go home and to get better and not to worry about anything. He recovered after eight months and came back to work, only to find himself travelling endlessly to Hong Kong and China. He said, 'Schroders went well beyond the call of duty and I have always been grateful to them for their support.' Being much liked he received great support and encouragement from all his colleagues who were thrilled to see him return fully fit albeit rather weak.

10. Essentially the problem was that, as the yuan was not convertible, the projects were un-financeable since the revenue in yuan could not be converted into dollars to repay the dollar denominated loans, there being no long-term domestic lending market. Also the provincial power bureaux responsible for purchasing the electricity had no balance sheets and no credit standing making it impossible to gauge their ability to perform under the long term power purchase agreements. Once the Bank of China realised that it would have to underwrite what was very expensive electricity it balked and only supported very few projects. The investors ultimately became jaded and withdrew.

CHAPTER 17

SOUTH EAST ASIA

1976 - 1994

In view of the success of Schroders & Chartered in Hong Kong, Schroders' natural partner for South East Asia was Standard Chartered Bank. However, it had existing merchant banking investments with other partners such as Arbuthnot Latham that could not be dissolved. Schroders therefore had to look elsewhere. Bulfield heard that the Crown Agents wished to withdraw from its merchant banking interests worldwide and therefore might be willing to sell its 24.5% shareholding in Singapore International Merchant Bankers Ltd (SIMBL). The majority shareholder, the Oversea-Chinese Banking Corporation (OCBC) – controlled by the prominent Lee family – was the second largest bank in Singapore. In addition it had a powerful presence in Malaysia with branches throughout the country. The Chairman, Tan Sri Tan Chin Tuan, had the complete confidence of the Lee family and ran the bank without interference. OCBC had considerable influence in Singapore and in Malaysia having very significant commercial investments in both countries – it was more of a universal bank than a commercial bank, with an interest in such companies as Great Eastern Life, the leading insurance company, Wearnes Brothers, the car distribution and engineering company, and Fraser & Neave, the brewers and soft drinks company. These and other less known companies were all regarded as being part of the OCBC stable. In 1976 Schroders acquired the Crown Agents' 24.5% shareholding in SIMBL and after some dithering increased it to 49% in 1980 by buying Continental Illinois' 24.5% stake. Michael Gleeson-White, currently the chief executive of Schroder Darling in Australia (see Chapter 18), was asked by Airlie to become the managing director with Yong Pung How as chairman. He got on well personally with Tan and was very impressed by Yong.[1]

Gleeson-White saw his task as being to 'assess future prospects and re-assemble the cast' – he saw huge potential for SIMBL and Schroders in the region with its unbounded growth prospects but this required intelligent, energetic and authoritative leadership. SIMBL's general manager Peter Russell was not up to the task of turning SIMBL into a competitive and leading merchant bank. Gleeson-White wanted a replacement from London to cover both roles as managing director and general manager. Airlie agreed to look for a suitable candidate and decided to send Nick Ferguson to fulfil the role – he was appointed chief executive reporting to Charles Tresise, the chairman.

Veronica Eng was head of Corporate Finance when Ferguson arrived. She had joined SIMBL's corporate finance department in 1974 straight from university and was the first female graduate to be employed – it was quite controversial at the time. The main business was IPOs and M&A for companies in Singapore, Malaysia and Indonesia and SIMBL was seen to be the number one house and to be absolutely straight. The companies in the OCBC stable provided a large amount of work. With a very small balance sheet there was little banking business, mainly small participations in syndicated loans arranged by SIMBL. Following Schroders taking its shareholding to 49%, London supported a greater effort in investment management under the energetic leadership of Maggie Hill.

Eng described Ferguson, the youngest managing director of SIMBL to date, as going at 100 miles an hour with incredible energy. He got on well with all the right people in the Singapore establishment and lifted SIMBL to a different level, encouraging business in Malaysia and Indonesia. He ran the business by units, each head having to prepare a business plan including the people they needed. He believed in growth and was not overly concerned about costs. He provided the vision and was the first person in Singapore to remunerate on the basis of performance rather than seniority and tenure – this was a major cultural change for Singapore.

Ferguson found SIMBL to be much like a firm of solicitors without much management. He liked Tan Chin Tuan from whom he learnt a lot, seeing him every Saturday morning – 'although very conservative, he was shrewd. Tresise was very experienced and thoughtful and a good mentor.' Ferguson introduced simple management systems that had been lacking and these gave the bank a sense of direction and priorities and encouraged everyone to get on with their jobs. Being keen on marketing, he installed a large board listing all the directors and executives down one axis and all the target clients on the other. In each box, a green mark indicated a telephone call, red a meeting and gold some new business. As the board was seen by all, the message was pretty quickly understood and it was taken down after three months. The other major contribution he made was to start up an investment management business. Through his friendship with Jeremy Hill, Jan Kingzett was sent out and Ferguson remembers him having a difficult time making progress in Indonesia. Ferguson thought he should help and so they visited a Mr Tan, who had made $100 million in trading sharks fin. He greeted them in a vest and baggy trousers and after Ferguson had made a presentation with all the charts, he asked Ferguson how much money he had. Ferguson said Schroders had $10 billion. 'No' said Tan, 'How much money you got Mr Fun-gun-son?' He replied that he had none. 'You want me give you my money when you got none?' They left, Ferguson realising it was not so easy.

In 1984 Ferguson was called back to London by Airlie with a view to taking over from Popham as head of Investment Management (see Chapter 2). He handed over to Richard Crowder. It was a difficult time with all the scandals in the region including political corruption in Bank Bumiputra, the dominant government owned bank in Malaysia, and all the companies being double listed on the Singapore and Kuala Lumpur Stock Exchanges. Business for SIMBL suffered as a result. Within a year Crowder decided he wanted to sail around the world with his family and left. He also secured the appointment as chairman of Smith New Court (Asia) in Hong Kong after his sailing trip. Subsequently being keen on islands he settled with his family in Guernsey where he became managing director of Schroders (CI). At about the same time Eng, who was married to an Englishman, decided to leave for London but delayed her departure until she managed to find a successor she was confident with – that was Robert Patterson from Lazards.

Mallinckrodt turned to Robin Tomlin, a banker in IBJ Schroder Bank & Trust Company in New York, to take over from Crowder in 1986.[2] Yong Pung How, 'bright, articulate and politically astute', was a great help and inspiration to Tomlin, who was totally green about Asia. Crowder had started loan syndication at SIMBL and Tomlin built on this by moving into the bond market and doing swaps – the same debt team carried out all these activities successfully unlike in London. In fact this team became the largest profit centre until the Asian debt crisis in 1997. SIMBL lead managed a S$400 million bond issue for Neptune Orient Lines, the national shipping company, which was the largest non-government bond ever issued in Singapore. It concentrated on the debt capital markets in Singapore and Malaysia including issues for Shell Malaysia. The corporate finance activities included M&A transactions, small IPOs and some rights issues for OCBC and Fraser & Neave. A unit trust was also launched for Singapore equities called Savers Capital Fund, which started at S$20 million.

There was a difference of opinion between the two shareholders regarding the future of SIMBL, OCBC wanting it to remain in Singapore and Schroders wishing to expand throughout South East Asia. Within a year of Tomlin's arrival, OCBC decided to set up its own merchant banking business to do all the capital raising for OCBC and its many clients. Being in direct competition created a lot of difficulty and confusion in the market and could not be resolved until Yong was appointed the managing director of the Monetary Authority of Singapore. Teo Cheng Guan, the new chairman of OCBC saw that the position was untenable and that it would be better to sell out to Schroders rather than taking over SIMBL. He therefore advised the Lee family, with its 26% controlling interest in OCBC, to sell. Mallinckrodt visited the senior staff at SIMBL and found that they were unanimously in favour of staying with Schroders and would move to Schroders if it were necessary to set up a new venture. It did not come to this as OCBC was prepared to sell its 51% shareholding. Mallinckrodt conducted the critical discussions with Teo and the Lee family member – being both principals made a big difference and an agreement on terms was agreed to without difficulty. Eric Henbrey, the head of tax in London, designed a tax efficient scheme involving the payment of a large franked dividend to OCBC that reduced the book value of SIMBL. The purchase price was then based on a premium over the reduced book value. With Schroders' acquisition of OCBC's 51% shareholding in 1989, SIMBL swapped the word Schroders for Singapore. Charles Tresise, who was 72 at the time and highly regarded as the former senior partner of Cooper Brothers in Singapore, remained chairman until he retired in the mid-1990s. Earlier, as a trusted adviser to Tan Chin Tuan, he had successfully held the ring between the two shareholders. He was a tremendous support to Tomlin and taught him all he needed to know – 'he was the best non-executive director in town.'

Following the acquisition, SIMBL's capital was sharply reduced, resulting in a significant increase in the return on equity. However, the lean capital had to be worked hard. Tomlin embarked on a gradual expansion throughout the region setting up offices in Jakarta followed by Kuala Lumpur and Bangkok. Each had to be presented to the GEC in London and was a tortuous process involving endless visits to London. It was not helped by Mallinckrodt, despite having already approved the proposals in detail, always playing the role of devil's advocate. The office in Jakarta was opened in 1991, with John Deloughery, a delightful but unworldly director from Schroders Australia, in charge, Bill Foo responsible for Corporate Finance and Teo Pek Swan, who married an Indonesian-Chinese, responsible for Investment Management. Debt capital markets business was directed by James Foo in Singapore. The following year, the KL office opened under Michael Sng, concentrating on the domestic corporate finance and debt capital markets. An investment management business was also started. All these activities did well in a thriving market. In 1994 an office was set up in Bangkok with joint ventures for securities with local brokers. Tomlin had thereby completed his plans to set up offices throughout South East Asia.

At the same time the Barings crisis erupted, with Nick Leeson breaking the bank by over extending himself in Nikkei futures contracts. With the fear that the British merchant banks were not invulnerable to going bust, their branches and subsidiaries were heavily scrutinised by the MAS and actions were taken to stop the co-mingling of their customers' money. Fortunately SIMBL had no involvement in Japanese futures contracts.

NOTES:

1. Following the introduction of the Malaysian government's Bumiputra policy requiring 40% of the country's assets to be controlled by Malays, resulting in the effective nationalisation of the leading businesses built up over many years by the Chinese and the British, many prominent Chinese business men left the country. Yong Pung How was one of these. Subsequently he went on to head the Government of Singapore Investment Corporation and become a member of the Securities Industry Council, the Singapore equivalent of the Take-over Panel in London, before finally being appointed the Chief Justice.

2. Robin Tomlin had joined Banking in 1969 working for Mallinckrodt and Michael Magdol on US business, spending a year in New York followed by being sponsored for an MBA at Harvard. He returned to the German desk in London in 1973 and worked on Middle East business and was part of the early team involved in the aborted Nigerian venture (see Chapter 1) in 1974/5. He then carried out a three-month survey of Iran following the earlier visit by Bruno and Dewe Mathews. While there he and Roditi took an interest in carpets and had a large stock shipped back to London for resale. He returned to Schrobanco in 1977 and remained there until after the sale to IBJ, at which time he told Mallinckrodt that he wished to return to Schroders in London. He and his wife Monica visited Singapore with some anxiety as they had two young children. They were impressed by what they saw, particularly with the high quality of the senior SIMBL staff. Monica, a Colombian by birth, also an MBA and 'more intelligent than me', was offered a job as a management consultant with Arthur D Little. They were able to acquire a 'Black and White House' through the connections of OCBC. These Tudor half-timbered houses were set in an acre of lush gardens and were wonderful for entertaining – a big element of the job. They had been built in the 1920s and 1930s by the army and the large British companies for the senior officers and expatriate staff and were much sought after by foreign bankers but not the Chinese, as they were old and full of not unfriendly insects.

CHAPTER 18

AUSTRALIA - ON THE PERIPHERY

1973 - 1999

Towards the end of 1971, Richardson came across Michael Gleeson-White walking down a street in the City. He had heard that Gleeson-White had recently retired as the senior partner of Ord, Minnett, and so he promptly offered him a director-ship of Schroder Wagg with responsibility for Darling & Company Limited (Darlings) in Australia and for developing Schroders' business in the Pacific – Hong Kong, Singapore, Malaysia, South Korea and Japan. He was the only Australian managing director of Schroder Darling to be made a director of Schroder Wagg. Gleeson-White had known Schroders for many years since Ord, Minnett had been one of the founding shareholders of Darlings in 1960 when Helbert, Wagg had a shareholding of 23.5%, the other share-holders being John Darling, a well-connected Sydney businessman, the Bank of New South Wales, Jardine Matheson & Co and Binder Hamlyn & Co. He had helped Charles Ord to build up Ord, Minnett from being a small stockbroker into one of the leaders in Australia next to Potters and JB Were. He arrived at Darlings to find that, despite having established a good reputation in the market, many of the best young directors had left – David Clarke and Mark Johnson for Hill Samuel and David Block to set up on his own. Tony Gorman, the respected head of the Melbourne office, left almost imme-diately afterwards.

Darlings had inserted itself successfully into the existing Australian financial system, dominated by the big stockbrokers, by establishing itself as an organisation which, at the time, came somewhere between an American investment bank and a British merchant bank. It was the brain-child of Charles Villiers of Helbert, Wagg and Gleeson-White, who thought from the outset that it should be seen in Australia as an Australian initiative managed by Australians. It got off to a very good start and before long a call came from Australia for some stiffening on the corporate finance side, and David Murison, a director of Schroder Wagg, was sent from London on a three-year secondment. He was by definition not seen as a candidate for the top job, which was reserved for Australians. This Australian policy could no doubt have been changed, as it eventually was, and Murison might have been a candidate for the top job but he finally opted, for personal reasons, to return to Schroder Wagg in London, where he continued his interest in Darlings, but did not have an effective voice until he left for the Bank of New South Wales in 1979.

David Clarke, chairman and founding director of Macquarie Bank, formerly Hill Samuel Australia, in 2002, described Darlings as a very exciting place to be at – a little bit before its time. It had lost a lot when Wolfensohn had left for London. John Darling, John Broinowski and Rupert Burge were all very different in personality, Broinowski being a formidable opponent you had to stand up to or you were dead in the water. Broinowski's excessively autocratic and ruthless style left the best young directors thoroughly frustrated with their prospects. Clarke and Johnson had joined Darlings, become directors and had left Darlings at the same time. Johnson, head of Corporate Finance, had been working for some time on the flotation of the Robe River iron ore project and the subsequent financial rescue of Mineral Securities and Clarke, as head of Banking, organised the banking syndicate in which Hill Samuel was a major participant. They therefore knew and liked Christopher Castleman, who had set up an office for Hill Samuel in Sydney the previous year. Clarke and Johnson, both barely 30 years old, had decided that they wanted to set up a merchant bank of their own, feeling that there were no opportunities within Darlings under Broinowski's dictatorial regime, and were thinking of securing backing from an American bank. One Sunday Clarke and Johnson were on their yacht in the harbour with Castleman when both parties independently raised the subject. The following morning Castleman, who was very able, a good judge of risk and excellent with people, telephoned Johnson and subsequently offered Clarke and Johnson the roles of joint chief executive of Hill Samuel in Australia with larger salaries and substantial share options – clearly their prospects were much better than they were at Darlings. This was the start of the most successful merchant banking venture in Australia. Broinowski had developed a shadow tax-free share option scheme for the directors, which did not penalise them if they left after five years – in fact its benefits had peaked and it was therefore in their interests to cash in their chips. Block, who was regarded by many as the most brilliant of all the corporate finance directors in Australia, set up his own firm taking with him a few of the younger executives and immediately wrote to all Darlings' clients, including CSR, offering to act for them in his own capacity, even sending a copy of the letter to Gleeson-White!

Broinowski, unlike John Darling who was an entrepreneur and a man of vision, had an eye for the detail – he was imperious, autocratic, tough and efficient, he was self-interested and saw his job as a personal fiefdom and had blazing rows with his directors. Wolfensohn, another protégé of Charles Ord, like Gleeson-White, and an inspiration to the young, left for London in 1967 and Block after a row with Broinowski left in 1972. On the other hand Broinowski was also likeable with a droll sense of humour and was a very concerned person doing a great deal of work for the Smith Family charity, which looked after poor and disadvantaged children. Gleeson-White in contrast was a mild-mannered stockbroker, a talker rather than a doer. He was exceptionally bright and creative but impractical and totally bewildering to his colleagues in that he could never hold a conversation for any length of time on the same subject and this drove people crazy. He had a great feel for the market, like all top-class brokers. He had great strategic thoughts but they were not necessarily relevant to the business – however, he was reputed to be the brains behind the development of the money market. Management was not his strong suit in that he was not good with people not having the sensitivity necessary to deal with the egos of the prima donnas so critical to the success of merchant banks. There was no focus on profits or budgets. He was a man of considerable charm and delightful to work with.

On instructions from Richardson, Gleeson-White went to see Broinowski at his farm and told him that he could stay on as a director – thereby avoiding more disruption and bad press – providing he kept out of the management. At the time, despite the departure of Clarke, Johnson, Block and Gorman, Darlings was still seen as the leading merchant bank – the most prestigious and best connected. Illustrative of the major transactions it was involved in was acting for CSR in respect of its purchase of Ready Mixed Concrete, the largest take-over of the time, involving businesses in Australia and in Britain. Darlings was an intellectual hot house where the brightest people worked. There was a fine lifestyle and it was a congenial and challenging place to work. Gleeson-White therefore found that there were a lot of good people at Darlings but no leaders.

However, his relaxed management style resulted in the younger people losing confidence in the future and being attracted by the better opportunities elsewhere. Mike Crivelli, a senior investment manager, also very bright, left for Bankers Trust where he helped Rob Fergusson to build up the best fund management business in Australia over the next 20 years. At this time Darlings' investment management business in equities and fixed interest stocks was on a par with that of BT Australia. It also had an excellent property fund second only to the General Property Trust of Lend Lease. Anthony Bailey, a seriously lightweight – intellectually rather than physically – corporate financier from London totally undermined the confidence of the young corporate financiers in London's interest in Darlings. Peter Mason, a highly regarded young executive in Corporate Finance, left to join Block. Arthur Charles, another executive with great potential recently returned from a very pleasant year with Schroder Wagg in London, found the reputation of the firm in decline and was disturbed by Mason's departure. It was at this time that John Darling, as opposed to Darlings, following the debacle of Scottish-Australian, was promoting the shares of a company called Austiran, which was exporting sheep to Iran. As many of his friends were persuaded to invest in the venture and as agriculture was one of the most important sectors of the economy, its failure severely damaged the reputation of Darlings, even though it was not directly involved.

In contrast to the declining position in Corporate Finance and Investment Management, Banking under Richard Griffin was doing relatively well with all the profits of Darlings in 1974, 1975 and 1976 coming from Banking – Banking never made a loss. The Australian economy at the time was experiencing considerable difficulties with a growth rate of 5% leading to inflation of 20%. Loans to the property sector had been avoided and a start had been made with Bulfield in London on a series of substantial limited-recourse loans to an alumina refinery joint venture between ALCOA and Western Mining – these loans were in some ways the start of Schroders' development of a project finance business, which was to thrive in the late 1980s and the 1990s. At the same time

Griffin persuaded Western Mining to issue a Eurobond in the London market with Schroders as the lead manager – later Credit Swiss First Boston became joint manager. Unfortunately it was not a success and the issue was reduced from US$25 million to US$15 million literally at the last minute – it was the last deal ever done for Western Mining (see Chapter 14). Griffin, who had joined the Melbourne office in 1969, was a sound and reliable banker who got to know most of the chairmen and finance directors of the established Australian companies. He maintained good relations with the directors in London, was loyal and always ready to help. He built up the loan book to A$800 million before reducing it to A$300 million and remained head of Banking until 1980 when he attended the Stanford Executive Program at the Stanford Business School.

During 1975, Darling & Company became Schroder Darling & Co as a result of Schroders increasing its shareholding to 50%, the remaining shareholders being OCBC 15%, Bank of New South Wales 10% and Bank of Nova Scotia 25%. Schroders had the opportunity to buy out all the minorities but decided against, which gave mixed signals to the market and was exploited by the competition – 'How can a merchant bank operate when it doesn't know who owns it?' At that time Gleeson-White was spending an increasing amount of his time in Asia culminating in a move to Singapore as managing director of SIMBL in which Schroders had purchased a minority shareholding in 1976 (see Chapter 17). He left the management of Darling to a triumvirate of John Ormandy, *primus inter pares*, a delightful extrovert corporate financier from Melbourne who was past his best, Griffin and John Gerahty, the head of Corporate Finance who was outstanding and very clever but a loner and not a good team player. It avoided having to take the unpalatable decision of selecting one of the three as the chief executive and therefore risking losing two of the three and it also left open the position of chief executive for Gleeson-White on his return from Singapore. It proved to be an unfortunate mix, which was exploited by all the staff that played one off against the others. No decisions were taken. Everyone did their own thing and the bank went sideways – all dynamism was lost and it became difficult to attract strong people. Schroders in London appeared to show no interest. In the meanwhile nobody was bothering about Investment Management. Gerahty, arguably one of the most brilliant corporate financiers of his generation, in demand from clients as a good thinker and a clever creator of financial structures, became irritated and left for Hill Samuel. Brian Gatfield, head of money markets under Griffin, left for Bank of America where he could spread his wings and take advantage of a huge balance sheet. And Charles, having seen the reputation of Schroder Darling almost in freefall, decided to join Block and Mason. At last Airlie in London realised that there was something radically wrong and towards the end of 1978, on the advice of Murison, sent out Ben Strickland to salvage what was left.[1] 'I felt they needed some discipline but perhaps he had this to a fault.' At the same time Gleeson-White became chairman of the holdings board. Gleeson-White went on to become an economic investment advisor to the Singapore Government and a member of a number of boards as well as president of the Art Gallery of New South Wales – in 1984, he was awarded

Officer of the Order of Australia (AO) for his contribution to the development of the financial markets in Australia and services to the arts and the community.

Strickland, who was seen within Schroder Darling to be a good man manager with whom everybody knew where they stood, initiated a strategic review and consulted very widely within the business community. He managed to stop the infighting, settle down the directors and staff and gave focus and impetus to the organisation. He took endless trouble over developing better structures and disciplines and introduced new management systems and controls. He and his wife Tessa worked assiduously cultivating the captains of industry in Sydney by entertaining them and their wives at the opera and at concerts and became well known in the business community. This did not noticeably lead to any new business but it halted the slide and the self-destruction of the triumvirate. Although Strickland stabilised the situation, his inflexible military management style resulted in another major defection – following a blazing row, Robin Crawford, the last top-class corporate financier, left for Hill Samuel with John Wilson. Despite being rather a loose canon at Schroder Darling, he proved to be a major asset to Hill Samuel having endless ideas only half of which were any good but these were brilliant. By this time the corporate finance business at Schroder Darling was decimated and approaching a point of irrelevance with the list of alumni being longer than those in the firm. Strickland, despite a huge effort, including considering the possibility buying David Block & Associates, failed to attract anyone of any stature to head up Corporate Finance. He did, however, have Ronnie Beevor, who had been seconded from Corporate Finance in London in 1979, to bolster the shrinking corporate finance team and run the Melbourne office prior to returning home. Before doing so he successfully completed the difficult task of organising a scheme of arrangement to put together four companies: Consolidated Goldfields; Renison; Mt Lyell Mining & Railway Company; and Associated Minerals. These became a naturalised Australian company, Renison Goldfields Consolidated, 49% owned by UK interests and 51% owned by Australian interests. This extremely complicated transaction, despite many attempts by others, was only the second such deal in Australia, the first being Rio Tinto and CRA.

Investment Management was going reasonably under Jeff Harrison until he retired and handed over to his well-thought-of deputy, Roger Bacon, who regrettably proved to be incapable of controlling the staff, not having the necessary backbone and steel. The policy and strategy were fine but not the way in which they were managed. Performance fell off and with this Schroder Darling's reputation in the market. Clients withdrew their funds and it became impossible to stop the slide.

Late in 1981, Gatfield received a call from Strickland's secretary asking him to visit him. 'It felt like being called to report to the headmaster.' He thought he was being approached to become head of Banking and was astonished when offered the job as the chief executive to take over from Strickland. He found it completely bizarre, knowing he was not in any way qualified to run a merchant bank. He knew nothing about corporate finance or investment management, the two most visible activities. In considering it, he knew Schroder Darling was in a chaotic position but it still had market empathy and was thought well of ethically – 'why not give it a go after all I had nothing to lose.' He was sent off to the Stanford Executive Program at the Stanford Business School where he learnt an enormous amount about management and how everything fitted together. (Adam Broadbent was on the same programme but they saw little of each other.) On his return to Sydney, Strickland left much sooner than expected – suddenly Gatfield found himself in charge in the middle of a recession – 'oh shit!'. A recent survey of the performance of all the major merchant banks in Australia ranked Schroder Darling the worst in terms of return on equity and on assets. As there were no profits it could hardly get worse. The firm still had a reputation for ethics and he was young and full of energy. Griffin, his old boss and always available for advice, became deputy chairman to Peter Baillieu who had taken over as chairman from Gleeson-White the previous year. Baillieu was an excellent mentor and always supportive of Gatfield in his dealings with London. It was during his watch in 1985 that Schroders bought out the minority shareholders of Schroder Darling and renamed the company Schroders Australia. Now that Schroders owned the whole company, the holdings board had less of a role. Griffin, who was chairman of the Australian Merchant Bankers Association, was awarded a Member of the Order of Australia (AM) in 1989 for his contribution to finance, industry, business and the community. When he retired from Schroders Australia Holdings in 2001 he was the longest serving director of the company.

Deregulation of the banking industry, leading to a complete revolution in the financial markets, was imminent. Margins on bank lending were being squeezed by a massive influx of new banks that were offering huge salaries to their new staff – it was difficult for Schroders Australia to retain staff at a time when it was being forced down the credit ladder. Gatfield decided that he should pull out of lending and move from a credit risk to a market risk organisation – acting as an intermediary in the market between the customers and the financial institutions – with a new risk management structure. He put a proposal to London, which was accepted, and sold the whole of his loan book, which was by now well below the A$300 million Griffin had reduced it to in 1980, to Midland Bank for 105% of its book value. The financial press had a field day saying Schroders Australia was at last closing its doors. Three or four years later following the market crash in 1987, most of the new entrants suffered substantial losses on their loans and closed down. Unlike the vast majority of the other Australian banks, Schroders Australia suffered no bad debts.

Gatfield set up a capital market committee under Bill Evans, the newly hired head of Capital Markets, and completely changed the culture of the bank. Schroders Australia became an intermediary in the domestic and international currency markets. On the international side Ken Stockton and Mark Hopkinson, who was on secondment from the Reserve Asset Management Programme (RAMP) in London that had been set up by Wolfensohn following the oil crisis in 1973, were developing a currency and gold forward-dealing business, which made good money. There were considerable opportunities in this area particularly following the currency crisis in December 1983 when the Labour government floated the Australian dollar. This led to currency swaps which were in their infancy. By 1986, a year of economic difficulties with a soft currency, near double digit inflation and continued high domestic interest rates, Schroders Australia had become the market leader in interest rate and currency swaps. Gatfield, who was well ahead of his time, was very supportive of his directors despite the risks involved but there was continual resistance from London, which wore everyone down not least Gatfield who had to field the calls in the middle of the night. On the other hand he always found Solandt, the chairman of the Group Market Risk Committee in London, to be receptive and helpful. This was not surprising, as Solandt never had any problems with Australia, which he regarded as a great success unlike Hong Kong. Macquarie Bank took over from Schroders Australia when it was forced to curtail its ambitions and made the profits Gatfield had aspired to.

In the meanwhile the corporate financiers, who were mostly old workhorses, continued to make no profits – they managed the flotation of Kidston Gold Mines and worked on a number of gold mining projects. They extended their work to New Zealand with an appointment to advise New Zealand Steel on the NZ$ 1.6 billion Glenbrook project. Investment Management with its dreadful track record was always at the bottom of the league tables and it was a constant struggle to keep clients. Bacon had not proved a successful head and was replaced by Peiter Franzen, a recruit from Prudential. The property fund, which had A$420 million under management, on the other hand, had good self-confident people, so much so that they threatened to leave with their business. Gatfield agreed an arrangement in which Jeremy Lewis, John Kelleher and David Allott acquired a 24.9% stake in the fund. He also separated them from Investment Management as they were a good differentiator in the market for Schroders Australia – they grew strongly thereafter.

By 1987 Gatfield was, 'getting increasingly fed up with all the travel to London and also the culture of greed encroaching on the investment banking industry' and he decided to leave. A survey of the leading merchant banks ranked Schroders Australia in the top ten for profitability and return on assets with a return on equity of 25% after tax. Gatfield had proved to be a good manager and analyser of the business – his selection of people was perhaps not so good. In view of the dire position of the fund management business it was felt that an investment manager should be appointed as the next chief executive. Gatfield who had met periodically with the other managing directors in Asia was impressed with Bolland and recommended that he be approached.

Bolland, an investment management director from London who had had a successful run as managing director of Schroders Asia in Hong Kong, was sent out (see Chapter 16). Bolland had been a safe pair of hands when managing compliant Chinese in a steady market of rising profits in Hong Kong but was soon out of his depth in Sydney where he had to manage Australians in a company where fund management, his area of expertise, was on the rocks. He found that Investment Management under Franzen had no clients and was losing money with forty staff. He reduced the team to ten and by the end of the year had almost doubled the funds under management. Corporate Finance under Jim Turnbull, who was well thought of by Bischoff when in Hong Kong, had seven ageing directors and no work to speak of. Bolland decided to hire a new head and found Bob Gallard who was duly interviewed by Mallinckrodt and Bischoff among others and then hired. Turnbull left and it became clear to Bolland within five weeks that Gallard was a disaster and so he too was fired. Corporate Finance went nowhere after that. He found the sophisticated treasury business under Evans and Hopkinson was a mystery. Hopkinson, who was disappointed by Gatfield's unexpected departure, was one of the first to leave. Banking under the cautious management of Griffin and David Fewtrell, during a disastrous period of bad debts for all the Australian banks, managed to only lose money on Quintex – owned by the infamous Christopher Skase – and that was because the collateral was from the wrong company. Great credit should be given to Griffin and Fewtrell since all the British merchant banks lost money in 1988/9 whereas Schroders Australia broke even. Bolland had a torrid time and was unpopular, as his management style was not felt to be compatible with managing Australians. His only friend and a great support was Baillieu, his non-executive chairman. Bolland had by then been abroad for eight and a half years was clearly keen to get back home.

Mallinckrodt realised something radical had to be done if Schroders Australia was to survive and on the advice of Baillieu, consulted with Broinowski who rang Charles who in turn spoke to Mason – the two corporate finance stars who had left Darlings to join David Block 15 years previously. After Block sold out to Lloyds, Mason and Charles had run the corporate finance business very successfully for many years and were now working as consultants effectively in semi-retirement. Mason was described by his colleagues as being 'charming, energetic and personable, intelligent, forthright, a brilliant tactician, deal-doer and negotiator, particularly in take-overs, who commands the confidence of clients, a well-known name in the market, extremely well-connected with a top-class reputation, and in many ways similar to Bischoff'. He was also seen as impulsive, short-tempered, extremely intolerant of laziness or disloyalty and not one who enjoyed the drudgery of day-to-day management. Charles was seen as the ideal partner and foil to Mason, complementing and counter-balancing him by keeping his feet on the ground and picking up the pieces he left behind. He was described as 'a charming and courteous patrician with a good presence, self-assured, articulate, relaxed and patient with a good sense of humour and a good administrator'.

Clearly it would be a remarkable coup if their services could be secured. After some heavy cultivation in London and a sense of genuine interest and commitment demonstrated by Mallinckrodt, they were more receptive to the request to take over the management of Schroders Australia. Their main concern was whether it was capable of being rescued. They were in a strong position to negotiate attractive financial packages for themselves, which took full account of the huge risk they were taking to their reputations. They were appointed joint chief executives sharing the same office with

Mason concentrating on the corporate finance business and Charles, effectively chief operating officer, looking after the rest. Bolland, who was desperate to get back to London, gave them what turned out to be misleading information about the state of the investment management business – the A$900 million funds under management turned out to be A$400 million and in no time they were A$140 million. Franzen proved to be no better than Bacon and had been fired before Mason and Charles took over. They decided to close this business down and start it again – it was effectively run thereafter on a care and maintenance basis. By 1995 they were winning a lot of new mandates and surprisingly reported that they were, 'among the leading managers of international pension fund assets'. All the directors of Corporate Finance were fired and replaced at considerable expense by former colleagues from Lloyds. The property fund continued to do well with Lewis now in London.

Financial Markets, under the ineffective management of Evans, was not helped by personal misbehaviour of many of the employees. The business was also not going too well as Evans, although brilliant and a very good dealer, proved to be not only difficult to manage but also to be an ineffective manager himself. He was found a job as the economist at Westpac, where he was able to take full advantage of his excellent brain. Hopkinson who had remained in touch with Bolland was recommended by Bolland to Mason. He was impressed by what Mason and Charles were doing for Schroders Australia and became head of Financial Markets. Fortunately the Australian economy was performing well and continued to do so throughout the decade, providing plenty of business opportunities. Mason concentrated on building up the corporate finance business and in restoring the reputation of the firm and in this he was very successful. An early success was undertaking the defence of Arnotts Limited, the national biscuit company, against Campbell Soup from America – this was a landmark transaction due to the emotion of the public against one of their leading companies being acquired by a foreign purchaser. Although Campbell Soup increased its shareholding from 33% to 58%, unusually a special voting agreement was upheld in the courts preserving control in the hands of the existing board. Ultimately it was acquired for A$1.4 billion but only after a protracted fight and for a significantly higher price.

In the early 1990s the government initiated an extensive privatisation programme in the transport and electricity sector and Brandler, the head of the project finance office in Singapore, worked with David Lowes and others in obtaining assignments from the government and foreign clients interested in construct, finance and operate projects in the transport sector and in acquiring power stations and distribution systems. Many mandates were secured and some successes achieved except that Macquarie were a formidable and better qualified competitor, having learnt remarkably quickly the necessary skills – in fact they took this business to a totally different level than any others by taking significant equity interests in these investments.

At about the same time Mason was appointed as head of investment banking in Asia and was seen by some to be a potential successor to Bischoff, having many of his good characteristics. However, this was not a success as being reluctant to move to Hong Kong from Sydney, where he had an idyllic lifestyle, he had to travel endlessly to the Far East and this was a distraction from his task in Australia. Hopkinson was disappointed and felt let down. Charles went to Hong Kong to take over the management of Schroder Securities, which was in a big mess – despite his lack of knowledge of the securities business he felt he could make a good contribution and enjoyed it.

Mason saw the need for an equity capability and proposed to London, with the support of Adam Broadbent and Philip Augar, the purchase of ANZ McLaughlin, a well-regarded securities business. When the proposal was turned down due to the perception of better opportunities in New York and concern about management problems, Mason saw this as a lack of trust in him and this demoralised the corporate finance group. Despite Corporate Finance doing well acting for Westpac on its acquisition of Challenge Bank and Caltex Australia on its merger with Ampol, Mason felt that if the business was to continue to grow it was necessary to incentivise the top five directors including himself and therefore negotiated an arrangement whereby they received half the profits after costs, which included their salaries. The effect on profits was quite noticeable but Baillieu the chairman insisted on Mason resigning as chief executive due to a perceived conflict of interest and Mason reluctantly agreed. The corporate finance profits responded well for a period but with a clear policy of containment Mason and the others decided to leave – he felt badly let down. Despite this he said Mallinckrodt had always supported him and Charles and that he was the only person he found in Schroders who had a long-term view of the firm. 'He was very determined, cared passionately for Schroders and was immensely determined on preservation as opposed to creation. He was kind personally and sincere and he and Charmaine were easy visitors to Australia. However I felt he never trusted me to run the business. Bischoff was in denial. It was sad. They were nice people.' Hopkinson who was then head of investment banking in Hong Kong came down to negotiate the severance packages. Whatever else happened they certainly were well compensated for the risks they had taken which once again was no comfort to Schroders Australia.

The finance director Kerry Smith was appointed chief executive in 1996. He found the property fund to be doing reasonably well, the investment management business on a caretaker basis with funds of between A$50 and A$100 million losing A$2 million a year, Financial Markets making some money but a poor quality business. The corporate finance business, which had not made profits of any significance for years, was now doing better, particularly since the profit-sharing arrangements agreed with Mason. In 1996, Schroders Australia made a profit of A$1 million. In 1997, they achieved a record profit of A$11 million made up by Corporate Finance, Financial Markets and the property fund – in their 37-year history they had never made a profit of over A$10 million! In 1998, there was a profit of A$25 million made up again of Corporate Finance, the property fund and Financial Markets. Mason left in early 1998 and this destroyed the corporate finance business, which was dissolved. In 1999, there was a profit after tax of A$65 million including extraordinaries arising from the sale of the property fund to AMP for 52 times its book value for A$112 million. In January 2000 the investment banking business, which was now simply Financial Markets, was sold to Salomon who took a few staff and dissolved the business. The investment management business, or what was left of it, remained with Schroders changing its name to Schroders Australia Management Ltd. Towards the end there had been a lot of referral business from London but there was a reluctance to provide any quality staff to help. As Kerry Smith, the last of a long line of chief executives, said, 'There was no commitment or interest from London and an absence of a long-term view. It was always a long way away and difficult to get heard.'

Conclusion

This is a sad story of opportunities missed through consistently inadequate management. It is of course easy in hindsight to be critical. At the time it would not have been seen in such extreme terms. After all, only one other British merchant bank, Hill Samuel, latterly Macquarie Bank, was and has continued to be a resounding success.

The list of those who came, tried and retired is legion. UBS Warburg, a relative latecomer, through its venture with Potters, became the leading investment bank in equities. Rothschild made a success of fund management. Why did Schroders show so little interest or commitment to an investment that had so much potential? For 15 years, it had a minority shareholding and very reluctantly increased it to 50% in 1975. But so had Ord, Minett but in contrast to Schroders its commitment in terms of quality staff provided was phenomenal. Maybe Australia was seen as being rather small in world terms and on the periphery of Schroders' world in London. It may not have made much money but Schroders' investment was modest and there was little risk financially until Gatfield got into market risk and that was well contained. Schroders may have stuck with the original policy of Australian only management for too long. The fact is that Schroders was never prepared or able to send to Australia anyone of real quality other than Strickland and he was removed before he could do more than halt the decline. Perhaps it simply did not have the people of the quality needed or the skills to identify them. There were many visitors from London most of whom were only interested in getting business for themselves rather than in assisting Schroders Australia with its business. There were no incentives to those in London to give up good staff to help Australia. All the judgements were on performance at home.

Verey had no interest in Australia. Airlie showed great commitment and was constantly concerned about the management and it was he who sent out Strickland but in the end he might have pulled him back too early. However, he had far greater and more challenging problems in New York. Francis Cator, the London director responsible for Australia between 1979 and 1983, visited twice a year but was not seen in London to be fighting for Schroder Darling's cause – he was liked as he took great trouble talking to all the directors and staff and could be guaranteed to provide the rations. When it came to business, however, his style was out of accord with Australian businessmen. Earlier on David Murison, who had a much greater affinity with Australian businessmen, had done a swap with Wolfensohn and spent three years working on corporate finance assignments for Darlings but on his return to London he found he had been away too long and had been overtaken by others and as a result he no longer had an effective voice for Schroder Darling. This may have sent out a message that it was best to remain at home. One of the jobs of Schroder Darling was to arrange meetings for visiting dignitaries from London and to entertain them – they knew that if they did this well the London directors would go back satisfied feeling they had done a good job in Australia. Mallinckrodt was passionately concerned but was risk averse – Gatfield was a casualty of this – but he secured the services of Mason and Charles after the disastrous tenure of Bolland. Another problem was the conundrum of whether or not to insert British management over Australians who rightly could regard themselves as being every bit as good as a 'pom'. Regrettably Schroders failed to find adequate management at home until possibly at the end when it was too late.

So why did Hill Samuel succeed so outstandingly when Schroders so resoundingly failed?

Darling was a nursery of some of the most talented young financial brains in Australia. Without exception they all left mostly for Hill Samuel who had identified very early on that the key to investment banking is the management of those seeking personal wealth. Clarke said he set out to do the same things as Darling. The difference was he installed an attractive compensation and share incentive package, which ensured that all those who did well for Hill Samuel became rich – as John Whitehead of Goldman Sachs wrote in his book, 'make sure you are long-term greedy not short-term.' The profit share scheme was fully transparent to all executives regarding how the pool was determined – how it was split between individuals was confidential. The only time after Clarke and Johnson left Darlings when Schroders Australia did well was when profit share arrangements were put in place for the property fund and for Corporate Finance at the end – confirmation that investment bankers have to be financially motivated to deliver of their best. They then sought out good people including John Gerahty, which took some years, and created an intellectually stimulating environment – an attractive mix. If staff were not up to scratch they were ruthless in getting rid of them. In terms of the competition they rigorously monitored and controlled the ratio of remuneration to gross revenue knowing that their top people could earn more in Hong Kong and New York but without the lifestyle.

Although initially wholly owned by Hill Samuel the senior people were given founder equity and a lot of independence. Of their competitors only Bankers Trust had the same attitude with similar results. Following the acquisition of Bankers Trust by Deutsche Bank in the late 1990s, Deutsche decided to sell its businesses in Australia. The investment management business, which was smaller than that of Darling in 1973, was sold for approximately A$2 billion to Westpac and the remainder including some excellent businesses and over 400 quality staff was picked up for a price below book value by Macquarie who surprisingly were the only buyers. Gerahty said it was all to do with management. 'Clarke was an outstanding manager of people, particularly the prima donnas so necessary to the success of the bank. He was a good picker, understood their needs, got on well with them and remunerated them well. They were given a lot of freedom to run their own businesses.'

In view of the shortage of and need to conserve capital, Clarke was brilliant at assessing risk and at establishing the guidelines necessary to allow his directors the freedom of action and responsibilities to create things. Importantly he put in place the management structures necessary to control what were effectively a series of franchises. Hill Samuel, which became a trading bank in 1985 and changed its name to Macquarie Bank, was known as 'the millionaires' factory' in which anyone of talent who worked hard became rich, as did Macquarie Bank. In every area of management they were highly professional not least in recruiting – they made a point of hiring the sons and daughters of leading business people particularly from Jewish families knowing many of them would go back to their family businesses and become important clients. During the 30 years from inception in 1971 to the end of the century there were only three chief executives – Clarke, Tony Berg and Alan Moss, all of whom in their different ways were outstanding – whereas at Darling through to Schroders Australia there were eight, forgetting those sharing the role. Schroders invariably appointed chief executives who were corporate financiers who at their best are good leaders but rarely good managers. Neither Clarke of Macquarie nor Chris Corrigan of Bankers Trust was a corporate financier – both were exceptional leaders and managers. Finally, non-executive directors were carefully selected for the contribution they could make to the bank and were expected to deliver or be asked to go. From an initial equity of A$2 million in 1971 Macquarie Bank had a market capital of A$7.5 billion in 2000, with A$242 million profits after tax, a return on shareholders funds of 26% and 4500 directors and staff. They had become the only world-class financial institution in Australia and in a comparable category to Goldman Sachs, albeit on a much smaller scale.

In contrast Schroders Australia was like a cricket team that played with style but lost gallantly and were good losers – not an analogy with which most Australians would be comfortable.

NOTES:

1. Ben Strickland, a meticulous chartered accountant, had been in Corporate Finance at Schroder Wagg since 1968 and had just completed the advanced management program at Harvard Business School. He was very proud of his father's military record – he commanded the tank regiment that finally broke the German line at the battle of Casino leading to the fall of Rome and later he was the director of strategic planning at the Ministry of Defence. He was seen to be honest, direct, determined, hard working, stubborn, school-masterish, slightly lacking in humour but pleasant.

CHAPTER 19

ENVY AND GREED

Prior to 1986 remuneration was almost entirely in the form salaries with bonuses only being introduced for directors and some senior staff that year. The bonuses at that time would have been around 25% of salaries and mostly notified to the individual by letter and occasionally an embarrassing interview with a superior, all directors being spoken to by the chairman. Essentially the individual was informed of his remuneration and thanked for his work to which the individual said thank you and changed the subject – after all it was bad manners to talk about money. Mallinckrodt brought a far more disciplined approach to remuneration with the recruitment of Desmond Boyle, Sue Cox and others. In 1987 a Group Compensation Committee (GCC) was set up under Sir Ernest Woodroofe who introduced disciplines to ensure that remuneration was reviewed in relation to that paid by the competitors. It oversaw the annual pay review including the level of salaries and bonuses. Broad policies were set for the Group as a whole and these were adapted to local conditions and tax consequences by separate compensation committees in each of the countries Schroders operated in. With Boyle, Cox and Elizabeth Warren, this became a highly professional process carried out independently by each of the businesses. Competitive information was provided by two firms of consultants, Towers Perrin followed by McLagan Partners, who by interviewing all the competitors were able to provide average statistics for every job within each business of the median and upper quartile salaries and bonuses paid the previous year. This information, together with the consultant's expectations of increases in the current year for each business, was used as the basis for the heads of each of the businesses to bracket their directors and staff into categories and work up their bid for the salaries and bonus payments for individual directors and staff. Backing up their views was a staff appraisal system in which all directors and staff were set and agreed objectives for the year against which their performance was reviewed. In advance of this Bischoff reviewed each business' performance and pinpointed where each business head should be positioning his people in relation to the median and upper quartile numbers – this could change from year to year depending on performance.

Salaries

The pay philosophy introduced by the GCC was based on the concept of total remuneration with salaries, which were part of the fixed costs, being kept to a minimum generally rising by no more than inflation. This resulted in salaries over time becoming well below the norm outside the City. Contract terms were also short, all directors being on a three months contract so that if they left they were only entitled to three months' salary. (Redundancy terms were more complicated and individually negotiated.) The variable element of the remuneration was bonuses that were dependent on profits and performance. Having worked out the numbers for his directors and staff with his senior directors, the business head discussed and secured the endorsement of Cox before they were put before Bischoff. At the same time recommendations for promotions were submitted. A meeting followed with Bischoff in which the numbers were challenged, adjusted and provisionally agreed. The salary numbers were not contentious at that level as an overall percentage increase, generally in line with inflation, had been decided and as this had to include improvements in individual performance the directors, who were receiving much larger bonuses, received a *de-minimus* rise leaving more for those below (for many years in the early and mid-1990s the salaries of the more senior directors were not increased). The problem with a policy that limited salaries was that it meant that pensions, which were based on the last year's salary, were reduced each year in real terms. For those not receiving large bonuses, generally the support staff, this was a severe penalty. Having said that they were receiving market pay and as most of them were very capable they could have got a job elsewhere. The secretaries in the City were relatively well paid receiving more than for example a lead cellist in one of the top national orchestras or a lecturer at the LSE. By contrast in industry salaries tended to be higher, contracts longer but bonuses lower resulting in significantly higher fixed costs.

Bonuses

The big debates were concerning the size of the bonus pool for each business and often this meant justifying the amount for each individual. Out of these discussions came the individual businesses' demands on the total bonus pool whose quantum nobody knew. Each head knew his own bonus pool and how it related to the profits his business had produced but not the total for the bank and therefore his share. The bonus scheme was based on the shareholders receiving an after bonus and after tax return on capital of 13% – the average of all the leading merchant banks over the previous five years – although this was eroded later with the bonus pool escalating. The objective was to align the interests of the management with those of the shareholders in regard to the profits and the capital of the firm. There was extraordinary secrecy with the numbers that were only known to Mallinckrodt and Bischoff and the GCC as well as to Morris who acted as its secretary – even MacAndrew, the finance director did not know. The GCC was provided with guidelines on the ratio of remuneration to total costs of the competitors – the US banks generally had a guideline of 65%. They also received details for each business for previous years of the bonuses received as a proportion of the profits earned. This showed that for businesses being developed the amount paid in bonuses was higher and a reduction was imposed when their profits increased. Against this information the committee discussed the numbers recommended by the management and various adjustments were made with no recourse to be had. Also included was a list of the remuneration of the top 20 people in each business.

When bonuses were still something of a novelty and the business heads had not learnt how to manage the process to their advantage there was little challenge to the equity of the system. However, with the increasing competition from the US investment banks, which were paying enhanced remuneration to attract good corporate finance people from the merchant banks (and subsequently, with their significantly greater profitability due to a wider range of products and substantially more capital enabling them to pay even more) there was increasing pressure by Corporate Finance to secure more of the pie for their people and by the other businesses heads not to have their share taken from them. At the same time the remuneration scales for each of the businesses were diverging with the corporate financiers getting the most and the lenders in Banking getting the least. Largely due to the system of allocation between the different businesses being clouded in secrecy with nobody knowing whether it was fair, the share of the bonus pool gave rise to a lot of dissention among the business heads. Throughout the 1990s the biggest profit contributors were Investment Management and Treasury with Corporate Finance coming a poor third. In terms of profit per head Investment Management, which had very large staff numbers, may have come behind Treasury. None of the business heads felt he had received sufficient for his people, suspecting but not knowing that the lion's share had gone to the corporate finance directors who they felt were making a less than proportionate contribution to the overall profits. These concerns and jealousies tended to overlook that Corporate Finance was probably getting no more than the market for their business. Turner, the chairman of the GCC, said the real problem was the fact that the corporate finance people thought they should receive bonuses in line with the US investment banks irrespective of the fact that they were making significantly less profits. This led to decreasing margins with the shareholders' take falling each year to a point that Corporate Finance was becoming totally unviable. This inability to compete for top talent became one of the main justifications for selling the investment bank.

The so-called non-productive directors and staff felt particularly aggrieved as they were invariably squeezed, with nobody standing up for them. These back office directors and staff worked hard to support the operational staff and without them the revenue earners would not have been able to earn as much revenue. Effectively the secrecy created an air of mistrust and envy. Perhaps if it was more open and the disparity, if there was any, was clearer it would have made people even more unhappy! Maybe it was better not to know. There is no doubt, however, that there was a growing irritation by Investment Management and Treasury against the demands made by Corporate Finance.

The way in which the bonus pool was shared was to some extent a matter for the individual businesses to decide. SIM and Corporate Finance approached the matter in an entirely different way. SIM developed a long-term incentive plan based on SIM's profits in which large numbers of directors and staff received some form of deferred remuneration (see Chapter 12). Much time was spent on this issue by Turner who observed the emphasis on long term compensation benefits for a wide variety of directors and executives rather than the 'star' approach adopted by Richard Broadbent of Corporate

Finance in which disproportionate payments were made to relatively few senior people (see Chapter 22).

The bonus round was an exercise universally loathed by the heads of the businesses. If the numbers were shaved, as they often were, the heads of the businesses had to allocate the cuts and once the numbers were agreed all the directors and staff were informed of their new salary and bonus invariably with individual interviews. In 1996 it was decided that in order to prevent people leaving as soon as they had received their bonus, the bonus would be divided into two, the second half only being paid in the following November despite the fact that it had been awarded for work completed almost a year earlier. This did not go down well, sowing much distrust in the senior management. It was a further indication that the firm had changed and that the senior management no longer trusted their staff.

There was one benefit in the process however, as save for the members of the GCC nobody knew what bonuses had been paid to individuals other than to the seven executive directors on the main board, whose remuneration was set out in the annual report. Regrettably this did not apply to the issue of share options.

Share Options

In 1983 Schroders introduced a share ownership scheme – which superseded an earlier scheme in 1971 – 'to reward eligible staff for their hard work in helping to create the profits on which the Group depends' that involved a free issue of Schroder shares each year equivalent to between 6 and 7% of the participant's basic salary up to a maximum of £5000. Long-serving staff were able to build up quite a few shares over their career. This was followed by a senior executive share option scheme in 1986 that involved the grant of an option to subscribe for non-voting ordinary shares which could be exercised after three years at the price granted. It was never made clear who was eligible or the basis on which they were distributed – it was totally opaque. Essentially the process lent itself to people feeling they were unfairly treated.

Non-voting shares were introduced in 1986 to enable the management to have an incentive without loss of control by the family, which thereby retained 48.01% of the voting shares. For every ordinary share each shareholder received four voting shares and one non-voting share. The restructuring had to be approved by the shareholders and Mallinckrodt played a large part in meeting the institutions and in securing their acceptance. Many of the institutional shareholders had objected to the issue of non-voting shares as a matter of principle and because of the harm it would do to the liquidity of the shares. Although not enamoured by the idea they gave sufficient support for the family not to have to use its votes to gain acceptance. Following the share exchange the senior executive share option scheme 1986 was initiated and non-voting shares were granted to certain directors of Schroders and Schroder Wagg at a price close to the current market value.

As a result of the issue of options over the years the ratio between voting and non-voting shares was to change from 4 to 1 to 3.25 to 1 by 1999. The family, being determined to maintain its control over the bank, insisted that non-voting shares were bought in advance of the issue of options to make sure that there was a minimal increase in the number of shares. There were continual difficulties with the family over the amount of these issues. As one of the non-executive directors said,

> at the root of the problem was the reluctance of the family to share its wealth with the senior management. It wanted more of the pie rather than being satisfied with a larger amount arising out of the growth of the pie. Had the senior managers become partners in the business it would have fundamentally changed their attitudes to costs and embedded in them a long term view of the business and thereby aligned the family interests with the key decision makers. Short-term bonuses and having the ability to exercise options after three years was not conducive to long term thinking.

Non-voting share options were issued to the directors annually. They were listed in the accounts each year together with the remuneration of the directors of Schroders. Unfortunately the issues of options to the directors of Schroder Wagg who were not on the main board was also published, it being legally necessary. This proved to be very divisive and badly damaged the collegiate atmosphere within Schroders. Options were given to some people every year, sometimes in significant amounts particularly those in Corporate Finance, other people received one issue and no more, and others, who might reasonably have expected one issue never received any. This was driven by the fact that the US investment banks provided as part of their package significant stock options to lock in their key people that were distributed to them throughout the world from the overall profits of the bank. With the reluctance of the family to release shares there was insufficient to go around and the lion's share went to the corporate financiers and those on the main board. The irony was that the value of these shares was driven up by the value created by SIM rather than Corporate Finance. People were deeply shocked at the size of the remuneration and the amount of share options being allocated to the few. It was clear that greed started at the top and this bred envy in those below.

CHAPTER 20

MALLINCKRODT PASSES THE BATON TO BISCHOFF

1995

G owi Mallinckrodt retired as chairman of Schroders in May 1995 having been with the Group for 41 years. Unusually he remained an executive director and was appointed to the new position of president. During his ten years as chairman profits increased by 8.8 times to £132 million, shareholders' funds 4.5 times to £731 million and market capitalisation 16 times to £1.85 billion. During the same period the FTSE All Share index increased by two and a half. In his final chairman's statement, Mallinckrodt praised Bischoff for his energy and business acumen and for being his closest colleague and great personal friend. In response Bischoff spoke of Mallinckrodt's leadership and strategic thinking and of his insistence on standards of integrity, prudence, quality and teamwork. In looking back on his chairmanship later, Mallinckrodt was most proud of the fact that he had always suppressed politics at Schroders. He was also pleased that there had been 'utter and total harmony' with Bischoff and that all issues had been discussed and worked out. He recognised that he was surrounded by cleverer people and was lucky to have participated with them in the development of the business.

Mallinckrodt was highly regarded outside but was perhaps less appreciated within Schroders. All agreed that his partnership with Bischoff was a remarkable one and that it took them both to achieve it. Airlie had been proved right that Bischoff had the flexibility to reach a *modus operandi* with Mallinckrodt. Mallinckrodt, although absolutely determined to be seen to be the executive chairman outside, was prepared to take on all the work Bischoff did not enjoy even though he had not expected or wished to do so but did it to ensure their joint success. These roles were difficult and by their nature did not bring popularity. The analogy of both being on the same motor bicycle was often used by Bruno and Mallinckrodt and this was reflected in the view of colleagues that Bischoff was the external face with his foot flat on the accelerator with Mallinckrodt being the internal manager, the disciplinarian with his foot on the brake. Together they reaped the fruits of Airlie's decisions. With Bischoff always in the limelight and given all the praise in the press it could not have been easy for Mallinckrodt.

The competition had a high regard for Mallinckrodt. Sir Siegmund Warburg used to meet Mallinckrodt twice a year over lunch to exchange confidences and being from the same part of Germany they got on very well. Sir David Scholey said Siegmund felt that Mallinckrodt was the only person who could revitalise Schroders and return it to its former glory. He respected Mallinckrodt finding him very German, unsentimental, prepared to share confidences, extremely trustworthy and playing the key role of owner and proprietor – a deeply rooted German characteristic – with a strong sense of authority and proprietorship. Simon Robertson of Kleinwort Benson saw him as 'the guardian of the family's position who understood longevity and was a trustee of the next generation always avoiding doing things that would jeopardise the future'.

James Kelly, who worked very closely with Mallinckrodt over the previous ten years said,

> He had good networking skills with a flair for talking people into being enthusiastic to buy what he wished to sell – Schrobanco with all its Latin American debts to IBJ. As the representative of the principal shareholder, he could speak authoritatively to the outside world. Although not as much of a people person, he had the ability to say 'No' when Bischoff wanted to say, 'Yes'. He proved to be a good statesman – no easy task being married to the largest shareholder's sister. Despite not having a very good start he emerged as an important player. He became the intermediary between the management and the family and in that respect he moved from a position of perceived insignificance to become critical to the success of the firm. He held the long-term view, as did the family.

Turner echoed this in saying they made a powerful team in some ways fulfilling each other's roles with Bischoff dealing with all the clients, with whom he was outstanding, and Mallinckrodt dealing with the difficult problems of firing and reassigning people, something Bischoff disliked. Mallinckrodt was always concerned about the next five years whereas Bischoff the next five days, but this was not a criticism. Each therefore operated in the areas they were most comfortable in. Bruno, who was so fortunate to have Gowi as his brother-in-law, thought it was 'a marvellous combination of complimentary skills with Win's good judgement and his ability to get in new business and encourage the people and Gowi, the long term thinker, strategist and carer of the pennies'.

Way also found them a marvellous team, 'Win the consummate relationship man and Gowi involved inside considering all the detail.' Having worked so closely with Mallinckrodt for more than 25 years and having participated in all the major decisions, Way described him as, 'good strategically and in operations, always taking a long term view'. Personally he found him 'extraordinarily ethical and honest, with a strong social conscience with all his charitable work for the disadvantaged and education, great loyalty and a wonderful family man'. Scholey said it was a great partnership in which both complimented each other, observing that there is always a need to have two or three people to balance and stimulate. Those inside said they complimented each other, the strengths of one covering the weaknesses of the other. Bischoff often deferred decisions so he could speak to Mallinckrodt and then passed on Mallinckrodt's negative reaction. Schroders flourished during their partnership and one has to ask whether it would have done so without Mallinckrodt. He would be the first to say that it certainly would not have done so without Bischoff.

Reflecting on his partner, Bischoff said

He had a conviction that his position as a member of the family, even though not a Schroder, was to hold the mantle with the duty to do his best for the family and safeguard it. Being a banker he was very risk averse. Personally he had a well developed sense of obligation, was religious and had a strong sense of family, he felt the need to repay society, had high moral standards, the family he had created with Charmaine meant a huge amount to him. He had delightful children. He was also generous in his private life.

Sedgwick said 'he was very shrewd and closely vetted strategy as well as being the disciplinarian and controller of the business, preventing the firm from doing anything stupid.'

One of Mallinckrodt's skills and enthusiasms was networking. He spent an enormous amount of his time travelling around the world calling on people in government and central banks as well as attending international conferences, often giving speeches. With his formidable early contacts in Germany and the USA he never had a problem calling on senior business and government leaders and through them he acquired an extensive knowledge of a very wide number of subjects. With his ability to retain and to absorb what he had heard he built up over the years a large number of personal contacts, particularly in Germany and the United States but also elsewhere. He was well known to them for always being courteous.

Mallinckrodt played very little part in the management of the revenue earning businesses and Bischoff always had to persuade him that the management were doing their best for the firm and should be trusted. He respected Bischoff, who told him everything after the Standard Chartered Bank perpetual FRN saga, spent masses of time and had endless patience with him as well as helping him to persuade the family.

He was felt to be naturally cautious and resisted expansion and this was ill-suited to the challenges faced by investment banks. However, he was the force behind the East European business and Harington proved to be the perfect person to be put in charge. He was mesmerised by China and had he been able to do so he would have thrown even more resources at it to no avail. His error was the purchase of Wertheim, his refusal to change its management and his failure to implement what was needed, that is, its full integration with London. Being so risk averse, he was also a permanent drag on the development of a securities business but maybe in hindsight he was correct in this. His appointment of Sedgwick as head of investment banking when he knew nothing about it was curious and did not help the resolution of the problems with Wertheim. He was seen to be a good seller of businesses – Schrobanco and Schroder Leasing – but a bad buyer – Wertheim and BPGF.

Throughout the book there are many references to the views of his colleagues and subordinates from which it can be seen he did not have an easy relationship with them largely due to his personality and his lack of knowledge about their businesses. Many of the personal qualities expressed by his family and outsiders above would not have been recognised by his colleagues other than Bischoff who knew him best. Most of the people who worked directly for him found him extremely demanding sometimes being vindictive with someone always having to suffer if things went wrong. Due to his conscientiousness, briefing him was exhausting and time consuming with his requirement that they go into great detail invariably having to go through each point two or three times. Those running the businesses had less to do with him invariably dealing directly with Bischoff. He was fiercely protective of the areas he was responsible for, that is, Australia, Singapore and the United States where he would not brook any interference and certainly not criticism from the other business heads. He had the courage of his convictions and invariably spoke his mind but tended to be negative. He did however achieve some good compromises.

His greatest success was in being an effective bridge between the management and the family. Throughout his chairmanship and subsequent presidency the previous tensions with the family were avoided. He said he never allowed the family's interests to influence his thinking on the running of the bank. Turner put it another way saying, 'Gowi felt that if the bank was properly run it was in the best interest of the shareholders and the family.' As a result he was able to persuade Bruno of the merits of decisions recommended by the management that affected the shareholders and in this he was greatly helped by Bischoff with his huge capacity for patience.

In November 1996, Gowi suffered a brain haemorrhage while at home. Although successfully operated on he had lost his abilities in numeracy and literacy and part of his vision. For the next 18 months he was visited everyday by a therapist and together they worked on him recovering his ability to read and write. Driven by the knowledge that if he did not use his brain it would die, and if he did not keep fit his body would go to sleep, he fought on and within three months he returned to the office. These characteristics, particularly his strength of character, self-discipline and great determination to overcome adversity, explain why and how he achieved what he did during his career. The other reason for his successful career and his recovery from his illness was the colossal support he received from his loyal and devoted wife Charmaine for whom all those in the firm who knew her, of which there were hundreds, had a very high regard and affection. It is interesting to speculate about the contribution she might have made to the board had she been a member. She was born too early.

Although many at Schroders might have felt Mallinckrodt spent all his time on Schroder business even when he stepped down as chairman, he had been an active non-executive director of Siemens plc and Allianz of America Inc as well as being on the advisory board of Bain & Co, the management consultants and McGraw Hill. He attended every annual meeting of the World Economic Forum in Davos from 1990, which suited his networking skills, and became the chairman of the council representing all the members.

His main interest outside business, apart from his close knit family, was creating a bridge between the leaders of different religions as a member of the Interfaith Foundation in which Christians, Muslims and Jews were involved and later joined by Buddhists and Hindus. Having always been a strongly committed Christian, he has real passion for this work, reads a lot on the subject and finds it very rewarding.[1] In line with his interest in ethics he was for many years on the advisory council of the Institute of Business Ethics and a trustee of Christian Responsibility in Public Affaires. In the academic field his interests include the *Incunabula* (referring to things 'belonging to the cradle') – manuscripts and books dating from the fifteenth century – in the Bodleian Library at Oxford, not least as the word was coined by a Canon of Munster Cathedral, Bernhard von Mallinckrodt, in 1640.

He always took a great interest in furthering good relations between Germany and Britain and maintained a close relationship with the German ambassadors in London. He was also president of the German-British Chamber of Industry & Commerce and president of the German YMCA. For his 'contribution (over 40 years) towards the enhancement of Anglo-German relations' he received successively the three classes of the Cross of the Federal Republic of Germany culminating in 1990 with the Great Cross – *Verdienstkreuz 1 Klasse des Verdienstordens* (FRG). This consistent service in support of German activities to some extent reflected that he saw himself as being a German living in England.

His greatest pride is his family, which is very close knit and a huge credit to him and Charmaine. Outside observers were impressed by how all the Mallinckrodt children clearly enjoyed each other's company. They had a wonderful relationship with their father and were impressed by his self-discipline, integrity and strong character, and for being kind, tolerant and open-minded and with a great interest in human beings. He clearly thrived on being an internationalist with his enthusiasm for inclusiveness and diversity and the virtues of different cultures and societies seeing diversity as a source of strength. The key to his character was blending enthusiasm and optimism with discipline. He had a few very good English friends who mainly came through Charmaine, but his closest personal friends were German, from his school days at Salem.

He continued to play an active role on the board as a director and was available to the Group Compensation Committee and met regularly with Way and Turner. He also came into the office everyday and for many it was as if he was still chairman.

In the New Year of 1997, Mallinckrodt was appointed by Her Majesty the Queen an honorary Knight Commander of the Most Excellent Order of the British Empire (KBE).

The honorary knighthood was conferred 'in recognition of outstanding services rendered over many years to banking and finance in the City of London'.

NOTES:

1. Charmaine was brought up in the Church of England and she and Gowi attend their local Anglican church. His mother and sisters converted to Catholicism, the Joest family having come from a long line of Catholics in Westphalia with a number of bishops in the family. His aunt Mother Pauline, who founded an Order of Christian Charity for Catholic teaching nuns that spread across the world, including Colegio Mallinckrodt based in Buenos Aires for children and youth education, was beatified by the Pope in Rome in 1985. Following on from previous generations of the Schroder family he supported Christus Kirche in Knightsbridge which was built and given by the Schröder family and other prominent German families in 1904 and the Hamburg Lutheran Church in Hackney in the East End, London's oldest German institution which was founded in 1699 as a place of worship for Hanseatic merchants residing in the City.

PART 3
BISCHOFF
1995 – 2000

CHAPTER 21

BISCHOFF BECOMES CHAIRMAN

1995 — 1999

On becoming chairman of Schroders in May 1995, Bischoff retained the responsibilities of the chief executive but dropped the title and Sedgwick was appointed vice-chairman, remaining group managing director of Investment Management. It was said that Sedgwick was there to play some of the role Mallinckrodt had played — the person at the top prepared to take the tough calls. Bischoff became less involved in the day-to-day work of Corporate Finance and Securities but remained involved with clients when needed. He also gave up the chairmanship of Schroder Wagg to Solandt but it had lost its prestige and power due to the chief executive and group managing directors having assumed responsibility for the activities of the operating companies. When he took over as chairman of the GEC from Mallinckrodt in 1992, Bischoff turned it into a forum for his colleagues to form a common view and avoid disputes, himself playing the role of a chairman rather than chief executive. Proposals from below were rarely turned down, the GEC simply questioning and doing supervisory testing. It was never an originator of business being essentially a management group.

In his first statement as chairman in the 1995 Annual Report, Bischoff emphasised the importance of the umbrella provided by the Schroder family,

As a result of the significant structural changes in the financial services industry in recent years, not only in the UK but also in the USA, and in particular the major changes within the London market since the beginning of 1995, commentators have questioned our ability to retain our independence. The stability of our shareholding structure has been of major value to Schroders over many years and we see it as a significant factor in differentiating us from our competitors. Management firmly endorses our continued independence, since we have a strategy which is capable of delivering increasing value to shareholders.

This statement confirmed the management's view that the controlling shareholding of the Schroder family was a major benefit in protecting the firm from predators. The family stake was to be the foundation of Bischoff's strategy as it guaranteed independence. Capital constraints were to be considered a blessing forcing staff to focus their thinking. Specialist, international, independent were the buzzwords.

In 1995, Schroders acted for SG Warburg and Kleinwort Benson in their loss of independence to Swiss Bank Corporation and Dresdner Bank respectively, and also for Barings in its abortive rescue negotiations with the Bank of England and the British commercial banks. Morgan Grenfell had been acquired by Deutsche Bank five years earlier and so all Schroders' major British competitors had lost their independence. Lazards, NM Rothschild and Robert Fleming, although top class in their activities, were not regarded as being of the same stature as Schroders as investment banks principally as they had all decided not to compete as fully integrated investment banks.

A strategic review was conducted by Boston Consulting Group, its main focus being on whether Schroders should be more active in the securities business – in this respect the study was inconclusive. There followed a greater commitment to a global functional organisation putting more teeth into the previous moves in that direction. There was a considerable argument about this change as it meant that the country heads would lose all their power. Mallinckrodt wanted to maintain the integrity of the group companies in case, *in extremis*, it might be necessary to sell them. Naturally he was strongly supported by Boyce in Hong Kong, Tomlin in Singapore, Tanaka in Japan and Gasser in Switzerland. Mason in Australia wanted to take over the whole of the businesses in Asia to form a regional group like the very successful Jardine Fleming but the other heads did not like this as they preferred reporting direct to London. In these circumstances the group managing directors would continue to carry out a co-ordinating and advisory role. Sedgwick and Solandt argued strongly for a functional structure, seeing the merits of being global players. Bischoff, although by inclination favouring a functional management structure, had as usual to avoid an unpleasant confrontation. A functional organisation would increase the power and independence of those in charge of the global businesses and isolate those who had previously overseen the individual companies, comprising a number of businesses. Clearly the Group was best served by a functional organisation and this was finally agreed but its implementation was fought tooth and nail and may have contributed towards the failure of many of the overseas companies (see Chapter 24). There was to some extent a compromise in that investment banking had three regional heads in Europe, Asia and the United States and this is dealt with later. In line with these moves there was an increasing emphasis on profit performance of each of the businesses and for the remuneration of those within each to be related to it.

At the same time three executive committees were formed to control and co-ordinate the main businesses worldwide: Investment Banking under Sedgwick which included Corporate Finance, Securities, and Project Finance; Asset Management under Govett including Investment Management and Private Equity; Financial Markets under Solandt including Treasury, Banking and Leasing. There was also another under MacAndrew dealing with finance, planning and administration including IT. Each of these heads was a member of and reported to the GEC. Within each functional committee were represented regional and business heads.

Although there was a true partnership between Mallinckrodt and Bischoff as equals, this was not the case with Bischoff and Sedgwick. Sedgwick, as vice-chairman was effectively Bischoff's deputy. There was a considerable difference in that if Bischoff was considering something difficult with a subordinate, say the head of Corporate Finance, he could always go and discuss it with Mallinckrodt and return to the head of Corporate Finance saying the chairman had said no. For Sedgwick if he said no to the head of Corporate Finance, he would go directly to Bischoff and persuade him otherwise. However, Sedgwick did take on all the difficult jobs Bischoff did not like, including the removal of many of the heads of overseas companies in Asia. Mallinckrodt was a strong supporter of Sedgwick saying,

> He was a natural leader, uncomplicated, straight and committed and extremely ambitious. He was impeccably ethical and honest. He was prepared to fight his corner and was clear on targets. He was also popular and engendered team spirit with superb judgement, clarity of thought. He was intuitive and had a flair for investment instilling trust and confidence in his clients.

Sedgwick, much to everyone's surprise, was made group managing director of Investment Banking in 1996, following the retirement of Adam Broadbent. It was an extraordinary appointment as he held Investment Banking in total contempt but he was the one person that the family trusted to keep control of the more extreme elements such as Richard Broadbent and Steven Kotler. He was seen by the family as having no axe to grind since he was looking to his retirement. Mallinckrodt saw him as being loyal and willing to protect the interests of the firm against the investment bankers who were solely interested in themselves. In fact Samuel and Richard Broadbent were keen to see Sedgwick in this role as they felt it was important to include the most sceptical person on the board fully involved and committed to the future strategy for the investment bank.

Bischoff asked Sedgwick to go to New York to sort out the problems with Wertheim. As he was 61 at the time and looking forward to his retirement, he had no wish to move home. He therefore agreed, at a price which Schroders was clearly prepared to pay for his inconvenience, to commit two to three years spending half his time in New York and half in London. Having a reputation for being a hard man much was expected of him in pulling Wertheim and particularly Kotler into line. Although previously having been seen to be anti-Kotler, when he got to New York he found,

> a well managed business which had never made a loss since being purchased by Schroders in 1986 – unlike the subsidiaries of other British merchant banks – with a dedicated and conscientious management team fully committed to Schroders' interests and led by a very able businessman, Kotler. The business was entirely incompatible with Schroders in London being a boutique that could not compete with Goldman Sachs and it was clearly despised by the arrogant corporate finance people in London.[1]

It was also quite clear to Sedgwick that Schroders in London had no idea of what it had bought and no understanding of the nature of its business. Schroders had also never been prepared to put any capital into Wertheim to change it and had thereby prevented its growth. He was impressed with the quality of the people and the business of Wertheim and from then on fully and vigorously supported their cause in his dealings with powerful mandarins in London. Many in London found him a great disappointment and thought he had 'gone native'. In fact he very shortly formed a close personal relationship with Kotler, who helped him develop a social life in New York.

Although a disappointment in New York to those in London, Sedgwick healed the rift between Investment Banking and SIM, which had been largely created by himself. Being a pro-active manager he was always keen to get things done. He also helped achieve a resolution of the sale of Investment Banking and was a good support to Bischoff when he was appointed deputy chairman in September 1997. It was not a golden time for him however.

1995 was a critical time for the British merchant banks seeking to become investment bankers since the US investment bankers were gaining more dominance in the market. How each of the businesses responded to these threats, particularly the investment bankers, as they became known, is set out in the chapters that follow.

NOTES:

1. In fact this was a complete misconception in the minds of the corporate financiers in Wertheim. Adam Broadbent, Carnwath and Heath, all of whom spent time with Wertheim, would never have despised the people at Wertheim. Neither would Grimstone or Challen. They all saw them for what they were, but that was no cause for contempt. It was a cause for regret that Schroders did not have strategically what it needed, or the management to turn it into what was needed. It may not have come over in that way in New York.

CHAPTER 22

INVESTMENT BANKERS AT LAST – BUT WHERE?

1994 – 1998

During 1994 Samuel became joint head with Netherton of a demoralised Corporate Finance team in danger of haemorrhaging. He had joined the research department in Investment Management under Richard Morgan at the end of 1977, from Coopers & Lybrand. He was interviewed by Popham in a room piled with paper but had no idea what was discussed and assumed that was the end of it. A few days later he was telephoned and asked whether he had accepted the job he had been offered during the meeting and was too embarrassed to say no. Morgan encouraged him to join the Strategy Group but it became clear it would never get anywhere as it was trying to compete with the major strategic consultants without the people or the resources and was adding no value to Schroders' other activities. After the 1984 strategic review it was incorporated within Corporate Finance and Adam Broadbent made it clear that he could either become a corporate financier or he could leave – there was no discussion. He trained with Hugh Evans and soon became involved in supporting BP in its successful bid for Brit Oil and got to know David Simon, the finance director, and this developed over the years to become a close working relationship (see Chapter 6). He also worked on other oil transactions including LASMO's successful bid for Tricentrol, which was a high profile transaction. During the M&A recession in the early 1990s he worked on the Rosehaugh-Stanhope joint venture for Broadgate. He was the obvious successor to Challen, having a natural gravitas and being highly regarded and respected by the clients and colleagues.

Corporate Finance had plenty of M&A activity in 1995, with Schroders enjoying a remarkably good year, particularly in regard to the restructuring of the electricity industry in the UK, acting for Northern Electric, SWEB, Manweb and National Power. At the same time closer to home, there were big changes in the investment banking business particularly with the US banks becoming increasingly competitive in the UK and on the continent of Europe. Corporate Finance acted in February for Barings in its unsuccessful rescue negotiations with the Bank of England, in May for SG Warburg and in December for Kleinwort Benson in the sale of their businesses to Swiss Bank Corporation (SBC) and Dresdner Bank respectively.

The Baring crisis showed Bischoff and Schroders at their best in the eyes of Andrew Tuckey, Barings' beleaguered chief executive.

INVESTMENT BANKERS AT LAST -BUT WHERE?

We were totally gob-smacked when we heard of the position in Singapore on the Friday night. We set in motion an internal review and the following morning I rang Win at Severalls (his house in Gloucestershire). He arrived in a sports jacket and fawn trousers with a full team including Will Samuel and others and they worked through to late on Sunday night. An early conclusion was that an internal solution was not possible. Win organised all the banks and was on the phone all day to their chairman who packed the Bank of England on Sunday. To reach an agreement we needed to know that the futures contracts had been closed – the sheer size of the liabilities, at something short of $6 billion were too large and unpredictable to close off in that it was not possible to find a counter party. We would have been rescued if the liability had been known. The loss went from £50 million to £900 million by the time it was finally closed by ING, who had taken us over for £1. We all felt that Win and his colleagues had acquitted themselves well with no effort spared – they never got paid. It was typical of Win – amazing. The following day Peter Baring and I received a wonderful letters of sympathy, which was truly heartfelt.

The failure of Barings was a great shock to the City and particularly to the old accepting houses as it showed that they were no longer inviolate in that it was now clear that the Bank of England would not rescue them should they get into difficulty. It also sent out a message that they were no longer critical to the success of the City and would have to fend for themselves. It was an ominous message. The main immediate effect on Schroders was the need to separate out SIM clients' cash balances from Schroder Wagg's treasury business, which had up to that point been a cheap and reliable source of funding. A cash pool was therefore created off Schroder Wagg's balance sheet to manage separately the cash element of SIM clients' portfolios.

Within three months SG Warburg, the UK's premier investment banking name had, as a distressed seller, been bought by SBC for an 8% premium above book value and by the year end Dresdner Bank had purchased Kleinwort Benson for twice its book value, but this included its asset management business that was valued at 2.5% of its funds under management, leaving the investment banking business to go at a premium of 20% over net assets.

SG Warburg's collapse was due to its costs running out of control, through an increasingly high headcount and the payment of excessive bonuses – a substantial number of staff being on guaranteed bonuses – in the face of falling revenues that had fallen by a third in 1994/5. 'They did not have the capital base or the earnings power to meet their aspirations globally', said the Charles McVeigh III, the head of Salomons in London. It had lost its unique European culture by trying to grow too fast and thereby became a collection of hired hands working for themselves first and the company second. As Loehnis said 'there was always insufficient capital and costs got out of control. Scholey's choice of Cairns, a good corporate broker, as chief executive was bad as he found it too difficult to manage so many prima donnas, always having to compete with the large US investment banks which with their huge capital could survive their mistakes.' Peter Stormonth Darling, the chairman of MAM, four years later saw SG Warburg's demise as being due to: its failure to establish a strong US presence; the move into proprietary trading; the loss of its distinctively European character through the acquisition of three British securities firms; the absence of what he called 'an employee ownership mentality', which led to the driving up of the cost structure; and an inadequate system of controls over a firm that had grown too large – 'those in charge simply forgot to apply the rules which Siegmund Warburg used to drum into our minds constantly and repetitively' (David Kynaston, *The City of London Vol. IV, A Club No More*). 'The acquisition of SG Warburg marked the end of Britain's last true hope of fielding a top-class merchant bank capable of competing on an independent basis with the financial powerhouses of the world' (Erik Banks, *The Rise and Fall of the Merchant Banks*).

With SG Warburg being acquired all the press attention moved to Kleinwort Benson, which had done reasonably well having recovered from back office disasters of Big Bang, the heavy losses on Premier Oil[1] and the defection of quality people like John Nelson. However, with the failure of Barings and the collapse of SG Warburg they were vulnerable with the family holding under a third of the votes. Kleinwort was less ambitious than SG Warburg, only seeking to be an international investment bank rather than a global leader, and so was pleased to be out of the public eye and part of a larger group, Dresdner providing it with capital and a position in European fixed income. For the senior management, maintenance of Kleinwort's culture and some autonomy were the key issues – they expected to become an autonomous and independent subsidiary operating under the Dresdner umbrella. Staff considerations were mercenary and short term. Simon Robertson, the chairman of Kleinwort, was very pleased with the price of £1 billion, nearly twice book value, saying, 'David (Challen) is somebody you want at your side when the going gets tough.'

Morgan Grenfell, which had been acquired by Deutsche Bank in 1989, had retained an individual identity until Deutsche Bank decided in 1995 to consolidate its own securities and capital markets activities with Morgan Grenfell to form a new subsidiary, DMG. The expansion which followed, designed to enhance its international investment banking capabilities, led to it effectively being run by American traders and capital market specialists with American-style hiring and compensation packages. This was to lead to it climbing the Eurobond and international equities league tables. At the same time DMG lost its focus on and its reputation for corporate finance and M&A. Morgan Grenfell (and DMG) became so integrated within Deutsche Bank that it lost all its independence including its name (Erik Banks, *The Rise and Fall of the Merchant Banks*).

At this stage Schroders found itself virtually alone. All the largest British merchant banks had been acquired by the well-capitalised Swiss and German banks in the hope of competing in the international markets with the US 'bulge bracket' firms[2] and those that remained, like Lazard and NM Rothschild, had decided not to compete head on and remain mainly corporate finance advisors – Robert Fleming was seen to be mainly an asset management house although strong in investment banking in the Far East. Schroders was therefore besieged on all sides by the US investment banks which were becoming ever more dominant. It had to bite the bullet and decide if it wanted to become a fully integrated investment bank or remain a corporate finance advisor. With its high market value – almost entirely due to its very successful asset management business – and the protection from takeover provided by the Schroder family with its controlling shareholding, Schroders regarded itself as having been too successful to revert to a Lazard and become the best of the survivors. It aspired to being a Goldman Sachs. What it overlooked was that in fact it was only a leader in the UK corporate finance market – 1995 was another record year for Corporate Finance in the UK. It had an indifferent position on the Continent, particularly in capital raising, and Wertheim was a second league player in New York with no prospects of raising its status. Schroders had to decide the route it should take if it was to survive in investment banking and in doing so to learn the lessons of SG Warburg and Kleinwort Benson.

Boston Consulting Group was taken on to review in 1995 whether Schroders should be in the securities business and whether it should be integrated – surprisingly the exercise was inconclusive and nothing changed. Samuel and Netherton arranged for Gary Davis, a former vicar and change consultant at the Results Partnership, to facilitate a discussion among the corporate finance directors to discuss the future of the business. It was part of the transition from partnership management to the recognition that one or two had to be in charge. There was general acceptance of the need for a securities business and a greater drive into Europe if they were to become a serious investment bank. At last after ten years of ambivalence, Corporate Finance faced with the abyss had come off the fence and embraced Securities, which was then incorporated with Corporate Finance to become Investment Banking. However, the family still had to be convinced. Consideration was first given to the sale of the investment bank by the board at this time, when it was raised by Way and Turner, two of the non-executive directors close to the Schroder family, with the encouragement of Sedgwick. For Turner it was inevitable that Schroders would fail to compete as revenues were being squeezed by the US investment banks and increasing remuneration costs were closing the gap. Mallinckrodt was neutral at the time although he was concerned about the competition becoming more of a principal than an intermediary, as this required a level of capital Schroders did not have. The views of the management, that is, Bischoff, Sedgwick, MacAndrew and Govett, were that they could succeed by building a securities business.

The Renaissance of Securities

The corporate finance directors having finally come down in favour of securities being a necessary means of their survival, Bischoff and Adam Broadbent initiated discussions with Philip Augar, the head of NatWest Securities, with a view to him building for Schroders a viable securities business. A year previously, Richard Wyatt, aged 35, was head of equity capital markets at Wood Mackenzie, recently acquired by NatWest Bank, when he came across Schroders in connection with the defence of LASMO against Enterprise. He liked what he saw of Challen and Richard Broadbent. Later he helped Schroders with the flotation of DFS, Lord Kirkham's family furniture stores company. He saw a fine corporate finance house with no capability in the equity business. Being a close personal friend and colleague of Augar, the chief executive of Wood Mac, now NatWest Securities, he promoted the idea of their team helping Schroders; particularly since, following NatWest's failure to buy SG Warburg, he felt NatWest had no future as an investment bank. Augar had similar views and a passionate wish to see a British house succeed as an integrated investment bank, the critical platform being a successful corporate finance team. One day Augar visited Wyatt at his home in Suffolk and said he was proposing to leave NatWest and had agreed to help Schroders to turn around its security business and would Wyatt like to join him by running the UK with Augar working on the continental European countries. A key member of their team, as head of research, was Patrick Wellington and the three of them came over together in 1995. Early the following year, JJ McNeill joined them. Together at NatWest they had been the number one rated equity team in the UK but they had no corporate finance capability. Effectively the NatWest team had been beheaded. With the arrival of the new team, Rupert Caldecott, who had been running Schroder Securities, moved to the private clients team under Roger Hills at SIM.

Augar unlocked the problem with the Schroder family as he was so convincing in his arguments for developing a successful securities business that they accepted. They were with the majority in being impressed if not spellbound by Augar. Augar was very smart with a high quality and good clarity of thinking and knew what made the securities business tick and how to build it using the aura of the Schroder name. He was good with people and had an ability to get his people to do what they were good at.

When Wyatt arrived at Cheapside and saw what was there, he wondered what on earth he had done. The only compensation was that they had a clean piece of paper to work from. So they hired the best team available plucking people out of Merrill Lynch, Goldman Sachs, NatWest, BZW, SG Warburg and James Capel. It was particularly helpful that following the acquisition of SBC Warburg by UBS there were a lot of good staff on the market. Within a year they were in profit, 'which cheered up Mallinckrodt', declared by the Excel Survey to be the most improved broker – hardly surprising as they had started from nothing! – but most importantly they had secured 2% of the market, the same as Cazenove.

In June 1995 Augar had approached Ruth Sack, who had been at James Capel for ten years as an investment analyst and sales person, to join him at Schroders. While at Manchester University her professor spoke with such awe about the City and its money earning that she thought she should drink at the trough. She quickly discovered that having a posh voice did not necessarily mean being smart. She had been in New York at the time Watkins was there and had a low opinion of him as a broker. She asked those who interviewed her, that is Bischoff, Augar, Samuel, Richard Broadbent and MacAndrew, why Schroders had got things wrong for so long? They admitted that there had never been an understanding of the need to integrate Securities with Corporate Finance. She knew that you had to have a real depth of understanding in order to recruit and to develop the business successfully. She felt that with Augar, Samuel, Broadbent and Bischoff, Schroders could be successful. She said she would only stay for three or four years. She started as head of sales and built a team to deliver a research product to the client base. Schroders had decided not to do trading, sticking to agency work. Mike Crawshaw from NatWest became head of research and Mark Edminston started to build non-US business into the United States. Edminston was very smart and spoke many languages and had been a very successful analyst.

We found the place a complete shambles with no discipline and an abuse of expense accounts, long lunches with entertaining on a 'please rather than thank you' basis – we sought to reverse this attitude. There was a good Italian team and also a good syndicate team led by Sauvary and Tassi, who had a good relationship with the Italians. Ivan Sedgwick, who was clearly very intelligent but cynical, was brought around to help the new team. We began to recruit high profile analysts with constant upgrading of the team – we needed to have good mid-field players and people with gravitas to match that of the clients.

Samuel took over capital markets in 1996 from Bill Slee, who had retired to become a senior adviser, and following the retirement of Adam Broadbent after 28 years' service, became group managing director of Corporate Finance. He had not made a success of managing Corporate Finance in London, as management and decisiveness were not his forte. He was a very able corporate finance practitioner and very good with clients – most felt he would have done better if he had continued to stay with his clients. Corporate Finance had chosen two heads in succession that were far better at advising clients than managing the business. Samuel was clever, the best strategic thinker, full of ideas and aware of all the possibilities facing Corporate Finance and had the ability to address the alternatives with determination. But as a manager and a leader he was not admired, being seen as a poor administrator and insufficiently tough in dealing with problems and people – like Bischoff, he was not good at dealing with conflicts – although he engendered great loyalty. He had more the qualities of a chairman than a chief executive.

On Samuel's elevation, Richard Broadbent became head of European Corporate Finance. He was a totally different kettle of fish. Broadbent (no relation to Adam Broadbent) joined Schroders in 1985, aged 34, from HM Treasury. Being one of his best officials, Sir Peter Middleton, the permanent secretary, was exceedingly annoyed to hear he was departing so much so that he told Bischoff of his displeasure with the implication that if Schroders hired anyone else from the Treasury it would not be to Schroders' advantage. The loss of Grimstone, despite being brighter, at more or less the same time was not regarded as seriously as the loss of Broadbent. It is interesting to compare the skills and personalities of these two adversaries. Both came from the Treasury, a very tough school requiring a strong intellect and an aggressive debating style in which they excelled. They were great catches for Schroders both being brilliant corporate financiers and exceptionally for civil servants they were very commercially aware and made Schroders a lot of money. As managers they were both bullies. Their personalities, however, were entirely different. Grimstone had charm, was more of a human being and a good companion socially. He needed the assurance of being stroked by his superiors and liked by his colleagues. Broadbent never relaxed, was ruthless and driven and uncomfortable to be with socially.

Under the consensual leadership of Challen and Samuel, Corporate Finance had become a bit loose and the pendulum had to swing back. It was run like a workers' cooperative with everybody's views being given equal weight. The management had to be tightened up and Broadbent was thought to be the right person for the task. He set about it with vigour, radically changing the organisation and its style. Essentially he decided to adopt the Goldman Sachs model[3], which by that time had become standard across the industry, and introduced industry teams and changed the compensation from being fairly equal and based on the overall performance of Corporate Finance to being based on the separate business units and individual performance. He was a great differentiator saying it was the only way to get the best – Bischoff spent a lot of his time on this issue. Bonuses jumped dramatically having an adverse effect on the cost base.

Building credibility on the Continent

To remain a viable force in Europe in face of the strengthening competition, Schroders' business on the Continent needed a radical overhaul. Broadbent put Tarantelli in overall charge of the offices on the Continent. He had a remuneration package based on the Italian team's revenue and this had to be unscrambled. Hans Bjerk did not have the knowledge and qualities to succeed in Germany. Arnaud Limal was too junior to be effective in France but Javier Salaverri was making progress in Spain. Broadbent placed a great deal of importance on building up a credible business on the Continent, bringing the heads of each country on to his management team. He had a very good relationship with Tarantelli, despite being very different in style. They respected each other and developed a good partnership. Tarantelli was impressed with Broadbent's decisiveness and his feel for the business. 'He took many decisions, 80% of them being right, which gave great momentum to the business. He had a good nose for people and we never had a disagreement over the choice of people.' Together they upgraded the capabilities of the offices in France and Germany by appointing Marc Vincent and Frank Muller, as country heads.

Both were in their early 30s and were not in charge of their offices for CSFB and Morgan Stanley in Paris and Frankfurt and so we placed a bet on them by giving them the top spot in their markets. Vincent was very French, extremely hard working and committed. As was Muller, who, although very German, had been brought up in the US and had a more international flavour

Both were more North European than Salaverri in Madrid. Tarantelli got them to concentrate on very large transactions in their countries for major companies so as to be noticed in their markets. The merger of Credit Swiss with Winterthur Life in 1997 was a major breakthrough for Vincent showing Schroders had become an important factor in Europe as well as in the UK. The cream on the cake was being appointed to advise Credit Lyonnais on its 4 billion euro privatisation.

The appointment by the German Government to advise on the relationship between Deutsche Post and Postbank was a great coup for Muller and his team as it was secured in the face of fierce international competition – Mallinckrodt's stature in senior German circles and being present at the early meetings made a critical difference. (The 22 billion euro third tranche of Deutsche Telecom privatisation IPO in 1999 showed Schroders had become a serious force in Germany.) Tarantelli and Broadbent built a strong presence in France, Germany and Spain to add to that of Italy, which continued to play a leading role in the many major M&A transactions and equity issues in the financial services sector over the next three years. The acquisition of Carnegie España in 1996 created a fully integrated investment banking capability in Spain. 1997 saw IPOs in Spain and Italy and a placing of equity for Pechiney in France. Revenues in continental Europe grew on average by 50% each year. This was one of Broadbent's great legacies to the firm. Impressively and unusually, he used to spend a day a week in each of the offices on the Continent running the business from there.

Running alongside the improved fortunes of the European corporate finance business, Securites was building up its position. Sack said,

The European business improved with the acquisition of Carnegie España, which had a higher rating internationally than the Italian team. It gave us a major presence in research and institutional broking. The product was being built up and SIM was very helpful being honest about what was good and not – we had the feeling that the whole bank was behind us. A lot of institutions were prepared to give us a hearing, as we were different and not competing with them. Our success was due to the quality of our people. The research was focused on identifying good companies for the clients to buy, rather than the normal maintenance done by the other larger brokers – our recommendations also tended to be better than others. The market was changing with the increasing strength of the Americans who were more performance orientated. Philip was a fantastic guiding light and inspirational, making you check yourself or he would have to set up checks himself. We had to have self-discipline and agreed actions with appropriate follow up. There was also regular dialogue with Tarantelli and Broadbent.

The French team acquired from Merrill Lynch in Paris was not seen to be of the same standing as the Italian and Spanish teams – 'they were seen as a build'. They looked at the German market but decided against it as they had teams in London who could deal with the German institutions. They wanted to build a Europe-to-Europe business with distribution across Europe. Good progress was being made in developing a well-integrated pan-European business. In 1996 the European securities division more than doubled revenues and market share achieving very good progress in the Excel ratings and repeated this in the following two years. At the same time Securities overall became profitable, before the payment of bonuses.

Project Finance

With the new organisation Project Finance became part of Investment Banking although still separately managed. This made sense as the business was moving closer to Corporate Finance with its industry specialisations and international corporate finance work. It did well from 1995 to 1997 with a multitude of financings being completed literally all over the world in Hong Kong, Indonesia, Malaysia, Bangladesh and Australia in Asia; Spain, Portugal, Hungary, Poland, Ukraine and UK in Europe; Argentina, Bolivia and Colombia in South America; and Qatar in the Middle East. It was a truly global business. Around 90 projects and privatisations were being advised with a value of $75 billion. Early in 1997 Dewe Mathews retired after 28 years with Schroders. The annual profits, during his 15-year tenure as head of Project Finance, had recovered from a loss of £240,000 in 1983, but remained below £1 million until 1989 and then jumped to £6 million in 1992 and rose steadily to £15 million in 1996. (A profit of £12 million was made in 1997 after which it fell as a result of the Asian debt crisis.) Virtually all the revenue came from advisory fees, which did not require any of the bank's capital. The worldwide professional staff only increased from 28 to 40 from 1990 to 1996. All this should of course be put into perspective as it only made a small contribution to Schroders' overall profits before tax, which were just short of £250 million.

In reviewing what had been achieved, Wadia was typically euphoric saying,

Bernard converted a dying export credit business into a world-class project finance and international corporate finance business. Being a great opportunist, he was able to move in quickly using his good connections and having the confidence to go in at the top of any company and government department. He formed an umbrella between Project Finance and the board's expectations. Although he started very hands on he changed his style later on to play more of a chairman's role. He took a huge calculated gamble in a market dominated by Morgan Grenfell and the large US banks and we finished up as an undisputed world leader (outside of the United States where there was little project finance business). He could not have done better. He managed to build a first class team without brutally firing anyone.

INVESTMENT BANKERS AT LAST – BUT WHERE?

James Kelly, the strategy consultant from MAC, who had watched developments from outside, observed,

Bernard was tenacious, tremendously optimistic like Bischoff, confident in the business and his people, not deterred by formidable competition, and determined to succeed regardless of the difficulties. Despite losing money in the early years he was not willing to give in and given the opportunity he used it and developed a world-class business and was a leader in the market. It was typical of Bischoff's willingness to support people he had faith in.

An indication of his style comes from the views of a long standing client and two colleagues from Corporate Finance. Ian Strachan, a client from Exxon, observed,

Bernard's strongest weapon was the threat of his latent anger being realised – he could be suitably histrionic when the occasion demanded it. He gave the impression of not listening often completing the point and immediately ridiculing it. He had a high level of impatience. These were all very effective negotiating tools

Adam Broadbent said, 'he fought his corner to a point where he frustrated his colleagues and did not make it his business to understand other Schroder business.' Grimstone was more direct saying,

Bernard was the most difficult person to deal with on a fee split negotiation – everyone was scared of him not knowing with his SAS background whether his anger was an act or real. Despite that, or because of it, he built a world class business based on intelligence rather than capital.

Dewe Mathews was consistently criticised for his dominant management style – not suffering from self-doubt he disagreed believing in strong leadership. The results, and the fact that nobody left spoke for themselves.

Personally I felt our success was due to us building a self supporting, totally committed, focused and loyal team of exceptionally able people who always maintained the highest standards – never accepting second best – in their work for our clients. There was never any question of the competitors being as good as we were and also there was no greed. It made all the hard work really worthwhile and immensely fulfilling. At the back of my mind I knew that Win Bischoff would always back us if I had to resort to him, which I never did save for the Lethbridge episode. This gave us a lot of confidence.

In order not to lose key people Samuel agreed to Dewe Mathews' recommendation to form two teams headed by John Burnham and Michael Sutcliffe covering project finance and energy respectively, both reporting to Samuel who would chair a management committee comprising themselves, Wadia and Broadbent, the European head of Corporate Finance. In view of the dying nature of the contractor finance business Philip Robinson decided to retire, aged 55. Wadia agreed to stay for two years to ensure a smooth transition with the clients. Wadia, who always had to stop himself from voicing his thoughts about the lesser art of contractor finance had a high regard for Robinson, 'Philip was the epitome of a traditional English merchant banker with all the social graces, charming and fun – very much the English gentleman, not often seen today. He anchored the contractor finance business which was highly cyclical and on the way out.' Dewe Mathews said, 'We would never had made it without Philip. He was utterly dependable, thorough and painstaking, never making an error having checked and rechecked to make sure everything was correct. He was also very loyal and a good friend despite having been put under much undue pressure by me.'

With Broadbent in charge of Corporate Finance there was a big cultural change. Corporate Finance was losing market share to the Americans and he totally reorganised the business into industry and geographic teams. He saw the merits of the project finance business and admired its international industry skills and sought to absorb Project Finance within Corporate Finance. Being so dominant and with nobody able to stand up to him, Broadbent got rid of the committee chaired by Samuel, and after speaking to all the directors at a planning session, removed the heads of Energy and Project Finance, firing Sutcliffe and transferring Burnham to a senior coverage role, and replacing them with Gomm and Houston, the most respected of the young directors both of whom had had successful periods running the offices in Asia. The old contractor finance business disappeared Robinson having retired. Sasha Chamberlain, after having done an outstanding job for fifteen years, was retired early without any finesse. The strong pipeline of business brought with it continuing revenues and profits, albeit no longer rising, from new power stations for BP and Intergen in the UK and an acquisition for RWE in Hungary, private hospitals under the government's PFI and electricity privatisations in South America and Eastern Europe. It looked too good to be true until being hit by the Asian debt crisis in 1998 that resulted in many projects at an advanced stage of development in the region being suspended and an adverse impact on profits in later years. It had been a very good run. Within Investment Banking, the qualities of the project financiers, who had become international corporate financiers, were more than appreciated and they all thrived. The style was not what they had been used to but their careers were secured.

Differences of opinion on the way ahead

Wyatt had known Broadbent for some years and Broadbent was very supportive of the efforts of Securities and so Wyatt and his team were brought into the Corporate Finance fold from the outset and encouraged to be involved in any of the distribution opportunities with clients. At the same time Wyatt added Capital Markets to his portfolio.

INVESTMENT BANKERS AT LAST -BUT WHERE?

And so for the next 18 months it was like a honeymoon. Alas, brewing up below was a major difference of opinion between Broadbent and Augar over the future direction of the investment banking business, which led to the investment bank having to be sold.[4] Broadbent believed in the US investment banking model in which securities and research were subservient to Corporate Finance, whereas Augar saw a more equal relationship. Broadbent with the support of Tarantelli wanted to expand very fast and were encouraged by the market to believe they could succeed. Augar on the other hand was for a more measured and cautious approach with a focus on selected products and markets. It started as a difference of views but this did not last long as the tension built up. Augar and Broadbent were both intellectuals but Broadbent was a bully and Augar would not tolerate being bullied. Instead of there being a reconciliation and an agreed course of action Augar effectively retired from the fight leaving Broadbent to pursue a flawed strategy that inevitably led to failure. Wyatt felt Augar was the best business problem analyst he had ever met but he was unwilling to commit to any organisation totally and so was not prepared to fight. Unfortunately the two people who should have resolved the issue, Samuel and Bischoff, both disliked dealing with confrontational issues and allowed or were brow beaten by Broadbent into letting him pursue his path unchallenged.

Augar never thought Broadbent understood the securities business and Broadbent never thought Augar thought big enough. They may well have both been right. Augar was a cleverer analyst of the situation and Broadbent more of a visionary. Augar and Wyatt wanted to see an evolutionary strategy of gradually building the securities business and waiting for a bear market to expand when the US investment banks would come under pressure allowing Schroders to plunder the other firms. Broadbent on the other hand was hell-bent on taking the US 'bulge bracket' firms head on by a big expansion buying in more and more top-rate talent.

By the beginning of 1997, Broadbent found Augar in his way and arranged for him to become chairman of Schroder Securities so he could put Tarantelli in charge of European securities, despite the fact he had no knowledge of the business. Sack found Tarantelli

chaotic and difficult to deal with – he had no idea how to manage his time. He had vision but it was Italy-centric. He did not have the same level of integrity as Augar. He allowed the Italians to go behind my back. With his man-management being so weak, fires broke out everywhere and Tarantelli found Machiavellian solutions. He was like Teflon – nothing sticks – and always pointed the finger at someone else. Being Broadbent's man, they needed each other.

Wyatt found Tarantelli to be a man with enormous push but with a flawed judgement, his business model having far too rosy a view of the future – 'he was an incurable romantic'. However, despite these reservations, the business went from strength-to-strength. It was not easy for Tarantelli being now in charge of a team recruited and loyal to Augar. He had to find a compromise between Broadbent and Augar. Augar was an advocate of a niche strategy; Broadbent was keener on going for the top. Tarantelli felt Schroders should always go for blue chips wherever they went and had failed where they had gone for the lesser option. He was pleased with the Carnegie España acquisition as it was one of the best in Spain and was focused on high quality. He negotiated the deal but not being good at the detail, he cut corners, which some said led to problems later on. Javier Salaverri had a reputation for being all image rather than ability and often appeared in the social pages of Olga magazine. He was not liked. The substantial losses incurred on the large stake Schroders was left with in the unsuccessful IPO for Obrascon, the Spanish construction company, did not help.

On the other side of the world in Asia, Securities was going from bad to worse with the debt crisis and the collapse of the markets leading to most of the directors and staff being made redundant and raising in Mallinckrodt's mind further doubts about the viability of the investment banking business and the need to invest more and more into the securities business (see Chapter 24).

Being in a bull market in Europe a lot of money was made from 1997 to 1999 with Securities revenues tripling and net profits after bonuses being made in 1998 and 1999. In 1998, much to the surprise of the competitors, Schroders was rated by the Excel Survey as number one for quality of research, sales and execution, an extraordinary success after only three years in operation. Tarantelli credited it to the remarkable team of Sack, Crawshaw and Glen Poulter: Sack for her common sense, the fact that she was not over aggressive and her attention to quality; Crawshaw for his intelligence, commitment, loyalty and integrity despite being a bit naïve; and to Poulter, the head of trading, who was one of the best in the market. All had been hired by Augar and aimed at being the best, never compromising on quality. They would never accept being average despite having no capital to play with.

There was some criticism of Tarantelli within the bank regarding the payment of excessively high salaries and bonuses to the securities people that had led to continuing losses. Sack said, 'we were paid the market rate and the business had agreed targets. The fact that the bonuses exceeded profits was not unusual. It was there to support Corporate Finance in capturing primary business rather than making profits. Securities was a low margin business making 10% margins whereas Corporate Finance made 30%.'[5] This was the essence of the problem. Corporate Finance had to cover the remuneration gap in Securities as well as meeting the demands of the corporate financiers and the shareholders. It could not satisfy them all. Sack had only intended to stay for three years but had stayed for four. She was with a good team, all of whom got on well. There was a great will to succeed. It was a wonderful experience and she learnt a lot about her own strengths and weaknesses. Unusually it was very apolitical until Tarantelli, but even so compared with others it was not at all political.

In the UK there continued to be plenty of corporate business, including advising on the demerger of British Gas and the sale of East Midlands and London Electricity. In the insurance sector, in which Schroders had always been very active, General Accident was advised on its merger with Commercial Union. Schroders remained high in the UK league tables for M&A and increasingly for equity issues.

In 1998, at a planning session at Leeds Castle, it was agreed that Schroders had to have a decent presence in New York and this was a matter of urgency. For Broadbent and Tarantelli to succeed in their strategy, the US business had to be sorted out and so Broadbent incorporated New York within his portfolio. What happened is covered in the next chapter.

NOTES:

1. Kleinwort Benson, having gone down the integrated route, encountered problems and lost a lot of money, including a much-publicised £34 million loss in 1990 through a misjudged £139 million block trade in Premier Consolidated Oilfields shares (David Kynaston, *The City of London Vol. IV, A Club No More*).

2. The 'bulge bracket' firms were a handful of US investment banks that were the principal underwriters of the largest issues – their capital raising capability required strong capitalisation.

3. Win Bischoff, like many others in Corporate Finance, had a high regard for Goldman Sachs and asked Peter Sachs and John Thornton some years before whether Schroders could visit them in New York to see how they did their business as he would like to model Schroders on Goldman Sachs. Adam Broadbent visited New York as part of the 1984 strategic review to report on the ways in which the leading investment banks were managed and spent much time with Goldman Sachs. Goldman Sachs was very open in answering his questions. Thornton observed later, 'Schroders had some smart and capable people and they built their own version. The quality of their work improved over the years, Schroders being the best example of those who pulled their socks up. Others, who did not, failed.'

4. Richard Broadbent and Philip Augar declined to be interviewed, regarding the end of their period at Schroders with a certain amount of bitterness.

5. Interestingly, in the early 1990s the profit margin for Corporate Finance was nearer 50%.

CHAPTER 23

WHAT ABOUT NEW YORK?

1995 – 1999

After eight years in which virtually no progress had been made in integrating the two companies, Schroders took full control of Wertheim, with Harmon remaining chairman and Kotler becoming the chief executive. Sedgwick, who had been against Schroders acquiring full control of Wertheim, was appointed deputy chairman agreeing to spend half his time in New York. Effectively the same people remained in charge despite the change in ownership. In 1996 Harmon was appointed chairman of the Export-Import Bank of the United States by President Clinton and moved to Washington having been appropriately compensated. Sedgwick became chairman. After he had been in New York for some months and had got to know Kotler and the Wertheim business he fundamentally changed his view of Kotler and in his direct way he fully defended Kotler's position even to the point of siding with Wertheim against London. His view was that Schroders did not understand the business, which was very well managed and had not incurred huge losses and that it should be left alone in the capable hands of Kotler. It was a totally inappropriate vehicle to turn into a 'bulge bracket' firm.

Barry Tarasoff, the head of research, observed that,

> although it was agreed by all that Schroders could not survive as an investment bank in Europe alone and had to be in New York as well, nothing happened at Wertheim following the outright purchase. It was too late to build from nothing following twenty years' consolidation of the investment banking industry. Schroders did not have the critical mass to succeed and could not attract and retain the highly talented people needed to build a viable business. Wertheim was a banker to mid-cap and small companies and if exceptionally it had a great analyst it might get a co-manager spot on a big issue. The big companies were dominated by Goldman Sachs and Morgan Stanley. This was the arena in which Schroders operated in Europe but it did not have the reputation and brand in New York to build and hire.

On the corporate finance side increasing efforts were made to build an integrated business by hiring Mack Rossoff, who had formerly been with Morgan Stanley, to head up Corporate Finance. His brief was to improve the corporate finance business and bring it closer to the UK. The perennial problem was that Wertheim had a very good and successful business with the small cap companies bringing in revenues of $120 million a year and was staffed accordingly. However, they were not suitable for carrying out cross-border big-ticket transactions. Rossoff, essentially a relationship banker not of the premier league, quickly alienated himself with all his colleagues, Tarasoff not being willing to be in the same room. Rossoff's attitude was that most if not all the corporate financiers at Wertheim were no good and so they left but could not be replaced. Following much internal argument with everyone threatening to leave, Rossoff resigned.

In May 1997 Grimstone was seduced by what may have been the largest remuneration package given to anyone in the Group to take on the job. Whereas his remuneration was clear for the next two years, his reporting lines were blurred. Stupidly he accepted as it proved to be an impossible job without receiving any additional assistance from London. He found a poisoned atmosphere, which was dysfunctional and torn apart by arguments, with the 80 staff in the department being reduced daily by departures. He braced himself and gave a big morale raising speech to the remaining staff. With the team falling apart, he needed to stabilise the position and then move forward. He rapidly came to the conclusion that it would be foolhardy to try and change the existing business but rather get it to hum and to build alongside it a new team to do the cross-border work as had been accomplished in Asia. Broadbent did not like his proposals and on the way by bus to a rugby match at Twickenham – during time off a group strategy meeting – he persuaded Sedgwick that trans-Atlantic corporate finance should come under a single management. Grimstone was prevented from carrying out his plan.

Within twelve weeks of Grimstone's appointment to New York, it was announced in January 1998 that Schroders had introduced a global management structure for its investment banking business. 'We're going more the American way,' said Bischoff. The changes, driven by the need to provide a global service to corporate clients, should end any 'regional profit-sharing phobia', he said. Budgets and profit and loss accounts would now be done globally by function and only then be cross-checked by region. Broadbent was appointed group managing director – Corporate Finance reporting to Kotler and Samuel, both joint group managing directors – Investment Banking. Grimstone, the bank's 'chief rain-maker', was appointed vice-chairman of Schroders' worldwide investment banking activities also reporting to Kotler and Samuel (*Financial Times*, 16 January 1998). Grimstone was effectively below Broadbent, with whom he had had a stormy and competitive relationship for some years. With Broadbent wishing to control everything, as was his custom, there were endless fights, which led to the question of who was in charge. Broadbent having charge of the corporate finance business in Europe, the only business that mattered, Grimstone lost out. Unfortunately titles did not matter much at Schroders – it was having control of resources and running a profitable business that mattered. Grimstone was soon marginalized. 'It was like being a prostitute in an Amsterdam window wearing one's best clothes in the hope that someone would visit one.' After six months of isolation and frustration he decided to quit, the money being no compensation. It was a sad day for Grimstone who left many colleagues that he liked and respected. Broadbent had by then seen off Grimstone and Augar and there appeared to be nobody in his way. He decided to move with his family to New York to manage global corporate finance from there.[1]

In Kotler's view the original deal was flawed, 50/50 not being a permanent solution. The integration therefore only started in 1994 but, 'there were cultural and personal differences and there was not a smooth transition' he tactfully said. His relationships with Bischoff, Sedgwick, Solandt and Adam Broadbent were very good – 'they were very smart and professional and could not have been nicer.' He and the others at Wertheim had a high regard for Grimstone, whom they found thoughtful and the only person from Schroders who spoke logically and accurately about the strategic things that might work. 'He came to the conclusion that there was nothing that could be done to improve the position. Regrettably he did not get on with Richard Broadbent.' Grimstone felt Kotler was a very good manager of an integrated investment bank – the only person who understood the interplay between corporate finance, capital markets and securities. Kotler refused to go into the high tech sector and was heavily criticised for staying with the old economy. He said

all those who went into the new economy subsequently failed – Robertson Stephens, which had been acquired by Bank of America for $540 million, was subsequently liquidated at a loss of $800 million. DLJ also failed.[2] In fact none of the middle sized firms survived as they could not compete with the giants, Alex Brown, Montgomery Securities and Oppenheimer being examples. Why should Schroders be any different? It was in the middle, being too small and too big.

With Broadbent's dominant views about the way forward for Investment Banking he had no alternative to going to New York despite having no experience of doing business in New York or managing Americans. Having reviewed the market in New York, he prepared an ambitious and high risk plan involving a proposal either to buy in people and teams or to acquire a corporate finance group in New York for $250 million and to sustain annual losses of $10-$20 million over the next few years. He made a full-scale presentation to the board and the plan that had received the blessing of Kotler and Sedgwick and their agreement to him carrying it out was accepted despite there being very little discussion. Samuel and Broadbent misinterpreted this as a lack of interest. In fact Bischoff had presented the plan to the non-executive directors before the board to avoid a disagreement and following an extensive debate they were happy to endorse the plan. There was, however, no clarity regarding Broadbent's position vis-à-vis Kotler. Broadbent expected to become chief executive of Schroders Inc but when he arrived in New York, Sedgwick openly backed Kotler against Broadbent who boiled over in fury. Kotler being a former partner of Wertheim and having run Wertheim autocratically for over ten years was not going to bossed about by this young Turk from London. Having befriended Sedgwick he knew he was on safe ground. Despite Kotler having made no changes since Schroders acquired full control five years previously, Sedgwick felt confident that Kotler could achieve the necessary changes better than Broadbent. Broadbent went on a family skiing holiday totally committed to the plan but must have had some misgivings about the difficulty of implementing it in view of Kotler's power base. He did not help himself by still having reporting directly to him all the heads of industry groups and countries in Europe. On his return in March, he insisted that unless he was given the power to shake up Wertheim, he would not be able to achieve his aim of building an effective and competitive trans-Atlantic corporate finance business. This was regarded as too high a risk due to Broadbent's dominant management style and the danger of a total collapse of Wertheim and its 1500 people. There was no meeting of minds and so he wrote an intemperate letter to Bischoff including his adverse views of Sedgwick, which was probably not intended as a resignation. Despite his admiration of Broadbent's achievements, Bischoff had no alternative to calling Broadbent back to London to settle his disengagement, particularly with Sedgwick taking a strong line not to allow Broadbent to withdraw his apparent resignation. Samuel was put in charge of cleaning up the mess. The reaction of the corporate finance directors in London to Broadbent's resignation was like an eruption – they were particularly critical that the top management had backed the lightweight people in New York against Broadbent, whom most of them admired if not wholly liked. A meeting was called by Samuel, Augar, Sykes and Hopkinson at which Bischoff was told by that Kotler had to go or the place would implode. Kotler was asked to go as he was resistant to change, a severance pay off of $8 million being agreed.

Schroders in the space of a few weeks had lost two of its strongest and most unmanageable managers and at a time when the business was looking very fragile. Bischoff and Samuel had some difficulties persuading some of the directors and senior staff in London to stay. On Broadbent's move to New York, Tarantelli had become head of European Investment Banking, Wyatt head of Securities and McNeil and Karen Cook co-heads of UK Corporate Finance.[3] Not long after Broadbent's demise, Cook, having lost all faith in Schroders' strategy generally and its ability to sort out New York, decided to leave for Goldman Sachs. This was a real body blow as with her high reputation she was issuing a verdict of no confidence in Schroders and also she looked after a number of important clients who could have followed her – fortunately none of the clients did but she was shortly followed by four young directors in the industry groups created by Broadbent.

The securities people did not care about the US. They wanted to build on the Augar/Wyatt model – small, profitable, focused and selective. They could easily set up in New York and sell UK and European securities there. Corporate Finance wanted to continue with Broadbent's strategy of competing with Goldman Sachs and Morgan Stanley. This dichotomy was the reason for the two groups then falling apart. To rescue the position, Augar had been offered the role of group managing director of Investment Banking before Broadbent went to New York, but he had declined. Seeing the way things were going some of the analysts started to leave. At a dinner attended by Samuel, Challen,

Tarantelli, Wyatt, McNeill and the heads of the French and German teams, the 'white flag was hoisted' saying the strategy had failed and there was no alternative but to sell the bank. Augar and Wyatt's view remained that Schroders could have gone on as a medium sized partnership. But without the family releasing more shares this was not on offer. Besides the corporate finance directors had no appetite for this. The remuneration packages and the career prospects offered by the Americans looked far more attractive and safe – they preferred to be highly paid employees rather than risk takers.

The departure of Broadbent was the turning point. If he had stayed there were some who felt the investment banking business could have survived but without him it was dead. It was a huge blow to morale and created insecurity. Despite that, the business in London was having its best year – 1999 being a record for Corporate Finance in the UK. Tarantelli was perhaps most affected. He was shocked, upset and emotionally against a sale. He thought mistakenly that Schroders could have carried on although he accepted in hindsight he was wrong.

Broadbent had a powerful and dominant personality and the views of him by his colleagues were therefore strong and mixed. Swannell, head of UK Corporate Finance, and Tarantelli, head of Securities, both of whom worked directly for him, were great admirers of his achievements and deeply upset by his departure, blaming Schroders for mismanagement. Swannell, known for his Panglossian enthusiasms, said,

> he was without doubt the most talented manager ever seen in an investment bank. He was very clear and decisive and did a huge amount to develop the business on the Continent and the industry groups and Securities. We never had a crossed word and he never interfered in the UK business. It was a big mistake to allow him to get lonely in New York. He was irrationally impatient but Schroders let him down as he was almost certainly right. He was very sad to leave.

Tarantelli, who had a particularly good working relationship with Broadbent, said,

> he was a very intense person, very tough, rough at the edges and not good with people but he did not need to kill everyone to win. He had no need to fight so acrimoniously and bitterly. Everything was too black and white. He had no need to break up with Augar. Everyone had to be a friend or a foe.

The views of his more senior colleagues such as Bischoff, Adam Broadbent, MacAndrew, Samuel and especially Sedgwick were less favourable. They all recognised his good brain, his tremendous capacity for work – always doing everything well and to high standards by being meticulous rather than intuitive, his great ability as a manager – always showing clear and committed leadership, and his good judgement in selecting and hiring people. He achieved a phenomenal amount in restructuring and re-orientating the business in Europe and had a strong following within Corporate Finance. On the other hand, the results came through bullying rather than persuasion and he had to have total control of everything, nobody ever being good enough – he never said we, always I. His views were uncompromising with little to no room left for dissuasion and anyone who crossed him was dead. Being so driven, his impatience, intolerance and lack of humour did not make him a comfortable colleague. Had he had more finesse he might have achieved the impossible. He was unusual for Schroders in being able to combine being an able manager and a good corporate financier. Wyatt, a long-standing friend, said, 'he was suffering from exhaustion and became so unreasonable that even his friends could not deal with him.' He made demands on himself that he could not meet. He insisted on keeping direct control of the European activities while still in New York and effectively drove himself to a standstill. He never thought anyone was as good as himself. Whatever is said about him however what he managed to achieve in Europe was remarkable and gave Schroders a huge asset.[4]

Kotler said he would not have changed anything. He liked everyone and had no negative words. He felt he had done his best and always looked out for the owners' interests – the partners and then Schroders. Kotler maintained that his return on equity was consistently and significantly higher that Schroders' non asset management business.[5] Of Sedgwick he said, 'I loved Peter. He was the best manager I ever worked with during my career, smart, focused, direct and honest – the best.'

From his office overlooking Central Park surrounded by dozens of photographs of himself with President Clinton and his administration, Harmon said,

In the end Schroders' capacity to assume risk was much less than was needed. The securities business is volatile and involves huge overheads. It requires the ability to risk capital on the trading markets. With the business growing and becoming increasingly more capital intensive, the bigger you are the more able you are to tolerate the volatility. Schroders was too small and had the wrong temperament being too risk averse. I found Mallinckrodt uneasy, very formal and austere. Being risk averse he found it very painful when there were bad months. You cannot be in the securities business without being a risk taker. He was tortured into buying a securities firm which forced him into selling his bank.

One of the big questions was why Bischoff, as the chief executive, did not do more to resolve the problems in New York. Apart from them being the responsibility of Mallinckrodt, he felt his time was best spent in Europe, which represented 80% of Schroders' profits, but in any case he did not think he could have done anything. He felt that,

Wertheim had worked hard to achieve a corporate finance activity on London lines with a strict delineation of who does what. The client base however was not appropriate. All the power was still with Kotler not those who went out to change things such as Grimstone and Sedgwick. Kotler was very jealous of his power and was a very good administrator but not a rainmaker. Rossoff who was hired to transform the corporate finance business was also a good organiser but again not a rainmaker. In the meanwhile the distance between Wertheim and the competitors was widening. When Schroders bought into Wertheim in 1986 it was making pre-tax profits of $50 million, whereas Morgan Stanley was making $400 million. By 1995, Wertheim was still stuck at $50 million whereas Morgan Stanley was making $4 billion. It had remained a small boutique.

Charles Sinclair ruefully observed, 'Wertheim sapped the energy of senior management including Bischoff and Sedgwick and the opportunity costs were never quantified.'

Samuel, the strategist, amazingly had no faith in Broadbent's plan and found it unworkable. (One has to ask why he had allowed it to go ahead.) There was a need for a radical solution but the issues were never debated. The family did not wish to sell the investment bank. It was clear, however, that a platform in New York was needed as without that the key people would leave and the right people could not be attracted. Time was not on his side.

NOTES:

1. The article headlined 'Schroders — Fear and Loathing on Cheapside' by Nick Kochan in the *Euromoney* magazine in January 2000 is the source of some of the information on Richard Broadbent's period in New York due to it being confirmed by those involved.

2. DLJ had been very sucessful and was bought by CSFB for about $10 billion and only failed under CSFB management (see Chapter 8).

3. Karen Cook was the mother of six children and married to Patrick Drayton, then director general of the Take-over Panel.

4. Richard Broadbent returned to the civil service as chairman of HM Customs and Excise and was subsequently knighted.

5. As stated earlier without access to financial information within Schroders the author was not able to make a judgement on the conflicting claims regarding Wertheim's profitability.

CHAPTER 24

THE ASIAN DEBT CRISIS BITES

1995 – 1999

The biggest issue facing the chief executives of the Asian companies in 1995 was the hotly disputed decision in London to advance to a wholly functional management, involving the loss of power of the country heads over the activities under them. This move was in line with industry market practices led by the US investment banks and so was not surprising. In fact many of the Schroders' activities had become centrally controlled. Asset management was well integrated with London and under the direction of the highly respected Jeremy Hill with his seasoned Asian experience. Project Finance had always been directed and controlled by London. Securities had similarly been the responsibility of London. Financial Markets, that is Treasury and Banking, had had its limits controlled from London and the treasury activities were well integrated although lending less so – Hopkinson had been in charge of the Asian treasury activities for some time albeit from his base in Sydney. Corporate Finance and Capital Markets were the exceptions and as they were the front window and the main link with local clients a transfer of control was unpopular at all levels. Grimstone was sent over to Hong Kong as regional head of Corporate Finance for Asia Pacific to achieve the change. Hopkinson moved to Hong Kong at the same time.

Further south in Singapore the transition from a geographic to a functional organisation was also causing difficulties, Tomlin being reluctant to give up his power over the businesses in his region. In 1991 he had agreed that his asset management activities would come under SIM in London and had thereby placed orders for SIM and collected S$2 million rebate commissions each year and this had worked very well. The securities business had been largely functionally controlled by Schroder Securities Asia in London from the beginning. Project Finance had always been a global business with all its regional offices reporting directly to London. He was now faced with having to hand over his corporate finance activities under Lawrence Wong to Grimstone and even worse his financial market activities to Hopkinson, both of whom were based in Hong Kong.

The position in Australia has been covered already in Chapter 18.

Investment Banking

The feeling in the local markets was that the people like Grimstone did not know the clients or the qualities of the corporate financiers and simply flew in to bag the fees. However he rapidly discovered that the Chinese do not like paying advisory fees and to succeed one needed to raise equity capital for them, regrettably not Schroders' strong suit. Also Schroders in Asia lacked any noticeable industry knowledge. Fee-sharing disputes arose and further soured relations. The HSBC acquisition of Midland Bank three years earlier had yielded negligible fees for Schroders Asia, despite the long-standing relationship and this was a continuing sore – maybe they did not know what a small fee had been paid. Clement Kwok, head of Corporate Finance in Hong Kong, left to become the finance director of MRTC and he was shortly followed by Lincoln Leong. The heavyweights from London had to justify their large remuneration packages, which dwarfed those of the other expatriates in Asia, by securing big transactions in direct competition with the US investment banks which had in the meanwhile been offering vast salaries to attract the best local talent.[1] Unfortunately Schroders was not equipped to compete as its securities business lacked the distribution capability. The big business was listings for the large Chinese corporations and Schroders also lacked the name awareness and capital of Morgan Stanley, JP Morgan, Lehman and Goldman Sachs, which swept the board picking up all the IPOs despite having very little knowledge of the market. Clearly *guanxi* was not that important. As a Chinese vice-minister had pointed out to Dewe Mathews, a decade earlier, when he was advising him on a large petrochemical project in Shandong province, 'it is strange how old friends are not as competitive as new friends.'

Grimstone found the business in a poor state with much political in-fighting and no management. His task was to develop a unified business across the region, like Jardine Fleming, when hitherto each of the centres had acted independently. He had to deal with the local barons who had not previously been managed. Corporate Finance was the heart of the business but was losing £12 million a year – nobody had looked at the accounts properly as it was cross-subsidised by the profits of Asset Management. Next year he took over as regional head of Investment Banking from Peter Mason, who had not been willing to move to the region from Sydney, and so took on the securities businesses. This proved to be more difficult as each of the securities businesses reported back to London resulting in an over complicated matrix management. Despite all the difficulties, some successes were achieved. An Asia Pacific Regional Advisory Group was set up in Singapore under Ian Carnegie-Brown to provide a pan-Asian service to large multinationals wishing to invest in Asia, giving advice on the best country and help in carrying out the transaction. This led to Schroders acting for companies it had not dealt with before, that could then be acted for in London.

Schroders returned to the top of the M&A league tables in the region in 1997 and the losses were turned into modest profits having advised on substantial reorganisations for China Light and Hutchison Whampoa. This involved Grimstone in 130 flights of 250,000 miles a year and the accumulation of 2 million personal air miles. He was enjoying himself and beginning to feel he was making progress when like a bolt out of the blue he received the call from Samuel in 1997 asking him to go to New York. He was succeeded as regional head of Corporate Finance by Philip Mallinckrodt who was not as experienced as Grimstone. Unlike Grimstone, he was not brazen enough, after meeting Deng Xiaoping at the Great Hall of the People with a cast of hundreds, to say to potential clients that he was an advisor to Deng. He was shy and less extrovert, not as pushy or confident, and this came through to the staff. Grimstone was with Bischoff and MacAndrew in feeling Schroders should seek to catch up with Jardine Fleming and others who had made a fortune in securities during the bull markets up to 1993 and then to 1997 by building up a strong and integrated securities business. Philip, however, like Samuel and Augar, felt that Schroders could not reasonably wage a war on three fronts in Europe, the USA and Asia and that it was a waste of money to make a late dash for growth. It was a difficult decision accepting the appointment, since his father had not yet recovered from his haemorrhage. Philip arrived in Hong Kong a week after the hand over to the People's Republic of China and within a few months the region was hit by the Asian debt crisis. With the combination of the changed competitive landscape and the debt crisis, Schroders had little competitive advantage over the big US investment banks, who had moved heavily into Hong Kong, and had to curtail its ambitions significantly focusing simply on corporate and project finance. Schroders was no longer seeking to be a dominant player in the market.

Philip's pessimistic views about securities were confirmed as Securities in Asia was going from bad to worse with the debt crisis and the collapse of the markets. In January 1998, Schroders announced that after losing money in Asian broking for two years it was closing down most of its Asian broking business, making 220 of its staff redundant – 70 being based in Hong Kong – predominantly from equity sales, research, settlement and back office staff. The Japan office, which had done well in recent years, was spared cuts (*South China Morning Post*). This raised in his mind further doubts about the viability of the investment banking business with its need to invest more and more into the securities business. Over the next two years the cost base was halved and the corporate finance revenue doubled. Philip returned to London in 1999 when he handed over to Andrew Brandler, the successful regional head of Project Finance.

Project Finance

Fortunately there was other work in the region that was more profitable. Schroders acted for Hong Kong Air Cargo Terminals (HACTL), a consortium comprising Swire, Jardine, Cathay Pacific and the China National Aviation Corporation, in bidding for the concession from the Hong Kong government to handle cargo at the new airport at Chek Lap Kok, involving the construction, operation and financing of the terminal. Gomm and his team arranged a HK$6.6 billion limited recourse financing secured on the anticipated cargo revenue – it was the largest such financing ever arranged in Hong Kong. Earlier, much to the annoyance of Gomm, Boyce had, for relationship reasons, agreed a derisory success fee of US$300,000 for this work. The finance director of HACTL, however, was so pleased with the work that he voluntarily agreed to increase the fee to US$1 million. Importantly it also lead to a further appointment to support the Asia Container Terminals consortium bid — owned by Jardine[2] and Sealand Terminals (a US company) and others — for a franchise to develop, construct and operate a new sea container terminal. The project was complicated by the PRC government objecting to Jardine's lead role in the consortium due to its unpopularity with the Chinese for having recently de-listed from Hong Kong to Singapore. A compromise was agreed with an existing container terminal of Jardine being swapped for the new terminal. The stalwart and energetic Richard Beales, who had worked with Gomm in carrying out this advisory work, successfully completed the HK$5 billion financing after Gomm returned to London. This was only one of many examples of the PRC government interfering in the award by the Hong Kong government of contracts associated with the new airport at Chep Lap Kok. In fact it lead to considerable delays which resulted in the airport not being completed before the British government lowered its flag at the end of June 1997. There were also other projects in South Korea, Taiwan and the Philippines to keep the six to eight man team busy.

Brandler and his team in Singapore were equally busy where they advised on the financing of the world's largest greenfield port — a $820 million container terminal in Malaysia — and arranged a $600 million debt financing for a zinc mine in Australia. However, the Asian debt crisis put a major dent in the work with many investors pulling out of a number of projects in an advanced stage of development throughout the region and so life was tougher and work more sporadic. Although the good backlog of work avoided the need to cut back on the staff, there was likely to be an adverse impact on the profits as Asia generally provided up to a third of Project Finance's profits.

Asset Management

Since Bischoff had left Hong Kong in 1982 and the management of pension funds was initiated, the number of funds under management in Hong Kong had grown from nothing to 300 and the total funds managed to HK$83 billion by 1999. This was 70% of the assets under external management in Hong Kong retirement schemes. Schroders Asia having been the market leader in pension fund management for many years, the Hong Kong government introduced a Mandatory Provident Fund (MPF) like the Singapore Provident Fund, which had been in operation for decades. At the same time Members Choice was introduced resulting in all the small companies having to provide pensions for their employees, who had to choose each month into which fund the contributions should be placed. One of the main reasons for this was that salary inflation had outgrown the investment returns throughout the 1990s and companies wanted to move away from defined benefit pension schemes, in which retirement benefits were effectively underwritten by the employers, towards defined contribution, where the employee received the benefits, but they were not underwritten by the employer. In the three years' run up to its implementation in 1999 new administration systems had to be developed and installed as well as expensive advertising being incurred by the fund managers who were now dealing with a totally different retail market. HSBC with its well known name, despite not being a leader in asset management, swept the board in

2000. Schroders Asia did very badly, much to the disappointment of Richard Haw, who had been seconded to Hong Kong for two years, 22 years previously, and had had such a good record up until then. Asset Management profits had also been significantly impacted by the fall in markets in the region in 1998, which reduced the funds under management and led to a fall off in sales of unit trusts.

Financial Markets

Sykes and Hopkinson, who succeeded Solandt as joint heads of Financial Markets in 1995, had a very good working relationship. They had grown up in parallel on different sides of the world. Hopkinson, a quiet Yorkshire man who had originally worked with Henry Blackie in RAMP, which had had successes in Venezuela and Singapore, was seconded to Schroders Australia where he became one of the leading thinkers under Gatfield in developing the derivatives market. He was arguably the leading player in the derivatives market in Australia and being highly able he turned around significant treasury losses in Australia into its largest profit centre (see Chapter 18). Subsequently he became an Australian citizen. Sykes had built the business in London (see Chapter 9) on the back of much of Hopkinson's work and so there was a great deal of mutual respect. They had lengthy debates on how to work together and agreed that Asia was extremely difficult to manage from London and should be separated from the rest of the world. Hopkinson continued to run Asia from Hong Kong and Sykes ran the rest from London. They talked all the time and all went well until the Asian debt crisis towards the end of 1997.

The Asian debt crisis arose out of excessive borrowing by companies and governments in South East Asia fuelled by the enthusiasm of investors and banks in search of the 'Asian Miracle'. Too much money flowed into the market and excess liquidity had to go somewhere – it went into real estate whose values escalated to ridiculous levels and into manufacturing capacity, which became excessive. Inevitably the bubble burst and Schroders found itself with many bad loans.

Before the debt crisis, Financial Markets in Hong Kong had been making an increasingly important contribution to profits under Hopkinson and Lee, but this was then reversed. Schroders Asia came out of the crisis relatively unscathed only wiping out its profits in one year, 1998, with a provision of HK$71 million. The main problem was a HK$10 million convertible bond with the Palliburg Group which could not be traded off the books. Hopkinson cleared up the other problems that were in the banking sector, a traditional area of strength. There were some bad loans but most of the exposure was in bank CDs that were all right. Also the loan book had been reduced to a relatively small amount, which had been conservatively managed. Lee, who had been punching well above his weight over the years, did well in a difficult period.

In Singapore it was a different matter. 90% of the loans and bonds, particularly in Indonesia, Thailand and South Korea, were in trouble. Tomlin was caught out. He had been managing director of SIMBL for twelve years under the fierce protection of Mallinckrodt and in Hopkinson's view was running an ill-disciplined crew for some time

– always painting a rosy picture of the position. The capital markets team, under the previously highly regarded James Foo, got stuck with many problems as well as those it had entered into voluntarily. (Being a banker by background, Tomlin always showed a greater interest in the debt rather than the equity capital markets.) Hopkinson took charge of debt capital markets which led to the independent-minded James Foo departing. He came to the view that SIMBL was over trading on its small capital and arranged for it to be increased, which led to far larger underwriting positions being taken in advance of the crisis that broke in the middle of 1997. It started with a run on the Thai baht leading to a devaluation of 40%-50%. Indonesia followed with the Rupiah falling from 2500 to the dollar to 17000, accompanied by terrible riots in Jakarta against Chinese business and the fall of the Suharto regime. Devaluations in Malaysia and Singapore followed at around 40% and 20% respectively. All the local corporations had been borrowing in US dollars because the interest rates were lower than in their domestic currencies. There was absolute turmoil in the markets and SIMBL was heavily exposed. Even worse, SIMBL was the agent and managed many loans and bonds in which it had no participation with 96 active syndicates requiring fiduciary duties. The full team became preoccupied by workouts, leaving no time or energy for origination, thus no revenue. In addition much of the debt had been off balance sheet but at the behest of Hopkinson these assets had been brought on to the balance sheet to use up SIMBL's increased capital, thereby increasing SIMBL's direct exposure. Provisions were made for 30% of the portfolio which would have wiped out the whole of SIMBL's capital had not Hopkinson arranged for the liabilities on the loans and bonds to be transferred to London.

The assets had to be renegotiated and sold with provisions and write-downs of £67 million being made in 1997 and 1998 against group exposure to counter parties domiciled in Asia (excluding Japan) of £427 million. Although Mallinckrodt got very exercised about the potential losses they were not that serious in that even if £67 million had been lost, which was assessed to be the worst position, it only represented 4% of the Group's net worth – in the end the losses were less but still of the order of £50 million. There was a recovery in 1999 with £18 million of the provisions written back and the exposure down to £229 million. However, the losses had a negative impact on the performance of Financial Markets in 1997 and 1998 and Solandt's previously high levels of profit were badly dented.

Tomlin was asked to depart on the thirtieth anniversary of his joining the company – a sad end for someone who had served the bank with such loyalty over so many years. With his wife Monica, he had established a leading position in the community, particularly its cultural life, where they were active supporters of the arts, including the Singapore Repertory Theatre and the Symphony Orchestra. They were an attractive couple who gave Schroders great credibility in Singapore over twelve years and, with his outgoing and somewhat laid-back personality, they were always welcoming to their many visitors. As is often the case with investment bankers, he did even better afterwards becoming chairman of UBS Warburg in Singapore, with significantly more professional resources at his disposal.

THE ASIAN DEBT CRISIS BITES

Boyce, seeing his role as now being largely ceremonial in the new functional management structure, had been in conversations with Michael Kadoorie with a view to joining Sir Elly Kadoorie & Sons and agreed to join them in early 1998 but at the request of Bischoff he stayed on until March 1999. During his decade at Schroders Asia, profits had trebled to HK$150 million and shareholder funds had increased from HK$200 million to HK$500 million. He had enjoyed his time with Schroders and did not suffer from coming from outside as SG Warburg and Schroders had a similar culture and values. He had not enjoyed the effects of the Big Bang with people looking after themselves rather than the firm. The style had changed and the increasing greed over bonuses depressed him. Not long afterwards, Bischoff approached the Kadoories to buy out its 25% interest and offered a price that did not satisfy them as they suspected Schroders might be planning to sell the company at a premium and so insisted on a premium to be paid in that eventuality. MacAndrew, who handled the negotiations, agreed to buy out at the higher price. Schroders Asia was a good investment for the Kadoories as well as Schroders itself, in which they had built up an important shareholding, when John Schroder had sold his shares in 1989.

On the other side of the world Schroders was considering the future of its decreasingly profitable investment bank. When the investment banking business was sold to Salomon Smith Barney (SSB) at the end of 1999 the Far East business was integrated within SSB's Asian business but due to a lack of interest by SSB, it lead to the disappearance of the well-regarded Asian business Schroders had painstakingly built up over 30 years.

NOTES:

1. Project Finance lost two of its top Chinese managers Chan Wing Leong and Sucher Yan to Bankers Trust and JP Morgan.

2. Interestingly both these advisory assignments were secured through Jardine who, after they had observed the quality and intensity of the work, were supportive of Project Finance being paid fees on international scales which was unusual in Hong Kong.

CHAPTER 25

WHAT WENT WRONG AT SIM?

1996 - 1999

Sedgwick had identified three candidates suitable to become his successor as head of what became known in the market as Asset Management, all of whom were tried, tested and proven in different parts of the business. Govett had been his loyal deputy for nine years and wanted the job and Sedgwick felt he deserved it. Govett very reasonably felt that he had a greater understanding of the business than any of his other colleagues and did not believe one needed to be an extrovert to run a successful business like SIM. Govett was admired as a great investor being one of the top investors Schroders ever had. He was by far the cleverest director and with Hill had the best brains. He had also played a leading part in the management of the business with heavy involvement in recruiting, marketing, finance and remuneration since becoming a director in 1980. However, for those outside SIM and on the Schroders board, he gave the impression of lacking charisma, being exceptionally shy, and of not being a natural leader or strong on people management, tending to be unusually quiet at meetings outside Investment Management. He was also seen to be commercially academic and too intellectual. Worst of all, he and Mallinckrodt did not see eye-to-eye and the fact that he, like Popham, Sedgwick and several others before him, thought Mallinckrodt had no understanding of the asset management business, and probably showed it, could not have helped.

Salisbury[1] had run the SCMI business in the States very well and was highly regarded by Mallinckrodt. He came across Mallinckrodt when he took over the management of Schroder Naess and Thomas in New York, after Jim Hocking had been finally fired. He and his wife lived in an apartment below the Mallinckrodts when Mallinckrodt was running Schrobanco, and became very friendly with them. Salisbury, by his own admission, was not an investor, unlike any previous head of Investment Management. He was seen to be a good manager and administrator but with little feel for the markets. He was intelligent, hard working and articulate, with presence and came across as international, which he was. In contrast to Govett, he tended to talk a lot and always liked to have the last word. He was clearly ambitious. He was thought to be a safe pair of hands with Bolland as his deputy. Bolland, the third candidate, had been managing director of Schroders Asia and Schroders Australia and had managed the unit trust and pension fund businesses in London. He had acquitted himself well in all areas, save possibly for in Australia.

Most members of the board and the GEC, particularly Mallinckrodt, had some unease about Govett's management style and wanted Salisbury to be Sedgwick's successor –

Sedgwick had earlier arranged a dinner party for Way to meet Salisbury and Bolland and Way had been most impressed by Salisbury who spoke well and with confidence but was a little cautious about his abilities to take decisions. At the same time consideration was being given to Bischoff's succession and Salisbury and Sykes were seen to be the favourites. Salisbury therefore had to be put in charge of something big. Mallinckrodt saw Govett as standing in the way, but Govett at 50 said he would not stay on under Salisbury. Sedgwick, who had a high regard for Govett as an investor and valued his loyalty, knew he was not bluffing and so he was appointed chairman of SIM with Salisbury and Bolland joint-chief executives. It was felt that Bolland's fund management experience would compliment Salisbury's administrative skills. As Sedgwick had the ear of the senior directors of SIM, Bischoff and the board looked to him for his judgement on matters related to SIM. Govett being rather unworldly was surprised at how ambitious Salisbury and Bolland were.

With SIM earning over half of the Group's profits, Govett felt not unreasonably that he should have a seat on the Schroders Plc board. He was reluctantly made group managing director of Asset Management in 1997 and put on the board moving to Cheapside. Salisbury became chairman of SIM with Bolland his deputy. Govett was isolated and resigned the following year. He was replaced by Salisbury as group managing director of Asset Management, but retained his chairmanship of SIM. SIM had lost its best investor – one of the two or three most highly respected in the City – and Salisbury downgraded the role of the fund managers to below that of the financial managers. It proved to be the undoing of SIM. Salisbury ignored Bolland who stepped aside as deputy chairman taking on some of his old clients and had no further involvement in the management. He left as early as he could. Despite the miserable end to his career he had had a remarkably good run. In hindsight a triumvirate with such disparate people was unlikely to succeed and would inevitably come apart.

One of the problems inherited by Salisbury was inadequate systems. The investment management business had been changing very fast with the introduction of a raft of new regulation during 1980s and 1990s and SIM was tremendously underinvested in computer systems. SIM had made no investment of its super profits in IT and support services, which provided valuations for clients and information systems for management and fund managers – up-to-date and reliable information for client valuations and advice had been barely changed since the early 1980s. The inefficiency of the systems resulted in much work having to be done through to midnight. It appeared that all the senior management wanted was to squeeze out more profits with increasingly difficult budgetary targets set by the Group. MacAndrew, however, said that investment in new systems had never been raised as an issue and certainly no requests to spend money on the systems had been rejected. On the contrary Strickland and MacAndrew and the board had warned SIM over a number of years of the need to up-date its technology. Whatever the truth the lack of up-to-date systems became a serious problem in serving clients.

Salisbury had many ideas about new organisational structures which were seen by many of the old guard to be complex and incompatible with the business. They made little sense to the investment managers who felt they could only be destructive. He created a culture where being a business manager was more important and better remunerated than being an investment manager. He insisted on being in charge of everything and despite not being an investor he appointed himself chairman of the UK Pension Fund Committee and allocated the balancing of the portfolio to the business managers, as he did not trust the investment managers. On being appointed chief investment officer, Nicola Ralston, previously head of research, was instructed to develop a logical investment process to determine how all client money should be invested – the idea was to create an intellectual property right for Schroders to replace individuals in terms of value. Salisbury was accused of believing in the triumph of the process over talent and feeling that good performance would result – science came first. It was seen as a vast philosophical error. For this purpose Ralston was expected to define a common ground for all investors. Needless to say she found it impossible as the diversity of different approaches, the key to successful investment management, lies with individuals not systems. As a result of this process everyone became thoroughly disenchanted. Salisbury had poisoned the atmosphere and lost the hearts and minds of all the investment managers – the popular and iconoclastic Cox, one of the best investors, was one of many who left.

In the late 1990s there was a fundamental change in the market's view of the leadership stocks with the traditional companies and large manufacturers faring badly with the rise in sterling. In the US market, growth oriented stocks became the fashion, focusing on the technology, media and telecommunications sector (TMT). There was much talk about the new economy. Within SIM there was an increasing and more vocal difference of view between Ralston and the younger and less experienced fund managers in favour of the momentum stocks of the new economy and the older and more experienced fund managers like Cox in favour of sticking to the tried and tested fundamentals. SIM had always been a value investor – stocks with low price/earnings ratios and high yields, rather than growth stocks with high price/earnings and low yields. Cox with his formidable record in the 1990s, his strong character, commitment and intelligence was difficult to challenge. He genuinely did not understand the merits of the so-called new economy as it did not make economic sense, which of course proved to be correct after the bubble burst. However, at this stage with the rapid emergence of the high tech companies, growth stocks became the rage for the next two years and SIM's performance suffered by not investing in them. SIM's pooled balanced fund, its flagship in which clients were effectively told how much to invest in different asset groups and in which stocks and shares, was heavily criticised by Combined Actuarial Performance Services (CAPS) for missing the rally in internet and telecommunication stocks that led markets to record levels in 1999 and early 2000 and this created a lack of confidence in the investment process. By missing the rally the fund's performance came in the bottom tenth of its competing products. Salisbury was in a quandary with the previously successful investment approach not leading to the right result and facing unprecedented criticism from clients and the consultants. MAM, Gartmore and Philips and Drew who were also under performing faced the same pressures as SIM.

An investment conference took place in March 1999, led by Ralston, the new chief investment officer, who strongly espoused tech stocks, at which they bowed to the pressure of the dissatisfied clients and consultants and decided to hug the index and move into growth stocks. Instead of sticking to its guns, SIM made the mistake of not holding its nerve and compromised its principles – under pressure it invested near to the top. When the TMT bubble burst and value stocks came back, SIM should have done well but it had 'lost the plot' and only did moderately thereafter. Fortunately they were unable to move that much money into TMT stocks as it was close to the top of the market and so the performance in 2000, 2001 and 2002 should not have been too adversely affected. However, the real damage was the perception of the clients who, despite their earlier criticism, were not impressed by the change in policy. By this time Cox had decided that it would be better to retire gracefully rather than to fight for his strongly felt principles and so he left. He had had 'twelve wonderful years, being given the opportunity to do things he never dreamt of doing in a lovely place to work'. With his departure there were very few experienced fund managers left, Ralston being a researcher rather than an investor. Salisbury and Ralston felt that investment decisions should be driven by the research department rather than the fund managers. The process, which became more mechanised, was driven by the young inexperienced analysts who became the fashion rather than the fund managers. This was a total reversal of the policy adopted by Govett. The changes introduced by Ralston caused a lot of distress in the organisation and she was subsequently fired.

These mistakes wiped out much of the good work over the previous two decades in building a formidable investment performance record. Performance started slipping and with so few experienced investors they did not know how to reverse the position. Salisbury publicly acknowledged SIM's pooled UK pension funds had underperformed (*Daily Telegraph,* 12 March) and attempted to counter the criticism by explaining that it was the first time since 1988 that SIM had under performed. At the same time, clients turned against portmanteau-balanced funds, preferring tracker funds, which shadowed stock market indices and were cheaper and seemed to lose nothing in performance. There were also specialist funds focusing on regions, industries or particular types of assets allowing trustees to decide how assets were allocated.

Schroders' Annual Report for 1998, in which it gave its view of the investment outlook, speaks for itself.

Last year was a challenging year for investment performance, as liquidity driven markets brought unprecedented disparities of valuations between perceived growth stocks and companies under competitive pressures. Against this background, many active mangers in Western markets, including ourselves, under performed market indices. However, we believe that our investment approach based as it is upon fundamental research, will produce satisfactory relative returns over the medium- and long-term as it has done in the past.

Salisbury wanted to take control of everything within SIM and was soon at loggerheads with Hill who was chairman of all the Asian activities. This was unacceptable to Salisbury who forced Hill to hand over all, even if in doing so he was undermining the business. Hill was demoted to deputy chairman. For Hill, who had had a brilliant 30-year career at Schroders, it was an ignominious end. It was also very sad. He had found Schroders an excellent place to work, had enjoyed the partnership and thought J Henry Schroder Wagg was the best club he had been a member of and therefore had refused to resign his directorship when the bank was restructured into functional entities in 1985 – it was at this point that he and many others felt that the old Schroders' style had disappeared.

At the same time Peter Wolton came back from Tokyo to head up the unit trust business as managing director of Schroder Unit Trusts Limited with responsibility for co-ordinating mutual funds globally. He replaced Clive Boothman, who took over the private client business from Roger Hills. Hill regarded Wolton as being by far the most able person in SIM but like many at Schroders he was difficult to manage and being very able he did not suffer fools and was quite abrasive and not liked by certain less able colleagues as he tended to call a spade a spade. Sedgwick had a high regard for Wolton too and saw him as a future head of SIM. When he left for Tokyo SIM was the 'top of the pops' but on his return it was losing clients fast and more money was going out of the unit trusts than coming in, for the first time in ten years. As he saw it, the management structure had not grown in line with the growth of the business and there was a lack of clarity about reporting lines and therefore a lot of unnecessary duplication especially on the investment side. Nicola Ralston was the chief investment officer but it was not clear whom the fund managers reported to. Investment performance declined as a result. Salisbury's weakness as a chief executive led to people behaving in strange ways. Not long afterwards, Salisbury wanted Wolton to move to private clients and he only reluctantly agreed after having said he felt his next move would be to becoming a chief executive. He was told to leave and did not take long to become the chief executive of Barings Asset Management (London) where he could bring to bear all, good and bad, that he had learnt at Schroders.

Wolton felt that strategically Salisbury had good ideas on the functional led business with a clear separation between retail, institutional and private clients. He thought SIM had the chance to be the pre-eminent asset management business by taking a longer-term approach and as a result could have competed with Fidelity, the leading US asset management house. The fact that senior management of Schroders was dominated by investment bankers rather than investment managers meant that this was not appreciated, the continuing flow of short-term profits being more important.

WHAT WENT WRONG AT SIM?

Salisbury was said to be more interested in status than money. When in 1998 Sedgwick imposed a pay freeze on SIM the entire management committee said SIM would lose people and goodwill. They felt that in rejecting their views, Salisbury was determined to show the board that his strong leadership was more important than supporting his own directors and staff. This was one of the defining moments in which it was seen that he was more interested in own position than that of his staff, whose confidence he completely lost. Salisbury was almost universally condemned by his colleagues and blamed for the increasing demise of SIM but it is difficult to believe that he was not supported in his actions by Sedgwick who knew the business so well.

There was still an impetus to the business from the good performance of the past and this hid the damage being done within SIM. In fact with the raging bull market the funds under management and profits after tax of Asset Management (including Private Equity) had increased by 92% and 74% respectively during the four years to 1999 much in line with the FT All Share index of 80%. From outside SIM it looked very impressive. In any case the eyes of the board and Sedgwick were focused elsewhere on the survival and the subsequent sale of the investment banking business. With all the problems at SIM it is quite extraordinary that it was not sold with the investment bank. Most of the directors of SIM including Salisbury, felt the asset management business would become very capital intensive and that it should have been sold with the investment bank. There had been a long debate at the board but the family was adamant that SIM should not be sold. Overall it was seen that Schroders was a big player in asset management but not a top player in investment banking, whose value was its people rather than its assets. As far as Bruno was concerned, 'it was a question of whether Schroders could hack it. The investment banking business could not compete and therefore it was sensible to sell it whereas the asset management business could continue to do well, so why sell?' With the Schroder family being against any sale, it was bad enough trying to get them to accept the sale of the investment bank without also having to fight another battle over SIM. Perhaps they did not appreciate that SIM had passed its best in the past two years.

NOTES:

1. Under the terms of his severance contract, David Salisbury was not permitted to speak about his time at Schroders and therefore was not able to give his side to the story to the author. Had he had been able to do so there would have been more balance.

CHAPTER 26

PRIVATE EQUITY BREAKS AWAY

1994 - 1999

Ferguson had taken advice from Joe Bower at Harvard Business School that investors in private equity funds were more interested in regional than country funds and this was confirmed by Schroder Ventures' investors who were pressing for a single European fund with one currency and no country allocations. Ferguson and Smitham therefore had to bring all the European businesses together and this took six years to accomplish as five barons had to be brought into one kingdom with a loss of independence and having to agree their future actions with others. Fortunately, because of the history of the partners from each country having been brought together annually for a planning and recreation session, there was a good deal of trust between them. Smitham critically put up a chart asking them, 'Do you want to raise more money, do larger deals and earn more money?' It did the trick. Confucius said that if you want to cross a chasm don't try and do it in two steps. Schroder Ventures ignored the maxim. As a first stage a federation was created in 1995 with each country partnership having rights, its share being dependent on the fees it contributed. The UK business had for the first time to combine with others to achieve what it wanted. It was the most complicated deal Smitham had ever done. Schroders from then on became a partner with no rights to fire anyone. At the same time it was decided that the business should be run as a meritocracy with the introduction of a flexible profit sharing system whereby the partners assessed each other annually and out of that came each partner's revised profit percentage. If a partner's stake reduced in two consecutive years he or she was expected to leave and this resulted in a number of the partners departing. Sherwood was an enormous fan of Smitham. He gave Moulton the credit for founding the business and Smitham the credit for the creation of a European business which Moulton would not have been able to do. None of the country heads, apart from Byrn, liked Moulton, who had the bigger business and therefore more perceived clout – he spoke so fast and with so much slang that none of them understood him or had any faith in him. Sherwood felt it was their destiny to become a European business – it was a natural progression. 'Peter had the skill to bring everyone together and to get positive results from us all.'

In 1996, Bischoff had the brilliant idea of setting up a quoted investment trust that could secure retail funds from the market and be completely liquid in that investors could sell at any time. He had to push Ferguson quite hard as he was desperately busy rushing around the world raising new funds. Schroder Ventures International Investment Trust (SVIIT), which raised £1.9 billion on the Stock Exchange, was designed to give access through a quoted vehicle to Schroder Ventures' international portfolio of investments in 18 countries in Europe, Asia Pacific and North America. It provided a permanent source of funds for a variety of venture and buy-out funds mainly managed by Schroder Ventures and at the same time solved the liquidity problems of the investors. Ferguson noticed that 95% of the $1 billion committed to the funds came from pension funds and life insurance companies and so he approached them all offering them the opportunity to convert their direct investments into units in the quoted investment trust. A total of 18% accepted which gave them $180 million to start the fund, which grew over the next few years to $450 million. It had an added importance to Schroders as there were no capital gains on the investments provided that there were no distributions. It was ground-breaking and a brilliant success and Schroders became one of the biggest investors in the funds, investing €220 million in the first European fund of €1 billion and €750 million in the second fund of €3.5 billion.

In 1997 investors wanted to make larger commitments to bigger funds and so it was agreed to amalgamate all the separate European funds into one entity and to raise the first European fund of €1 billion, with no specified allocation to individual countries. The European entities thereby became a single business. With the closing of the €1 billion European fund, the business was thoroughly reviewed and in the process five of the UK partners left. With the exception of Spain, all the European partnerships were merged within Schroder Ventures Limited and became controlled by the four European countries (UK, France, Germany and Italy) based on the proportion of each country's contribution of management fees negotiated and carried interest earned, reflecting their success as a business. The Spanish business was excluded as it had never been a success since its country head, Jaime Grego, was not a venture capitalist and risk averse – not surprisingly the business was a failure. At the same time Schroders' stake in the carried interest earned on the funds was reduced from 5% to 4%.

The following year the investors became increasingly concerned about the management fees not being wholly employed in the business and its staff. This lead to many venture businesses becoming independent of their corporate umbrella companies – Doughty Hanson became independent from Chartered WLB, Electra Kingsway from Electra, Cinven from the Coal Board and Schroder Ventures from Schroders. The Schroder carry was further reduced to 3%. To some extent this separation became inevitable following the confusion in the market created by SIM insisting on setting up a venture capital internet fund which was felt to be in competition with the European partnership. With the investors continuing to ask what contribution Schroders was making for its share of the carry and the management fees, Smitham asked Ferguson to justify his role. It was acknowledged that Schroders was not contributing sufficient to justify receiving a carried interest in funds raised after 2002. It would, however, continue to receive carries on the existing funds over the following ten years or so. These arrangements were finally negotiated between Challen and Smitham in 1999 with the total separation of Schroders from Schroder Ventures Europe, which changed its name to Permira, Schroders retaining an economic interest in the event of a sale of the business. The organisation moved from a federation of businesses into a fully integrated business with one balance sheet and profit and loss account. At the time of separation the European business had 75 professionals and $4 billion under management.

Looking back, Smitham who handed over to Buffini said he had wonderful partners all with a great sense of fairness. Contrasting a few of them he said,

Damon was energetic and bright with a wonderful feel for people and an ability to take quick decisions. He was also a real leader. Richard (Winkles) was grand, arrogant, outspoken, self-important and was very good with the companies and did a great job as a non-executive director of Appledore. He also had good investment judgement. Veronica (Eng) was brilliant, very intelligent, very quick with a great sense of responsibility having spent seventeen years handling difficult problems. In such an organisation things go wrong but she manages to get them right.

Eng had a huge following Byrn having said, 'Everyone was impressed by Veronica who always knew as much if not more about a company's accounts than the finance director of the company.' Speaking of Sherwood, Smitham said 'Charles is intelligent, sees both sides of an argument, is persuasive, a good salesman, has made a great contribution, is dispassionate and always has a smile on his face and is gracious and never nasty.' His final word was for Ferguson. 'Nick has huge enthusiasm and energy but tends to talk a lot and not listen. He has completed more start-ups than anyone – each new and independent and all with a relationship with Schroders. He did wonders but never focused on performance. He accomplished more than most would even think about.' The criticism over monitoring performance may have been rather harsh as Ferguson spent much of his time with the investors and had to explain the performance to them. Colleagues at Schroders not involved in the business said he had created a very valuable asset, built up a team of good people and made a lot of money for Schroders and for himself. He was seen to be very bright, arrogant, *de haute en bas*, highly ambitious, with a good manner and sound common sense, but slightly lazy.

At the same time all the non-European businesses went their own way. Ferguson and Andrew Williams, who had come from Capital Markets to help with investor relations, and the remainder of the central team at SVH went to manage SVIIT. At the time of the break away in 1999, over 30 funds had been raised with $4.2 billion committed funds (that were to double the following year) in ten countries with 160 professional staff. The aggregated net internal rate of return on the $4.2 billion committed to all the Schroder Venture funds by the investors (net of all fees and carried interest to the partnerships) from inception in 1983 to the end of 1999 was 21.5% compared with a weighted stock market return of 14.5% – a remarkable achievement. And so Schroders parted from the brilliant business it had created. It had received nearly £300 million in management fees and carried interest over the 15 years and was greatly indebted to Ferguson.

CHAPTER 27

THE SALE OF THE INVESTMENT BANK

1999 - 2000

Following the ignominious departure of Broadbent and Kotler, it was clear to Bischoff that there were three alternatives open to him: 'hire a major hitter with a firm attached, hire a major hitter without a firm or finally think the unthinkable tie up with a major Wall Street house – a European house would not do. We needed the strength of Wall Street to take on the large US investment banks. Could we buy a boutique?' Bischoff and MacAndrew called on Bruce Wasserstein of Wasserstein and Perella at his palatial apartment in New York for a three- to four-hour meeting at which Wasserstein spoke for 98% of the time saying that Schroders would make an ideal partner but he wanted $1 billion for his business but his chemistry with Bischoff was not good – he subsequently received $1.4 billion from Dresdner Bank.

In September Bischoff turned to Geoffrey Boisi to discuss the possible acquisition of Beacon Group. Broadbent, Samuel and Bischoff had met Boisi on a number of previous occasions and liked him. He a tall and impressive American, a highly rated and serious figure in New York, who had been head of M&A at Goldman Sachs responsible for the merger of Philip Morris with General Foods and KKR take-over of RJR Nabisco, and had with him a strong body of colleagues, including Dick Herbst, his second in command, Lloyd Bentsen, the ex-US Treasury Secretary and David Coulter, former president of BankAmerica, who felt confident they could take on the challenge. They had the force of personality and drive. There followed intense negotiations to reach an agreement. Beacon was a relatively small M&A and private equity business, with the venture capital side being more important. Terms were agreed to pay $400 million for a business with $100 million assets with the strong prospect of Boisi becoming Bischoff's successor. However, payments would be made in stages making a discounted price of $320 million. Samuel felt it was a very full price and that there would have to be a positive response from the market in the share price, which in turn would lead to a positive response from clients and then employees – a virtuous circle so to speak. He could not see this happening. There was a potential problem, since to succeed it was necessary to have a global profit and loss account whereas to calculate the performance payments, which were to be based on New York, it would be necessary to have a separate account. They all undertook to stay for three years. The terms of the deal were somehow leaked through Wertheim – it was too accurate to have come from any other source. This raised anxiety inside the firm with questions of what the management was doing in New York. When the senior directors in London heard the details of the deal they were upset and felt a sense of injustice as they had slaved away to create the investment banking business and all the rewards were being given to the new people on the block who had as yet done nothing. It was therefore decided not to go ahead and Bischoff had to go and tell Boisi. On the same plane was Bruno, who was deeply upset by events, probably fearing the alternative of a sale. He left a note by Bischoff's seat saying 'please don't listen to the colleagues' and offered to buy Beacon with his own money. However, it was not possible as there definitely would have been a strong exit from London.

The Times of 19 October perceptively analysed the thinking behind the deal,

> Schroders is starting to worry that it cannot maintain its state of independence in the face of challenges from Goldman, Merrill and the two Morgans and so it is willing to take a potentially fatal gamble. A botched integration could see Schroders lose not only financially but also in reputation, including key directors following Steven Kotler and Richard Broadbent out of the door. There is an atmosphere within Schroders that 'something must be done' about its US operations. But betting the farm to solve a problem in the chicken coup may only hasten the end of Schroders as an independent entity.

The Sunday Times five days later, following a statement by Schroders saying discussions had been terminated said, 'Officially Schroders is looking for an alternative US deal but Bischoff also knows that the debate about the firm's independence will now explode.'

There was a lively debate at the GEC at which it was agreed that the game was up for Investment Banking at Schroders. The bank had failed to get New York right. The cost base was running away through excessive remuneration in relation to revenue. Capital was beginning to be used up in the United States and in Europe. Finally the product base was insufficiently broad with too much dependence on equity due to having no capability in debt. Having pulled out of the Beacon deal there was no alternative other than to sell. If a deal was not completed by the bonus round in February, the firm would implode. All the potential buyers had already been identified.

Mallinckrodt was persuaded and agreed there was no point in pussy-footing around – it had to be done quickly and at the top. He had come to the conclusion that Schroders had inadequate capital to compete with the big New York houses, Schroders having recently lost a major transaction on the Continent to a bank that was willing to underwrite the whole transaction itself. Mallinckrodt had been approached by endless suitors over the years and had politely rejected them. However, he had kept up all these relationships and so was able to go straight to the top. Bischoff saw Goldman Sachs, Morgan Stanley, Citigroup, Chase and Lehman. He explained that the board was considering the future and felt there was a need to make a further consolidation either by combining with another or by a big acquisition in the United States. Some were keen to buy the whole of Schroders but this was not on the table as the family had decided to keep the asset management business. One or two expressed an interest in the investment bank but would prefer the whole. The banks with the biggest gaps in Europe, which was essentially where Schroders had strength, were Chase and Citigroup – Salomon Smith Barney (SSB) was particularly weak in Europe.

Towards the end of 1998, Jim Boshart and Michael Klein were sent by Citigroup to London as the head of Europe and head of Investment Banking respectively to improve SSB's position in the market where it was languishing behind its principal competitors. Its reputation had suffered from the bond trading scandals in New York in 1991 and led to the removal of its mandate for the British Telecom bond privatisation by HM Treasury. With this setback and the lack of any immediate prospects for privatisation business from the government, on which its profits were heavily dependent, all building of the business stopped at a time when the competition was expanding. Whereas in the US Citigroup was well balanced between commercial and investment banking, in Europe it was overweight in commercial banking with investment banking having a collection of businesses that lacked a fundamental infrastructure on the continent of Europe. There were plenty of people but no strategy. SSB was not in the top ten in any of its businesses in Europe at a time when it was one of the top investment banks in New York. Effectively SSB was simply a strong domestic player in the US and if it remained as it was Citigroup would fail to reach its goal of being a top global player.

Having reviewed the competitive position in detail, Boshart and Klein prepared their plan, 'Project Europe 1', and made a presentation in London to the top executives in Citigroup and SSB, including Sandy Weill and John Reid, the joint chief executives of Citigroup, Deryck Maughan, vice-chairman of Citigroup, who had been the chief executive of Salomon before it was acquired by Citigroup, and Michael Carpenter, the chairman and chief executive officer of SSB Holdings. They set out the current position, the opportunities in Europe and their plan for the future. In Europe, SSB was not profitable on revenues of $150 million (SSB's world-wide revenue was only $600 million) with 17 managing directors. It had a 40% annual turnover of its staff and had insufficient scale in any part of Europe and in any of its products to succeed against the competition. Unless it could close the gap between its position in the European and US markets it would never become a global bank. The gap could be closed organically or by acquiring a major player in Europe. Their first choice was Schroders. They were given approval to go ahead with the plan and hired 1000 new staff as SSB needed to have the scale in equity and bond dealing if it was to be complimentary to an acquisition should they pursue that route later. They also needed to develop the investment banking products to match the commercial banking products of Citibank in Europe so that they could to offer a comprehensive range of products to the best clients in Europe. This had been achieved in the US and so they had a successful model to follow. They hired an executive search firm to investigate the market for key people and among the many interviewed were a couple of dozen of the top 40 investment bankers at Schroders, all of whom said they would never join a US investment bank.

Schroders having clearly made some major errors in New York, with the failed discussions with Beacon having been publicly aired in the press, Samuel had invited Klein to lunch in November and asked him what Schroders should do now. Klein suggested that he should see Carpenter in New York. In fact SSB knew a few of the senior people at Schroders, including Bischoff and Samuel, as they had asked Schroders to look at Barings for them following its demise. To SSB, Schroders' investment bank was the inverse of themselves as they struggled in Europe with a collection of assets.

When Bischoff told Boisi that he could not go ahead with the Beacon acquisition, he offered him the job of advising Schroders with a substantial fee. There was some concern that Biosi might try and steer Schroders towards Chase. However, the meeting with Chase went very badly – Schroders performed poorly and did not like the people at Chase. The body language did not work and neither side fired up the other. Boisi said to Bischoff that the Schroder team of Bischoff, MacAndrew, Samuel, Augar and Sykes should be far more positive with Citigroup and not afraid to sell themselves. Bischoff returned to London. The meeting with Citigroup was completely different. The Schroder team arrived at Citigroup's out-of-town executive suite to be greeted with a sumptuous breakfast, which they ate despite having breakfasted already. They sat down at 9.30am in a circle in comfortable armchairs. Citigroup fielded their top investment banking team headed by Deryck Maughan and Michael Carpenter. Curiously both were Englishmen and Maughan was knighted in the New Year. Sanford Weill, the chief executive of Citigroup, arrived for lunch having flown in in his private jet. The Schroder presentation was far more polished and more assured and, after a few questions, was followed by a full exposition of the Citigroup investment banking business. The Citigroup team were wholly committed and of a very high quality. The European people performed very well and there was a matching of minds. The two businesses were complimentary and a deal made sense. The meeting broke up at 3.30pm as Bischoff and MacAndrew had to catch a flight to London. Detailed negotiations then commenced and Samuel and Sykes were able to secure some good concessions. Although there were no deal breakers, there were important issues like management positions, warranties and conditions and also the amount of money Citigroup was prepared to put in to ensure that the key directors and staff remained in the new investment bank. Bischoff returned to London totally exhausted and briefed the board. He said he could not close the gap with Carpenter due the key directors and staff not having an incentivised share in the business. The US investment banks provided their senior staff each year with substantial amounts of shares in the bank which locked them in and was one of the reasons why the British merchant banks found it too expensive to attract US investment bankers, it being too expensive to buy them out. He seemed completely defeated. Sinclair quietly suggested that this could surely be provided in Citigroup shares. Way picked it up and developed the argument and it led to an acceptable and workable solution.

Sufficient progress was made by Boxing Day to allow Citigroup to start its due diligence in earnest. Citigroup was planning to announce its results on 18 January and wanted to include a statement on the merger and this gave greater momentum to the process and a clear dead line. MacAndrew, who was responsible for the execution, and his team worked all day and night as is usual for such transactions. Dealing with the New York lawyers and tax experts was a nightmare with so many details to tie up. Breaking up Schroders was like dividing Siamese twins. It was the most complex transaction MacAndrew had undertaken but he managed to reach agreement without a *force majeure* clause – Schroders could not take the business back if there was material adverse change. Instead there was a clause saying the price would be renegotiated in those circumstances. He also had to get irrevocable commitments from Bruno and the trustees of the Schroder family settlements in respect of shares representing 47.6% of the voting shares to vote in favour of the sale. On 17 January Bischoff started to tell the most senior staff of the agreement to sell. In the afternoon the shares started to rise and early the following morning the Stock Exchange asked Cazenove for a reason, saying they had a mind to suspend the shares. Gaulter, the company secretary, said there would be an announcement soon. The lawyers were still causing difficulties until the last minute. At 1.30pm on 18 January the agreement was signed by both parties and an announcement was made to the Stock Exchange. The document sent to shareholders succinctly summarised the problem for Schroders,

The board concluded that a stronger North American presence and an enhanced capability in the debt market were necessary prerequisites of an attractive and viable investment banking business, particularly given the cost pressures in the industry. In the circumstances, the board decided that it was in the best interests of the business and shareholders to combine it with SSBH.

The press coverage was favourable. The *Financial Mail on Sunday* on 23 January 2000 described Schroders as,

The most blue-blooded of City houses, with a reputation for being the most old school and Protestant of banks. The Schroders deal provides Salomon and its parent, Citigroup, with the elusive link across the Atlantic that provided the thinking behind many investment banking deals of the Nineties. Bischoff recognised the limits of the bank's growth in a mega-market. The deal was made even more necessary by the internecine strife within the bank. Schroders was ranked sixteenth in UK, Euroland and eastern European deals in 1999 to Salomon's eleventh.

IFR (22 January 2000) quoted Michael Carpenter, Citigroup's co-head of corporate and investment banking, as saying, 'We've been pretty open about the fact that Europe has been the weak link in our investment banking operation. Schroders gives us the kind of presence in Europe that we have elsewhere in the world.' *The Economist* (22 January 2000) said,

On top of the £1.35 billion, SSB is putting aside £250 million to entice Schroders 200 top staff to stay. America, indeed, was the rock on which Schroders ambitions foundered. The principal reason for the sale of its investment banking operations, says one closely involved in the decision, was its inability to build or buy an American presence. Schroders' American operation was based on Wertheim, an M&A boutique in which it invested in 1986. Its performance has been lacklustre. 'It doesn't make any money. That's pretty hard in the present environment', says Mr Carpenter with some understatement.

Prior to going with Citigroup, Schroders had asked Citigroup and Chase for a price for the investment bank but only received an offer from Citigroup. Chase needed to do a really large transaction and Schroders' investment banking business was too small. They may have been panicked into buying Robert Fleming and paid £4.88 billion, a very high price. However they were attracted by Fleming's very successful asset management business and by Jardine Fleming's integrated pan-Asian investment banking business (something Schroders never achieved). Had Schroders sold the whole bank, including its asset management business, it would have received approaching £6 billion. Roddie Fleming, who was the main strategist and driving force behind the sale, was also a brilliant negotiator. Sir John Craven who acted for the Fleming family, which had a capital base of £1 billion, said,

Fleming was all things to all people and too big to shrink back. It required more capital so that the family shareholding would gradually reduce over time. With the family owning 28% (seven shareholders, none with more than 7%) and Matheson owning 20% – through selling its 50% stake in the successful Jardine Fleming in Hong Kong for shares in Robert Fleming – together they created a controlling interest of 48%. Within three weeks of the bank being sold to Chase Manhattan the market collapsed with the cracks in the dot com boom and also JP Morgan became available.

The timing was near perfect and the execution particularly well handed.

The sale of Schroders' investment bank for £1.35 billion was well-regarded in the press, not least for having been at a premium over net assets after taking into account transaction and reorganisation costs of just under 50%. This compared with premiums of 20% and 8% achieved by Kleinworts and SG Warburg respectively five years earlier (see Chapter 22). It was also well executed and the Schroder people have stayed together which is unusual in the investment banking business.

The timing of the sale was near perfect as commented on by the press following the publication of Schroders' last Annual Report as one entity. On 12 March the *Wall Street Journal* commented,

The investment banking profits have been flat for the last four or five years and we have been in a bull market. In 1993 investment banking made pre tax profits of £139 million and we've never seen that again. Schroders had a pre-tax return on equity of 25% but the investment banking business had a return of only 10% – that's far below the industry average which ranges from 14% to 16%.

THE SALE OF THE INVESTMENT BANK

The extent of Schroders competitive decline in Europe in the 1990s is illustrated by the M&A league tables compiled by Thomson Financial Securities data. It was eleventh overall in global M&A activity in 1990-1995 but sank to thirteenth in 1996, fifteenth in 1997 and 1998 and twenty-seventh in deals in 1999. Schroders had a tendency to concentrate on the UK league tables where it was generally near to if not at the top.

Following agreement to terms with Citigroup, Bischoff had to carry the key people. He spoke very defensively in long sentences, as was his want when nervous about the outcome, to Swannell who cut him short saying it was the right thing to do. Swannell had found himself having to work alongside SSB for the de-merger of National Power and was not concerned about the cultural difference – 'after all it was better than gentle decline'. Being rather proud of his achievements as head of UK Corporate Finance since 1995, with Corporate Finance being at the top of the league tables in the UK if not in Europe overall, he did not want to see it all go to waste. A dinner was arranged for Bob Rubin, vice-chairman of Citigroup, at which the top ten Salomon and Schroder people were present and they found each other compatible. Rubin explained why he had joined Citigroup after being Clinton's Secretary of the Treasury. A series of meetings followed at Michael Klein's home. At 35 he was one of the most impressive investment bankers you could meet. Michael Carpenter convinced everybody there was a good future and rapid steps were taken to put together a genuine merger. The strengths of Schroders' culture – team working and no backstabbing – were put into a much stronger organisation.

With the sale, Augar decided to retire. Although defeated he left with his reputation high. He had done something not done before – he had created a valuable asset by starting an equity business from scratch, which had become profitable in three or four years. In this he had absolute drive and clarity of vision and gave the business his undivided attention for two years but academia always beckoned. Curiously for someone so highly respected the view of his close colleagues was that he had an enormous social and educational chip on his shoulder, hence his need to obtain a PhD to prove himself. This came through very strongly in his book *The Death of Gentlemanly Capitalism*.

Reviewing the transaction and its implementation thereafter, Michael Klein was very enthusiastic.

> The net purchase price agreed was very fair to both parties and to Citigroup it was a very attractive transaction for a great bank that could never have been created organically by SSB – the continuity and consistency and position within the establishment would have taken decades to achieve. Although the asset management business was attractive it was never on the table and the first priority for Citigroup was the investment bank.

> Being aware of the failures of many such acquisitions, particularly Deutsche Bank's purchase of Morgan Grenfell, Klein was anxious to get it right with Schroders and adopted the approach that it should not be an acquisition of Schroders by SSB, rather it should be

the reverse with the SSB activities and people being folded into Schroders. By this means the combined entity, Schroder Salomon Smith Barney (SSSB) – it had been agreed that Citigroup could use the Schroder name for five years – under Schroders' leadership could keep and increase its market position by having access to the extra products available from SSB and the capital of Citigroup and thereby combine to provide a better service to global clients. Having agreed to the transaction, Klein and his colleagues moved rapidly on to the difficult structural and social issues with Bischoff and Samuel with meetings at the Berkeley Hotel and Klein's home to go through every detail, all having to be completed before the announcement on 18 January. During this period the senior people from both sides met, including Challen and Tarantelli. The SSB people realised from their earlier interviews that the Schroder people had all said they would never join a US investment bank and so all the discussions were based on the new entity SSSB being led by the Schroder culture and those at Schroders feeling they were leading the new business with access to all the new products. Of the 70 Schroder directors, 68 joined and they operated as a single entity immediately from 19 January with the first piece of new business being secured in the third week of January. It was extraordinarily successful. There was a press campaign together with personal letters being sent by Bischoff to all the Schroder clients explaining why Schroders had joined SSB.

With the sale of the investment bank all the international project financiers became European corporate financiers heading up and working within energy and infrastructure industry groups. Showing their adaptability and skills, they had over the years moved with the market from project finance through international corporate finance and privatisation and now to M&A. They were all retained and welcomed by SSB. In Klein's view,

The acquisition of Schroders' investment bank was absolutely critical to the success of Citigroup and SSB's investment banking business in Europe. The main reasons for the success were: the strength of Schroders position in the UK and its relationship with the main UK corporates; the decision was taken at the right time and in a good market environment; the strategy to merge SSB into Schroders rather than the reverse; the rapidity of the move, which had not been seen elsewhere – Citigroup was very adept at such mergers having gone through the same when SSB was acquired by Citigroup; and finally the total commitment of Bischoff to the success of the merger. Bischoff led in sending out the message that the merger would succeed. He knew that all his colleagues would have preferred to remain independent but he was able to persuade them of the power of the new organisation. Salomon had a terrible trading culture and so he brought over from New York Rubin, who had come from outside and carried huge weight within Citigroup, to sell the deal. He gave all the team exposure to us at SSB. He was the first person to move to Canary Wharf and was followed by everyone by May with each of the Schroder and SSB people sitting next to each other. The business was previously barely recognised but now it has a good momentum and can hire anyone. Bischoff has since played an important role on the nine-man executive committee of Citigroup where he is greatly valued in a highly competitive environment – this says a lot for his skills and personality.

Schroders brought with it a wonderful UK franchise with large and medium companies. The business on the Continent was very small relative to the market with revenues of only £60 – £70 million although not bad in quality. The securities business was also quite small, being a niche good quality player – after combining the securities businesses of Schroders and SSB, SSSB was still only a mid tier player. All Schroders activities in Europe were kept save for the fixed income side.

In Challen's view the most interesting and valuable thing that came out of Wertheim was a rehearsal of what not to do in implementing the sale of the investment bank to SSB. It showed how a lack of trust and mutual respect could destroy a merger. This was never allowed to happen at Schroder Salomon Smith Barney (SSSB) – no polarisations or divisions were allowed. Explaining the concerns of his colleagues in London he said,

At Schroders we had worked very hard and effectively at developing enduring relationships with clients based upon their trust in the independence and quality of our advice. Our problem was that we could not capitalise on these relationships as fully as we wished because clients doubted our capabilities in the United States and because we lacked many of the financing products, which were becoming such an important (and remunerative) part of investment banking business. As a result (and often rather reluctantly, I believe) clients introduced other banks into the relationship. So we were not only losing revenues but also allowing competitors to achieve a bridgehead. Even more troubling, some of our best younger people were becoming restless and doubting that it made sense for them to make a career at a competitively disadvantaged bank, however much they admired it.

It became clear to many of us that these shortcomings would have to be tackled and that the only timely solution was likely to be a combination with another group, despite the great emotional attachment long-standing Schroder professionals had to the group's independence. I began to be worried that we might run out of potential partners while this realisation was sinking in. When Citigroup made its approach it was clear that it had to be taken very seriously, provided we could satisfy ourselves that the Schroder approach to business would be maintained within the larger group.

Many outsiders, familiar only with the history of the two groups, doubted that this would be possible. The article in the *Financial Times* on 20 January 2000 headed, 'Culture clash may spark Schroders exodus' with a cartoon of a Salomon shark with rolled up shirt sleeves and wide suspenders grabbing a worried-looking bespectacled man in a dark suit captioned, 'This is a marriage made in hell', was a typical reaction. But our careful investigations had persuaded us that this was a mis-judgment. In addition to the sensitivity which we found in our discussions to cultural issues there was a strong pragmatic reason why this should be so. Citigroup's need was for the

European client relationships which they largely lacked, so they could not jeopardise those relationships and the commitment of the people who had created them if they were to buy the business.

In practice the merger has worked better than any other combination in investment banking of which I am aware – not a field in which there is much good competition, I must admit. This is because the professionals in each part of the merger have recognised in their new colleagues high quality people with completely different and complementary skills to their own. As a result, ex-Schroder professionals felt a real sense of relief in their dealings with clients that there were no longer any no-go areas. The new group had credibility wherever it was needed.'

Of course there had to be some painful adjustments. Some areas of obvious overlap had to be dealt with at the time of the merger. In other areas, especially in view of the downturn in markets, numbers of people have had to be reduced where the merger resulted in more than we really needed. Nevertheless, to the great credit of those principally responsible for putting these two apparently disparate organisations together, the result is a confident and unified organisation, comparatively free from internal rivalries. And out of two organisations each with serious competitive handicaps a single group has been created which is increasingly recognised as one of the leading forces in investment banking in Europe.

Elsewhere there was less success. In Asia the Schroder staff were told by the Salomon people that they would decide whom they wished to keep and then did nothing for three months. Salomon was quite satisfied with its Asian operations and did not need Schroders' people. It was therefore not a priority. Schroders, with its main interest in Europe, had done nothing to secure their future. Most of the staff had been with the Schroders for many years having resisted the attempts of head hunters to lure them away feeling a loyalty to Schroders despite having been paid marginally less. Seeing that there was no interest in them they answered the call of the head hunters. Effectively the investment banking business throughout Asia simply withered away. It was not the proudest moment in Schroders' history.

In New York, Wertheim was completely duplicated by SSB and so there was no benefit. Only ten people got offered jobs. Besides Citigroup was totally focused on Europe and concentrated on making that a success. Commenting later Tarasoff said,

There was no consultation on the sale of the investment bank or consideration of the people at Wertheim, which was understandable. Of the 900 staff only ten were offered jobs by SSB, the remainder being fired as all their jobs were duplicated – five of the 120 in research were offered jobs. SSB only needed Europe where it was weak. Schroders was remarkably considerate and generous to the staff. Mallinckrodt was a real gentleman speaking to everyone, explaining why the sale had to happen and thanking them for their efforts. We never saw or heard anything from Bischoff or Samuel.

Kotler went into business on his own. Tarasoff became head of research at SG Cowan and Rebell moved to Loews Corporation to manage a $40 billion mixed fund.

There were differing views among the competitors about the reasons for Schroders having to sell the investment bank. Sir John Craven felt Schroders had sown the seeds of failure by not having any meaningful plans for the Big Bang when it decided not to build a securities business as SG Warburg had done with its acquisition of Akroyd & Smithers, Rowe & Pitman and Mullens. To succeed it had to have the ability to underwrite and distribute primary and secondary debt and equity securities. SG Warburg had learnt through its Eurobond experience what securities were all about whereas Schroders had no knowledge of Eurobonds and did not know how to react to the Big Bang. Instead it had a single capacity advisory product that became increasingly irrelevant. SG Warburg had done spectacularly well until Sir David Scholey had taken his eyes off the ball and mismanagement had brought about its demise. Simon Robertson, who had left Kleinwort after its acquisition by Dresdner Bank for Goldman Sachs, felt Schroders' mistake was to seek to build a securities business in the 1990s by buying Wertheim which was the wrong vehicle. Having seen Kleinwort fail he could not understand why Schroders made the same mistake. Wertheim was known to be the Klingenstein's vehicle to do private business and not at all a suitable base to build an M&A business in New York. From this point it was inevitable that Schroders would have to sell out to a US investment bank.

On the fact that no UK merchant bank succeeded globally, Thornton said it was principally due to not having built a credible business in the States. He believed it could have been achieved had it been started earlier and the right people had been hired. There was a race against time in being able to react to the change in the market. It was a question of 'those who adapted the fastest survived' rather than the Darwinism 'the survival of the fittest'. He did not believe one had to be big to be successful. The Americans had two big advantages – a big and richer home market, which yielded the funds to finance growth and being already integrated they understood the markets and how to take risks.

The failure of Barings triggered the decline of the British merchant banks and all save Schroders fell within two years. It was structural in that all the merchant banks were trying to get into the security business and not be banks. The US investment banks on the other hand had started as securities houses and it was in their blood. None of the British merchant banks succeeded in becoming integrated houses save for SG Warburg. Schroders had to either retreat back to being a boutique advisory house like Lazards and Rothschild or become an integrated house like SG Warburg. The US investment banks were able to capture all the economics – M&A fees became squeezed down to about 25% of the total fees on a large transaction. Rothschild, wholly owned by the family and with its wonderful name, did not have to make a profit. Schroders never succeeded in New York – Wertheim was seen in the market to be a hugely bad purchase.

In contrast the US investment banks took their time in establishing themselves in London. Morgan Stanley did quite badly for five years but when approached by SG Warburg, when it was failing, it was only interested in Mercury Asset Management, which was not for sale. Goldman Sachs struggled originally but with its amazing presentations, industry specialists and sheer professionalism unknown in the City at that time, it inevitably broke through without the need to buy a British merchant bank. The US investment banks which succeeded[1] were also better managers – the people who did the deals and made the money (revenue earners) were the best paid and were kept clear of management responsibilities. In contrast the UK managers were given the status and the pay – everyone wanted to be called something grand. In Goldman Sachs the top ten earners had nothing to do with management and never worried about costs.

Looking at the rejected alternative of remaining an advisory business, Schroders' undoubted strength, Jones at Lazards felt the only way to make a success of the corporate finance advisory business was through a partnership since outside shareholders are always demanding increasing dividends and the participants pay themselves too much when in a plc. Schroders became stranded between the US investment banks dominating the securities market and the advisory groups like Lazard. Costs got out of control and it became too expensive for Schroders to compete. Robertson echoed the same thoughts saying,

> If Schroders had reverted to being a high quality M&A boutique it would only have survived as a partnership. Plcs tend to take more of the cake. Once Schroders went public and into the securities business where there is a constant demand for capital it was inevitable that Schroders would fail. They were never tricky, had good manners and always did what they said they would.

Sinclair felt the key mistake was the family not being prepared to share its wealth. Its instinct was to want more of the pie than to grow the pie. Had the revenue-earning directors become the owners of the business it would have severely changed their attitude to costs including the headcount and remuneration with a focus on profits as opposed to bonuses. Schroders was mesmerised by its perceived stature whereas it could have had overwhelming force in the advisory business.

In-house, Way saw the sale of the investment bank as being inevitable as Schroders was in a double squeeze – revenue being hit by the fierce competition of the supremely able US investment banks and costs being out of hand due to excessive compensation in relation to profitability. There was no way out and it was therefore important to get some value before it was too late. He described Schroders as being a firm of quality people with integrity, collegiality and family spirit and without being extraordinarily selfish and greedy. Sinclair felt the key to the success was the fact that it was a very good business.

NOTES:

1. Many of the US investment banks were not well managed and failed, including Lehman in the 1980s, First Boston, Shearson and Salomon. With the enormous market and capital available in New York, unlike in London, they were often able to survive mismanagement and recover and recreate themselves under well capitalised new management.

CHAPTER 28

WIN BISCHOFF

2000

Win Bischoff left Schroders after 34 years to become chairman of Citigroup Europe and a member of the management committee of Citigroup. At the same time he was given a knighthood for his services to banking and the City. His 15-year record since becoming chief executive speaks for itself: after tax profits had increased from £15 million to £244 million; shareholders' funds from £164 million to £1370 million; and the market capitalisation from £114 million to £3551 million, a multiple of 31 compared to the FTSE All Share index of 5.5. During his five-year chairmanship, Schroders' market capitalisation and the FTSE All Share index both doubled showing that the best performance was during his ten-year partnership with Gowi Mallinckrodt.

The story behind these results and those who helped Bischoff to achieve them has been fully described in this book. It is unlikely that they would have been possible without his inspiring leadership and his light touch with colleagues. Gowi Mallinckrodt, Bischoff's partner for ten years and board member for a further five, said,

it was wonderful to work with Win who was immensely stimulating, positive and constructive. He was intuitive in dealing with people and situations and had great people skills, never being confrontational or taking a rigid position and always enjoining people into discussions to achieve progress. He was driven by success and did not like not to succeed but always for the common good. He was a person for the moment with a short time horizon but was good strategically on clearly identifiable issues, not a visionary. He was also quick off the mark and could digest issues immediately. He was unusually talented and delightful and we respected each other. I had not expected when asked to be chairman to have to spend so much time on administrative matters, which Win had no interest in, but it worked well.

They were an effective partnership.

Being so busy and committed to Schroders, Bischoff only took on one non-executive role. In 1992, he was invited to become a non-executive director of Cable and Wireless by its chairman, Lord Young of Graffham. It turned out to be a roller coaster ride with the share price rising from 240p to £13 only to fall to 120p. All went well for a number of years with Young and James Ross, as chief executive officer, at the helm, with profits and the share price steadily increasing. In 1995 Ross, formerly a managing director of

BP, decided that Young should go and be replaced by a non-executive chairman, their style of management being at variance, and approached the non-executive directors on the subject. As the senior non-executive director Bischoff informed Young of Ross' views and invited him to meet the non-executive directors following which it was agreed that Ross should go with Young staying on to supervise the recruitment of a new chief executive and non-executive chairman. The following day the interim results were announced as well as the departure of Ross. Over the next few days the press became increasingly critical of Cable and Wireless and Young's performance. The board decided to sack Young as well as Ross and to call back Brian Smith (later knighted), chairman of Lister & Co and BAA plc and a former non-executive director of Cable and Wireless, to become chairman with Bischoff as deputy chairman.

Despite the shock and his public humiliation, Young remained a friend of Bischoff always having been impressed by his marvellous manner and ability to 'work a room'. 'He is the consummate international banker and likely to be seen as the leading banker in the City. He may have had a rather sheltered life in the City and not be up to the toughness required in the real commercial world.'

Following the appointment of Graham Wallace as chief executive (after Dick Brown had left for EDS) the major monopolies in Hong Kong, Australia and the UK were sold for very high prices, which led to the share price rising to £13. Unfortunately the proceeds were unwisely invested in the US and proved to be a major disaster, the share price dropping to 120p. Reflecting on the events Bischoff said 'as a member of the board I was wholly behind both strategies.'

The views of Win Bischoff can be divided between those of his family, his colleagues, his competitors, his clients and the press.

Win was fortunate in having a wife who, apart from bringing up their two sons and managing their homes in London, Gloucestershire and Tuscany, supported him by entertaining his clients and often accompanied him on his endless travels abroad. Their sons Christopher and Charlie were very proud of their father. Although they did not at first understand what he did they observed his ambition and will to succeed and learnt to appreciate his values of hard work, loyalty and duty – they noticed how disappointed he was when any of his colleagues left Schroders – and his strong sense of family. He had very few close personal friends concentrating all his rare free time on his family. Not having been educated in England he did not have friends around from his youth but was always loyal to those he had known in the past, however well or badly they had done in life. Within the family he was not naturally extrovert, being quieter than with friends and clients – they saw the way he could turn on the charm with clients. Business was never discussed at home. They saw him as being smart, intelligent and very thoughtful with a great intuitive memory and much like his mother. He never read any books acquiring his wide knowledge of the arts through reading magazines. Clearly work was what he loved most and he would find it difficult to stop being involved in business. Apart from music and especially opera, his other great love was Tuscany where they built a home from scratch in the hills above Sienna – he loved the people and their language, the atmosphere, the food and the wine and this was where he relaxed most of all, even though he may well have been thinking about work!

Much has been said about Bischoff's competitiveness on the golf course but not much about his prowess. Gary Brass, a strong supporter of the Wagtail Golf Society, in which Schroder and former Schroder people get together twice a year at Swinley Forest and the Berkshire, recalls playing with Bischoff who holed out in two shots on a par 5 dogleg of 476 yards on the sixth hole of the Blue Course at the Berkshire by hitting his ball with a 2 iron off the tee and holing it with a 3 iron off the fairway, scoring 6 stableford points due to receiving a stroke on his handicap of 13. Brass was so impressed by this remarkable achievement that he wrote to Michael Bonallack, the secretary of the Royal and Ancient Golf Club at St Andrews, who wrote a letter of congratulations to Bischoff, which can be found framed in his downstairs lavatory at Severalls, his house in Gloucestershire.

Bischoff's colleagues were remarkably unanimous in their views. His weaknesses were that he was a poor manager – weak and disinterested – and was not good at taking decisions, particularly on personnel matters and especially on people he knew well – it was not in his character to fire. He hated confrontation and shied away from it – he was too nice. In this respect he was fortunate in having as his partners up to 1994 Gowi Mallinckrodt and thereafter Peter Sedgwick who were both strong in these areas. Bischoff's strengths were his enthusiastic, inspiring and charismatic leadership – always leading by example – and his ability to build a team, as well as his capacity to attract people and to maintain their loyalty. Although not brilliant he had a good mind with a strong commercial instinct and was tremendously quick with good mental arithmetic. He never interfered with the businesses that were going well, particularly investment management. He had a phenomenal capacity for hard work and the physical strength to travel extensively, often going into a meeting straight off an aeroplane. He had a huge and unselfish commitment to Schroders, tirelessly putting its interests before anything else. His greatest asset, however, was as a marketer and relationship builder, being more admired in the City than anyone else. He was turned on by big deals, taking on an almost boyish character in his enthusiasm. He was also universally liked, admired and respected by his colleagues at every level.

Nobody could have read this book without asking why things were beginning to slide in the two most important businesses Investment Banking and Asset Management in the late 1990's. The unremitting pressure from the US investment banks was a critical factor in that sector but the lack of control over Richard Broadbent and his bitter disputes with Augar and Kotler must be put at the door of Bischoff and Samuel, both of whom were uncomfortable dealing with confrontational situations. There was nobody around sufficiently tough to knock heads together, Sedgwick having lost his objectivity by siding with Kotler. The problems brewing up within Asset Management were hidden by the good results and the rampant bull market and may have been overlooked due to the more obvious problems with Investment Banking. What was remarkable, however, was how Bischoff faced with an investment bank in danger of disintegration was able so quickly to arrange its sale to the better capitalised Citigroup for a very handsome profit and to secure for those involved in Europe a future with Schroders' culture preserved within the new organisation. The execution of the merger and its durability would appear to have no parallel.

Bischoff's competitors were equally complimentary about him, Sir John Craven saying, 'he was a superb client man, a leader of men, hardworking and tireless in his efforts for Schroders. The Schroder family owe him a huge debt. He was strategically challenged and should have sold the whole bank.' Sir David Scholey would not be drawn, comparing him with chief executives rather than chairmen. Andrew Tuckey of Barings felt Scholey and Bischoff were very similar with Scholey in his day a touch better and Craven was very effective, 'but you could always go to Win and get objective and unbiased advice.' David Mayhew of Cazenove said he was,

the supreme figure in the advisory business, with great leadership, culturally compatible with successful business and with an appetite for business. In his area he was the equal of any. Craven was a great money maker in buying and selling companies. Scholey had a very high set of standards in his day and was a great leader but had an eye on the Bank of England. Bischoff made the transition better than the others.

John Thornton had a high regard for Bischoff.

He was better than anyone as a client person and a person to work with as a joint adviser. He was prepared to realistically assess where Schroders was, create change, bind difficult people and encourage teamwork as a culture. He had great 'EQ' emotional intelligence as opposed to IQ and a sense of dynamics. He was not a technician. He was much more prepared to listen than Scholey and Craven and would go for the best idea even if it did not come from his own people. He really fought his corner for his clients and for Schroders.

In comparing Scholey, Craven and Bischoff, Thornton said,

Scholey was very bright, charismatic and shrewd but was more focused on his future in the City than Bischoff who was more obviously committed to Schroders. Scholey was also more of an internationalist. Craven was a better principal, knowing how to make money by understanding the economics and how to get a deal done. Bischoff by contrast makes you feel he is focused on your problem by empathy and trust – you knew he was in your corner.

The clients' views have been well covered in the book. In essence they all said they knew he was on their side and that their interests were paramount in all the advice he gave, always coming before the financial interests of Schroders.

WIN BISCHOFF

The press were equally enthusiastic, some more personal than others. In an article in the *Sunday Telegraph* headed 'The perfect international banker' Judi Bevan wrote, 'tall and stylish, Bischoff has the air of someone equally at home in Zurich or New York. With his silver hair, gold Rolex, designer glasses and piercing blue eyes, set just a fraction too close together, he looks decidedly un-British. His shirts have curiously long collars and are monogrammed with all four initials standing for Winfried Franz Wilhelm Bischoff.' On greeting her at lunch at Schroders, unlike his colleagues he noticed her suntan and exclaimed, 'you've been skiing.' 'He is superb with clients,' says one colleague. 'He has an almost chameleon-like ability to get on with anybody' – she had already noticed!

The Times (11 September 1999), said Bischoff was,

> unusual in the City in winning unanimous admiration of both his competitors and peers. Such is the respect that he garners from his peers that, in what is an increasingly cut-throat game, competitors have been known to consult Bischoff informally about their plans, safe in the knowledge that they will get good advice and their information will be entirely confidential.

The *Daily Telegraph* (31 December 1999) reviewing the business people receiving knighthoods in the New Years Honour's List, said, 'Win Bischoff, 58, who restored the gloss to the name of Schroders and is regarded as one of the best investment bankers of his generation, finally makes the list for his services to banking.'

Win's father, Helmut[1], from whom Win inherited his client relationship skills, sadly had died before his son's achievements were publicly recognised. However his mother, Hildegard, from whom he inherited his intelligence and drive, was alive and immensely proud of his knighthood.

NOTES:

1. Helmut Bischoff was appointed a Grand Master of the Order of Good Hope by Nelson Mandela and given the *Grosse Deutsche Bundesverdienstkreuz* by the German government for his services to South Africa and to Germany.

LOOKING BACK

2003

At the risk of being thought to be wise after the event it is perhaps worth looking back to consider if things could have been managed better.

And so the great Schroder house was split in two with the family carrying on as an asset management house having disposed of the glamorous and risky investment bank. To some it might appear to have been a failure but on the other hand the family could be proud that in other hands, with more capital at its disposal, its investment bank, with its strength in Europe, formed an important part of its new owner's capacity to compete as a global player. Unlike many of the other leading British investment banks that had been acquired by other larger banks, it did not disintegrate and lose its culture and style. It thrived and those involved were able to continue with their careers always feeling proud of their origins. As Michael Klein of SSSB said, 'the merger of Schroders with SSB in Europe, with the preservation of the Schroder culture, has been a phenomenal success. From not being in the top ten in Europe in debt, equities, M&A, research, sales and trading in 2000, by 2002 SSSB was in the top four in all businesses and number one in the UK across the board.' With the merger holding together, SSSB surpassed all its principal competitors including Goldman Sachs and Morgan Stanley, becoming the largest corporate and investment banker in Europe. Speaking for his Schroder colleagues David Challen said,

> The merger has worked better than any other combination in investment banking of which I am aware. To the great credit of those principally responsible for putting these two apparently disparate organisations together, the result is a confident and unified organisation, comparatively free from internal rivalries. And out of two organisations each with serious competitive handicaps a single group has been created which is increasingly recognised as one of the leading forces in investment banking in Europe.

So why was it that Schroders, having enjoyed the benefits of protection from potential predators through the controlling family shareholding and having survived the disappearance of its main British competitors in the mid-1990s, failed to maintain its independence five years later. There were probably three main reasons. First Schrobanco was sold ten years too late and this lay at the door of the Schroder family. Secondly, Schroders' efforts in developing a securities business were extraordinarily badly handled by the management. And finally, in the face of overwhelming competition from the better capitalised US investment banks, Schroders was unable to retain its best corporate financiers due to not being able to afford to remunerate them competitively.

Central to these issues was that as a result of the family's determination to maintain control of the bank, which afforded protection to the management from predators, the bank's strategy was constrained by having insufficient capital to achieve growth. At the same time there was the misconception within Schroders that it could compete with the large US investment banks when it had nothing like the same capital and was so weak in the United States, the most important market in the world. Schroders' aspirations were not feasible in view of its lack of capital and so its strategy was fundamentally flawed.

It was quite clear to Richardson by 1970 that as the New York commercial banks increased their overseas activities, Schrobanco would be gradually squeezed out of the market and fail. Schroders had decided that it wished to become an investment bank and could only do so, owing to the restrictions contained in the Glass-Steagall Act, if it sold Schrobanco. At that time the US investment banks were relatively small and only operating in their domestic market. The opportunity to move into investment banking in New York at the ideal time was denied to the management due to the family's refusal to contemplate a sale. They only agreed to it 15 years later when faced by the inevitable failure of Schrobanco. There was then a further opportunity to develop a meaningful investment banking presence in New York but the board took a decision to make a totally inappropriate acquisition without consulting those who understood and were expected to manage the business.

As Charles Sinclair, the well regarded and thoughtful non-executive director said, 'Schroders' ultimate failure to remain totally independent was due to the failure of the Schroder family to agree to the sale of Schrobanco for nearly a decade and to then use the proceeds to purchase a second tier US investment bank which had no prospects of becoming more than that.' When Schrobanco was finally sold in 1986 the hasty and ill-thought-through purchase of Wertheim prevented Schroders from developing an effective investment banking business in New York. Without management control and a lack of willingness to enforce the necessary management changes, failure was inevitable. Had Schroders invested the money in hiring top quality and respected investment bankers in New York, as suggested by John Thornton of Goldman Sachs, it might have succeeded but it would still have been handicapped by the family not having the capital to deal with the huge capital raising needed to become a global player. This ill-fated move relegated Schroders to being a non-global player in the second division. Its effect was that Schroders would never be a force in the market that most mattered – New York. DLJ, much the same size and type of business as Wertheim, was able to develop a highly successful integrated investment bank in New York.

At the same time in London, Schroders, particularly the corporate financiers, completely misjudged the Big Bang. It did not appreciate that it was all about raising capital for its clients that would become an essential adjunct to its advisory function particularly for M&A transactions. The problem was that Schroders lacked the depth of skills in capital raising, only having true competence as an underwriter. It therefore failed to appreciate, until too late, that capital raising was all about the link with research and distribution. Capital raising in the UK market, which had hitherto been by underwriting with the distribution through the brokers, became more akin to the US market that was similar to the Euro market requiring reciprocation. Gordon Richardson may have been a brilliant and charismatic corporate financier but he totally mishandled the Euro market business and was dismissive of continental Europe. As a result Schroders' capital market activity was virtually non-existent in debt. Schroders always focused on equity. More importantly Schroders failed to develop the reciprocity and knowledge of distribution that was necessary to grasp fully the implications of the Big Bang, unlike SG Warburg which was more European in culture.

Schroders therefore wasted the next ten years dithering over the securities business with nobody understanding where it should fit and avoiding responsibility for it. When the corporate financiers finally woke up to the reality that the integration of securities with corporate finance was critical to their survival, it was virtually too late. The competition had already established itself in such strength globally that Schroders could not catch up. A valiant effort was made by Philip Augar to build a securities business that was integrated with corporate finance and this was achieved to a limited extent in Europe but then the uncontrolled infighting between him and Richard Broadbent over what to do in New York destroyed the last hopes of success. The investment bank was sold just in time to save it disintegrating but at a very good price.

The view from outside was that Schroders' strategy for securities was misconceived. Cazenove, the leading UK broking house, felt that Schroders had made a huge mistake attempting to build its own distribution business from scratch by hiring a few people and was bound to fail. Buying a bigger broker would have given Schroders the benefit of an established structure. Later under Augar with the focus on the agency function and research, Schroders had more of a chance, not least because of the good former Wood Mackenzie people. Cazenove watched the deteriorating position of Schroders in New York that was clearly requiring more and more management time. SG Warburg also felt 'it was a disastrous mistake trying to build a securities business from scratch. Schroders clearly had no idea of how much money and effort was needed to run a securities business and more importantly the phenomenal change in culture.' In the end, of course, SG Warburg failed and never achieved anything in New York.

By culture Schroders was always more comfortable as an advisor than as a financier and a risk taker and what mattered was the M&A tables rather than the equity and debt capital raising tables. Another problem was that decisions were being driven by the perceived stature of the business. Schroders thought it was too big to revert to being an advisory business, which was its real and only strength. Everyone aspired to being on the same level as Goldman Sachs and Morgan Stanley. In fact with the overwhelming force of its advisory skills Schroders would have been the leader and head and shoulders over its competitors. It had not learnt that it should fight on its own ground and never go into battle without knowing it would win (as recommended by Sun Tzu 2500 years before in *The Art of War,* his classic essays on the conduct of war). Schroders was brilliant at advising its clients but was not as good at advising itself. But in order for this strategy to succeed, the Schroder family would have had to share its wealth with the senior management, something it was reluctant to do. Had the senior management become partners in the business it would have fudamentally changed their attitudes to costs and embedded in them a long-term view of the business and thereby aligned the interests of the key decision makers with the family. Short-term bonuses and the ability to exercise share options after three years are not conducive to long-term thinking.

There was also a certain amount of complacency within Corporate Finance with the judgement of their performance continually being based on the UK market rather than elsewhere. Strangely, although Schroders had an executive committee in which most of the time the British were outnumbered by foreigners (two Germans, a Frenchman, a Swiss, replaced by a Dutchman, and an American and three to four British), it was still remarkably British in attitude and invariably judged itself by its domestic market. When it came down to it Schroders was really a UK corporate financier of the top grade and this was what Citigroup wanted. On the Continent it was passable but nothing special, especially in capital raising. In New York it was nothing and in Asia it had drifted into the sand.

Having said all that, Schroders had had a good run under the umbrella of the hugely successful asset management business. The financial performance from 1985 to 1999 was nothing short of outstanding.

And so Schroders, following the sale of the investment bank, has entered another stage with the full backing of the Schroder family. Peter Sedgwick became chairman with Gowi and Bruno remaining on the board and Philip leaving investment banking to rejoin the family firm in its new guise. The asset management business in the face of a sharp downturn in the market had many problems, most of which were self-inflicted. This required significant changes in the top and middle management involving substantial restructuring costs and new investment. That led to the first losses in Schroders' history in 2001. With the signs of a recovery under the new management and an improvement in investment performance, there is no reason to believe that Schroders will not continue to thrive. With Bruno and Gowi becoming less active, Philip will be taking on the family's crusade to pass on to the next generation his inheritance in a better condition than he received it by continuing to bring to Schroders 'stability, protection and independence and the ability to plan a long way ahead without fear of a take-over' as promised by his uncle (1997 *Schroder Wagtail*).

ANNEX 1

PRINCIPAL SUBSIDIARY AND ASSOCIATED COMPANIES OF SCHRODERS PLC BEFORE AND AFTER 1985

Principal Subsidiary and Associated Companies to 1985

Americas	Europe	Asia

Schroders Inc
J Henry Schroder Bank &
  Trust Company
J Henry Schroder Banking
  Corporation
J Henry Schroder
  Corporation
Schroder Capital
  Management Inc
Schroder Venture Managers
  Ltd
Schroder Real Estate Assoc [1]
	J Henry Schroder Wagg &
	  Co. Ltd
	Schroder Leasing Ltd
	Schroder Securities (UK)
	  Ltd
	Schroder Life Assurance Ltd
	Schroder Properties Ltd
	Schroder Asseily & Co Ltd
	Schroder Venture Advisors [2]
	J Henry Schroder Bank AG
		Schroders Asia Ltd
		Schroder Securities (Hong
		  Kong) Ltd
		Singapore International
		  Merchant Bankers Ltd [1]
		Schroder, Darling and
		  Company Ltd [1]

	Representative offices	
Rio de Janeiro/Sao Paulo Bogotá Caracas	Frankfurt-am-Main	Singapore Tokyo

Principal Subsidiary and Associated Companies from 1986

Americas	Europe	Asia

Schroders Inc
Wertheim Schroder &
  Co Inc. [1]
Schroder Capital Management
  International Inc
Schroder Real Estate Assoc [2]
Schroder Venture Managers
  Ltd
IBJ Schroder Bank & Trust
  Company [1]
	J Henry Schroder Wagg &
	  Co. Ltd.
	Schroder Investment
	  Management Ltd
	Schroder Leasing Ltd
	Schroder Securities Ltd
	Schroder Properties Ltd
	Schroder Asseily & Co Ltd
	Schroder Venture Advisors [2]
	J Henry Schroder Bank AG
		Schroders Asia Ltd
		Schroder Securities (Hong
		  Kong) Ltd
		Schroder International
		  Merchant Bankers Ltd
		  (from 1989) [1]
		Schroders Australia Ltd
		SIM (Japan) Ltd
		Schroder Securities (Japan)
		  Ltd

	Representative offices	
Bogotá Caracas Sao Paulo		Singapore Seoul

[1] Affiliate   [2] Partnership

ANNEX 2

SCHRODERS' PERFORMANCE
1973 - 1999

Year	Profit after Tax £m	Shareholders' Funds £m	Market Capitalisation £m	Funds under Management £m	Number of Staff
1973	2.4	25.9	33.0		
1977	3.5	44.9	31.8		
1984	15.1	164.0	114.3	10.3	
1985	29.2	171.6	182.5	11.0	
1986	72.2	221.1	214.4	15.0	2500
1987	27.1	227.4	284.1	16.0	2667
1988	30.1	254.7	264.6	17.5	3094
1989	46.6	313.1	489.7	22.5	3225
1990	31.6	310.2	410.0	21.0	3311
1991	54.4	360.6	640.7	27.7	3429
1992	69.6	545.6	816.1	36.1	3658
1993	140.3	674.5	1,732.5	52.9	3911
1994	132.3	731.3	1,853.0	56.7	4357
1995	139.0	849.3	2,556.0	74.0	4700
1996	179.2	941.1	2,880.0	87.6	5128
1997	170.9	1046.3	3,684.3	106.9	5762
1998	167.8	1170.5	3,120.4	119.0	6004
1999	243.8	1370.4	3,550.9	142.6	6067

Source: Schroders Plc. Annual Report and Accounts

1985 £12.9 million profit on part sale of Schrobanco

1986 £51.3 million profit on sale of Schroder Life and the remainder of Schrobanco.

1992 Full disclosure of profits was started.

PROFIT BEFORE TAX BY BUSINESS
1993 - 1999

Year	Asset Management		Merchant and Investment Banking [1]		Total
	£m	%	£m	%	£m
1993	56.8	29	139.0	71	195.8
1994	85.4	44	110.0	56	195.4
1995	93.0	47	104.3	53	197.3
1996	132.0	55	106.7	45	238.7
1997	154.1	63	90.8 [3]	37	244.9
1998	146.6	63	85.1 [3]	37	231.7
1999	186.7 [2]	58	137.3 [3]	42	324.0

Source: Annual Report and Accounts

Note: Profits were not split between businesses until the 1993 Annual Report.

[1] Corporate Finance, Securities, Project Finance, Banking and Financial Markets

[2] Includes £24.9 million profit on the sale of the Australian Property Fund.

[3] After provisions for Asian debts of £23.9m in 1997, £43.2m in 1998, and a write back of £18m in 1999.

ANNEX 4

STOCK MARKET INDICES AT YEAR END
1973 - 1999

Year	FTSE All Share index	Nikkei 225 index	Hang Seng index
1973	150	4307	433
1977	215	4866	404
1984	593	11543	1200
1985	683	13083	1752
1986	835	18821	2568
1987	870	21564	2303
1988	927	30159	2687
1989	1205	38916	2837
1990	1032	23849	3025
1991	1188	22984	4297
1992	1364	16925	5512
1993	1682	17417	11888
1994	1521	19723	8191
1995	1803	19868	10073
1996	2014	19361	13451
1997	2411	15259	10723
1998	2674	13842	10049
1999	3242	18934	16962

Source: Datastream

INDEX OF NAMES